My Name
in
Books

My Name in Books

A GUIDE TO CHARACTER NAMES IN CHILDREN'S LITERATURE

Katharyn E. Tuten-Puckett

1993
Libraries Unlimited, Inc.
Englewood, Colorado

Libraries Unlimited, Inc.
P.O. Box 6633
Englewood, Colorado 80155-6633

Library of Congress Cataloging-in-Publication Data

Tuten-Puckett, Katharyn E.
  My name in books : a guide to character names in children's literature / Katharyn E. Tuten-Puckett.
    xvi, 242 p. 22x28 cm.
    Includes indexes.
    ISBN 0-87287-979-8
    1. Children's literature--History and criticism--Dictionaries.
2. Characters and characteristics in literature--Dictionaries.
3. Names, Personal, in literature--Dictionaries. I. Title.
PN1008.5.T87 1993
809'.927'03--dc20   93-2660
                                                               CIP

To the staff of the Children's Department
at Monroe County Public Library,
Bloomington, Indiana.
Their love and knowledge
of children and books is contagious.

CONTENTS

ACKNOWLEDGMENTS

The author has many people to thank for assistance with this book. First and foremost, I am grateful to Virginia (Ginny) Richey, Children's Department Head at Monroe County Public Library, for sharing her idea and allowing me to work on it, for her generosity of spirit, and for her continuous encouragement and support.

Deep appreciation goes to William Hamlin, Indiana University undergraduate and computer whiz. His knowledge of hardware and software and his patience with Carmelita the Wonder Computer has made this project possible.

I am grateful for the expertise and cheerful assistance of the librarians and staff in the Children's Department at Monroe County Public Library: John Anderson, Patty Callison, Mary D'Eliso, Pat Firenze, Mary Frasier, Jim Grace, Lenny Kim, Jean Schelm, and Nissy Stetson.

Support and encouragement for this project have been offered in a variety of ways by many others and I am grateful to all of them.

Thanks go to my editor, Dr. David Loertscher; my children, Marliece Puckett and James Puckett; Linda Cornwell, Consultant, Learning Resources Unit, Indiana State Department of Education; Judith Dye, School of Library and Information Science Library, Indiana University; Sara Laughlin, Coordinator, Stone Hills Library Network, Bloomington, Indiana; Denise Ogren, Bloomington, Indiana. Thanks also go to all of those who responded promptly with current lists of book awards: James Hester, Arkansas Elementary School Council, Arkansas Department of Education; California Library Association; University of Georgia, College of Education, Department of Language Education; Linda Cornwell, Indiana State Department of Education; William White Library, Emporia State University; Jennifer Smith, Northern Kentucky University, Learning Resource Center; Flo Starkey, Coordinator of Library/Media Services, Roswell Independent School District, New Mexico; Children's Services Consultant, State Library of Ohio; Oklahoma State Department of Education; Cherie Bussert, Youth Services Librarian, Boise Public Library, Idaho; South Carolina Association of School Librarians; Janelle Paris, Texas Bluebonnet Award Committee; Katherine Olsen, Specialist, Library Media Education, Utah State Department of Education; Gail Fusnaj, Vermont Congress of Parents and Teachers; Kathy Leland, Bothell, Washington; C. Himmons, Suncrest Primary School, Morgantown, West Virginia; Jane Addams Peace Association; Office for Outreach Services, American Library Association.

INTRODUCTION

Children enjoy reading about characters that have the same first name as the reader. They also like characters with the names of their friends and family members or characters that have unusual names. The purpose of this book is to motivate youngsters to read by arranging entries by the character's first name. The names of major characters are used and a book may have more than one entry. Fiction, nonfiction (including biographies), picture books, and easy readers are included because the purpose is to encourage readers to locate characters with a particular name.

The body of the guide consists of an alphabetical listing by characters' first names. Citation information was determined by the information printed in each book and from standard reference sources including *Children's Books in Print, 1991-1992*, *The Elementary School Library Collection*, 17th edition, and *Children's Catalog*, 15th edition. Information for each title includes author, title, illustrator, publisher, publication date, number of pages, type of book, Library of Congress catalog number (LC), International Standard Book Number (ISBN), and a brief annotation. Book awards follow the annotation.

A combined author/title index and a title index are included to assist in determining the availability of titles in a collection. The books selected for inclusion in this guide should be found in most children's library collections. Included are selected award-winning books, Reading Rainbow titles, phase 1 and 2 titles from *The Elementary School Library Collection*, 17th edition, and titles from *Children's Catalog*, 15th edition.

Book Awards

Books that have been given well-known children's book awards and reader's choice book awards are included. Some titles have received multiple awards, which are cited. Some award-winning books have not been included because they do not have character names or because the book was unavailable for review.

Adult Selected Awards

JANE ADDAMS CHILDREN'S BOOK AWARDS. Presented annually since 1953 by the Women's International League for Peace and Freedom and the Jane Addams Peace Association for a book "that most effectively promotes the cause of peace, social justice, world community, and the equality of the sexes and all races." Honor books may be included.

MILDRED L. BATCHELDER AWARD. Presented annually since 1968 by the Children's Services Division (now Association for Library Services to Children) of the American Library Association to an American publisher of the most outstanding English translation of a foreign-language book published in a foreign country in the preceding year.

BOSTON GLOBE-HORN BOOK AWARDS. Presented annually since 1967 by the *Boston Globe* and *Horn Book Magazine*. Two awards were given through 1975—for outstanding text and for outstanding illustration. In 1976 the award categories were changed to Outstanding Fiction or Poetry, Outstanding Nonfiction, and Outstanding Illustration.

RANDOLPH CALDECOTT MEDAL. Presented annually since 1938 by the Association for Library Service to Children, a division of the American Library Association, to "the artist of the most distinguished American picture book for children."

CARNEGIE MEDAL. Presented annually since 1936 by the British Library Association for an outstanding children's book written in English and published in the United Kingdom.

CHILD STUDY CHILDREN'S BOOK AWARD. Presented annually since 1943 by Child Study Children's Book Committee at Bank Street College of Education. This award is given to a book of fiction or nonfiction that "deals realistically with the problems of the world."

CHRISTOPHER AWARD. Presented annually since 1969 by "The Christophers" to children's authors and illustrators "whose works have achieved artistic excellence—affirming the highest values of the human spirit," and have wide public acceptance.

DUTTON JUNIOR ANIMAL BOOK AWARD. Presented annually from 1965 to 1969 by E. P. Dutton and Company. The award was presented for a fiction or nonfiction book about animals.

GOLDEN KITE AWARD. Presented annually since 1973 by the Society of Children's Book Writers. Fiction, nonfiction, and picture/illustration categories are included. "The winning titles are those which exhibit excellence in writing and genuinely appeal to the interest and concerns of children."

JEFFERSON CUP AWARD. Presented annually since 1983 by the Children's and Young Adult Round Table of the Virginia Library Association to "encourage the writing of quality books on history, biography and historical fiction."

CORETTA SCOTT KING AWARD. Presented annually since 1969 by the Coretta Scott King Task Force of the American Library Association's Social Responsibilities Round Table. Awarded to African-American authors and illustrators "whose distinguished books promote an understanding and appreciation of the culture and contribution of all people to the realization of the 'American Dream.' "

NATIONAL JEWISH BOOK AWARDS. Presented annually since 1952 by the Jewish Welfare Board and the Jewish Book Council to "authors and illustrators who have made outstanding contributions to Jewish Literature for children."

JOHN NEWBERY MEDAL. Presented annually since 1922 by the Association for Library Service to Children, a division of the American Library Association, to the author "of the most distinguished contribution to American literature for children."

SCOTT O'DELL AWARD FOR HISTORICAL FICTION. Presented annually since 1981 by the Advisory Committee of the Bulletin of the Center for Children's Books to a book of historical fiction "set in the new world," which has literary merit and has been published by a U.S. publisher.

EDGAR ALLAN POE AWARD. Presented annually since 1961 by the Mystery Writers of America for the best juvenile mystery of the year.

Reader's Choice Awards

ALASKA: See Pacific Northwest.

ARIZONA: ARIZONA YOUNG READERS AWARD. Sponsored by Arizona State University, Tempe, and the University of Arizona (Department of Elementary Education, College of Education), Tucson, to "stimulate the interest of young readers in outstanding literature written primarily for them." Awards presented annually since 1977.

ARKANSAS: CHARLIE MAY SIMON BOOK AWARD. Sponsored by the Arkansas Elementary School Council of the State Department of Education to promote reading and the discussion of books and to honor an Arkansas author. Awards presented annually since 1970.

CALIFORNIA: CALIFORNIA YOUNG READER MEDAL. Sponsored by the California Reading Association, California Library Association, California Media & Library Educators Association, and California Association of Teachers of English to "encourage California children to become better acquainted with 'good literature' and to honor a favorite book and its author." Awards presented in four categories since 1983.

COLORADO: COLORADO CHILDREN'S BOOK AWARD. Sponsored by the Colorado Council of the International Reading Association to "encourage children's active involvement with books and reading." Awards presented annually since 1976.

FLORIDA: SUNSHINE STATE YOUNG READER'S AWARD. Sponsored by the School Library Media Services Office, Florida Department of Education, and the Florida Association for Media in Education to "encourage students to read for personal satisfaction . . . to help students become discriminating in their personal selection of books . . . and to give recognition to those who write books for children and young people." Awards presented annually since 1981.

GEORGIA: GEORGIA CHILDREN'S BOOK AWARDS. Sponsored by the University of Georgia, College of Education. Awards presented annually since 1969.

HAWAII: NENE AWARD. Sponsored by the Hawaii Association of School Librarians and the Children's and Youth Services Section, Hawaii Library Association to "help the children of Hawaii become acquainted with the best contemporary writers of fiction for children, become aware of the qualities that make a good book, and to choose the best rather than the mediocre." Awards presented annually since 1964.

IDAHO: See Pacific Northwest.

INDIANA: YOUNG HOOSIER AWARD. Sponsored by the Association for Indiana Media Educators to "encourage boys and girls to read and enjoy good books." Awards presented annually since 1975.

IOWA: IOWA CHILDREN'S CHOICE AWARD. Sponsored by the Iowa Educational Media Association to "provide an avenue for positive dialogue between teacher, parent, and children about books and authors." Awards presented annually since 1980.

KANSAS: WILLIAM ALLEN WHITE CHILDREN'S BOOK AWARD. Sponsored by Emporia State University, William Allen White Library, to "encourage the boys and girls of Kansas to read and enjoy good books." Awards presented annually since 1953.

KENTUCKY: THE BLUEGRASS AWARD. Sponsored by Northern Kentucky University, Learning Resources Center to "encourage Kentucky children to read and enjoy a variety of books and select their favorite." Awards presented annually since 1983.

MASSACHUSETTS: MASSACHUSETTS CHILDREN'S BOOK AWARDS. Sponsored by Salem State College to retain children's interest in reading once they have learned to read. Awards presented annually since 1976.

MICHIGAN: MICHIGAN YOUNG READERS' AWARDS. Sponsored by the Michigan Council of Teachers of English to "interest children in reading literature and to express their feelings and ideas." Awards presented annually since 1980.

MINNESOTA: MAUD HART LOVELACE BOOK AWARD. Sponsored by the Friends of Minnesota Valley Regional Library and endorsed by the Minnesota Educational Media Organization and the Minnesota Library Association to "motivate kids to read, introduce books that people may have missed, and encourage interaction between public and school librarians." Awards presented annually since 1980.

MISSOURI: MARK TWAIN AWARD. Sponsored by the Missouri Association of School Librarians to "provide the children of Missouri with their very own source to enrich their lives through reading and to find the joys that lie in being able to read." Awards presented annually since 1972.

MONTANA: See Pacific Northwest.

NEBRASKA: NEBRASKA GOLDEN SOWER AWARDS. Sponsored by the Nebraska Library Association to "encourage Nebraska children to read widely in several areas of picture books and fiction." Awards presented annually since 1981.

NEW HAMPSHIRE: GREAT STONE FACE AWARD. Sponsored by CHILIS, a Division of the New Hampshire Library Association-Children's Librarians to "promote reading for fun and enjoyment among the children of New Hampshire by having them select and honor the books that have given them the most pleasure." Awards presented annually since 1980.

NEW MEXICO: LAND OF ENCHANTMENT CHILDREN'S BOOK AWARD. Sponsored by the New Mexico Library Association and the New Mexico State International Reading Association. Awards presented annually since 1981.

OHIO: BUCKEYE CHILDREN'S BOOK AWARDS. Sponsored by the International Reading Association, Ohio Council, Ohio Council of Teachers of English Language Arts, Ohio Department of Education, Ohio Educational Library Media Association, the Ohio Library Association, and the State Library of Ohio to "encourage children to read literature critically, encourage teacher involvement in children's literature programs in their schools, and to commend authors." Awards presented annually since 1982.

OKLAHOMA: SEQUOYAH CHILDREN'S BOOK AWARD. Sponsored by the Oklahoma State Department of Education, Library Resources. Awards presented annually since 1959.

OREGON: See Pacific Northwest.

PACIFIC NORTHWEST: YOUNG READER'S CHOICE AWARD. Sponsored by the Children's and Young Adult Services Division, Pacific Northwest Library Association. Awards presented annually since 1940.

PENNSYLVANIA: CAROLYN W. FIELD AWARD. Sponsored by the Youth Services Division of the Pennsylvania Library Association. Awards presented annually since 1984.

SOUTH CAROLINA: SOUTH CAROLINA CHILDREN'S BOOK AWARD. Sponsored by the South Carolina Association of School Librarians, the State Department of Education, and the College of Librarianship, University of South Carolina to "expose students in grades 4-8 to contemporary and realistic literature concerned with a variety of subjects that relate to children's lives today." Awards presented annually since 1976.

TEXAS: TEXAS BLUEBONNET AWARD. Sponsored by the Texas Library Association, Texas Association of School Librarians, and Children's Round Table to "encourage Texas children to read more books, explore a variety of books, develop powers of discrimination, and to identify the authors of their choice." Awards presented annually since 1981.

UTAH: UTAH CHILDREN'S BOOK AWARD. Sponsored by the Children's Literature Association of Utah, Department of Educational Studies, University of Utah to "encourage the love of reading on the part of children and to introduce children to good books by outstanding authors." Awards presented annually since 1980.

VERMONT: DOROTHY CANFIELD FISHER CHILDREN'S BOOK AWARD. Sponsored by the Vermont Department of Libraries and the Vermont Congress of Parents and Teachers to "encourage Vermont school children to become enthusiastic and discriminating readers." Awards presented annually since 1957.

WASHINGTON: WASHINGTON CHILDREN'S CHOICE PICTURE BOOK AWARD. Sponsored by the Washington Library Media Association. Awards presented annually since 1982.

WEST VIRGINIA: WEST VIRGINIA CHILDREN'S BOOK AWARD. Sponsored by an award committee to "enrich the lives of children in grades 3 through 6 by encouraging the reading of books of literary quality." Awards presented annually since 1985.

WISCONSIN: GOLDEN ARCHER AWARD and LITTLE ARCHER AWARD. Sponsored by the Department of Library Science, University of Wisconsin-Oshkosh. Awards presented annually since 1974.

KEY TO ENTRIES

Under each name, you'll find a list of books that have characters with that name. Each listing includes the author's name, the book's title, and information such as when the book was published, its length, and the type of book, followed by a short description of the book and any awards it won.

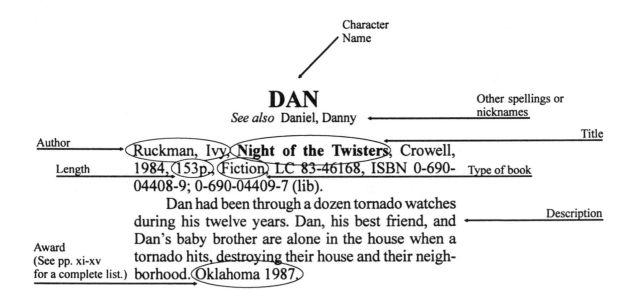

Character Name

DAN
See also Daniel, Danny

Other spellings or nicknames

Title

Author

Ruckman, Ivy, **Night of the Twisters**, Crowell, 1984, 153p., Fiction, LC 83-46168, ISBN 0-690-04408-9; 0-690-04409-7 (lib).

Length

Type of book

Dan had been through a dozen tornado watches during his twelve years. Dan, his best friend, and Dan's baby brother are alone in the house when a tornado hits, destroying their house and their neighborhood. Oklahoma 1987.

Description

Award
(See pp. xi-xv for a complete list.)

-A-

AARON
See also Aerin, Erin

Fleischman, Paul, **Half-a-Moon Inn**, illustrated by Kathy Jacobi, Harper & Row, 1980, 88p., Fiction, ISBN 0-06-021918-1.

Aaron was born mute and uses writing to communicate. He is left alone when his mother goes to the village, and when she doesn't return, Aaron searches for her in a blizzard. He becomes entrapped by the evil manager of the Half-a-Moon Inn.

Gilson, Jamie, **Dial Leroi Rupert, DJ**, illustrated by John Wallner, Lothrop, Lee & Shepard, 1979, 126p., Fiction, ISBN 0-688-51888-5.

Aaron is a sixth-grade boy who is constantly getting into mischief with two of his friends. The boys get into trouble with adults and finally meet a disc jockey who helps them with their problems.

ABBIE
See also Abby, Abigail

Eager, Edward, **Seven-Day Magic**, illustrated by N. M. Bodecker, Harcourt Brace Jovanovich, 1962, 156p., Fiction, ISBN 0-15-272922-4.

Abbie finds a book of magic at the library. She and her friends have many exciting adventures with it, until the book is due and has to be returned.

Giff, Patricia Reilly, **Have You Seen Hyacinth McCaw?**, illustrated by Anthony Kramer, Delacorte, 1981, 134p., Fiction, ISBN 0-385-28389-X.

Abbie and her friend discover there are several mysteries to solve when they look for Hyacinth McCaw. There is another book about Abbie and her friend.

Roop, Peter and Connie Roop, **Keep the Lights Burning, Abbie**, illustrated by Peter E. Hanson, Carolrhoda, 1985, 40p., Nonfiction, LC 84-27446, ISBN 0-87614-275-7 (lib); 0-87614-454-7 (pbk).

Abbie Burgess and her family live in a lighthouse on an island off the coast of Maine. Abbie's father is the lighthouse keeper and when a terrible storm delays his return to the island for several weeks, Abbie must keep the lights burning. Based on a true incident that happened in 1856. A Reading Rainbow book.

ABBY
See also Abbie, Abigail

Doty, Jean Slaughter, **Dark Horse**, illustrated by Dorothy Haskell Chhuy, Morrow, 1983, 122p., Fiction, ISBN 0-688-01703-7.

Abby works as a volunteer at a horse stable. She discovers that an unusual-looking horse is good at jumping and Abby is allowed to compete with him.

O'Connor, Jane, **Yours Till Niagara Falls, Abby**, illustrated by Margot Apple, Hastings House, 1979, 128p., Fiction, ISBN 0-803-886-012.

Ten-year-old Abby is concerned about how she is going to survive two months of summer camp without her best friend. Nebraska 1982.

Thomas, Joyce Carol, **Marked by Fire**, Avon, 1982, 172p., Fiction, ISBN 0-380-793-27X (pbk).

Abby was born in an Oklahoma cotton field after a tornado. As she grows up, she learns the secrets of folk medicine from a healer. 1983 Jane Addams Award book.

ABE
See also Abraham

Lexau, Joan M., **Striped Ice Cream**, illustrated by John Wilson, Lippincott, 1968, 95p., Fiction, LC 68-10774, ISBN 0-590-4290-5.

Abe's sister is resigned to the fact that their mother cannot afford anything special for her birthday, but she does not understand why the family seems to have turned against her, until the big day finally arrives. Arkansas 1971.

ABEL

Steig, William, **Abel's Island**, Farrar, Straus & Giroux, 1976, 117p., Fiction, ISBN 0-374-30010-0.

Abel the mouse and his wife have lived happily until a great flood takes Abel to an uninhabited island where he spends a year. 1977 Newbery Honor book.

ABIGAIL
See also Abbie, Abby

Cox, David, **Bossyboots**, illustrated by David Cox, Crown, 1985, 26p., Picture Book, LC 86-16799, ISBN 0-517-56491-2.

Abigail is the bossiest girl in all of Australia. While taking the stagecoach across the bush to her home in Narrabi, she orders around the horses, the other passengers, and the driver. Abigail's bossiness comes in handy when the stagecoach is held up by Flash Fred the outlaw. A Reading Rainbow book.

Park, Ruth, **Playing Beatie Bow**, Atheneum, 1982, 196p., Fiction, ISBN 0-689-30889-2.

Fourteen-year-old Abigail is unhappy with her parents and their decision to move to Norway from Australia. While watching youngsters play a game called 'Beatie Bow', Abigail is transported to an earlier century and meets the girl that the game is named for. 1982 Boston Globe-Horn Book Award. 1981 Best Australian Book of the Year.

ABRAHAM
See also Abe

Freedman, Russell, **Lincoln: A Photobiography**, illustrated by Photos and Prints, Clarion, 1987, 150p., Nonfiction, LC 86-33379, ISBN 0-89919-380-3.

A warm, appealing biography of Abraham Lincoln. Beginnning with a lively account of his boyhood, the book continues with Lincoln's courtship of and marriage to Mary Todd. The focus is on the presidential years (1861-1865), with explanations of the many complex issues that Lincoln faced during the Civil War years. Numerous photographs and prints illustrate the book. 1988 Newbery Award book. 1988 Jefferson Cup Award.

ABYSSINIA

Thomas, Joyce Carol, **Bright Shadow**, Avon, 1983, 144p., Fiction, ISBN 0-380-845-091.

Abyssinia Jackson has to learn to cope with tragedy when peace is shattered in the Oklahoma countryside and her boyfriend disappears. 1984 Coretta Scott King Honor book.

ADAM

Aliki, **Feelings**, illustrated by Aliki, Greenwillow, 1984, 32p., Picture Book, LC 84-4098, ISBN 0-688-03831-X; 0-688-03832-8 (lib).

Adam is just one of the children who is portrayed showing the various emotions that everyone feels: sadness, fear, jealousy, anger, love, and so forth. Poems, dialogues, pictures, and stories. A Reading Rainbow book.

Brittain, Bill, **Wish Giver: Three Tales of Coven Tree, The**, illustrated by Andrew Glass, Harper & Row, 1983, 181p., Fiction, LC 82-48264, ISBN 0-06-020686-1; 0-06-020687-X (lib).

Thaddeus Blinn was a funny little man who appeared from out of nowhere and put his tent by the annual Coven Tree Church Social. He said he had the power to give people exactly what they asked for. Adam is one of the characters who finds that wishes often have unexpected results when they come true. 1984 Newbery Honor book.

Bulla, Clyde Robert, **Cardboard Crown**, illustrated by Michele Chessare, Crowell, 1984, 78p., Fiction, ISBN 0-690-04361-9.

Adam sells his most prized possession to get money to help a mysterious girl return to her father.

Gray, Elizabeth Janet, **Adam of the Road**, illustrated by Robert Lawson, Viking, 1942, 317p., Fiction, LC 42-10681, ISBN 0-670-10435-3.

Adam is the son of a minstrel in thirteenth-century England. His father told him that roads are important because they bring all kinds of people together and they provide a home to a minstrel. When Adam's dog is stolen and his father disappears, Adam takes to the road to search for them both. 1943 Newbery Award book.

Greene, Constance, **I and Sproggy**, illustrated by Emily McCully, Viking, 1978, 155p., Fiction, ISBN 0-670-38980-3.

Ten-year-old Adam lives in New York, and when his stepsister comes to visit he is asked to take care of her. Through their adventures, Adam learns that making friends with someone is better than being rivals.

Levinson, Marilyn, **And Don't Bring Jeremy**, illustrated by Diane de Groat, Holt, 1985, 122p., Fiction, ISBN 0-8050-0554-4.

Eleven-year-old Adam has trouble making friends in his new neighborhood because of their attitudes toward his older brother who has neurological impairments.

Martel, Cruz, **Yagua Days**, illustrated by Jerry Pinkney, Dial, 1976, 40p., Fiction, ISBN 0-8037-9766-4.

Adam makes numerous discoveries about the differences in life in New York City and on an island when he goes to Puerto Rico to visit relatives.

Moore, Lilian, **I'll Meet You at the Cucumbers**, illustrated by Sharon Wooding, Atheneum, 1988, 63p., Fiction, ISBN 0-689-31243-1.

Adam is a country mouse. When he goes to the city to visit a friend he discovers new sights and sounds and has many experiences.

Smith, Janice Lee, **Monster in the Third Dresser Drawer and Other Stories about Adam Joshua, The**, illustrated by Dick Gackenbach, Harper & Row, 1981, 86p., Fiction, ISBN 0-06-025739-3.

Six humorous short stories about Adam Joshua include an imaginary monster in his room, and the addition of a new baby sister to the family. There are several other books about Adam Joshua.

Tapp, Kathy Kennedy, **Den 4 Meets the Jinx**, Macmillan, 1988, 118p., Fiction, ISBN 0-689-50453-5.

Adam is frustrated with his five-year-old sister who gets into everything, although he discovers that it can be helpful having a sister who knows what is going on.

ADDIE

Rock, Gail, **House Without a Christmas Tree, The**, illustrated by Charles Gehm, Knopf, 1974, 87p., Fiction, ISBN 0-394-92833-4.

Ten-year-old Addie wants a Christmas tree, but her father refuses to buy one even though their house is the only one without a tree. There is another book about Addie and her family.

AERIN
See also Aaron, Erin

McKinley, Robin, **Hero and the Crown, The**, Greenwillow, 1984, 246p., Fiction, LC 84-4074, ISBN 0-688-02593-5.

Aerin is the daughter of a Damarian king and a witch-woman of the mysterious demon-haunted north. In this fantasy tale, Aerin is able to claim her birthright with the guidance of a wizard and the help of the blue sword. 1985 Newbery Award book.

AGATHA

Brittain, Bill, **Wish Giver: Three Tales of Coven Tree, The**, illustrated by Andrew Glass, Harper & Row, 1983, 181p., Fiction, LC 82-48264, ISBN 0-06-020686-1; 0-06-020687-X (lib).

Thaddeus Blinn was a funny little man who appeared from out of nowhere and put his tent by the annual Coven Tree Church Social. He said he had the power to give people exactly what they asked for. Agatha is one of the characters who finds that wishes often have unexpected results when they come true. 1984 Newbery Honor book.

AGBA

Henry, Marguerite, **King of the Wind**, illustrated by Wesley Dennis, Rand McNally, 1948, 174p., Fiction, LC 48-8773, ISBN 0-02-743629-2.

This story follows the adventures of the Arabian stallion who was taken to England to become one of the founding sires of the Thoroughbred breed, and the mute Arab stable boy, Agba, who tended him with loyalty and devotion all of his life. 1949 Newbery Award book. Pacific Northwest 1951.

AL
See also Alan, Albert, Aldo, Alec, Alex, Alexander, Alexandra, Alfred, Allen, Almanzo

Hurd, Thacher, **Mama Don't Allow: Starring Miles and the Swamp Band**, illustrated by Thacher Hurd, Harper & Row, 1984, 40p., Picture Book, LC 83-47703, ISBN 0-06-022689-7; 0-06-022690-0 (lib); 0-06-443078-2 (pbk).

Al and the Swamp Band have a great time playing at the Alligator Ball, until they discover the dinner menu. 1985 Boston Globe-Horn Book Award. A Reading Rainbow book.

Yorinks, Arthur, **Hey, Al**, illustrated by Richard Egielski, Farrar, Straus & Giroux, 1986, 28p., Picture Book, LC 86-80955, ISBN 0-374-33060-3.

Al is a janitor. He and his dog, Eddie, live a simple life in a single room. They struggle until a mysterious bird offers them a change of fortune. 1987 Caldecott Award book. Kentucky 1988.

ALAN
See also Al, Allen

Levoy, Myron, **Alan and Naomi**, Harper & Row, 1977, 192p., Fiction, LC 76-41522, ISBN 0-06-023799-6; 0-06-023800-3 (lib).

Set in New York in the 1940s, Alan tries to befriend Naomi, a girl traumatized by Nazi brutality in France. 1978 Jane Addams Honor book.

Pinkwater, D. Manus, **Alan Mendelsohn, the Boy from Mars**, Dutton, 1979, 248p., Fiction, ISBN 0-525-25360-2.

As a new student, Alan befriends the class creep. The two boys buy a mind control system that takes them on hilarious adventures through time and space.

Rockwell, Thomas, **How to Eat Fried Worms**, illustrated by Emily McCully, Watts, 1973, 115p., Fiction, LC 73-4262, ISBN 0-531-02631-0.

Billy is willing to eat anything and agrees to eat fifteen worms to win a bet with Alan. Arizona 1979. California 1975. Hawaii 1976. Indiana 1977. Iowa 1980. Massachusetts 1976. Missouri 1975. Oklahoma 1976. South Carolina 1976.

Rockwell, Thomas, **How to Fight a Girl**, illustrated by Gioia Fiammenghi, Watts, 1987, 112p., Fiction, ISBN 0-531-10140-1.

Although Alan lost the worm-eating contest in another book, he is determined to get the best of his friend and comes up with a plan that involves two girls.

Van Allsburg, Chris, **Garden of Abdul Gasazi, The**, illustrated by Chris Van Allsburg, Houghton Mifflin, 1979, 30p., Picture Book, LC 79-016844, ISBN 0-395-27804-X.

When Alan takes the dog he is caring for on a walk, Fritz escapes. Fritz runs into the forbidden garden of a retired magician who hates dogs and Alan is convinced that a spell has been cast over his charge. 1980 Caldecott Honor book. 1980 Boston Globe-Horn Book Award. A Reading Rainbow book.

ALANNA
See also Elana, Elena

Pierce, Tamora, **Alanna: The First Adventure**, Atheneum, 1983, 241p., Fiction, ISBN 0-689-30994-5.

Alanna wants to be a knight so she trades places with her twin brother who wants to live a quiet life. There are several books about Alanna and her adventures during the Middle Ages.

ALBERT
See also Al

Brown, Marcia, **Stone Soup: An Old Tale**, illustrated by Marcia Brown, Scribner, 1947, 40p., Picture Book, ISBN 0-684-92296-7; 0-684-16217-2 (pbk).

Albert and the other peasants hid their food when they saw three hungry soldiers coming down the road. The soldiers taught the villagers how to make soup from three stones and soon a village feast was prepared. An old folktale. 1948 Caldecott Honor book.

Isenberg, Barbara and Marjorie Jaffe, **Albert the Running Bear's Exercise Book**, illustrated by

Diane de Groat, Clarion, 1984, 63p., Picture Book, LC 84-7064, ISBN 0-89919-294-7; 0-89919-318-8.

Violet has been trained as a gymnast and a stunt bear. She knows numerous exercises to teach Albert so he can become a better runner. Pictures show the reader how to do the exercises with Albert. A Reading Rainbow book.

McGinnis, Lila, **Ghost Upstairs**, illustrated by Amy Rowen, Hastings House, 1982, 1982p., Fiction, ISBN 0-8038-9286-1.

When an old mansion is demolished, a lively young ghost moves into Albert's bedroom and gets him into humorous trouble.

Meyer, Edith Patterson, **Champions of Peace: Winners of the Nobel Peace Prize**, Little, Brown, 1959, 216p., Nonfiction, LC 59-7355.

Dr. Albert Schweitzer was a medical missionary in French Equatorial Africa. He won the Nobel Peace Prize in 1952 for his respect for all human life. 1960 Jane Addams Award book.

ALDO
See also Al

Hurwitz, Johanna, **Aldo Applesauce**, Morrow, 1979, 127p., Fiction, ISBN 0-688-32199-2.

When fourth grader Aldo Sossi moves from the city to the suburbs there are many changes, and making friends in a new school is one of the most difficult. There are other books about Aldo.

ALEC
See also Al, Alexander

Farley, Walter, **Black Stallion Returns, The**, Random House, 1945, 199p., Fiction, LC 45-8763, ISBN 0-394-80602-6; 0-394-90602-0 (lib); 0-394-83610-3 (pbk).

Alec Ramsey is heartbroken when his beloved horse, the Black Stallion, is taken by an Arab chieftain. Alec's love for his horse takes him halfway across the world to the Great Central Desert of Arabia on an adventure of intrigue. Pacific Northwest 1948.

Kingman, Lee, **Luck of the Miss l**, Houghton Mifflin, 1986, 153p., Fiction, ISBN 0-395-40421-5.

Eleven-year-old Alec has many problems to overcome as he trains for a rower's race, including the capsizing of his boat.

ALEX
See also Al, Alexa, Alexis, Alexander, Alexandra

Bawden, Nina, **Finding**, Lothrop, Lee & Shepard, 1985, 153p., Fiction, ISBN 0-688-04979-6.

Alex was found in the arms of a statue as a baby and adopted by a family who raised him. He becomes fearful that he will be taken away when an elderly woman thinks that he may be her grandson.

Graeber, Charlotte, **Mustard**, illustrated by Donna Diamond, Macmillan, 1982, 42p., Fiction, LC 81-20764, ISBN 0-02-736690-1.

Eight-year-old Alex and his family think Mustard is the most wonderful cat in the world. Mustard is fourteen and has been with the family since before Alex was born. It is hard for the family to accept the realization that Mustard is old and losing his health. West Virginia 1986.

Jukes, Mavis, **Like Jake and Me**, illustrated by Lloyd Bloom, Knopf, 1984, 30p., Picture Book, LC 83-8380, ISBN 0-394-85608-2; 0-394-95608-7 (lib).

Alex wants to be like Jake, his big, strong, stepfather. But when a large, hairy spider crawls into Jake's clothes, Alex finds that there are some things that even cowboys are afraid of. Alex becomes the brave one as he searches for the spider. 1985 Newbery Honor book.

Orlev, Uri, **Island on Bird Street, The**, Houghton Mifflin, 1984, 162p., Fiction, ISBN 0-395-33887-5.

Alex is an eleven-year-old Jewish boy who is left alone in the Warsaw ghetto for five months when his mother disappears and his father is sent to an unknown destination by the Germans. 1985 Jane Addams Honor Book.

Park, Barbara, **Skinnybones**, Knopf, 1982, 112p., Fiction, ISBN 0-394-849-884; 0-394-949-889 (lib).

Alex Frankovitch has been in Little League for six years and is the smallest team member. His wisecracking and bragging get him into a humorous battle of skills with a pitcher who has a perfect record. Georgia 1985. Minnesota 1985. Texas 1985. Utah 1987.

Roberts, Willo Davis, **Magic Book, The**, Atheneum, 1986, 150p., Fiction, ISBN 0-689-31120-6.

Alex and his friends try magic spells from an old book but the spells don't give the anticipated results.

ALEXA
See also Alex

Savage, Deborah, **Rumour of Otters**, Houghton Mifflin, 1986, 156p., Fiction, ISBN 0-395-41186-6.

Fourteen-year-old Alexa lives on a remote New Zealand sheep station. She has heard rumours of otters that only the Maori tribesmen have seen and decides she will find them.

ALEXANDER
See also Al, Alec, Alex

Boston, Lucy, **Children of Green Knowe**, illustrated by Peter Boston, Peter Smith, 1955, 157p., Fiction, ISBN 0-8446-6288-7.

Alexander is one of the children who lived in the ancient house of Green Knowe during the seventeenth century. The children meet a boy from the present and they have many adventures. There are five books in this series.

Garden, Nancy, **Prisoner of Vampires**, illustrated by Michele Chessare, Farrar, Straus & Giroux, 1984, 213p., Fiction, ISBN 0-374-36129-0.

Twelve-year-old Alexander Darlington meets a vampire while he is researching a school project and soon sinister events take place. Alexander and his friend Mike decide they have to stop the vampire in this suspenseful and scary tale set in Cambridge, Massachusetts.

Keller, Mollie, **Alexander Hamilton**, Watts, 1986, 72p., Nonfiction, ISBN 0-531-10214-9.

A biography about Alexander Hamilton, a famous statesman who was involved in the Constitutional Convention of the United States.

Lasker, Joe, **Great Alexander the Great, The**, Viking, 1983, 32p., Nonfiction, ISBN 0-670-34841-4.

As a boy Alexander overcame a frightened horse and became determined to not let anything overcome him. As a man, he conquered one of the greatest kingdoms of his time and was known as a leader and a warrior. A biography of this famous and feared leader.

Lionni, Leo, **Alexander and the Wind-Up Mouse**, Pantheon, 1969, 31p., Picture Book, ISBN 0-394-82911-5.

Alexander is a small mouse who makes friends with a toy mouse and wants to be just like him, until he makes a discovery about the toy. 1970 Caldecott Honor book.

Peck, Richard, **Ghost Belonged to Me; A Novel, The**, Viking, 1975, 183p., Fiction, ISBN 0-670-33767-6.

Alexander and his friend Blossom Culp become involved with an elderly man and a ghost and have humorous adventures. There are other books about Alexander and Blossom.

Raskin, Ellen, **Westing Game, The**, Dutton, 1978, 185p., Fiction, LC 77-18866, ISBN 0-525-42320-6.

Alexander is one of the sixteen people invited to the reading of the very strange will of the very rich Samuel W. Westing. Alexander could become a millionaire depending on how he plays the tricky and dangerous Westing Game. 1979 Newbery Award book. 1978 Boston Globe-Horn Book Award. Michigan 1982.

Ross, Josephine, **Alexander Fleming**, illustrated by Edward Mortelmans, Hamish Hamilton, 1984, 60p., Nonfiction, ISBN 0-241-11203-6.

Dr. Alexander Fleming discovered penicillin while working as a researcher in a bacteriology department. As a result, he won the Nobel Prize for medicine for this important medical contribution.

Viorst, Judith, **Alexander and the Terrible, Horrible, No Good, Very Bad Day**, illustrated by Ray Cruz, Atheneum, 1977, 28p., Picture Book, LC 72-75289, ISBN 0-689-30072-7.

Alexander knows it will be a bad day when he awakes with gum in his hair and trips on his skateboard getting out of bed. As the day continues everything goes wrong. Georgia 1977. A Reading Rainbow book.

ALEXANDRA
See also Al, Alex

Greene, Constance, **Your Old Pal, Al**, Viking, 1979, 149p., Fiction, ISBN 0-670-79575-5.

Alexandra, known as Al, is waiting for two special letters when her best friend comes to visit. There are other books about Al.

ALEXIS
See also Alex

Hodges, Margaret, **Avenger**, Scribner, 1982, 178p., Fiction, ISBN 0-684-17636-X.

Set in ancient Greece, fifteen-year-old Alexis is determined to avenge his father who had his ship attacked by pirates and received no help from the neighboring king. Alexis becomes involved in the Olympic games and has dangerous and exciting adventures.

ALFIE
See also Al, Alfred

Byars, Betsy, **Cartoonist, The**, illustrated by Richard Cuffari, Viking, 1978, 119p., Fiction, ISBN 0-670-20556-7.

Alfie treasures his private room in the attic where he can escape from his family and draw his cartoons. When his privacy is threatened, Alfie is determined to keep his room.

ALFRED
See also Al, Alfie

Meyer, Edith Patterson, **Champions of Peace: Winners of the Nobel Peace Prize**, illustrated by Eric

von Schmidt, Little, Brown, 1959, 216p., Nonfiction, LC 59-7355.

Alfred Nobel was the Swedish inventor of dynamite who left his fortune to establish the Nobel Foundation to give an international peace prize in his honor. 1960 Jane Addams Award book.

ALICE

Adams, Laurie and Allison Coudert, **Alice and the Boa Constrictor**, illustrated by Emily Arnold McCully, Houghton Mifflin, 1983, 87p., Fiction, ISBN 0-395-33068-8.

Alice studies snakes at school and she is determined to buy a boa constrictor for a pet. She has many humorous ideas for making money to buy the snake and a cage. When she finally gets her snake there is havoc.

Burchard, Peter, **Sea Change**, Farrar, Straus & Giroux, 1984, 117p., Fiction, ISBN 0-374-36460-5.

Stories about Alice, Ann, and Lisa who are grandmother, mother, and daughter. The stories tell about how family members deal with problems and with one another.

Carroll, Lewis, **Alice's Adventures in Wonderland**, illustrated by Anthony Browne, Knopf, 1988, 118p., Fiction, ISBN 0-394-80592-5.

The classic story of Alice and her many adventures in an unusual land after she falls down a rabbit hole.

Cooney, Barbara, **Miss Rumphius**, illustrated by Barbara Cooney, Viking, 1982, 32p., Picture Book, LC 82-2837, ISBN 0-670-47958-6.

As a young girl, Alice Rumphius wanted to visit faraway places, live by the sea, and make the world a more beautiful place. By the time Alice is elderly, she had done all three. 1983 Jane Addams Award book.

Lindbergh, Anne, **Worry Week**, illustrated by Kathryn Hewitt, Harcourt Brace Jovanovich, 1985, 131p., Fiction, ISBN 0-15-299675-3.

Thirteen-year-old Alice and her two younger sisters spend a week by themselves in their beach cottage in Maine and make many discoveries.

Naylor, Phyllis Reynolds, **Agony of Alice, The**, Atheneum, 1985, 119p., Fiction, ISBN 0-689-31143-5.

Eleven-year-old Alice has a difficult time in sixth grade with one uncomfortable experience after another until she's not sure she will ever become a self-confident teen.

Robinson, Barbara, **Best Christmas Pageant Ever, The**, illustrated by Judith Gwyn Brown, Harper & Row, 1972, 80p., Fiction, LC 72-76501, ISBN 06-025043-7; 06-025044-5.

The six Herdman kids are so awful it is hard to believe they are real. When they decide to participate in the church Christmas pageant, Alice thinks it will be the worst one ever. Georgia 1976. Indiana 1978. Minnesota 1982.

Skurzynski, Gloria, **Minstrel in the Tower**, illustrated by Julek Heller, Random House, 1988, 60p., Fiction, ISBN 0-394-99598-8.

Set in the medieval times, Alice and her brother are kidnapped and held captive in a tower when they set out to find their uncle.

ALICIA

Pope, Elizabeth Marie, **Perilous Gard, The**, illustrated by Richard Cuffari, Houghton Mifflin, 1974, 280p., Fiction, ISBN 0-395-18512-2.

Alicia is beautiful but unwise, and when she sends a letter to the queen, her sister is punished and sent to a mysterious castle where she has fantastic adventures. 1975 Newbery Honor book.

ALISON

Krensky, Stephen, **Ghostly Business**, Atheneum, 1980, 144p., Fiction, ISBN 0-689-31048-X.

Alison is one of the Wynd children who uses her magic powers to prevent ghosts from taking over houses in Boston.

ALLEGRA

Lindbergh, Anne, **Worry Week**, illustrated by Kathryn Hewitt, Harcourt Brace Jovanovich, 1985, 131p., Fiction, ISBN 0-15-299675-3.

Eleven-year-old Allegra and her two sisters make many discoveries when they spend a week by themselves at the family beach cottage in Maine.

ALLEN
See also Al, Alan

Gardiner, John Reynolds, **Top Secret**, illustrated by Marc Simont, Little, Brown, 1985, 110p., Fiction, ISBN 0-316-30368-2.

Allen Brewster decides to experiment with human photosynthesis for a science project. In this humorous story, Allen surprises everyone when he turns green.

ALMANZO
See also Al

Wilder, Laura Ingalls, **Farmer Boy**, illustrated by Garth Williams, Harper & Row, 1953, 371p., Fiction, ISBN 0-06-026421-7.

Almanzo Wilder is a young boy growing up on his father's farm in northern New York in the 1800s. His life and that of the Ingalls family will intertwine in later books in this popular series.

Wilder, Laura Ingalls, **These Happy Golden Years**, illustrated by Garth Williams, Harper & Row, 1953, 288p., Fiction.

Laura Ingalls begins teaching and Almanzo Wilder begins courting her in this book in the popular series about the Ingalls family. 1944 Newbery Honor book.

ALVIN
See also Al

Dorros, Arthur, **Alligator Shoes**, illustrated by Arthur Dorros, Dutton, 1982, 22p., Picture Book, LC 82-2409, ISBN 0-525-44428-9.

Alvin the Alligator is locked in a shoe store by mistake. He tried on a large variety of shoes before deciding to keep a very special pair. A Reading Rainbow book.

Greenwald, Sheila, **Alvin Webster's Surefire Plan for Success (And How It Failed)**, Little, Brown, 1987, 95p., Fiction, ISBN 0-316-32706-9.

Alvin is a very bright student who learns to be a sympathetic and decent person when he is forced to help another student to learn math.

Hicks, Clifford, **Wacky World of Alvin Fernald**, illustrated by Laura Hartman, H. Holt, 1981, 143p., Fiction, ISBN 0-03-057783-7.

In this humorous story, Alvin is determined to outdo the mayor with his April Fool's joke. There is another book about Alvin.

Manes, Stephen, **Hooples' Horrible Holiday, The**, illustrated by Wally Neibart, Avon, 1986, 121p., Fiction, ISBN 0-380-89740-7 (pbk).

Alvin Hoople becomes involved in a series of misadventures when he and his family fly to his grandparents' home for Thanksgiving.

AMANDA

Adler, C. S., **Good-Bye Pink Pig**, Putnam, 1985, 176p., Fiction, ISBN 0-399-21282-5.

Amanda is shy and finds it difficult to attend a new middle school. She retreats into a fantasy world and confides in a small rose quartz pig until she makes friends with the school custodian and begins to face the real world.

Bromberg, Andrew, **Computer Overbyte; Plus Two More Codebreakers**, illustrated by Mary Kornblum, Greenwillow, 1982, 47p., Fiction, ISBN 0-688-00943-3.

Amanda and Sherlock Jones solve three mysteries by breaking codes and identifying clues.

Bulla, Clyde Robert, **Lion to Guard Us**, illustrated by Michele Chessare, Crowell, 1981, 117p., Fiction, ISBN 0-690-04097-0.

Amanda's father went to the Jamestown colony in Virginia, leaving his family in London. When their mother dies, the children decide to join their father and experience a shipwreck.

Lyon, George Ella, **Borrowed Children**, Orchard, 1988, 154p., Fiction, ISBN 0-531-08351-9.

Amanda lives in the mountains of Kentucky during the Depression years. She has to assume adult responsibilities when her mother becomes ill and requires lengthy bedrest. 1989 Golden Kite Award.

Snyder, Zilpha Keatley, **Headless Cupid, The**, illustrated by Alton Raible, Atheneum, 1972, 203p., Fiction, LC 78-154763, ISBN 0-689-20687-9.

Amanda is an unusual person. A student of the occult, she wears her ceremonial costume and takes her crow to meet her new stepfamily. When she discovers a headless cupid on the stairwell of their house, Amanda is certain that the house once had a poltergeist. 1972 Newbery Honor book. Kansas 1974.

AMBROSIA

Rohmer, Harriet, **Uncle Nacho's Hat**, illustrated by Veg Reisberg, Children's Book Press, 1989, 32p., Picture Book, LC 88-37090, ISBN 0-89239-043-3.

Ambrosia gives her Uncle Nacho a new hat, but he spends so much time worrying about his old hat that he doesn't enjoy the new one. Adapted from a Nicaraguan folktale, this story is written in both English and Spanish. A Reading Rainbow book.

AMELIA

Lauber, Patricia, **Lost Star: The Story of Amelia Earhart**, Scholastic, 1988, 106p., Nonfiction, ISBN 0-590-41615-4.

Amelia Earhart was a pioneer woman flyer who believed that women were capable of doing what men could do. She disappeared on a flight around the world. This biography provides information about her education and interests.

AMIFIKA

Clifton, Lucille, **Amifika**, Dutton, 1977, 32p., Picture Book, ISBN 0-525-25548-6.

When his father returns from the army, little Amifika hides because he is afraid that his father won't remember him. 1978 Jane Addams Special Recognition book.

AMOS

Lawson, Robert, **Ben and Me; A New and Astonishing Life of Benjamin Franklin as Written by His Good Mouse, Amos, Lately Discovered**, illustrated by Robert Lawson, Little, Brown, 1939, 113p., Fiction, ISBN 0-316-51732-1.

Amos Mouse moves into Benjamin Franklin's hat and begins advising the historical figure and helping to make him famous.

Seligson, Susan, **Amos: The Story of an Old Dog and His Couch**, illustrated by Howie Schneider, Little, Brown, 1987, 32p., Picture Book, ISBN 0-316-77404-9.

Amos is an old dog that finds adventures when he discovers that his favorite couch has a motor and can be driven. Washington 1990.

Yates, Elizabeth, **Amos Fortune, Free Man**, illustrated by Nora S. Unwin, Aladdin, 1951, 178p., Nonfiction, ISBN 0-14-34158-7.

The biography of At-Mun, a young African prince, from the time he was taken from his jungle village by white slave dealers in 1725. Included are his years of slavery in America and his purchase of his own freedom. In 1801, he divided up the remainder of his money for bequests to a church and a school. 1951 Newbery Award book. Kansas 1953.

AMY

Alcott, Louisa M., **Little Women, or Meg, Jo, Beth and Amy**, Little, Brown, 1968, 372p., Fiction, ISBN 0-316-03090-2.

The classic story of four sisters and their family life in New England at the time of the Civil War.

Blume, Judy, **It's Not the End of the World**, Bradbury, 1972, 169p., Fiction, ISBN 0-02-711050-8.

Amy, her brother, and sister are very upset when their parents decide to get a divorce. Karen, the older sister, tries to get the parents back together.

Cleaver, Vera, **Sugar Blue**, Lothrop, Lee & Shepard, 1984, 155p., Fiction, ISBN 0-688-02720-2.

Amy is a loner and tries to keep everyone out of her life but she discovers she loves her little niece.

Kennedy, Richard, **Amy's Eyes**, illustrated by Richard Egielski, Harper & Row, 1985, 437p., Fiction, ISBN 0-06-023220-X.

Ten-year-old Amy has been changed into a doll and is taken along when the toys who came to life crew a ship looking for pirate treasure.

Levoy, Myron, **Magic Hat of Mortimer Wintergreen, The**, HarperCollins, 1988, 211p., Fiction, ISBN 0-06-023842-9.

A melodramtic and humorous story set in 1893. Eleven-year-old Amy and her older brother meet a famous magician when they run away from their wicked aunt.

Wright, Betty Ren, **Dollhouse Murders, The**, Holiday House, 1983, 149p., Fiction, LC 83-06147, ISBN 0-823-40497-8.

Amy is fascinated with the old dollhouse that she finds in the attic. It's exactly like the house that she and her aunt are staying in. When strange things begin to happen in the dollhouse, Amy knows that the dolls are trying to tell her something important. California 1987. New Mexico 1988. Pacific Northwest 1986. Texas 1986.

ANASTASIA

Lowry, Lois, **Anastasia Krupnik**, Houghton Mifflin, 1979, 114p., Fiction, LC 79-18625, ISBN 0-395-28629-8.

Anastasia Krupnik finds being ten years old very confusing. She has an awful teacher, difficult parents who are going to have a baby, and there is an interesting sixth-grade boy who has not noticed her. Fortunately, she has her secret green notebook to write in. Michigan 1983.

ANATOLE

Willard, Nancy, **Sailing to Cythera, and Other Anatole Stories**, illustrated by David McPhail, Harcourt Brace Jovanovich, 1974, 72p., Fiction, ISBN 0-15-269961-9.

Three stories about Anatole, an ordinary looking little boy who has the most extraordinary experiences including the ability to run on the air and sail through the wallpaper.

ANDREI
See also Andy

Rosenberg, Maxine B., **Being Adopted**, illustrated by George Ancona, Lothrop, Lee & Shepard, 1984, 44p., Nonfiction, LC 83-17522, ISBN 0-688-02672-9; 0-688-02673-7 (lib).

Ten-year-old Andrei was born in India and adopted by an American family. He and two other children tell about their experiences as adopted members of families who have different cultural and racial roots than they do. A Reading Rainbow book.

ANDREW
See also Andy

Beatty, Patricia, **I Want My Sunday, Stranger**, Morrow, 1977, 254p., Fiction, ISBN 0-688-22118-1.

Andrew Laney runs away from his California home to search for Sunday, his prized race horse. Set in 1863, the horse had been stolen and sold to Civil War troops.

Blume, Judy, **Freckle Juice**, illustrated by Sonia O. Lisker, Four Winds, 1971, 40p., Fiction, ISBN 0-02-711690-5.

Andrew wants to have freckles and he tries a recipe that is given to him for freckle juice, with humorous results.

Gretz, Susanna and Alison Sage, **Teddy Bears Cure a Cold**, illustrated by Susanna Gretz and Alison Sage, Four Winds, 1984, 32p., Picture Book, LC 84-4015, ISBN 0-590-07949-2.

William the bear feels sick and spends several days in bed while Andrew and the other bears take care of him. A Reading Rainbow book.

Haskins, James, **Andrew Young: Man With a Mission**, Lothrop, Lee & Shepard, 1979, 192p., Nonfiction, LC 79-1046, ISBN 0-688-41896-1; 0-688-51896-6 (lib).

The biography of Andrew Young who became U.S. Ambassador to the United Nations. As a child, Andrew learned to use diplomacy instead of his fists to defend himself in a white society hostile to blacks. As an adult his activities include being a clergyman, a civil rights worker, and a legislator. 1980 Coretta Scott King Honor book.

Hilton, Suzanne, **World of Young Andrew Jackson, The,** illustrated by Patricia Lynn, Walker, 1988, 118p., Nonfiction, ISBN 0-8027-6815-6.

This biography of Andrew Jackson begins with the tragic death of his father when Andrew was a child. As an adult, he became a frontier statesman and was later elected to be president of the United States.

Rubinstein, Gillian, **Space Demons,** Dial, 1988, 198p., Fiction, ISBN 0-8037-0534-4.

Andrew, his brother, and friends are drawn into a computer game where they experience danger as they attempt to get out.

ANDY
See also Andrei, Andrew

Burch, Robert, **King Kong and Other Poets**, Viking Kestrel, 1986, 123p., Fiction, ISBN 0-670-80927-6.

Andy is a sixth grader who befriends the quiet new girl in his class who writes poetry.

Calhoun, Mary, **Night the Monster Came**, illustrated by Leslie Morrill, Morrow, 1982, 64p., Fiction, ISBN 0-688-01168-3.

Nine-year-old Andy is certain that Bigfoot is trying to get into his house in the country. He overcomes his fear of monsters through an act of courage.

Cameron, Eleanor, **Beyond Silence**, Dutton, 1980, 197p., Fiction, ISBN 0-525-26463-9.

Andy and his father go on vacation to the Scottish castle where his father was born. At the castle, Andy goes back in time, meets ancestors, and has numerous adventures.

Daugherty, James, **Andy and the Lion**, illustrated by James Daugherty, Viking, 1938, 79p., Picture Book, ISBN 0-670-12433-8.

In this classic story, Andy wins a lion as a friend and then protects the lion from other people. 1939 Caldecott Honor book.

Krumgold, Joseph, **Onion John**, illustrated by Symeon Shimin, Crowell, 1959, 248p., Fiction, LC 59-11395, ISBN 0-690-59957-9.

Andy's conflict with the odd-jobs man, Onion John, causes a conflict between Andy and his father. 1960 Newbery Award book.

Morey, Walt, **Kavik, the Wolf Dog**, illustrated by Peter Parnall, Dutton, 1968, 192p., Fiction, ISBN 0-525-33093-3.

Andy Evans is the only master that had ever loved Kavik, the wolf dog, and the dog searches for Andy through numerous hardships. Kansas 1971. Vermont 1970.

Naylor, Phyllis Reynolds, **Beetles, Lightly Roasted**, Atheneum, 1987, 134p., Fiction, ISBN 0-689-31355-1.

Fifth-grader Andy Moller wants to win an essay contest and decides upon an unusual way to promote conservation. He uses insects as the main ingredient for recipes!

Smith, Carole, **Hit-and-Run Connection**, illustrated by Marie DeJohn, Whitman, 1982, 126p., Fiction, ISBN 0-8075-3317-3.

Andy is determined to find the driver that hit his friend, then left. A chance encounter leads him to believe that the driver is a member of the Chicago White Sox baseball team.

ANEGO

Wosmek, Frances, **Brown Bird Singing**, illustrated by Ted Lewin, Lothrop, Lee & Shepard, 1986, 120p., Fiction, ISBN 0-688-06251-2.

Set in the early 1900s, Anego is a nine-year-old Chippewa Indian who has lived for several years with a white family in rural Minnesota. Anego worries about the time when her father will come to get her since she has forgotten a great deal about her own family.

ANGELA
See also Angie

Raskin, Ellen, **Westing Game, The**, Dutton, 1978, 185p., Fiction, LC 77-18866, ISBN 0-525-42320-6.

Angela is one of the sixteen people invited to the reading of the very strange will of the very rich Samuel W. Westing. She could become a millionaire, depending on how she plays the tricky and dangerous Westing Game. 1979 Newbery Award book. 1978 Boston Globe-Horn Book Award. Michigan 1982.

Robinson, Nancy, **Oh Honestly, Angela!**, Scholastic, 1985, 114p., Fiction, ISBN 0-590-41287-6.

Angela is a precocious youngster who causes her older sister many problems in this humorous story of family life.

Skurzynski, Gloria, **Dangerous Ground**, Bradbury, 1989, 151p., Fiction, ISBN 0-02-782731-3.

Angela lives with her aged great-aunt and has enjoyed it until the older woman starts behaving erratically. The two take an unplanned trip across Wyoming.

ANGELINA
See also Angie, Angela

Holabird, Katharine, **Angelina Ballerina**, illustrated by Helen Craig, Potter, 1983, Picture Book, ISBN 0-517-55083-0.

As a young mouse Angelina takes ballet lessons and through her talent and hard work, she becomes a famous ballerina. There are other books about Angelina. Kentucky 1985.

ANGELO

McCaffrey, Mary, **My Brother Ange**, illustrated by Denise Saldutti, Crowell, 1982, 86p., Fiction, ISBN 0-690-04195-0.

Seven-year-old Angelo irritates his older brother who is bored by life in their cramped London flat. When an accident happens, the family is brought together.

ANGIE
See also Angela, Angelina

Lasky, Kathryn, **Sugaring Time,** illustrated by Christopher G. Knight, Macmillan, 1983, 58p., Nonfiction, LC 82-23928, ISBN 0-02-751680-6.

Angie and her family live on a farm that has a small maple grove. In March, it is time to harvest the sap for maple syrup. Photographs show the family gathering sap and making syrup. 1984 Newbery Honor book.

ANITA

Perl, Lila, **Dumb Like Me, Olivia Potts**, Clarion, 1976, 181p., Fiction, ISBN 0-395-28870-3.

Anita and her friend Olivia become involved in solving a mystery and Olivia discovers that she isn't as dumb as she would like to pretend that she is.

ANN
See also Anna, Annabel, Annabelle, Anna Marie, Annemarie, Anne, Annie, Mary Ann

Bailey, Carolyn Sherwin, **Miss Hickory,** illustrated by Ruth Gannett, Viking, 1946, 123p., Fiction, ISBN 0-670-47940-3.

Ann thought of her country doll, Miss Hickory, as a real person and made a corncob house for her under the lilac bush. Miss Hickory had a head made from a hickory nut and a body made from an applewood tree. When Ann went away to school for the winter, Miss Hickory spent her time with the farm creatures. 1947 Newbery Award book.

Burchard, Peter, **Sea Change**, Farrar, Straus & Giroux, 1984, 117p., Fiction, ISBN 0-374-36460-5.

Stories about Ann, Lisa, and Alice, who are mother, daughter, and grandmother. The stories tell about how the family members deal with problems and with one another.

Carlson, Natalie Savage, **Ann Aurelia and Dorothy**, illustrated by Dale Payson, Harper & Row, 1968, 130p., Fiction, ISBN 0-06-020959-3.

Ann Aurelia lives with a foster family and becomes friends with a girl she meets on the playground. The two girls have many adventures in the neighborhood.

Fritz, Jean, **Cabin Faced West, The**, illustrated by Feodor Rojankovsky, Coward-McCann, 1958, 124p., Fiction, ISBN 0-698-20016-0.

Ann and her family live on the frontier of western Pennsylvania in 1784. Ann has a very lonely life until she makes new friends and the family has a special visitor.

O'Brien, Robert, **Z for Zachariah**, Atheneum, 1975, 249p., Fiction, ISBN 0-689-30442-0.

Ann Burden is a teenager who thinks she is the only person left alive after a nuclear war. When she sees a man wearing a safe-suit enter her valley she is thrilled until she realizes that he is dangerous and not the companion she had hoped for. 1976 Jane Addams Honor Book.

ANNA
See also Ann, Annabel, Annabelle, Anna Marie, Anne, Annie

Ames, Mildred, **Anna to the Infinite Power**, Scribner, 1981, 198p., Fiction, ISBN 0-684-16855-3.

Anna is a mathematical genius but she does not seem to have any feelings for anyone else. Life is disrupted when she accidently discovers that she is a clone.

Bunting, Eve, **Wednesday Surprise, The**, Clarion, 1989, 32p., Fiction, ISBN 0-899-197-213.

Grandma comes to visit on Wednesday nights and everyone thinks that she is teaching Anna to read. 1990 Jane Addams Honor Book.

Byars, Betsy, **Glory Girl, The**, Viking, 1983, 122p., Fiction, ISBN 0-670-34261-0.

Anna feels like a misfit in her family since she doesn't sing in their gospel group. When her misfit uncle is paroled from prison, Anna becomes friends with him.

Gehrts, Barbara, **Don't Say a Word**, Macmillan, 1986, 169p., Fiction, ISBN 0-689-50412-8.

Anna is the daughter of a high-ranking German official during the Nazi regime. She tells of the terror of the times as her father becomes a victim of the dictator's rule. Based on the author's experiences this title has been translated from German.

Haugaard, Erik Christian, **Little Fishes, The**, illustrated by Milton Johnson, Houghton Mifflin, 1967, 215p., Fiction, LC 67-14701, ISBN 0-395-06802-9.

The story of Guido, an orphaned twelve-year-old, and his friend Anna. Guido is a begger in occupied Italy during World War II. He develops compassion and understanding that help him survive as he searches for food each day and witnesses the tragedy of war. 1968 Jane Addams Award book. 1967 Boston Globe-Horn Book Award.

Kerr, Judith, **When Hitler Stole Pink Rabbit**, illustrated by Judith Kerr, Coward-McCann, 1971, 191p., Fiction, ISBN 0-698-20182-5.

Nine-year-old Anna tells of her family's life as German Jewish refugees fleeing from their home in Berlin. They escape to Switzerland, then go to Paris, before finally arriving in London. Based on the author's personal experiences.

Little, Jean, **From Anna**, illustrated by Joan Sandin, Harper & Row, 1972, 201p., Fiction, ISBN 0-06-023912-3.

Anna felt very awkward and homely. When her family moved to Canada from Germany in 1933, she began to find herself and her own friends.

MacLachlan, Patricia, **Sarah, Plain and Tall**, Harper & Row, 1985, 58p., Fiction, LC 83-49481, ISBN 0-06-024101-2; 0-06-024102-0 (lib).

When their father invites a mail-order bride named Sarah to come live with them in their prairie home, Anna and Caleb learn to appreciate her and want her to stay. 1986 Christopher Award. 1986 Golden Kite Award. 1986 Newbery Award book. 1986 Jefferson Cup Award. 1986 Scott O'Dell Award. Arkansas 1988.

ANNA MARIE
See also Ann, Anna, Anne, Annemarie, Annie

Aiken, Joan, **Midnight Is a Place**, Viking, 1974, 287p., Fiction, LC 74-760, ISBN 0-670-47483-5.

Anna Marie is an unusual little French girl. Her arrival completely changes the lonely, monotonous life of a fourteen-year-old boy who lives in the house of his unpleasant guardian. Set in England in the nineteenth century.

ANNABEL
See also Ann, Anna, Annabelle, Anne, Annie

Brock, Betty, **No Flying in the House**, illustrated by Wallace Tripp, Harper & Row, 1970, 139p., Fiction, ISBN 0-06-020643-8.

A mystery-fantasy about Annabel and the tiny talking dog that accompanies her to the rich Mrs. Vancourt's home where they decide they will live.

Rodgers, Mary, **Billion for Boris, A**, Harper & Row, 1974, 211p., Fiction, ISBN 0-06-025054-2.

When Annabel's brother repairs the television set it begins showing what will happen the next day. Her friend Boris decides to use the information to earn money to fix up his apartment with unexpected and humorous results.

Rodgers, Mary, **Freaky Friday**, Harper & Row, 1972, 145p., Fiction, LC 74-183158, ISBN 06-025048-8; 06-025049-6.

At thirteen, Annabel Andrews is self-willed and has constant disagreements with her mother over her appearance, her room, her eating habits, and her freedom. One Friday, she awakens to discover that she has changed into her mother, and her mother has become her. A humorous fantasy that allows Annabel to see herself as others see her. California 1977. Georgia 1978. Hawaii 1977.

ANNABELLE
See also Ann, Anna, Annabel, Anne, Annie

Perl, Lila, **Annabelle Starr, E.S.P.**, Clarion, 1983, 147p., Fiction, ISBN 0-89919-187-8.

Annabelle is convinced that she has extrasensory perception and makes predictions based on what could be her overactive imagination.

ANNE

See also Ann, Anna, Annabel, Annabelle, Anna Marie, Annemarie, Annie, Mary Anne

Chadwick, Roxane, **Anne Morrow Lindbergh, Pilot and Poet**, Lerner, 1987, 56p., Nonfiction, ISBN 0-8225-0488-X.

Biographical information about Anne Morrow Lindbergh, a shy young woman who married the famous aviator, Charles Lindbergh, and went on to become famous as a writer and poet.

Hurwitz, Johanna, **Anne Frank: Life in Hiding**, illustrated by Vera Rosenberry, Jewish Publication Society, 1988, 62p., Nonfiction, ISBN 0-8276-0311-8.

This biography of the well-known young Jewish girl, Anne Frank, explains the political situation that drove Anne's family to Holland and into hiding.

Montgomery, Lucy, **Anne of Greene Gables**, illustrated by Jody Lee, Grosset & Dunlap, 1983, 382p., Fiction, ISBN 0-448-06030-2.

Anne is an orphan who is taken in by a lonely middle-aged brother and sister who live on a farm on Prince Edward Island. Anne is imaginative and full of mischief. Set in the late 1800s, there are several other books about Anne as she grows up.

Peare, Catherine Owens, **Helen Keller Story, The**, Crowell, 1959, 183p., Nonfiction, LC 59-10979, ISBN 0-690-37520-4.

This biography tells the story of Helen Keller who was born deaf and blind yet became an advocate for the blind as an adult due to the influence of her teacher, Anne Sullivan. Kansas 1962. Oklahoma 1962.

ANNEMARIE

See also Ann, Anna Marie, Anne, Annie

Lowry, Lois, **Number the Stars**, Houghton Mifflin, 1989, 137p., Fiction, LC 88-37134, ISBN 0-395-51060-0.

Set in 1943, during the German occupation of Denmark. Ten-year-old Annemarie and her family take in Ellen Roser, Annemarie's best friend, when all of the Jews in Denmark are being relocated. Annemarie learns to be brave and courageous as she helps to shelter her friend from the Nazis. 1990 National Jewish Book Award. 1990 Newbery Award book. 1990 Jane Addams Honor book. Vermont 1991.

ANNIE

See also Ann, Anna, Annabel, Annabelle, Anna Marie, Anne, Annemarie

Clymer, Eleanor, **My Brother Stevie**, Dell, 1967, 72p., Fiction, ISBN 0-440-40125-9.

When their mother deserts them, Annie and her brother live with their grandmother. Annie is supposed to watch over her brother but he gets into a great deal of trouble with the older boys.

Henry, Marguerite, **Mustang, Wild Spirit of the West**, illustrated by Robert Lougheed, Rand McNally, 1966, 222p., Nonfiction, ISBN 0-528-82327-2.

The biography of Annie Bronn, a young woman who overcame great odds to become an expert horse rider. Later in life she led the crusade to stop the slaughter of wild horses for pet food, and to prevent the cruel hunting practices that nearly led to the extinction of wild mustangs. Oklahoma 1970.

Mearian, Judy Frank, **Two Ways About It**, Dial, 1979, 166p., Fiction, ISBN 0-8037-8797-9.

Annie is an only child who has resented her cousin spending summers with the family. When Annie's mother has to have surgery for cancer, the two girls grow closer.

Miles, Miska, **Annie and the Old One**, illustrated by Peter Parnall, Little, Brown, 1971, 44p., Picture Book, LC 79-129900.

Annie is a young Navajo Indian girl. When her grandmother, the old one, says she will die when the rug they are weaving is finished, Annie does everything she can to keep the rug from being completed in order to keep her grandmother alive and with her. 1972 Newbery Honor book.

Morpurgo, Michael, **Twist of Gold**, Heinemann, 1987, 226p., Fiction, ISBN 0-7182-3971-7.

Annie O'Brien and her brother left Ireland during the potato famine in 1847 to try to locate their father who had immigrated to California.

Quackenbush, Robert, **Quick, Annie, Give Me a Catchy Line: A Story of Samuel F. B. Morse**, Prentice-Hall, 1983, 36p., Nonfiction, ISBN 0-13-749762-8.

A brief biography about Samuel Morse, the man who invented the telegraph.

Quackenbush, Robert, **Who's That Girl With the Gun? A Story of Annie Oakley**, Prentice-Hall, 1987, 36p., Nonfiction, ISBN 0-13-957671-1.

Annie Oakley learned to shoot a gun as a young girl and went on to use her skills to entertain as a sharpshooter in a Wild West Show. This brief biography provides background information about the woman and her career.

Reiss, Johanna, **Upstairs Room, The**, Crowell, 1972, 196p., Nonfiction, ISBN 0-690-85127-8.

The experiences of Annie de Leeuw and her family's experiences as Dutch Jews during the German occupation of Holland during World War II are told in a simple and moving story. The story begins in 1938 when Annie is the six-year-old daughter of a prosperous family and ends with the liberation in 1945. 1973 Newbery Honor book. 1973 Jane Addams Honor book. Winner of the Buxtehuder Bulle, International Peace Prize.

Rostkowski, Margaret, **After the Dancing Days**, HarperCollins, 1986, 217p., Fiction, ISBN 0-06-025078-X.

Thirteen-year-old Annie becomes aware of the wounded men that return from World War I. Her father is a doctor and Annie wants to help a badly wounded young man adjust to his new life. 1987 Golden Kite Award. 1987 Jefferson Cup Award.

Selden, Bernice, **Story of Annie Sullivan, Helen Keller's Teacher, The**, illustrated by Eileen McKeating, Dell, 1987, 86p., Nonfiction, ISBN 0-440-48285-2.

This biography includes Annie Sullivan's unhappy childhood, her education as a teacher for the blind, and her amazing success with Helen Keller, a girl who was deaf, mute, and blind.

Sharmat, Marjorie Weinman, **Nate the Great and the Phony Clue**, illustrated by Marc Simont, Coward-McCann, 1977, 48p., Easy Reader, LC 76-42461, ISBN 0-698-20405-0.

A piece of paper with the letters VITA printed on it appears on Nate's doorstep. The boy detective Nate the Great looks for the missing pieces and sees Annie and Finley along the way. A Reading Rainbow book.

ANTHONY
See also Tony

Bellairs, John, **Dark Secret of the Weatherend**, Dial, 1984, 182p., Fiction, ISBN 0-8037-0074-1.

Fourteen-year-old Anthony Monday and sixty-eight-year-old Miss Eells explore a decrepit mansion and discover a diary, which leads them on an exciting adventure. There are other books about these two friends.

Hamilton, Virginia, **Anthony Burns: The Defeat and Triumph of a Fugitive Slave**, Knopf, 1988, 193p., Nonfiction, ISBN 0-394-88185-0; 0-394-98185-5 (lib).

Anthony Burns was a slave who escaped to Boston in 1854. He was arrested under the Fugitive Slave Acts and his trial caused a furor. 1989 Jane Addams Honor Book. 1989 Jefferson Cup Award. 1988 Boston Globe-Horn Book Award.

ANTON
See also Tony

Kumin, Maxine, **Microscope, The**, illustrated by Arnold Lobel, Harper & Row, 1984, 28p., Easy Reader, LC 82-47728, ISBN 0-06-023523-3; 0-06-023524-1 (lib).

The Dutch scientist Anton von Leewenhoek really lived in the Netherlands from 1632-1723. This rhymed verse tells of his interest in looking through his homemade microscopes where he saw interesting sights. A Reading Rainbow book.

ANTONIA
See also Tony

Klein, Norma, **Confessions of an Only Child**, illustrated by Richard Cuffari, Knopf, 1988, 93p., Fiction, ISBN 0-394-80569-0.

Eight-year-old Antonia isn't too sure that she wants a sibling but when there are problems with the baby she feels sad.

ANTONIO
See also Tony

Baylor, Byrd, **Coyote Cry**, illustrated by Symeon Shimin, Lothrop, Lee & Shepard, 1972, 28p., Fiction, ISBN 0-688-51624-6.

Antonio herds sheep with his grandfather. He believes that coyotes are his enemy even though his grandfather says that coyotes only kill to survive. Antonio changes his thoughts about coyotes after a particular incident.

Konigsburg, Elaine, **Throwing Shadows**, Atheneum, 1979, 151p., Fiction, ISBN 0-689-30714-4.

The story of Antonio as he sells his weavings in Ecuador is one of the five short stories in this book.

APRIL

Duncan, Lois, **Don't Look Behind You**, Delacorte, 1989, Fiction, ISBN 0-440-501-393.

April's father is a witness in a federal case and the family is forced to go into hiding when a hired killer threatens their lives. Indiana 1992. Utah 1992. Virginia 1992.

Snyder, Zilpha Keatley, **Egypt Game, The**, illustrated by Alton Raible, Atheneum, 1967, 215p., Fiction, LC 67-2717, ISBN 0-689-30006-9; 0-689-70297-3.

When April Hall is sent to live with her grandmother, she becomes friends with eleven-year-old Melanie Ross and her little brother Marshall. The three children become interested in ancient Egypt and play the Egypt Game until there is a murder in the neighborhood. 1968 Newbery Honor book.

ARCHIE

Keats, Ezra Jack, **Goggles**, illustrated by Ezra Jack Keats, Macmillan, 1969, 32p., Picture Book, LC 70-78081, ISBN 0-02-749590-6.

Archie and his friend have to outsmart the neighborhood bullies before they can enjoy playing with the motorcycle goggles that they have found. 1970 Caldecott Honor book.

Keats, Ezra Jack, **Hi, Cat!**, illustrated by Ezra Jack Keats, Macmillan, 1970, 35p., Picture Book, LC 71-102968, ISBN 0-87499-180-3.

The new cat on the block gives Archie a bad start on his morning. 1970 Boston Globe-Horn Book Award.

Keats, Ezra Jack, **Pet Show!**, illustrated by Ezra Jack Keats, Macmillan, 1974, 38p., Picture Book, LC 86-17225, ISBN 0-02-749620-1.

Archie can't find his cat to enter in the neighborhood pet show, so he has to do some quick thinking to win a prize. A Reading Rainbow book.

ARI
See also Ariel

Pascal, Francine, **Hand-Me-Down Kid, The**, Viking, 1980, 172p., Fiction, ISBN 0-670-35969-6.

Ari Jacobs is the youngest member of the family and gets tired of getting hand-me-downs from her brother and sister. Ari encounters one problem after another after she borrows her sister's bicycle for a race and it gets stolen. Vermont 1982.

ARIEL
See also Ari

Coerr, Eleanor, **Big Balloon Race, The**, illustrated by Carolyn Croll, Harper & Row, 1981, 62p., Easy Reader, LC 80-8368, ISBN 0-06-021352-3; 0-06-021353-1 (lib).

Ariel Myers lives on Balloon Farm in Mohawk Valley, New York. Her father makes hot air balloons and her mother is a famous balloonist. When Ariel accidentally stows away on her mother's balloon during a big race, her mother is afraid they will lose. Set in the 1880s, this book is based on a real family. A Reading Rainbow book.

Pierce, Meredith Ann, **Darkangel, The**, Little, Brown, 1982, 1982p., Fiction, ISBN 0-316-70741-4.

Set on a distant planet, Ariel goes to the castle of the twelve-winged vampire to make a rescue. While there she successfully breaks the spell that changed a prince into a vampire. There is another book about Ariel. California 1986.

ARLISS

Gipson, Fred, **Old Yeller**, illustrated by Carl Burger, Harper & Row, 1956, 158p., Fiction, LC 56-8780, ISBN 0-06-011546-7.

Five-year-old Arliss, his fourteen-year-old brother, and his parents live on Birdsong Creek in the Texas hill country during the 1860s. Life isn't easy but they have a snug cabin, their own cattle and hogs, and they grow most of their food. When a big, ugly, yellow dog comes out of nowhere and steals a whole side of pork, Arliss wants to protect it. 1957 Newbery Honor book. Hawaii 1966. Kansas 1959. Oklahoma 1959. Pacific Northwest 1959.

ARLO

Birdseye, Tom, **I'm Going to Be Famous**, Holiday House, 1986, 160p., Fiction, ISBN 0-8234-0630-X.

Arlo Moore is in fifth grade and determined to set a record and get his name in a book of records. The results are hilarious when he tries to eat seventeen bananas in less than two minutes.

ARMAND

Carlson, Natalie Savage, **Family Under the Bridge, The**, illustrated by Garth Williams, HarperCollins, 1958, 97p., Fiction, LC 58-5292, ISBN 0-06-020991-7.

Armand, the old hobo, disliked children until Suzy, Paul, and Evelyne moved to his bridge with their mother after being evicted from their apartment. Bridges were the only free shelter in Paris, but Armand didn't think it was the proper place for a family to live. Armand learned that when families

stay together they make a home no matter where they live. 1959 Newbery Honor book.

ARNE
See also Arnie, Arnold

Fife, Dale, **North of Danger**, illustrated by Saether Haakon, Dutton, 1978, 72p., Fiction, ISBN 0-525-36035-2.

Twelve-year-old Arne Kristiansen decides he must warn his father that the Nazis have occupied Norway and evacuated people from its capitol. His father is working on a glacier 200 miles away near the Arctic and Arne has many adventures as he struggles to reach him. Based on a factual incident from World War II.

ARNIE
See also Arne, Arnold

Brookins, Dana, **Alone in Wolf Hollow**, Clarion, 1978, 137p., Fiction, ISBN 0-395-28849-5.

Arnie and his brother are orphans. The two are sent to live with one relative after another until they are finally sent to their alcoholic uncle who lives in the woods of Wolf Hollow. The boys become involved in a murder mystery while struggling to stay together.

Carlson, Nancy, **Louanne Pig in Making the Team**, illustrated by Nancy Carlson, Carolrhoda, 1985, 28p., Picture Book, LC 85-3775, ISBN 0-87614-281-1 (lib).

Louanne Pig plans to try out for cheerleading and her friend, Arnie, plans to try out for football. They practice together and when they get to try-outs, something surprising happens. A Reading Rainbow book.

ARNOLD
See also Arne, Arnie

Cole, Joanna, **Magic School Bus Inside the Earth, The**, illustrated by Bruce Degen, Scholastic, 1987, 40p., Picture Book, LC 87-4563, ISBN 0-590-40759-7.

Arnold and the rest of Mrs. Frizzle's class learn firsthand about different kinds of rocks and the mation of the earth when they take a field trip in the magic school bus. A Reading Rainbow book.

ARTHUR
See also Artie

Beckman, Delores, **My Own Private Sky**, Dutton, 1980, 154p., Fiction, ISBN 0-525-35510-3.

Eleven-year-old Arthur has numerous allergies and fears. When he moves to California with his mother, his new sitter encourages him to overcome his fears and Arthur is able to help her when she has an accident.

Brown, Marc, **Arthur's Eyes**, illustrated by Marc Brown, Little, Brown, 1979, 32p., Picture Book, LC 79-11734, ISBN 0-316-11063-9.

Before Arthur got eyeglasses, he had problems seeing the math problems on the board and couldn't shoot a basketball in the basket. After he gets glasses, his friends tease him and Arthur becomes so embarrassed that he decides to hide his glasses. A Reading Rainbow book.

MacLachlan, Patricia, **Arthur, for the Very First Time**, illustrated by Lloyd Bloom, Harper & Row, 1980, 117p., Fiction, ISBN 0-06-024047-4.

Ten-year-old Arthur has an unusual summer when his parents send him to live with an eccentric great-aunt and great-uncle. 1981 Golden Kite Award.

Pinkwater, D. Manus, **Hoboken Chicken Emergency**, Prentice-Hall, 1977, 83p., Fiction, ISBN 0-13-92514-5.

Arthur can't find a turkey for Thanksgiving dinner so he buys a 266-pound chicken and the humorous incidents begin.

Ruckman, Ivy, **Night of the Twisters**, Crowell, 1984, 153p., Fiction, LC 83-46168, ISBN 0-690-04408-9; 0-690-04409-7 (lib).

Arthur and his friend have been through many tornado watches during their twelve years. Arthur is at Dan's house with Dan and Dan's baby brother when a tornado hits and destroys the house and the neighborhood. Oklahoma 1987.

ARTIE
See also Arthur

Korman, Gordon, **No Coins Please**, Scholastic, 1984, 184p., Fiction, ISBN 0-590-33466-2 (pbk).

Artie manages to accumulate a large amount of money through his selling activities as he and five other boys go across the country camping out with their counselors.

ASA

Stolz, Mary, **Belling the Tiger**, illustrated by Beni Montresor, Harper & Row, 1961, 64p., Fiction, LC 61-5776, ISBN 0-06-025811-X.

The fierce chief mouse decides that the cat should be belled and all the other mice agree. Asa is one of the two smallest and least important of the mice chosen for the task. 1962 Newbery Honor book.

ASHLEY

Hahn, Mary Downing, **Doll in the Garden: A Ghost Story**, Clarion, 1989, 160p., Fiction, ISBN 0-899-198-481.

An antique doll that Ashley and her friend find buried in a garden leads the girls to an eerie adventure. By going through the hedge, the girls enter the ghostly world of an earlier time. Virginia 1992.

Morpurgo, Michael, **King of the Cloud Forests**, Viking Kestrel, 1988, 145p., Fiction, ISBN 0-670-82069-5.

Fourteen-year-old Ashley and his uncle set out on foot to leave China when the Japanese armies invade during World War II. After facing terrible weather and near starvation, Ashley has a fantasy adventure.

AT-MUN

Yates, Elizabeth, **Amos Fortune, Free Man**, illustrated by Nora S. Unwin, Aladdin, 1951, 178p., Nonfiction, ISBN 0-14-34158-7.

The biography of At-Mun, a young African prince, from the time he was taken from his jungle village by white slave dealers in 1725. Included are his years as an American slave and his purchase of his own freedom. In 1801 he divided up the remainder of his money for bequests to a church and a school. 1951 Newbery Award book. Kansas 1953.

ATTEAN

Speare, Elizabeth George, **Sign of the Beaver, The**, Houghton Mifflin, 1983, 135p., Fiction, LC 83-118, ISBN 0-395-33890-5.

During the early 1700s, the young Indian boy Attean meets the white settler Matt. Matt was left alone to guard his family's newly built home while his father went to get the rest of their family. Attean and Matt learn from one another, develop a friendship, and begin to appreciate each other's cultures. 1984 Child Study Children's Book Award. 1984 Christopher Award. 1984 Newbery Honor book. 1984 Scott O'Dell Award.

ATTILA

Seredy, Kate, **White Stag, The**, illustrated by Kate Seredy, Viking, 1937, 95p., Fiction, LC 37-37800, ISBN 0-670-76375-6.

The epic story of the migration of the Huns and Magyars from Asia to Europe. Included is the story of Attila the Hun who was born in 408. 1938 Newbery Award book.

AUGUST

See also Augusta, Auguste

Lindbergh, Anne, **People in Pineapple Place**, Harcourt Brace Jovanovich, 1982, 153p., Fiction, ISBN 0-15-260517-7.

Ten-year-old August is bored and unhappy that his mother has moved him to Georgetown, in Washington, D.C. He meets children from another time who provide August with many interesting experiences before they move on.

AUGUSTA

See also August, Auguste

Chambers, John W., **Colonel and Me**, Atheneum, 1985, 190p., Fiction, ISBN 0-689-31087-0.

The summer that she is fourteen, Augusta takes horseback riding lessons and learns a lot about herself and her needs.

AUGUSTE

See also August, Augusta

Cunningham, Julia, **Silent Voice**, Dutton, 1981, 145p., Fiction, ISBN 0-525-39295-5.

Auguste is a mute orphan who performs as a mime. His chance at learning from a great actor are almost destroyed by a street bully.

AUSTIN

Jukes, Mavis, **Blackberries in the Dark**, illustrated by Thomas Allen, Knopf, 1985, Picture Book, ISBN 0-394-97599-5.

Nine-year-old Austin has a difficult time visiting his grandmother after his grandfather dies, until the two begin sharing very special memories.

AVIVA

Bethancourt, Jeanne, **Rainbow Kid**, Avon, 1983, 108p., Fiction, ISBN 0-380-84665-9 (pbk).

Aviva Granger is ten years old when her parents divorce and she is concerned about how it will affect her life. There are several other books about Aviva.

AXEL

Verne, Jules, **Journey to the Center of the Earth**, Dodd, Mead, 1979, 226p., Fiction, ISBN 0-396-08429-X.

A revised edition of the classic science fiction story. Axel travels with his uncle to the center of the earth where they find huge forests, prehistoric monsters, and amazing adventures.

-B-

BABS
See also Barbara

Howard, Elizabeth Fitzgerald, **Train to Lulu's The**, illustrated by Robert Casilla, B
ook, LC 86-33429, ISBN 0-02-744620-4.

Babs and her older sister take the long train ride from Boston to Baltimore by themselves. Their parents put them on the train and their relatives, including Lulu, meet them when they get off.

BARBARA
See also Babs, Bobby

Allard, Harry, **Miss Nelson Has a Field Day**, illustrated by James Marshall, Houghton Mifflin, 1985, 32p., Picture Book, LC 84-27791, ISBN 0-395-36690-9.

The football team hasn't won a game all year and everyone at school is down in the dumps. Miss Nelson and her sister, Barbara, call upon Miss Viola Swamp, the meanest substitute in the world, to get the team in shape. A Reading Rainbow book.

Campbell, Barbara, **Girl Called Bob and a Horse Called Yoki**, Dial, 1982, 168p., Fiction, ISBN 0-8037-3150-7.

During World War II, Barbara's father is serving in the navy and her mother works in a factory. Barbara's best friends are a neighbor boy and the horse that is used to deliver milk. When the children discover that the horse is going to be sold to the glue factory, they decide to take action to save him.

Miles, Betty, **Real Me, The**, Knopf, 1974, 122p., Fiction, ISBN 0-394-92838-5.

Barbara Fisher is a normal girl trying to be herself but finds that her interests aren't always the ones that other people think she should have.

Roberts, Naurice, **Barbara Jordan: The Great Lady from Texas**, Children's Press, 1984, 31p., Nonfiction, ISBN 0-526-03511-8.

Biographical information about Barbara Jordan. She learned to work hard and study when she was young and used that knowledge to become a lawyer, a state senator, a congresswoman, and a professor.

BARNABY

Mahy, Margaret, **Haunting, The**, Atheneum, 1982, 135p., Fiction, ISBN 0-689-50243-5.

Barnaby and his family learn that there is a member of each generation of their family who has the gift of ESP and magic. Set in New Zealand.

BARNEY

Carrick, Carol, **What a Wimp**, illustrated by Donald Carrick, Clarion, 1983, 89p., Fiction, ISBN 0-89919-139-8.

Barney's parents have divorced and he and his mother and brother move to a new home. Barney has trouble adjusting and making friends until he realizes that he has to solve his own problems.

Cooper, Susan, **Over Sea, Under Stone**, Harcourt Brace Jovanovich, 1966, 252p., Fiction, ISBN 0-15-259034-X.

Barney is one of the characters who battles the dark forces of evil while searching for the treasures that will permanently vanquish them.

Sleator, William, **Interstellar Pig**, Dutton, 1984, 197p., Fiction, ISBN 0-525-44098-4.

During a boring summer at the beach, Barney becomes involved with strange neighbors and their board game, which has them roam the galaxies of the universe. California 1988.

Wells, Rosemary, **Through the Hidden Door**, Dial, 1987, 264p., Fiction, ISBN 0-8037-0276-0.

Barney is an outsider at school. When he and another outsider explore a mysterious cave they come upon a fantasy adventure involving miniature people.

BART
See also Bartholomew

Brookins, Dana, **Alone in Wolf Hollow**, Clarion, 1978, 137p., Fiction, ISBN 0-395-28849-5.

Bart and his brother Arnie are orphans. The two are sent from one relative to another until they are sent to live with an alcoholic uncle in the woods of Wolf Hollow. The boys become involved in a murder mystery while struggling to stay together.

BARTHOLOMEW
See also Bart

Seuss, Dr., **Bartholomew and the Oobleck**, illustrated by Dr. Seuss, Random House, 1949, 46p., Picture Book, LC 49-11423, ISBN 0-394-80075-3; 0-394-90075-8 (lib).

The king was tired of the same things coming down from the sky and ordered his magicians to create something new. When the oobleck that comes down threatens to destroy the kingdom, Bartholomew Cubbins teaches the king how to apologize and helps to stop the menace. 1950 Caldecott Honor book.

BAXTER

Kalb, Jonah, **Goof That Won the Pennant, The**, illustrated by Sandy Kossin, Houghton Mifflin, 1976, 103p., Fiction, LC 76-21678, ISBN 0-395-24834-5.

Baxter is one of the members of the Blazer's baseball team, a team of oddballs and misfits who do not even try to win. When their coach gives them the idea that winning is more fun than losing, the team decides to try. Indiana 1981.

BEATRICE
See also Beatrix, Betty

Cleary, Beverly, **Ramona the Brave**, illustrated by Alan Tiegreen, Morrow, 1975, 190p., Fiction, LC 74-16494, ISBN 0-688-22015-0; 0-688-32015-5 (lib).

Ramona Quimby is feeling quite grown-up since she will be entering first grade at the same school that her older sister Beatrice attends. Beatrice, known as Beezus by her family, is not as excited. The Quimby family has many humorous moments and Ramona discovers many things about herself and other people. Missouri 1978.

Schwartz, Amy, **Bea and Mr. Jones**, illustrated by Amy Schwartz, Bradbury, 1982, 29p., Picture Book, LC 81-18031, ISBN 0-02-781430-0.

Beatrice is tired of going to kindergarten, and her father is tired of going to work. The two decide to trade places for a day and both discover what they really enjoy doing. A Reading Rainbow book.

BEATRIX
See also Beatrice, Betty

Collins, David R., **Country Artist: A Story About Beatrix Potter**, illustrated by Karen Ritz, Carolrhoda, 1989, 56p., Nonfiction, ISBN 0-87614-344-3.

Beatrix Potter created her famous story of Peter Rabbit to amuse a sick child. This biography tells about the author/illustrator and her works.

BECKY
See also Rebecca

Bond, Nancy, **String in the Harp**, Atheneum, 1984, 370p., Fiction, LC 75-28181, ISBN 0-689-50036-8.

After their mother dies, ten-year-old Becky, her older sister, and brother are taken to Wales for a year by their dad. One of the youngsters finds an ancient harp-tuning key that takes him back to the time of the great sixth-century bard, Taliesin. 1977 Newbery Honor book.

Dessent, Michael, **Baseball Becky**, Oak Tree, 1982, 150p., Fiction, ISBN 0-916392-80-5.

Becky learns to play baseball when a softball league begins in her hometown and her father agrees to be a coach.

Rice, Eve, **Remarkable Return of Winston Potter Crisply, The**, Greenwillow, 1976, 185p., Fiction, ISBN 0-688-84145-7.

Becky and her younger brother are suspicious of their older brother's activities and suspect him of being a spy. A humorous story about a family.

Siegel, Robert, **Alpha Centauri**, illustrated by Kurt Mitchell, Crossways, 1980, 255p., Fiction, ISBN 0-89107-180-6.

When Becky visits England, she becomes involved in an adventure set in a far distant past when centaurs are being hunted by an ancient tribe.

BELINDA

Winthrop, Elizabeth, **Belinda's Hurricane**, illustrated by Wendy Watson, Dutton, 1984, 54p., Fiction, ISBN 0-525-44106-9.

Belinda learns a great deal about a cranky neighbor when he and his dog take shelter with Belinda and her grandmother during a hurricane on Fox Island.

BELLE

Alcock, Vivien, **Travelers by Night**, Delacorte, 1983, 182p., Fiction, LC 85-1663, ISBN 0-385-29406-9.

Belle and Charlie are determined to save an old elephant from the slaughterhouse. The two circus children kidnap the animal and begin a dangerous journey to a safari park 100 miles away where they hope to find the elephant a home.

Cleaver, Vera, **Belle Pruitt**, Lippincott, 1988, 169p., Fiction, ISBN 0-397-32305-0.

Eleven-year-old Belle is sent to live with relatives after her baby brother dies and the family begins having problems coping. Belle decides she will have to help get the family together again.

BEN

See also Benjamin, Benjie, Benjy, Benny

Bosse, Malcolm, **Cave Beyond Time**, Crowell, 1980, 187p., 1980, ISBN 0-690-04076-8.

While walking in the Arizona desert, Ben is transported back in time after being bitten by a rattlesnake. He has unique experiences living with tribes of mammoth hunters, bison hunters, and early farmers.

Collier, James Lincoln and Christopher Collier, **Bloody Country**, Four Winds, 1976, 183p., Fiction, ISBN 0-02-722960-2.

Ben Buck and his father have many struggles when they emigrate to western Pennsylvania at the time of the Revolutionary War.

Eckert, Alan W., **Incident at Hawk's Hill**, Little, Brown, 1971, 173p., Fiction, ISBN 0-316-20866-3.

Sixteen-year-old John has a younger brother who is shy and withdrawn. Six-year-old Ben rarely speaks to people but has an amazing ability to communicate with animals. Ben develops a bond with a badger and lives in the badger's burrow for several months. Set on a homestead in the Canadian West prairies in 1870, this book is based on an actual incident. 1972 Newbery Honor book.

Gondosch, Linda, **Who Needs a Bratty Brother?**, illustrated by Helen Cogancherry, Lodestar, 1985, 112p., Fiction, ISBN 0-525-67170-6.

Ben drives his older sister crazy with his many antics including putting worms in her cup and a dried mouse tail in her book. Kentucky 1988.

Isadora, Rachel, **Ben's Trumpet**, illustrated by Rachel Isadora, Greenwillow, 1979, 32p., Picture Book, LC 78-12885, ISBN 0-688-80194-3.

Ben wants to be a trumpeter. At night he sits on the fire escape of his apartment building and plays an imaginary trumpet as he listens to the jazz from a nearby club. The other kids laugh at him, but one of the musicians takes an interest in Ben. 1980 Caldecott Honor book. A Reading Rainbow book.

Keats, Ezra Jack, **Apt. 3**, illustrated by Ezra Jack Keats, Macmillan, 1971, 34p., Picture Book, LC 78-123135, ISBN 0-02-749510-8.

Ben and his older brother Sam hear someone playing a harmonica in their apartment building. When they search for the source of the music, they make a new friend. A Reading Rainbow book.

Konigsburg, Elaine, **George**, Dell, 1970, 150p., Fiction, ISBN 0-440-42847-5 (pbk).

Ben is a very intelligent sixth grader who has a little being named George living inside him and offering advice.

Lawson, Robert, **Ben and Me; A New and Astonishing Life of Benjamin Franklin, as Written by His Good Mouse, Amos, Lately Discovered**, illustrated by Robert Lawson, Little, Brown, 1939, 113p., Fiction, ISBN 0-316-51732-1.

Amos Mouse moves into Benjamin Franklin's hat and begins advising the historical figure and helping him to become famous.

Little, Jean, **Different Dragons**, illustrated by Laura Fernandez, Viking Kestrel, 1987, 123p., Fiction, ISBN 0-670-80836-9.

Ben has many fears and insecurities to conquer when he goes to spend the weekend with his aunt.

Mauser, Pat Rhoads, **Bundle of Sticks, A,** illustrated by Gail Owens, Atheneum, 1982, 169p., Fiction, ISBN 0-689-30899-X.

Eleven-year-old Ben has a difficult time in fifth grade because of a bully. Ben is enrolled in a martial arts school, gets a purple belt, and surprises the bully with his new skills. Mississippi 1985. Missouri 1985. Vermont 1984.

Morey, Walt, **Gentle Ben,** illustrated by John Schoenherr, Dutton, 1965, 191p., Fiction, ISBN 0-525-30429-0.

Ben is a huge, five-year-old bear that has been ignored and half starved by the man who found him as a cub. Ben is befriended by Mark Anderson, a frail, sensitive thirteen-year-old boy growing up in the outskirts of an Alaskan fishing village. An exciting adventure. Dutton Jr. Animal Award book. Oklahoma 1968.

Rubinstein, Gillian, **Space Demons,** Dial, 1988, 198p., Fiction, ISBN 0-8037-0534-4.

Ben, his brother, and friends are taken into a new computer game where they experience danger as they attempt to get out.

Van Allsburg, Chris, **Ben's Dream,** illustrated by Chris Van Allsburg, Houghton Mifflin, 1982, 31p., Picture Book, ISBN 0-395-32084-4.

While studying for a geography test, Ben falls asleep and dreams that a flood takes his house past monuments and landmarks.

Walker, David, **Big Ben,** illustrated by Victor Ambrus, Houghton Mifflin, 1969, 134p., Fiction, LC 74-82477, ISBN 0-395-07167-4.

Big Ben is a gentle, bumbling St. Bernard puppy that is acquired by a brother and sister. The two children discover that living with a fast-growing dog has its hazards as well as joys. Arkansas 1972.

BENJAMIN
See also Ben, Benjie, Benjy, Benny

Aliki, **Many Lives of Benjamin Franklin, The,** illustrated by Aliki, Simon & Schuster, 1988, 32p., Nonfiction, ISBN 0-671-66119-1.

Benjamin Franklin lived during the colonial period and became famous for his statesmanship and numerous inventions. This biography provides basic information about the man.

Aliki, **Many Lives of Benjamin Franklin, The,** illustrated by Aliki, Prentice-Hall, 1977, 30p., Easy Reader, LC 77-5508, ISBN 0-13-556019-5.

Factual information about the famous American Benjamin Franklin. He was born in Boston in 1706 and learned quickly as a child. Benjamin became a printer's apprentice at the age of twelve. As a man, Franklin was a printer, a writer, an inventor, a statesman, and a diplomat. He helped to write the Declaration of Independence. A Reading Rainbow book.

Garfield, Leon, **Mister Corett's Ghost,** illustrated by Antony Maitland, Viking Kestrel, 1982, 64p., Fiction, ISBN 0-670-81652-3.

Young Benjamin Partridge is an apprentice to an apothecary. When he runs an errand for his master on New Year's Eve, Benjamin encounters criminals and ghostly beings in a story about revenge and forgiveness.

Henry, Marguerite and Wesley Dennis, **Benjamin West and His Cat Grimalkin,** Macmillan, 1987, 147p., Fiction, ISBN 0-02-743660-8.

A fictionalized account of the artist Benjamin West and the influence of his Quaker upbringing.

Patterson, Lillie, **Benjamin Banneker: Genius of Early America,** Abingdon, 1978, 142p., Nonfiction, ISBN 0-687-029-007.

This biography of Benjamin Banneker tells of his many accomplishments in the eighteenth century, including being an astronomer, a mathematician, a surveyor, and a farmer. 1979 Coretta Scott King Honor book.

Rayner, Mary, **Mrs. Pig's Bulk Buy**, illustrated by Mary Rayner, Atheneum, 1981, 30p., Picture Book, LC 80-19875, ISBN 0-689-30831-0.

Benjamin and his nine brothers and sisters like to put ketchup on everything they eat. Mrs. Pig has a plan to cure the piglets of this habit, which changes their skin from white to pink. A Reading Rainbow book.

Rodgers, Mary, **Summer Switch**, Harper & Row, 1982, 185p., Fiction, ISBN 0-06-025059-3.

As he is traveling to summer camp, Benjamin wishes he could be like his father. When the two find that they have switched bodies, the results are hilarious.

BENJIE

See also Ben, Benjamin, Benjy

Byars, Betsy, **Eighteenth Emergency, The**, illustrated by Robert Grossman, Viking, 1973, 126p., Fiction, LC 72-91399, ISBN 670-29055-6.

Twelve-year-old Benjie is known as Mouse. When the toughest bully in school threatens to kill him, Mouse gets little help from friends or family and he has to prepare for the emergency by himself. Vermont 1975.

Childress, Alice, **Hero Ain't Nothin' But a Sandwich, A**, Coward-McCann, 1973, 126p., Fiction, LC 73-82035, ISBN 0-698-20278-3.

Benjie Johnson is thirteen and well on his way to being hooked on heroin although he doesn't see the problem. 1974 Jane Addams Honor Book.

BENJY

See also Ben, Benjamin, Benjie, Benny

Hancock, Mary, **Thundering Prairie**, illustrated by H. Tom Hall, Macrae Smith, 1969, 191p., Fiction, ISBN 0-8255-4101-8.

Shortly before the Oklahoma land run in 1893, Mr. Bryan is injured. Fourteen-year-old Benjy, who is small for his age, and his mule are the only hope the family has of getting their own farm.

Van Leeuwen, Jean, **Benjy and the Power of Zingies**, illustrated by Margot Apple, Dial, 1982, 103p., Fiction, ISBN 0-8037-0380-5.

Benjy is a third grader who wants to be an athlete and eats Zingies, a breakfast cereal that builds muscles, as a way to improve his life. There is another book about Benjy.

BENNY

See also Ben, Benjamin, Benjie, Benjy

Baird, Thomas, **Finding Fever**, Harper & Row, 1982, 213p., Fiction, ISBN 0-06-020353-6.

Fifteen-year-old Benny sets out to solve the mystery of why his sister's dog, and all the other dogs along their road, have been stolen.

Warner, Gertrude Chandler, **Boxcar Children, The**, illustrated by L. Kate Deal, Whitman, 1950, 154p., Fiction, ISBN 0-8075-0851-9.

Benny and the other three Alden children take refuge in an old boxcar to avoid being sent to an institution. This is the first in a series of books about these children.

BERNADETTE

Underwood, Betty, **Tamarack Tree, The**, illustrated by Bea Holmes, Houghton Mifflin, 1971, 230p., Fiction, ISBN 0-395-12761-0.

Bernadette is a fourteen-year-old orphan who lives in 1833. She carefully examines her feelings about many things when her community comes in conflict with its values. 1972 Jane Addams Award book.

BERNIE

Naylor, Phyllis Reynolds, **Bodies in the Bessledorf Hotel, The**, Atheneum, 1986, 132p., Fiction, ISBN 0-689-31304-7.

Bernie Magruder becomes involved in a humorous mystery as bodies disappear in the hotel managed by his father.

BERT
See also Burt

Hurd, Thacher, **Mama Don't Allow: Starring Miles and the Swamp Band**, illustrated by Thacher Hurd, Harper & Row, 1984, 40p., Picture Book, LC 83-47703, ISBN 0-06-022689-7; 0-06-022690-0 (lib); 0-06-443078-2 (pbk).

Bert and the Swamp Band have a great time playing at the Alligator Ball, until they discover the dinner menu. 1985 Boston Globe-Horn Book Award. A Reading Rainbow book.

Rounds, Glen, **Wild Appaloosa**, Holiday House, 1983, 79p., Fiction, ISBN 0-8234-0482-X.

Alternating chapters tell the story of a wild Appaloosa and a young boy who is helping to round up wild horses and dreams of catching the Appaloosa.

BERTHA
See also Berthe

Dutton, Sandra, **Magic of Myrna C. Waxweather, The**, illustrated by Matthew Clark, Atheneum, 1987, 61p., Fiction, ISBN 0-689-31273-3.

Bertha has a fairy godmother who helps her to adjust to school and to become popular.

Meyer, Edith Patterson, **Champions of Peace: Winners of the Nobel Peace Prize**, Little, Brown, 1959, 216p., Nonfiction, LC 59-7355.

Baroness Bertha Kinsky von Suttner won the Nobel Peace Prize in 1905. She wrote a famous antiwar novel and was the only woman among ninety-six delegates to the 1899 International Peace Conference. 1960 Jane Addams Award book.

BERTHE
See also Bertha

Raskin, Ellen, **Westing Game, The**, Dutton, 1978, 185p., Fiction, LC 77-18866, ISBN 0-525-42320-6.

Berthe is one of the sixteen people invited to the reading of the very strange will of the very rich Samuel W. Westing. She could become a millionaire, depending on how she plays the tricky and dangerous Westing Game. 1979 Newbery Award

book. 1978 Boston Globe-Horn Book Award. Michigan 1982.

BETH
See also Bethany, Elisabeth, Elizabeth, Maybeth

Adorjan, Carol, **Cat Sitter Mystery**, Avon, 1985, 74p., Fiction, ISBN 0-380-70094-8 (pbk).

Beth wonders how she is going to make friends in a new town at the beginning of the summer. She also wonders if the eccentric old lady next door is a witch. Mysterious events, involving cats, help her with both questions.

Alcott, Louisa M., **Little Women, or Meg, Jo, Beth and Amy**, Little, Brown, 1968, 372p., Fiction, ISBN 0-316-03090-2.

The classic story of four sisters and their family life in New England at the time of the Civil War.

Greene, Bette, **Get on out of Here, Philip Hall**, Dial, 1981, 150p., Fiction, ISBN 0-8037-2871-9.

When Beth loses two important events, she goes to stay with her grandmother and learns what leadership really means. There is another book about Beth.

Greene, Bette, **Philip Hall Likes Me, I Reckon Maybe**, illustrated by Charles Lilly, Dial, 1974, 135p., Fiction, LC 74-2887, ISBN 0-8037-6098-1; 0-8037-6096-5 (lib).

Eleven-year-old Beth thinks that Philip Hall likes her, but their on-again, off-again relationship sometimes makes her wonder. 1975 Newbery Honor book.

BETHANY
See also Beth

Beatty, Patricia, **Behave Yourself, Bethany Brant**, Morrow, 1986, 172p., Fiction, ISBN 0-688-05923-6.

Set in Texas in 1989, eleven-year-old Bethany Brant is the daughter of a preacher. She is intelligent and spunky, but no matter how hard she tries to be good, she is always getting into trouble.

BETSY
See also Elisabeth, Elizabeth

Haywood, Carolyn, **'B' Is for Betsy**, illustrated by Carolyn Haywood, Harcourt Brace Jovanovich, 1939, 159p., Fiction, ISBN 0-15-204975-4.

Betsy attends her first year in school and spends her vacation on a farm. There are several other books about Betsy.

Lovelace, Maud Hart, **Betsy-Tacy**, illustrated by Lois Lenski, Crowell, 1940, 113p., Fiction, ISBN 0-690-13805-9.

Set at the turn of the century, this story tells about Betsy and her life and her friendship with Tacy. There are several other books about the two young friends.

BETTY
See also Beatrice, Beatrix

Meltzer, Milton, **Betty Friedan: A Voice for Women's Rights**, illustrated by Stephan Marchesi, Viking Kestrel, 1985, 57p., Nonfiction, ISBN 0-670-80786-9.

Betty Friedan became well known for her outspoken support of women's rights during the 1970s. This biography gives information about Ms. Friedan and the causes she supports.

BEVERLY

Cleary, Beverly, **Girl from Yamhill**, Morrow, 1988, 279p., Nonfiction, ISBN 0-688-07800-1.

The popular children's author, Beverly Cleary, tells about her childhood and family struggles during the Depression years.

BILL
See also Billie, Billy, William

Atwater, Richard and Florence, **Mr. Popper's Penguins**, illustrated by Robert Lawson, Little, Brown, 1938, 140p., Fiction, ISBN 0-316-05842-4.

Bill and Janie Popper's father is a housepainter; he is also a dreamer. Mr. Popper is always absent-mindedly dreaming of countries faraway and he regrets that he hasn't traveled, even though he loves his family very much. Mr. Popper's adventures begin when he receives an Air Express package from Antarctica that containes a penguin! 1939 Newbery Honor book. Pacific Northwest 1941.

Cleary, Beverly, **Socks**, illustrated by Beatrice Darwin, Morrow, 1973, 156p., Fiction, ISBN 0-440-48256-9 (pbk).

Bill and Marilyn Bricker are a young couple who buy Socks, a kitten with white paws. Socks is taken to the Bricker's home where he is petted, pampered, and loved. When the Bricker's have a baby, Socks is no longer the center of attention and then the problems begin. Kansas 1976.

dePaola, Tomie, **Bill and Pete Go Down the Nile**, illustrated by Tomie dePaola, Putnam, 1987, 28p., Picture Book, LC 86-12258, ISBN 0-399-21395-3.

When Bill the crocodile and his bird friend Pete begin the new school year, they wonder what they will learn. On an exciting class trip to a Cairo museum they encounter a jewel thief. A Reading Rainbow book.

Haskins, James, **Bill Cosby: America's Most Famous Father**, Walker, 1988, 138p., Nonfiction, ISBN 0-8027-6786-9.

The famous American comedian, Bill Cosby, was constantly encouraged by his mother to get a good education. While pursuing his career on the stage and on television, Cosby continued his education. Biographical information provides an insight into the man as actor, educator, and family man.

Kellogg, Steven, **Pecos Bill**, illustrated by Steven Kellogg, Morrow, 1986, 32p., Fiction, ISBN 0-688-05872-8 (lib); 0-688-05871-X.

A tall tale about Bill who fell out of his family's covered wagon and was raised by wolves before being discovered by a cowboy. New Mexico 1991.

Meader, Stephen W., **Boy With a Pack**, illustrated by Edward Shenton, Harcourt Brace Jovanovich, 1939, 297p., Fiction, ISBN 0-15-211240-5.

Seventeen-year-old Bill has taken a job as a peddler and is going to the wilderness country with a pack of goods on his back. 1940 Newbery Honor book.

Peet, Bill, **Bill Peet: An Autobiography**, illustrated by Bill Peet, Houghton Mifflin, 1989, 190p., Nonfiction, LC 88-37067, ISBN 0-395-50932-7.

This autobiography of the well-known author and illustrator includes numerous black-and-white illustrations. Bill Peet was born in Grandview, Indiana, and has had a long and interesting career including working with Walt Disney on several animated movies. 1990 Caldecott Honor book. Utah 1991.

Wibberley, Leonard, **Perilous Gold**, Farrar, Straus & Giroux, 1978, 135p., Fiction, ISBN 0-374-35824-9.

Bill and his father build a small submarine to explore deep water so they can search for buried treasure near a California island.

BILLIE
See also Bill, Billy, William

De Veaux, Alexis, **Don't Explain: A Song of Billie Holiday**, Harper & Row, 1980, 151p., Nonfiction, ISBN 0-060-216-298; 0-060-216-301 (lib).

The life of the American jazz singer, Billie Holiday, is told in a prose poem. 1981 Coretta Scott King Honor book.

George, Jean Craighead, **Talking Earth**, Harper & Row, 1983, 151p., Fiction, ISBN 0-06-021976-9.

Thirteen-year-old Billie Wind questions the teachings of her Seminole ancestors and goes into the Everglades to discover for herself whether the animals and land can speak to her.

BILLY
See also Bill, Billie, William

Cox, David, **Tin Lizzie and Little Nell**, illustrated by David Cox, Bodley Head, 1982, 30p., Picture Book, ISBN 0-370-30922-7.

Billy Benson has an old grey mare named Little Nell. His neighbor, William Winterbottom, owns an old blue car called Tin Lizzie. Each of the Australian farmers think that his form of transportation is best and so they have a Saturday race. A Reading Rainbow book.

Dana, Barbara, **Zucchini**, illustrated by Eileen Christelow, Harper & Row, 1982, 122p., Fiction, LC 80-8448, ISBN 0-06-021394-9; 0-06-021395-7 (lib).

Billy is very shy but he loves Zucchini, the young ferret. Zucchini was escaping to the prairie when he and Billy met. When a misunderstanding occurs between the two, Zucchini feels hurt and rejected and runs away again. New Mexico 1987.

Morpurgo, Michael, **Little Foxes**, illustrated by Gareth Floyd, Kaye & Ward, 1984, 108p., Fiction, ISBN 0-7182-3972-5.

Billy Bunch is a lonely boy who befriends an orphaned fox. The two have many near-disasterous adventures.

Pomerantz, Charlotte, **Piggy in the Puddle, The**, illustrated by James Marshall, Macmillan, 1974, 32p., Picture Book, ISBN 0-02-774900-2.

Billy is a little pig whose younger sister is in a mud puddle and refuses to get out with humorous results. A Reading Rainbow book.

Rawls, Wilson, **Where the Red Fern Grows: The Story of Two Dogs and a Boy**, Doubleday, 1961, 212p., Fiction, ISBN 0-385-02059-7.

Billy Colman lives in the Ozark Mountains. He wanted a pair of coon hounds so he worked for two years to save up the money for them. He trained his dogs and won an award before a tragedy strikes.

Rockwell, Thomas, **How to Eat Fried Worms**, illustrated by Emily McCully, Watts, 1973, 115p., Fiction, LC 73-4262, ISBN 0-531-02631-0.

Billy is willing to eat anything and even agrees to eat fifteen worms to win a bet. Arizona 1979. California 1975. Hawaii 1976. Indiana 1977. Iowa 1980. Massachusetts 1976. Missouri 1975. Oklahoma 1976. South Carolina 1976.

Smith, Alison, **Billy Boone**, Scribner, 1989, 119p., Fiction, ISBN 0-684-18974-7.

Twelve-year-old Billy Boone has a mind of her own, and she wants to play the trumpet. However, her parents want Billy to be more ladylike.

BINNIE

Lord, Athena, **Spirit to Ride the Whirlwind**, Macmillan, 1981, 205p., Fiction, ISBN 0-02-761410-7.

Twelve-year-old Binnie wanted to work in the mills in Lowell, Massachusetts, during the 1830s. The unfair treatment of women and the terrible working conditions lead her to join a strike. 1982 Child Study Children's Book Award. 1982 Jane Addams Award.

BIRDIE

Lenski, Lois, **Strawberry Girl**, illustrated by Lois Lenski, Lippincott, 1945, 194p., Fiction, LC 45-7609, ISBN 0-397-30110-3.

Birdie Boyer and her family moved near the Slater family farm in Florida and Birdie found a new friend. A regional tale of a family of Florida Crackers who live in the backwoods. It includes their speech, customs, folk songs, and superstitions. 1946 Newbery Award book.

BLANCHE

Souci, Robert D., **Talking Eggs, The**, illustrated by Jerry Pinkney, Dial, 1989, 30p., Picture Book, LC 88-33469, ISBN 0-8037-0619-7; 0-8037-0620-0 (lib).

A Creole folktale about two very different sisters. Rose is spoiled and lazy while Blanche is sweet and hard-working. Rose is their mother's favorite and Blanche is required to do all the work. When Blanche meets an old witch-woman she enters a wondrous world and her life is changed. 1990 Caldecott Honor book. 1990 Coretta Scott King Honor book.

BOB
See also Bobby, Robert

Joyce, William, **Dinosaur Bob and His Adventures with the Family Lazardo**, illustrated by William Joyce, Harper & Row, 1988, 32p., Picture Book, LC 87-30796, ISBN 0-06-023047-9; 0-06-023048-7 (lib).

While on a family safari to Africa, young Scotty Lazardo finds a dinosaur who the family names Bob. When Bob returns to America with the family he creates quite a sensation. A Reading Rainbow book.

BOBBY
See also Barbara, Bob, Robert, Roberta

Christopher, Matt, **Fox Steals Home**, illustrated by Larry Johnson, Little, Brown, 1978, 178p., Fiction, ISBN 0-316-13976-9.

Bobby has two great challenges in his life. He wants to succeed in baseball, and he has to learn to adjust to a different way of life when his parents divorce.

BONNIE

Aiken, Joan, **Wolves of Willoughby Chase, The**, illustrated by Pat Marriott, Doubleday, 1962, 168p., Fiction, LC 63-18034, ISBN 0-385-03594-2.

Bonnie, her cousin, and a faithful friend conquer the many obstacles that surround them in Victorian England, including a grim governess and wicked wolves.

BORIS

Rodgers, Mary, **Billion for Boris, A**, Harper & Row, 1974, 211p., Fiction, ISBN 0-06-025054-2.

Boris needs money to remodel his apartment and decides to use information from his friend's television set that is giving tomorrow's news today. He meets with unexpected and humorous results.

Zhitkov, Boris Stepanovich, **How I Hunted the Little Fellows**, illustrated by Paul O. Zelincky, Dodd, Mead, 1979, 64p., Fiction, ISBN 0-396-07692-0.

In this translated Russian story, Boris believes that tiny sailors live in the model ship at his grandmother's house. In trying to see them, Boris wrecks his grandmother's most prized possession.

BOY-STRENGTH-OF-BLUE-HORSES

Martin, Bill, Jr. and John Archambault, **Knots on a Counting Rope**, illustrated by Ted Rand, H. Holt, 1987, 30p., Picture Book, LC 87-14858, ISBN 0-8050-0571-4.

Sitting under the desert sky, a Navaho Indian grandfather and his grandson Boy-Strength-of-Blue-Horses reminisce about the boy's birth, his first horse, and an exciting horse race. A Reading Rainbow book.

BOYD

Cleary, Beverly, **Dear Mr. Henshaw**, illustrated by Paul O. Zelinsky, Morrow, 1983, 134p., Fiction, LC 83-5372, ISBN 0-688-02405-X; 0-688-02406-8 (lib).

Boyd Henshaw is an author and Leigh has been a fan for four years. When Leigh's teacher assigns a letter-writing project, Leigh writes to Mr. Henshaw about his many personal and family problems and Mr. Henshaw responds with some surprising answers. 1984 Christopher Medal. 1984 Newbery Award book. Oklahoma 1986. Vermont 1985.

BRAD
See also Bradley

Christopher, John, **Fireball**, Dutton, 1981, 148p., Fiction, ISBN 0-525-29738-3.

Brad goes to England to visit his cousin for the summer. The two boys become involved in an exciting adventure when they find themselves in the Roman Britain of 2,000 years ago.

Green, Phyllis, **Eating Ice Cream with a Werewolf**, illustrated by Patti Stren, Harper & Row, 1983, 121p., Fiction, ISBN 0-06-022141-0.

Twelve-year-old Brad is left with a babysitter when his parents go on a trip. The humor begins when Brad discovers his sitter is a part-time witch.

BRADLEY
See also Brad

Sachar, Louis, **There's a Boy in the Girls' Bathroom**, Knopf, 1987, 195p., Fiction, LC 86-20100, ISBN 0-394-88570-8; 0-394-98570-2 (lib).

Bradley is an eleven-year-old misfit who is unmanageable but also lovable. He learns to believe in himself when he gets to know the school counselor, who is also a misfit of sorts. Arkansas 1990. Georgia 1990. New Mexico 1990. Ohio 1991. Pacific Northwest 1990. Texas 1990. Utah 1992. Virginia 1991.

BRAN
See also Brandon

Voight, Cynthia, **Building Blocks**, Atheneum, 1984, 128p., Fiction, ISBN 0-689-31035-8.

Twelve-year-old Bran finds himself going back in time to become a childhood friend of his father. The incident provides insight into his father and into Bran's family life.

BRANDON
See also Bran

Pitts, Paul, **Racing the Sun**, Avon, 1988, 150p., Fiction, ISBN 0-380-75496-7 (pbk).

Twelve-year-old Brandon Rogers lives in the suburbs. When he hears about the Navajo heritage of his father, Brandon faces a conflict in values.

BRENDON

Duncan, Lois, **Gift of Magic**, illustrated by Arvis Stewart, Little, Brown, 1971, 183p., Fiction, ISBN 0-316-19545-6.

Brendon and his siblings each have a special gift, which was predicted by their grandmother. Brendon's gift is one of music.

BRIAN

Adler, David A., **Eaton Stanley and the Mind Control Experiments**, illustrated by Joan Drescher, Dutton, 1985, 88p., Fiction, ISBN 0-525-44117-4.

Brian tells the story of his friend Eaton Stanley and their plan to take control of their sixth-grade teacher's mind.

Newman, Robert, **Merlin's Mistake**, illustrated by Richard Lebenson, Peter Smith, 1985, 237p., Fiction, ISBN 0-8446-6187-2.

Brian is the son of a dead knight. In order to prove himself, Brian joins another in a quest to search for magical powers.

Nixon, Joan Lowery, **Gift, The**, illustrated by Andrew Glass, Macmillan, 1983, 86p., Fiction, ISBN 0-02-768160-2.

While visiting Irish relatives, Brian sees the magical fairy folk that his grandfather has told him about.

Paulsen, Gary, **Hatchet**, Bradbury, 1987, 195p., Fiction, LC 87-6416, ISBN 0-02-770130-1.

After a plane crash, thirteen-year-old Brian Robeson spends fifty-four days in the wilderness alone. Initially he has to survive with only the aid of a hatchet, which had been given to him by his mother. 1988 Newbery Honor book. Georgia 1991. Indiana 1991. Kansas 1990. Ohio 1991. Vermont 1989.

Wallace, Bill, **Trapped in Death Cave**, Holiday House, 1984, 170p., Fiction, ISBN 0-823-405-168.

Brian's friend is convinced that his grandfather was murdered, and the two boys search for both a buried treasure and a killer. Utah 1989.

BRIGHT MORNING

O'Dell, Scott, **Sing Down the Moon**, Houghton Mifflin, 1970, 137p., Fiction, LC 71-98513, ISBN 0-395-10919-1.

Bright Morning, a young Navaho woman, tells of her life herding sheep, being kidnapped by Spaniards, and hiding from the soldiers that come to burn her village. This book is based upon the history of the Navaho Indians during the period of 1863-1865 when they were forced off their lands by soldiers and taken on The Long Walk to Fort Sumner. 1971 Newbery Honor book.

BRUCE

Peet, Bill, **Big Bad Bruce**, Houghton Mifflin, 1977, 38p., Picture Book, LC 76-062502, ISBN 0-395-2515-08.

Bruce the bear is a bully who never picks on anyone his own size. A small witch teaches Bruce a lesson he doesn't forget. California 1980. Georgia 1979.

BUDDY

Hamilton, Virginia, **Planet of Junior Brown, The**, Macmillan, 1971, 210p., Fiction, ISBN 0-02-742510-X.

Buddy Clark is one of the unusual characters in this book. He and his friends play hooky from school and when they are caught their private world is destroyed. 1972 Newbery Honor book.

Marshall, Edward, **Space Case**, illustrated by James Marshall, Dial, 1980, 38p., Picture Book, LC 80-13369, ISBN 0-8037-8005-2; 0-8037-8007-9 (lib).

On Halloween night, a strange creature joins Buddy McGee and his friends. The creature is from outer space and followed Buddy home to learn about Earthlings. Their experiences have humorous results. California 1988. Colorado 1983. Washington 1983. A Reading Rainbow book.

Roy, Ron, **Where's Buddy?**, illustrated by Troy Howell, Ticknor & Fields, 1982, 95p., Fiction, ISBN 0-89919-076-6.

Seven-year-old Buddy goes cave exploring with a friend and forgets to take an insulin injection for his diabetes, causing serious problems.

BURT
See also Bert

McCloskey, Robert, **Burt Dow, Deep-Water Man; A Tale of the Sea in the Classic Tradition**, Viking, 1963, 61p., Fiction, ISBN 0-670-19748-3.

A tall tale about Burt Dow, an old fisherman who catches a whale by its tail and has other adventures.

BWEELA

Steptoe, John, **Daddy Is a Monster...Sometimes**, illustrated by John Steptoe, Lippincott, 1900, 30p., Picture Book, LC 77-4464, ISBN 0-397-31762-X; 0-397-31893-6 (lib).

Bweela and her brother, Javaka, have a nice daddy who sometimes seems to turn into a scary monster when the children are too messy or noisy. A Reading Rainbow book.

-C-

CADDIE

Brink, Carol Ryrie, **Caddie Woodlawn**, illustrated by Trina Schart Hyman, Macmillan, 1973, 275p., Fiction, LC 73-588, ISBN 0-02-713670-1.

Caddie was the author's grandmother and this story comes from tales that she told of her pioneer childhood in Wisconsin in the 1860s. Caddie refused to be a 'lady' and preferred running in the woods with her brother. 1936 Newbery Award book.

CALEB

MacLachlan, Patricia, **Sarah, Plain and Tall**, Harper & Row, 1985, 58p., Fiction, LC 83-49481, ISBN 0-06-024101-2; 0-06-024102-0 (lib).

When their father invites a mail-order bride named Sarah to come live with them in their prairie home, Caleb and Anna learn to appreciate Sarah and hope she will stay. 1986 Christopher Award. 1986 Golden Kite Award. 1986 Newbery Award book. 1986 Jefferson Cup Award. 1986 Scott O'Dell Award. Arkansas 1988.

CALPURNIA

Rawlings, Marjorie Kinnan, **Secret River, The**, illustrated by Leonard Weisgard, Scribner, 1955, 54p., Fiction, LC 55-6916, ISBN 0-684-12636-2.

Calpurnia lives in a dark green forest in Florida. When hard times come to the forest, the young girl is led to a secret river to catch fish to help make times easier. 1956 Newbery Honor book.

CAM

Adler, David A., **Cam Jansen and the Mystery of the Stolen Diamonds**, illustrated by Susanna Nalti, Viking, 1980, 58p., Fiction, ISBN 0-670-200039-5.

Cam and her photographic memory help to solve the mystery of the hold-up at a jewelry store. There are other books about Cam Jansen.

CANDY
See also Constance

DeJong, Meindert, **Hurry Home Candy**, illustrated by Maurice Sendak, Harper & Row, 1953, 244p., Fiction, ISBN 0-06-021486-4.

Candy is a small dog wandering from one misadventure to another before making a home with an old sea captain. 1954 Newbery Honor book.

CAREY
See also Carrie, Kerri

Eyerly, Jeannette, **Seeing Summer**, Lippincott, 1981, 153p., Fiction, ISBN 0-397-31966-5.

Ten-year-old Carey becomes friends with her new neighbor who is blind. When her friend is kidnapped, Carey attempts to rescue her but finds that the girl is capable of taking care of herself.

Norton, Mary, **Bed-Knob and Broomstick**, illustrated by Erik Blegvad, Harcourt Brace Jovanovich, 1957, 189p., Fiction, ISBN 0-15-611500-X.

Carey Wilson and her siblings meet a woman who is studying to become a witch. The children are given magical powers and have unusual adventures.

CARL
See also Karl

Aaseng, Nathan, **Carl Lewis: Legend Chaser**, Lerner, 1985, 56p., Nonfiction, ISBN 0-8225-0496-0.

A biography about the famous track-and-field athlete, Carl Lewis.

Milhous, Katherine, **Egg Tree, The**, illustrated by Katherine Milhous, Scribner, 1950, 30p., Picture Book, ISBN 0-684-12716-4.

On Easter morning, Carl and his sister Katy search for colored Easter eggs. Katy finds beautiful decorated eggs in the closet, and their grandmother shows them how to decorate more eggs and how to make an egg tree. 1951 Caldecott Award book.

Sandin, Joan, **Long Way to a New Land, The**, illustrated by Joan Sandin, Harper & Row, 1981, 63p., Easy Reader, LC 80-8942, ISBN 0-06-025193-X; 0-06-025194-8 (lib).

In 1868, there was a drought in Sweden and no food for winter. Carl's family decides to emigrate to America and begin a new life. Their long journey is taken by cart, train, and steamship. A Reading Rainbow book.

CARLA

Kessler, Leonard, **Old Turtle's Baseball Stories**, illustrated by Leonard Kessler, Greenwillow, 1982, 55p., Easy Reader, LC 81-6390, ISBN 0-688-00723-6; 0-688-00724-4 (lib).

In the summer, Old Turtle and his friends play baseball and in the winter they tell baseball stories. Old Turtle tells a story about the best outfielder, Carla Kangaroo and a game in which she played right field, left field, and center field. A Reading Rainbow book.

CARLIE

Byars, Betsy, **Pinballs, The**, Harper & Row, 1977, 136p., Fiction, LC 76-41518, ISBN 0-06-020917-8; 0-06-020918-6 (lib).

Pinballs don't get to settle where they want to, and neither do foster children. Carlie, Harvey, and Thomas are three lonely children who have been disappointed by their own parents. But under the influence of their foster parents and each other, they decide that they aren't really pinballs. Arkansas 1980. California 1980. Georgia 1979. Kansas 1980. Minnesota 1981. Mississippi 1980.

CARMELA

Taha, Karen T., **Gift for Tia Rosa, A**, illustrated by Dee deRosa, Dillon, 1985, 38p., Picture Book, LC 85-6969, ISBN 0-87518-306-9.

Carmela has learned many things from her elderly neighbor, including how to knit. When her neighbor becomes very ill and dies, Carmela finds a way to express her love. A Reading Rainbow book.

CAROLINE
See also Carolyn

Clymer, Eleanor, **Horse in the Attic**, illustrated by Ted Lewin, Bradbury, 1983, 87p., Fiction, ISBN 0-02-719040-4.

Caroline discovers a painting of a horse in the attic of the stable of her family's new home. The discovery leads her to a mystery.

Lowry, Lois, **One Hundredth Thing about Caroline, The**, Houghton Mifflin, 1983, 150p., Fiction, ISBN 0-395-34829-3.

Eleven-year-old Caroline is suspicious of the man who lives upstairs and gets her brother to help her investigate the man's motives. There is another book about this family.

Paterson, Katherine, **Jacob Have I Loved**, Crowell, 1980, 244p., Fiction, LC 80-668, ISBN 0-690-04078-4; 0-690-04079-2 (lib); 0-06-440368-6 (pbk).

Louise reveals how she has felt that her twin sister, Caroline, has robbed her of everything: her hopes for schooling, her friends, her mother, and even her name. Alone and unsure, Louise finally begins to find her own identity. 1981 Newbery Award book.

Wilder, Laura Ingalls, **By the Shores of Silver Lake**, illustrated by Garth Williams, Harper & Row, 1953, 290p., Fiction, ISBN 0-06-026416-0.

The Ingalls didn't do well in Plum Creek, Minnesota, so Pa went west to the Dakota Territory. Caroline Ingalls took her children by train to meet Pa, and the family became the first settlers in a new town. When the family catches scarlet fever, Mary becomes blinded. There are other books about this family. 1940 Newbery Honor book. Pacific Northwest 1942.

CAROLYN
See also Caroline

Raskin, Ellen, **Mysterious Disappearance of Leon (I Mean Noel), The**, illustrated by Ellen Raskin, Dutton, 1980, 160p., Fiction, ISBN 0-525-35540-5.

Carolyn Fish is married when she is five years old to protect a family investment. Her young husband is sent to boarding school and Carolyn spends the next twenty years searching for him in this humorous mystery.

CARRIE
See also Carey, Kerri

Bawden, Nina, **Carrie's War**, Lippincott, 1973, 159p., Fiction, ISBN 0-397-31450-7.

As an adult, Carrie takes her children to see the house she had loved as a child when she was evacuated from war-torn London. As Carrie remembers those times, a mystery is slowly revealed.

Collier, James Lincoln and Christopher Collier, **Who Is Carrie?**, Delacorte, 1984, 158p., Fiction, ISBN 0-440-49536-9 (pbk).

Carrie is a kitchen slave in New York during the late part of the sixteenth century. She was orphaned as a small child and wonders who she really is and if she was born free.

Greenberg, Jan, **Season In-Between**, Farrar, Straus & Giroux, 1979, 149p., Fiction, ISBN 0-374-36564-4.

Twelve-year-old Carrie has many problems including school adjustments and finding out that her father has cancer.

Wilder, Laura Ingalls, **On the Banks of Plum Creek**, illustrated by Garth Williams, Harper & Row, 1953, 338p., Fiction, ISBN 0-06-026470-5.

Carrie Ingalls and her family move to Minnesota and live in a dugout until a new house can be built. The family is faced by many natural disasters including a flood, a blizzard, and grasshoppers. There are many other titles about this family. 1938 Newbery Honor book.

CASEY

Bottner, Barbara, **Dumb Old Casey Is a Fat Tree**, illustrated by Barbara Bottner, Harper & Row, 1979, 42p., Fiction, ISBN 0-06-020617-9.

Casey wants to be the evil prince at the ballet recital, but is assigned to be a tree because she is so overweight.

Bridgers, Sue Ellen, **All Together Now**, Knopf, 1979, 238p., Fiction, ISBN 0-394-94098-9.

Casey Flanagan spends the summer with her grandparents in a small town in North Carolina. She meets some interesting people and makes new friends.

Giff, Patricia Reilly, **Fourth-Grade Celebrity**, illustrated by Leslie Morrill, Delacorte, 1981, 117p., Fiction, ISBN 0-385-28303-3.

Being president of her fourth-grade class is not enough for Casey Valentine, she decides she must also be a celebrity in order to show up her older sister. There is another book about Casey.

Yep, Laurence, **Child of the Owl**, Harper & Row, 1977, 217p., Fiction, ISBN 0-06-026743-7.

Casey is a Chinese-American who learns about her mother and her Chinese heritage when she is sent to stay with relatives while her father is in the hospital. 1978 Jane Addams Award. 1977 Boston Globe-Horn Book Award.

CASSIA
See also Cassie

Yep, Laurence, **Serpent's Children**, Harper & Row, 1984, 277p., Fiction, ISBN 0-06-026812-3.

Cassia lives in a Chinese village in the nineteenth century. Her mother has died while her father has been fighting, and when he returns he continues to dream of a free China. There is another book about Cassia and her father.

CASSIE
See also Cassia

Alcock, Vivien, **Haunting of Cassie Palmer**, Delacorte, 1982, 149p., Fiction, ISBN 0-440-43370-3.

Cassie Palmer is the seventh child of a seventh child and supposedly has psychic powers. When she has to try to use those powers to save the family fortunes, a ghost from the eighteenth century appears.

Danziger, Paula, **Pistachio Prescription, The**, Delacorte, 1978, 123p., Fiction, ISBN 0-440-96895-X (pbk).

Thirteen-year-old Cassie has frequent asthma attacks due to the frequent fighting that goes on in her family. She is also a hypochondriac and eats pistachio nuts whenever things go wrong. She learns that her life is not as unbearable as it seems and her compulsion for pistachios doesn't help.

Taylor, Mildred, **Friendship, The**, illustrated by Max Ginsburg, Dial, 1987, 53p., Fiction, LC 86-29309, ISBN 0-8037-0417-8; 0-8037-0418-6 (lib).

When Cassie Logan and her three brothers are sent to a small rural store, trouble begins as an old black man keeps calling the white storekeeper by his first name. Set in Mississippi in 1933. 1988 Boston Globe-Horn Book Award. 1988 Coretta Scott King Award book.

Taylor, Mildred, **Let the Circle Be Unbroken**, Dial, 1981, 394p., Fiction, LC 81-65854, ISBN 0-8037-4748-9.

The saga of the Logan family is continued in this sequel. Set in 1935 during the Depression, Cassie and the other three Logan children and their parents watch their poor sharecropper neighbors in Mississippi being victimized by the large landowners. Racial tensions increase with the hard times and their friend is charged with murder. 1982 Coretta Scott King Award book. 1982 Jane Addams Honor book.

Taylor, Mildred, **Roll of Thunder, Hear My Cry**, Dial, 1976, 276p., Fiction, ISBN 0-8037-7473-7.

Cassie Logan and her family live a hard life in the backcountry of Mississippi during the Depression years. 1977 Newbery Award book. 1977 Jane Addams Award book. Pacific Northwest 1979.

Taylor, Mildred, **Song of the Trees**, illustrated by Jerry Pinkney, Dial, 1975, 48p., Fiction, ISBN 0-8037-5453-1.

Cassie and her family live on a small Mississippi farm during the Depression. The old trees on the farm offer the children protection until they are cut for lumber.

CATHERINE
See also Cathy, Kate, Katherine, Kathy, Katie, Katy, Kay

Blos, Joan W., **Gathering of Days: A New England Girl's Journey, 1830-1832, A**, Scribner, 1979, 145p., Fiction, LC 79-16898, ISBN 0-684-16340-3.

The journal of thirteen-year-old Catherine Hall records the last year that she lived on the family farm in New Hampshire. The year turns out to be quite memorable as her father remarries, a runaway slave opens Catherine's eyes to racial injustice, and she is grieved at her best friend's death. 1980 Newbery Award book. 1990 Jane Addams Award book.

CATHY
See also Catherine, Kate, Katherine, Kathy, Katie, Katy, Kay

Holland, Isabelle, **Now Is Not Too Late**, Lothrop, Lee & Shepard, 1980, 159p., Fiction, ISBN 0-688-51937-7.

While eleven-year-old Cathy is visiting with her grandmother on a small island, she meets a woman artist who is called names by the local residents. Cathy wants to pose for her to earn money for a bicycle, but it is hard to keep a secret from her family and friends.

Nesbit, E., **Enchanted Castle**, illustrated by H. R. Millar, Puffin, 1985, 252p., Fiction, ISBN 0-14-035057-8 (pbk).

Cathy is one of the children who spends her summer investigating an enchanted castle and having magical adventures.

CECI
See also Cecily

Ets, Marie Hall and Aurora Labastida, **Nine Days to Christmas**, illustrated by Marie Hall Ets, Viking, 1959, 48p., Picture Book, LC 59-16438, ISBN 670-51350-4.

Ceci is anxious to have her first posada, a special Christmas party held nine days before Christmas. Her brother and their servant help her keep track of the days and her mother helps Ceci buy a very special pinata. 1960 Caldecott Award book.

CECILY
See also Ceci

Lexau, Joan M., **Striped Ice Cream**, illustrated by John Wilson, Lippincott, 1968, 95p., Fiction, LC 68-10774, ISBN 0-397-31047-1.

Cecily's sister is resigned to the fact that their mother cannot afford anything special for her birthday, but she does not understand why the family seems to have turned against her, until the big day finally arrives. Arkansas 1971.

CEDRIC

Burnett, Frances Hodgson, **Little Lord Fauntleroy**, Dell, 1986, 223p., Fiction, ISBN 0-440-44764-X (pbk).

A classic story about Cedric Errol who moves from his widowed mother's simple house in New York to his grandfather's castle in England.

CESAR

Roberts, Naurice, **Cesar Chavez and la Causa**, Children's Press, 1986, 31p., Nonfiction, ISBN 0-516-03484-7.

Cesar Chavez's family emigrated from Mexico and had a difficult time in the United States. Chavez has a great sympathy for migrant workers and has

dedicated his life to their plight. This brief biography provides information about his life.

CHAD
See also Charles

Adler, C. S., **Cat That Was Left Behind**, Clarion/Ticknor & Fields, 1981, 146p., Fiction, ISBN 0-395-31020-2.

Chad feels rejected and resentful from being moved around to several foster families. Although his new foster parents do their best, Chad remains isolated until he finds a stray cat.

Graeber, Charlotte Towner, **Fudge**, illustrated by Cheryl Harness, Lothrop, Lee & Shepard, 1987, 123p., Fiction, ISBN 0-688-06735-2.

Ten-year-old Chad promises to care for the younger child, Fudge, to help out the family when his mother is expecting twins. Indiana 1990. Oklahoma 1990. West Virginia 1990.

Steele, William O, **Flaming Arrows**, illustrated by Paul Galdone, Harcourt Brace Jovanovich, 1957, 178p., Fiction, LC 57-6791, ISBN 0-15-228424-9.

Eleven-year-old Chad and his family, along with other settlers, have to go to the fort for protection during raids by the Chickamauga Indians. Kansas 1960.

CHARLES
See also Chad, Charley, Charlie, Chip, Chuck

Bishop, Claire Huchet, **Pancakes—Paris**, illustrated by Georges Schreiber, Viking, 1947, 64p., Fiction, LC 47-2541, ISBN 670-53783-7.

Charles lives with his mother and younger sister in a small apartment in France shortly after World War II. Charles remembers how holidays were celebrated before the war and is excited to meet two Americans who give him pancake mix to make a special meal. 1948 Newbery Honor book.

Byars, Betsy, **Winged Colt of Casa Mia**, illustrated by Richard Cuffari, Avon, 1973, 128p., Fiction, ISBN 0-380-00201-9 (pbk).

Charles and his uncle discover a winged colt and have many misadventures trying to save it.

Gretz, Susanna and Alison Sage, **Teddy Bears Cure a Cold**, illustrated by Susanna Gretz and Alison Sage, Four Winds, 1984, 32p., Picture Book, LC 84-4015, ISBN 0-590-07949-2.

William the bear feels sick and spends several days in bed while Charles and the other bears take care of him. A Reading Rainbow book.

L'Engle, Madeleine, **Swiftly Tilting Planet, A**, Farrar, Straus & Giroux, 1978, 278p., Fiction, LC 78-9648, ISBN 0-374-37362-0.

A companion volume to *A Wrinkle in Time.* Charles Wallace, the youngest Murry, travels through time and space in a battle against an evil dictator who would destroy the entire planet. His sister, Meg, goes with him in spirit by entering his thoughts and emotions. 1980 Jane Addams Award book.

L'Engle, Madeleine, **Wind in the Door, A**, Farrar, Straus & Giroux, 1973, 211p., Fiction, ISBN 0-374-38443-6.

Charles Wallace has problems at school where he is disliked and bullied by his classmates. His health is also deteriorating and he is certain there are dragons in the garden. His sister discovers there really are dragons and other aliens, and the two become involved in a series of terrifying adventures.

L'Engle, Madeleine, **Wrinkle in Time, A**, Dell, 1962, 211p., Fiction, ISBN 0-440-498-58.

On a dark and stormy night Charles Wallace Murray, his sister, and his mother go down to the kitchen for a midnight snack. An unearthly stranger arrives and the children are taken through a wrinkle in time as they search for their missing scientist father. 1963 Newbery Award book. Oklahoma 1965.

Norton, Mary, **Bed-Knob and Broomstick**, illustrated by Erik Blegvad, Harcourt Brace Jovanovich, 1957, 189p., Fiction, ISBN 0-15-611500-X.

Charles Wilson and his siblings meet a woman who is studying to become a witch. The children are given magical powers and they have unusual adventures.

Park, Barbara, **Don't Make Me Smile**, Knopf, 1981, 114p., Fiction, ISBN 0-394-94978-1.

Eleven-year-old Charles goes through a difficult time with his emotions when his parents tell him that they are getting a divorce.

Quackenbush, Robert, **Beagle and Mr. Flycatcher, a Story of Charles Darwin**, Prentice-Hall, 1983, 36p., Nonfiction, ISBN 0-13-071290-6.

A biography about Charles Darwin who started out with little career direction and went on to become famous for his controversial theories on evolution and natural selection.

Quackenbush, Robert, **Oh, What an Awful Mess. A Story of Charles Goodyear**, illustrated by Robert Quackenbush, Prentice-Hall, 1980, 40p., Nonfiction, ISBN 0-13-633404-0.

Charles Goodyear was an inventor who believed that rubber could be used to make useful products. This biography includes the many failures he had before he met success.

Wells, Rosemary, **Shy Charles**, illustrated by Rosemary Wells, Dial, 1988, 32p., Picture Book, ISBN 0-8037-056-38; 0-8037-056-46 (lib).

Charles is a very shy little mouse who overcomes his timidness when there is an emergency. 1989 Boston Globe-Horn Book Award.

Wilder, Laura Ingalls, **Long Winter, The**, illustrated by Garth Williams, Harper & Row, 1953, 334p., Fiction, ISBN 0-06-026460-8.

Charles Ingalls decides to move his family from their claim to town after an October blizzard and the prediction that winter will be seven months long. There are numerous titles about this family. 1941 Newbery Honor book.

CHARLEY
See also Charles, Charlie, Chuck

Beatty, Patricia, **Charley Skedaddle**, Morrow, 1987, 186p., Fiction, ISBN 0-688-0668-79.

Charley Quinn is a twelve-year-old boy who has grown up in the Bowery area of New York City. When he joins the Union Army as a drummer he is sent to Virginia, where he becomes a deserter and meets a hostile mountain woman. 1988 Scott O'Dell Award.

CHARLIE

See also Charles, Charley, Chuck

Alcock, Vivien, **Travelers by Night**, Delacorte, 1983, 182p., Fiction, LC 85-1663, ISBN 0-385-29406-9.

Charlie and Belle are determined to save an old elephant from the slaughterhouse. The two circus children kidnap the animal and begin a dangerous journey to a safari park 100 miles away where they hope to find the elephant a home.

Bulla, Clyde Robert, **Charlie's House**, illustrated by Arthur Dorros, Crowell, 1983, 81p., Fiction, ISBN 0-690-04260-4.

When he leaves England for America in the eighteenth century, twelve-year-old Charlie is sold as an indentured servant.

Callen, Larry, **Muskrat War**, Little, Brown, 1980, 132p., Fiction, ISBN 0-316-12498-2.

During hard financial times in their rural area, Charlie and his best friend and their fathers become involved in a muskrat war and other humorous incidents.

Dahl, Roald, **Charlie and the Great Glass Elevator**, illustrated by Joseph Schindelman, Knopf, 1972, 163p., Fiction, LC 72-2434, ISBN 0-394-82472-5; 0-394-92472-X (lib).

The further adventures of Charlie Bucket and Willy Wonka, the great chocolate maker. Charlie, his family, and Mr. Wonka find themselves launched into space in the great glass elevator. Hawaii 1978.

Kamen, Gloria, **Charlie Chaplin**, Atheneum, 1982, 70p., Nonfiction, ISBN 0-689-30925-2.

Charlie Chaplin was a world-famous actor, director, and producer. He had a difficult childhood which provided background for his film portrayals. This biography provides information about the well-known man.

Roberts, Willo Davis, **What Could Go Wrong?**, Atheneum, 1989, 167p., Fiction, ISBN 0-689-31438-8.

Charlie and his cousins fly from San Francisco to Seattle and become involved in a mystery filled with suspense.

Vivelo, Jackie, **Beagle in Trouble: Super Sleuth II**, Putnam, 1986, 109p., Fiction, ISBN 0-399-21325-2.

Charlie is one of the two partners in the Beagle Detective Agency. The two twelve-year-olds solve crimes using logic and deduction. There are other books about these detectives.

Wright, Betty Ren, **Pike River Phantom**, Holiday House, 1988, 153p., Fiction, ISBN 0-8234-0721-7.

Charlie Hocking is unhappy about moving to Pike River to be reunited with his father who is an ex-convict. When he encounters a ghost that wants revenge, Charlie becomes involved with a thrilling adventure that is almost too much for him.

CHARLOTTE

Avi, **True Confessions of Charlotte Doyle, The**, Orchard, 1990, 224p., Fiction, ISBN 0-531-084-930.

Charlotte is the only young woman on a transatlantic voyage in 1832. Her adventure includes learning that the crew is rebellious and the captain is murderous. 1991 Boston Globe-Horn Book Award. 1991 Golden Kite Award. 1991 Newbery Honor book.

Farmer, Penelope, **Charlotte Sometimes**, Dell, 1987, 174p., Fiction, ISBN 0-440-41261-7.

Charlotte falls asleep and when she awakens in the middle of the night she discovers she has slipped through forty years of history to become Clare, a girl who had been at the same boarding school during World War I.

White, E. B., **Charlotte's Web**, illustrated by Garth Williams, Harper & Row, 1952, 184p., Fiction, LC 52-9760, ISBN 0-06-026385-7.

Charlotte, a beautiful grey spider, is the special friend of Wilbur the pig. Wilbur had been the runt of the litter and was saved and raised by the little girl Fern. 1953 Newbery Honor book. Massachusetts 1984. Michigan 1980. Missouri 1980.

CHELSEA

Burke, Susan, **Island Bike Business**, illustrated by Betty Greenhatch and Graeme Base, Oxford, 1982, 78p., Fiction, ISBN 0-19-554297-5.

Chelsea and her friends have dangerous adventures when they attempt to recover missing bicycles.

CHERYL

Battles, Edith, **Witch in Room 6**, HarperCollins, 1987, 144p., Fiction, ISBN 0-06-020413-3.

Sean becomes friends with Cheryl, an eleven-year-old apprentice witch, although her family does not want her to associate with 'regular' kids.

CHESTER

Howe, Deborah and James Howe, **Bunnicula: A Rabbit Tale of Mystery**, illustrated by Alan Daniel, Atheneum, 1979, 98p., Fiction, LC 78-11472, ISBN 0-689-30700-4.

Chester, the cat, and Harold, the dog, become concerned about the baby bunny that the Monroe children found at the movie and brought home. The rabbit only sleeps from sunup to sundown and the family finds two fang marks on vegetables that have been drained of their color. Harold and Chester suspect the rabbit is a vampire. Florida 1984. Hawaii 1983. Iowa 1982. Nebraska 1981. New Mexico 1982. Oklahoma 1982. Pacific Northwest 1982. South Carolina 1981. Vermont 1981.

Selden, George, **Cricket in Times Square, The**, illustrated by Garth Williams, Farrar, Straus & Giroux, 1960, 151p., Fiction, ISBN 0-374-31650-3.

Chester is a musical cricket that spends his summer in a New York City subway where he is befriended by a boy, a mouse, and a cat. There are several other books about Chester and his friends. 1961 Newbery Honor book. Massachusetts 1979.

CHI

Chrisman, Arthur Bowie, **Shen of the Sea: Chinese Stories for Children**, illustrated by Else Hasselriis, Dutton, 1953, 219p., Fiction, LC 68-13420, ISBN 0-525-39244-0.

Ching Chi is just one of the characters that appears in these sixteen Chinese short stories. 1926 Newbery Award book.

CHIP

See also Charles

Simon, Seymour, **Chip Rogers, Computer Whiz**, illustrated by Steve Miller, Morrow, 1984, 84p., Fiction, ISBN 0-688-03855-7.

Chip and his friend become involved in a mystery when a jewel thief strikes in the museum where the children have their computer club. Readers can solve the mystery by reading the book or by using their computers and the program that Chip develops.

CHRIS

See also Chrissie, Christina, Christine, Christopher, Christos

Corbin, William, **Smoke**, Coward-McCann, 1967, 253p., Fiction, LC 67-24218, ISBN 0-698-20131-0.

Chris dislikes his new stepfather, even though the man tries hard to win Chris' respect and affection. Chris develops a relationship with Smoke, a half-starved, wild German shepherd, and finds that he has to turn to his stepfather for help. Pacific Northwest 1970.

Morey, Walt, **Lemon Meringue Dog**, Dutton, 1980, 165p., Fiction, ISBN 0-525-33455-6.

Twenty-year-old Chris and his dog search for drugs. When the dog discovers his favorite pies he ruins a drug bust and the two are demoted.

Norton, Andre, **Red Hart Magic**, illustrated by Donna Diamond, Crowell, 1976, 179p., Fiction, ISBN 0-690-01147-4.

Chris and his stepsister don't consider themselves to be part of the same family until they travel back to the seventeenth century and have adventures together.

Raskin, Ellen, **Westing Game, The**, Dutton, 1978, 185p., Fiction, LC 77-18866, ISBN 0-525-42320-6.

Chris is one of the sixteen people invited to the reading of the very strange will of the very rich Samuel W. Westing. Chris could become a millionaire, depending on how he plays the tricky and dangerous Westing Game. 1979 Newbery Award book. 1978 Boston Globe-Horn Book Award. Michigan 1982.

Steele, William O, **Perilous Road, The**, illustrated by Paul Galdone, Harcourt Brace Jovanovich, 1990, 189p., Fiction, ISBN 0-152-606-475.

Fourteen-year-old Chris hates the Yankees for invading his Tennessee mountain home. He learns a difficult lesson when he discovers that his brother is probably part of a Yankee supply troop that he has reported to the Confederates. 1958 Jane Addams Award book. 1959 Newbery Honor book.

CHRISSIE
See also Chris, Christina, Christine

Waldron, Ann, **House on Pendleton Block**, illustrated by Sonia O. Lisker, Hastings House, 1975, 151p., Fiction, ISBN 0-8038-3033-5.

When Chrissie's family moves to a large Texas mansion, she becomes interested in the dead owner and the mystery surrounding missing paintings.

CHRISTINA
See also Chris, Chrissie, Nina, Tina

Wright, Betty Ren, **Christina's Ghost**, Holiday House, 1985, 105p., Fiction, LC 85-42880, ISBN 0-8234-0581-8.

Christina had looked forward to spending part of her summer with her grandmother but becomes miserable when she has to stay with her grumpy uncle in a spooky, isolated Victorian house. Her summer changes when she sees the ghostly figure of a small, sad boy and feels an evil presence in the attic. Georgia 1988. Indiana 1989. Oklahoma 1988. Texas 1988.

CHRISTINE
See also Chris, Chrissie

Adler, C. S., **Silver Coach**, Avon, 1979, 103p., Fiction, ISBN 0-380-75498-3 (pbk).

Christine spends the summer with her grandmother and has fantasy adventures about her father with the help of a silver coach. She has to learn to accept her real life as it is, without her father.

CHRISTOPHER
See also Chris

Milne, A. A., **House at Pooh Corner**, illustrated by Ernest Shepard, Dutton, 1956, 180p., Fiction, ISBN 0-525-44444-0.

In this classic story, Christopher Robin visits his good friends at Pooh Corner, including Pooh Bear, Eeyore, Piglet, and Tigger.

Milne, A. A., **Winnie-the-Pooh**, illustrated by Hilda Scott, Dutton, 1974, 161p., Fiction, ISBN 0-525-44443-2.

The classic story of Christopher Robin and his toy bear, Winnie-the-Pooh, and their friends.

Soule, Gardner, **Christopher Columbus: On the Green Sea of Darkness**, Watts, 1988, 128p., Nonfiction, ISBN 0-531-10577-6.

The famous Italian explorer, Christopher Columbus, sailed four voyages across the Atlantic Ocean during the fifteenth century.

Taylor, Mildred, **Friendship, The**, illustrated by Max Ginsburg, Dial, 1987, 53p., Fiction, LC 86-29309, ISBN 0-8037-0417-8; 0-8037-0418-6 (lib).

When Christopher Logan, his two brothers, and sister are sent to a small rural store, trouble begins as an old black man keeps calling the white storekeeper by his first name. Set in Mississippi in 1933. 1988 Boston Globe-Horn Book Award. 1988 Coretta Scott King Award book.

Taylor, Mildred, **Let the Circle Be Unbroken**, Dial, 1981, 394p., Fiction, LC 81-65854, ISBN 0-8037-4748-9.

The story of the Logan family is continued in this story. Set in 1935 during the Depression, Christopher-John and his family watch their poor sharecropper neighbors in Mississippi being victimized by the large landowners. Hard times increase racial tensions and their friend is charged with murder. 1982 Coretta Scott King Award book. 1982 Jane Addams Honor book.

CHRISTOS
See also Chris

Raskin, Ellen, **Westing Game, The**, Dutton, 1978, 185p., Fiction, LC 77-18866, ISBN 0-525-42320-6.

Christos is one of the sixteen people invited to the reading of the very strange will of the very rich Samuel W. Westing. Christos could become a millionaire, depending on how he plays the tricky and dangerous Westing Game. 1979 Newbery Award book. 1978 Boston Globe-Horn Book Award. Michigan 1982.

CHUCK
See also Charles, Chip

Gaffney, Timothy, **Chuck Yeager: First Man to Fly Faster Than Sound**, Children's Press, 1986, 126p., Nonfiction, ISBN 0-516-03223-2.

Chuck Yeager showed courage as a pilot when he broke the sound barrier while flying a test plane. This biography contains information about his career and his many contributions to aviation.

CINDY
See also Cynthia, Lucinda

Kassem, Lou, **Middle School Blues**, Houghton Mifflin, 1986, 181p., Fiction, ISBN 0-395-39499-6.

Twelve-year-old Cindy spends her summer worrying about how she will do in seventh grade.

CLARA

Bawden, Nina, **Kept in the Dark**, Lothrop, Lee & Shepard, 1982, 160p., Fiction, ISBN 0-688-00900-X.

Clara and her siblings have many adjustments to make when they are left with grandparents that they do not know. Life becomes frightening when a stranger appears.

Boylston, Helen Dore, **Clara Barton: Founder of the American Red Cross**, illustrated by Paula Hutchinson, Random House, 1955, 182p., Nonfiction, ISBN 0-394-90358-7.

A biography of Clara Barton who was a courageous young woman involved in nursing education and founder of the American Red Cross.

Byars, Betsy, **Animal, the Vegetable, and John D. Jones, The**, illustrated by Ruth Sanderson, Delacorte, 1982, 150p., Fiction, ISBN 0-440-40356-1.

Clara and her sister are unhappy when their father brings a friend and her son on a vacation at the ocean. A tragedy changes the girl's outlook.

Pevsner, Stella, **Cute Is a Four-Letter Word**, Houghton Mifflin, 1980, 190p., Fiction, ISBN 0-395-29106-2.

Clara has many growing up experiences during her eighth-grade school year as she deals with her own problems and learns about friendship.

CLAUDE

Robinson, Barbara, **Best Christmas Pageant Ever, The**, illustrated by Judith Gwyn Brown, Harper & Row, 1972, 80p., Fiction, LC 72-76501, ISBN 06-025043-7; 06-025044-5.

Claude is one of the six Herdman children—kids so awful it is hard to believe they are real. When they decide to participate in the church Christmas pageant, people think it will be the worst one ever. Georgia 1976. Indiana 1978. Minnesota 1982.

Sharmat, Marjorie Weinman, **Nate the Great and the Lost List**, illustrated by Marc Simont, Coward-McCann, 1975, 48p., Easy Reader, LC 75-2543, ISBN 0-698-30593-0.

Claude was always losing things. When he lost the grocery list that his father had made, Claude went to Nate the Great, boy detective, to help him find it. While helping Claude, Nate got to try eating cat pancakes. Claude is in other Nate the Great books as well. A Reading Rainbow book.

CLAUDIA

Konigsburg, Elaine, **From the Mixed-Up Files of Mrs. Basil K. Frankweiler**, illustrated by E. L. Konigsburg, Atheneum, 1980, 162p., Fiction, LC 67-18988, ISBN 0-689-20586-4.

When Claudia decides to run away, she plans it very carefully. She takes her brother, Jamie, and they go to live at the Metropolitan Museum of Art. In the museum, they find a beautiful statue and a mystery to solve. 1968 Newbery Award book. Kansas 1970.

Martin, Ann, **Kristy's Great Idea**, Scholastic, 1986, 153p., Fiction, ISBN 0-590-41985-4 (pbk).

Claudia and her friends form a babysitting club. There are many books about this group of friends.

Smith, L. J., **Night of the Solstice, The**, Macmillan, 1987, 231p., Fiction, ISBN 0-02-785840-5.

Claudia, her sisters, and their brother encounter ghosts, monsters, and serpents when they go through the mirrors of the abandoned mansion to enter Wildwood in order to prevent evil from overtaking the Earth.

Wolitzer, Meg, **Dream Book, The**, Greenwillow, 1986, 148p., Fiction, ISBN 0-688-05148-0.

Eleven-year-old Claudia and her neighbor share strange dreams. The two girls become friends as they attempt to decipher the message and to determine whether they are experiencing ESP or magic.

CLEO

Kessler, Leonard, **Old Turtle's Baseball Stories**, illustrated by Leonard Kessler, Greenwillow, 1982, 55p., Easy Reader, LC 81-6390, ISBN 0-688-00723-6;0-688-00724-4 (lib).

In the summer, Old Turtle and his friends play baseball and in the winter they tell baseball stories. Old Turtle tells a story about Cleo Octopus, the best pitcher, and why she quit baseball. A Reading Rainbow book.

Mazer, Harry, **Island Keeper, The**, Dell, 1981, 165p., Fiction, ISBN 0-440-94774-X (pbk).

After her sister's death, Cleo runs away to live alone on an island in Canada. She survives by learning new skills and using what the environment has to offer.

CLIFF
See also Clifford

Giff, Patricia Reilly, **Rat Teeth**, illustrated by Leslie Morrill, Delacorte, 1984, 130p., Fiction, ISBN 0-385-29309-7.

Ten-year-old Cliff acts tough because he is sad about his parent's divorce, lonely attending a new school, and miserable about his two front teeth.

CLIFFORD
See also Cliff

Heinlein, Robert, **Have Space Suit—Will Travel**, Scribner, 1958, 276p., Fiction, ISBN 0-684-14857-9.

Although Clifford Russell is very intelligent, he had just loafed through school until his sophomore year in high school when he decides he wants to go to the moon. When he wins a contest his wishes come true and he has exciting adventures in outer space.Oklahoma 1961.

CLINT

Fleischman, Sid, **Me and the Man on the Moon-Eyed Horse**, illustrated by Eric von Schmidt, Little, Brown, 1977, 57p., Fiction, ISBN 0-316-28571-4.

A humorous story of Clint and the way that he manages to fool an outlaw in the wild, wild West.

CLIVE

Christopher, John, **Wild Jack**, Macmillan, 1974, 147p., Fiction, ISBN 0-02-718300-9.

Clive Anderson lives in London in the twenty-third century. Exiled to an island, Clive meets Wild Jack who is similar to Robin Hood.

CLYDE

Bulla, Clyde Robert, **Grain of Wheat: A Writer Begins**, Godine, 1985, 49p., Nonfiction, ISBN 0-87923-717-1.

This autobiography of a well-known children's author tells about his early life on a Midwestern farm during the early 1900s.

McCloskey, Robert, **Time of Wonder**, illustrated by Robert McCloskey, Viking, 1957, 63p., Picture Book, ISBN 0-670-71512-3.

Clyde Snowman, Harry Smith, and Ferd Clifford are a few of the people that live on the island where the children and their parents vacation in the summer. 1958 Caldecott Award book.

CODY

Rodgers, Raboo, **Magnum Fault**, Houghton Mifflin, 1984, 185p., Fiction, ISBN 0-395-34558-8.

Cody is concerned because his favorite river is drying up. He becomes involved in an even more serious mystery when the engineer father of a friend disappears after an accident, which the sheriff claims didn't happen.

COLLETTE

McKenna, Colleen O'Shaughnessy, **Too Many Murphys**, Scholastic, 1988, 140p., Fiction, ISBN 0-590-41731-2.

Eight-year-old Collette Murphy is tired of being part of a large family and wonders what it would be like to be an only child. There is another book about Collette.

COMFORT

Kaye, Geraldine, **Comfort Herself**, illustrated by Jennifer Northway, Dutton, 1984, 160p., Fiction, ISBN 0-233-97614-0.

When Comfort's British mother dies, she is sent to live with her black father in Ghana where she learns about her heritage and meets her African family.

CONRAD

Avi, **Sometimes I Think I Hear My Name**, Pantheon, 1982, 144p., Fiction, ISBN 0-394-95048-8.

Conrad is sent to live in St. Louis with an aunt and uncle when his parents get divorced. After deciding that his parents no longer care about him, he and a friend plan a visit to New York with humorous results.

Davies, Andrew, **Conrad's War**, Crown, 1980, 120p., Fiction, LC 79-28289, ISBN 0-517-54007-X.

Conrad is fascinated with guns and war. As he builds a tank from cardboard and spare parts, a time change takes place and Conrad finds himself at the controls of a real tank during World War II. 1980 Boston Globe-Horn Book Award.

CONSTANCE
See also Candy

Verheyden-Hilliard, Mary Ellen, **Constance Tom Noguchi: Scientist and Puzzle Solver**, illustrated by Marian Menzel, Equity Institute, 1985, 32p., Nonfiction, ISBN 0-932469-05-1.

A brief biography about Connie Noguchi, a researcher at the National Institute of Health. As a child, she was interested in how things work so she majored in physics in school.

COPPER

DeClements, Barthe, **No Place for Me**, Viking Kestrel, 1987, 136p., Fiction, ISBN 0-670-81908-5.

Twelve-year-old Copper Jones is sent from one relative to another while her mother is at an alcoholic rehabilitation center. Copper learns to accept responsibility for herself when she stays with her aunt who practices witchcraft.

CORETTA

Patterson, Lillie, **Coretta Scott King**, Garrard, 1977, 96p., Nonfiction.

A biography about Coretta Scott King, the wife of the famous civil rights leader Martin Luther King, Jr. 1978 Coretta Scott King Honor book.

CRAIG

Lampman, Evelyn, **City Under the Back Steps, The**, illustrated by Honore Valincourt, Doubleday, 1960, 210p., Fiction, LC 60-13539.

After being stung by a strange insect, Craig and his sister find themselves shrinking until they are the size of ants. The two children become pets of the ant queen and have unusual adventures in their own backyard. Vermont 1962.

CUSI

Clark, Ann Nolan, **Secret of the Andes**, illustrated by Jean Charlot, Viking, 1952, 130p., Fiction, ISBN 0-670-62975-8.

Cusi, the Indian boy, lives in a beautiful hidden valley high in the Andes Mountains of Peru. He and an old Incan llama herder live by themselves and Cusi doesn't see any other people for the first eight years of his life. When Cusi leaves the valley to see the Spanish world filled with people, he discovers his heart's desire. 1953 Newbery Award book.

CYBIL

Byars, Betsy, **Cybil War, The**, illustrated by Gail Owens, Viking, 1981, 126p., Fiction, LC 80-26912, ISBN 0-670-25248-4.

Simon fell in love with Cybil Ackerman, his redheaded schoolmate, the first time he saw her cross her eyes. The road to romance with Cybil is rocky and Simon has a lot to learn about friendship and loyalty. Oklahoma 1984.

CYNTHIA
See also Cindy

Mills, Claudia, **One and Only Cynthia Jane Thornton, The**, Macmillan, 1982, 110p., Fiction, ISBN 0-02-767090-2.

Ten-year-old Cynthia struggles to find her own identity and has to learn not to be threatened by other people and their talents.

Rylant, Cynthia, **When I Was Young in the Mountains**, illustrated by Diane Goode, Dutton, 1982, 26p., Picture Book, ISBN 0-525-42525-X.

These memories of the author's childhood in the Appalachian Mountains include her family and their community. 1983 Caldecott Honor book.

-D-

DALE

Roberts, Willo Davis, **Girl with the Silver Eyes, The**, Atheneum, 1982, 181p., Fiction, LC 80-12391, ISBN 0-689-30786-1.

Dale, Katie, and several other children have paranormal powers. They can move things with their minds and understand what animals are thinking. California 1986. Mississippi 1983.

DAMIAN

Aliki, **Feelings**, illustrated by Aliki, Greenwillow, 1984, 32p., Picture Book, LC 84-4098, ISBN 0-688-03831-X; 0-688-03832-8 (lib).

Damian is one of the children who is portrayed showing the various emotions that everyone feels: sadness, fear, jealousy, anger, love, and so forth. Poems, dialogues, pictures, and stories. A Reading Rainbow book.

DAN
See also Daniel, Danny

Ruckman, Ivy, **Night of the Twisters**, Crowell, 1984, 153p., Fiction, LC 83-46168, ISBN 0-690-04408-9; 0-690-04409-7 (lib).

Dan had been through a dozen tornado watches during his twelve years. Dan, his best friend, and Dan's baby brother are alone in the house when a tornado hits destroying, their house and their neighborhood. Oklahoma 1987.

DANIEL
See also Dan, Danny

Collier, James Lincoln and Christopher Collier, **Jump Ship to Freedom**, Delacorte, 1981, 198p., Fiction, ISBN 0-440-44323-7 (pbk).

Fourteen-year-old Daniel Arabus is determined to buy his freedom and his mother's freedom from slavery after his father dies fighting in the Revolutionary War. An exciting adventure takes place when Daniel is sent to sea and escapes during a storm.

Cookson, Catherine, **Lanky Jones**, Lothrop, Lee & Shepard, 1981, 158p., Fiction, ISBN 0-688-00431-8.

Daniel Jones and his father make friends with a farm family, which provides opportunities for later mysteries.

Daugherty, James, **Daniel Boone**, illustrated by James Daugherty, Viking, 1939, 95p., Nonfiction.

Historical information about the famous American frontiersman, Daniel Boone. Daniel was born near Reading, Pennsylvania, in the 1730s. His parents moved their eleven children to North Carolina in Conestoga wagons. 1940 Newbery Award book.

Kennedy, John F., **Profiles in Courage**, illustrated by Emil Weiss, Harper & Row, 1955, 164p., Nonfiction, LC 64-17696.

Daniel Webster showed political courage under pressure. He is one of the eight statesmen featured in this book. 1964 Jane Addams Award book.

Lawlor, Laurie, **Daniel Boone**, illustrated by Bert Dodson, Whitman, 1989, 160p., Nonfiction, ISBN 0-8075-1462-4.

Daniel Boone was a famous frontiersman who settled in Kentucky. This biography tells about both his life and the time period in which he lived.

Speare, Elizabeth George, **Bronze Bow, The**, Houghton Mifflin, 1961, 255p., Fiction, ISBN 0-395-07113-5.

This book is set in biblical times. Daniel bar Jamin is an eighteen-year-old Galilean. He has lived in hiding in the mountain stronghold of an outlaw gang after a childhood filled with tragedy. Daniel becomes dedicated to freeing Israel from oppressors and meets the young preacher named Jesus. 1962 Newbery Award book.

DANNY
See also Dan, Daniel

Dahl, Roald, **Danny, the Champion of the World**, illustrated by Jill Bennett, Knopf, 1975, 196p., Fiction, LC 75-8971, ISBN 0-394-83103-9; 0-394-93103-3 (lib).

Danny's mother died when he was a baby, so he lives with his dad in an old gypsy caravan behind a filling station. When he discovers that his dad leaves him at night to poach, Danny decides to help with humorous results. California 1979.

Kjelgaard, Jim, **Big Red: The Story of a Champion Irish Setter and a Trapper's Son...**, illustrated by Bob Kuhn, Holiday House, 1945, 254p., Fiction, ISBN 0-8234-0007-7.

Danny is the son of a trapper. He and his dog have many adventures as they track a great bear and roam the wilderness together.

Roberts, Willo Davis, **Minden Curse, The**, illustrated by Sherry Steeter, Atheneum, 1978, 226p., Fiction, ISBN 0-689-30603-2.

After being tutored by his father, Danny is not happy about having to live with his grandfather and go to a regular school. When his grandfather tells him that they share a curse, Danny's life becomes more interesting as he tries to avoid the accidents that often occur.

Sleator, William, **Blackbriar**, Scholastic, 1972, 217p., Fiction, ISBN 0-590-40308-7 (pbk).

Danny becomes involved in a mystery when his guardian takes him to a cottage in a remote area of England.

Slote, Alfred, **My Robot Buddy**, illustrated by Joel Schick, Lippincott, 1975, 92p., Fiction, ISBN 0-397-31641-0.

Danny wants a robot for his tenth birthday so he will have someone to play with. Hawaii 1981.

Williams, Jay, **Danny Dunn and the Homework Machine**, illustrated by Ezra Jack Keats, McGraw-Hill, 1958, 141p., Fiction, LC 58-10015, ISBN 07-070520-8; 07-070519-4.

Danny and his mother live at the home of an inventor and physicist. With the aid of a computer, Danny invents a homework machine that can give the correct answers and write two papers at the same time. Pacific Northwest 1961.

Williams, Jay, **Danny Dunn on the Ocean Floor**, illustrated by Brinton Turkle, McGraw-Hill, 1967, 156p., Fiction, ISBN 0-07-070524-0.

Danny goes to Mexico with the professor to record fish sounds, test a plastic diving ship, and make scientific discoveries on the ocean floor. Pacific Northwest 1963.

DAPHNE

Hahn, Mary Downing, **Daphne's Book**, Clarion, 1983, 177p., Fiction, LC 83-7348, ISBN 0-89919-183-5.

Jessica is not happy to be paired with Daphne for the seventh-grade Write-a-Book contest, since the other students think that Daphne is strange. A friendship develops between the two girls as Jessica gets to know Daphne and she discovers the tragic secret that Daphne is hiding. Kansas 1986.

DARCY

Muskopf, Elizabeth, **Revenge of Jeremiah Plum, The**, illustrated by David Christiana, H. Holt, 1987, 212p., Fiction, ISBN 0-8050-0203-0.

Darcy and her friend become involved in solving an old mystery when a ghost refuses to rest until his murder is solved.

Roberts, Willo Davis, **Baby-Sitting Is a Dangerous Job**, Atheneum, 1985, 161p., Fiction, ISBN 0-689-31100-1.

Thirteen-year-old Darcy babysits for three spoiled children of a wealthy family and when the four of them are kidnapped, Darcy has to use all of her wits. Indiana 1988. South Carolina 1988.

DAVE
See also Davey, David, Davidson, Davie, Davy

Erwin, Betty, **Go to the Room of the Eyes**, illustrated by Irene Burns, Little, Brown, 1969,180p., Fiction, LC 71-77446, ISBN 0-316-24946-7.

When they move into an old house in Seattle, Dave and the other five Evans children discover a strange message left by children who lived there thirty years earlier. The message leads them on a treasure hunt. Vermont 1971.

Neville, Emily Cheney, **It's Like This, Cat**, illustrated by Emil Weiss, Harper & Row, 1963, 180p., Fiction, LC 62-21292, ISBN 0-06-024390-2.

Fourteen-year-old Dave Mitchell lives in New York City. As he grows toward adulthood, he develops an affection for a stray tomcat, has his first shy friendship with a girl, and grows to understand his father as a human being and not just a parent. 1964 Newbery Award book.

DAVEY
See also Dave, David, Davidson, Davie, Davy

Blume, Judy, **Tiger Eyes**, Bradbury, 1981, 206p., Fiction, ISBN 0-87888-1859.

Davey Wexler has a difficult time adjusting to her father's murder outside his store in Atlantic City. The family goes to New Mexico to stay with a relative while they work out their grief. California 1983. Iowa 1985. Ohio 1983. Vermont 1983.

Callen, Larry, **If the World Ends**, Atheneum, 1983, 128p., Fiction, ISBN 0-689-31372-1.

A gunman forces their plane to land and Davey, his father, and his uncle become unwillingly involved in a plot to end the world. Set in Louisiana.

DAVID
See also Dave, Davey, Davidson, Davie, Davy

Brookins, Dana, **Who Killed Sack Annie?**, Clarion, 1983, 150p., Fiction, ISBN 0-89919-137-1.

David and a friend see someone try to kill Sack Annie, the bag lady. The police are unsure that a crime has taken place so the boys decide to solve the crime on their own.

Jarrell, Randall, **Fly by Night**, illustrated by Maurice Sendak, Farrar, Straus & Giroux, 1976, 30p., Picture Book, ISBN 0-374-32348-8.

David lives near the edge of the forest and one night he flies out into the forest and becomes an owlet for the night.

Johnson, Annabel and Edgar Johnson, **Grizzly, The**, illustrated by Gilbert Riswold, Harper & Row, 1964, 160p., Fiction, LC 64-11831, ISBN 0-06-022871-7.

David and his father had been estranged for a long time. While on a camping trip they find themselves united, for the first time, when they face the sinister threat of a grizzly bear. Kansas 1967.

Meltzer, Milton, **Ain't Gonna Study War No More: The Story of America's Peace Seekers**, Harper & Row, 1985, 282p., Nonfiction, ISBN 0-060-241-993; 0-060-242-000 (lib).

This book presents a history of pacifism and those people who have protested against war in the United States from colonial times to the present. In 1815, David Dodge resisted war and founded the New York Peace Society. 1986 Child Study Children's Book Award. 1986 Jane Addams Award.

Paulsen, Gary, **Voyage of the Frog, The**, Orchard, 1989, 141p., Fiction, ISBN 0-531-08405-1.

After inheriting his uncle's sailboat, fourteen-year-old David has to fight for survival at sea while learning to accept his uncle's death.

Sleator, William, **Duplicate**, Dutton, 1988, 154p., Fiction, ISBN 0-525-44390-8.

Sixteen-year-old David duplicates himself so he can be two places at once, then discovers there are many problems to be solved with two of him to deal with.

Snyder, Zilpha Keatley, **Headless Cupid, The**, illustrated by Alton Raible, Atheneum, 1972, 203p., Fiction, LC 78-154763, ISBN 0-689-20687-9.

David's new stepsister Amanda was a year older and quite unusual. A student of the occult, she wore her ceremonial costume and took her crow to meet her new stepfamily. When Amanda discovered the headless cupid on the stairwell of their house, she was certain that the house had once had a poltergeist. 1972 Newbery Honor book. Kansas 1974.

Stevenson, Robert Louis, **Kidnapped: Being the Memoirs of the Adventures of David Balfour in the Year 1751**, illustrated by N. C. Wyeth, Scribner, 1982, 289p., Fiction, ISBN 0-684-17634-3.

The classic story of the young orphan, David Balfour, who is kidnapped and sent to sea during the 1750s.

Wier, Ester, **Loner, The**, illustrated by Christie Price, David McKay, 1963, 153p., Fiction, LC 63-9334, ISBN 0-679-20097-5.

The boy had no home and no family to care for him. He wandered from place to place catching rides and picking crops. In Montana, he meets people who teach him how to believe in himself and that he doesn't need to be a loner. He is also given a name. 1964 Newbery Honor book.

DAVIDSON
See also Dave, Davey, David, Davie, Davy

Wojciechowska, Maia, **Hey, What's Wrong With This One?**, illustrated by Joan Sandin, Harper & Row, 1969, 72p., Fiction, LC 67-14071, ISBN 0-06-026579-5.

After their mother dies, Davidson and his two brothers live with their father and a succession of housekeepers. Housekeepers keep quitting because of the boys' messes, noise, and pranks. The boys know they need a mother. Georgia 1973.

DAVIE
See also Dave, Davey, David, Davidson, Davy

DeJong, Meindert, **Shadrach**, illustrated by Maurice Sendak, Harper & Row, 1953, 182p., Fiction, ISBN 0-006-021546-1.

Due to illness, Davie spends afternoons with his grandparents at their farm. He receives a pet rabbit and becomes devoted to it. 1954 Newbery Honor book.

DAVY
See also Dave, Davey, David, Davidson, Davie

Quackenbush, Robert, **Quit Pulling My Leg! A Story of Davy Crockett**, Prentice-Hall, 1987, 36p., Nonfiction, ISBN 0-671-66516-2.

Davy Crockett was raised on the frontier and had little education; nevertheless, he became well known and was elected to Congress. This brief biography gives background information on the famous frontiersman.

DEBBIE
See also Deborah

Goffstein, M. B., **Two Piano Tuners**, illustrated by M. B. Goffstein, Farrar, Straus & Giroux, 1970, 65p., Fiction, ISBN 0-374-38019-8.

When Debbie is orphaned, she goes to live with her grandfather who tunes pianos. Debbie decides she wants to be a piano tuner, not a concert pianist like her grandfather wants her to be.

DEBORAH
See also Debbie

McGovern, Ann, **Secret Soldier, the Story of Deborah Sampson**, illustrated by Ann Grifalconi, Four Winds, 1987, 62p., Nonfiction, ISBN 0-02-765780-9.

Factual information about Deborah Sampson who fought for a year and a half in the Continental Army, disguised as a boy.

DEENIE

Blume, Judy, **Deenie**, Bradbury, 1973, 159p., Fiction, ISBN 0-02-711020-6.

Deenie is a beautiful thirteen-year-old girl and her mother wants her to become a fashion model. When it is discovered that Deenie has a spinal deformity and will have to wear a brace for four years, there are numerous difficulties for her to overcome.

DELPHINE

Bang, Molly, **Delphine**, illustrated by Molly Bang, Morrow, 1988, 24p., Picture Book, LC 87-34958, ISBN 0-688-05636-9; 0-688-05637-7 (lib).

Delphine lives in a cabin high on a mountaintop with three companions: a guinea pig, a wolf, and a lion. When her grandmother sends her a package, Delphine and her companions journey down the steep mountainside wondering about the gift. A Reading Rainbow book.

DENCEY

Snedeker, Caroline, **Downright Dencey**, illustrated by Maginel Wright Barney, Doubleday, 1927, 314p., Fiction, ISBN 0-385-07284-8.

Dencey is one of the Quaker children who live in Nantucket during the early part of the twentieth century. His life revolves around family, school, friends, and religion. 1928 Newbery Honor book.

DENNIS

Collins, Meghan, **Willow Maiden**, illustrated by Laszlo Gal, Dial, 1985, 38p., Picture Book, ISBN 0-8037-0218-3.

In this original fairy tale, Dennis falls in love with the Willow King's daughter but they can only be together for a short time.

DENTON

Raskin, Ellen, **Westing Game, The**, Dutton, 1978, 185p., Fiction, LC 77-18866, ISBN 0-525-42320-6.

Denton is one of the sixteen people invited to the reading of the very strange will of the very rich Samuel W. Westing. Denton could become a millionaire, depending on how he plays the tricky and dangerous Westing Game. 1979 Newbery Award book. 1978 Boston Globe-Horn Book Award. Michigan 1982.

DEREK

Roos, Stephen, **My Favorite Ghost**, illustrated by Dee deRosa, Atheneum, 1988, 123p., Fiction, ISBN 0-689-31301-2.

When thirteen-year-old Derek loses his job, he decides to earn money by convincing kids that there is a ghost in a local mansion with unexpected results.

DESDEMONA
See also Didi

Keller, Beverly, **No Beasts, No Children!**, Lothrop, Lee & Shepard, 1983, 127p., Fiction, ISBN 0-688-01678-2.

After their mother leaves, Desdemona and the rest of the family move into a rickety old house where they meet a cranky neighbor and other new people who keep their life interesting. There are other books about Desdemona.

DESIRE

Clifton, Lucille, **Don't You Remember?**, illustrated by Evaline Ness, Dutton, 1973, 32p., Picture Book, ISBN 0-525-288-406 (lib).

Desire is a young girl with an excellent memory who is convinced that everyone else is forgetful of their promises. 1974 Coretta Scott King Honor book.

DEWEY

Byars, Betsy, **Trouble River**, illustrated by Rocco Negri, Viking, 1969, 158p., Fiction, ISBN 0-670-73257-5.

Dewey and his grandmother escape from Indians using the raft that he builds.

DIANA

Haskins, James, **Diana Ross, Star Supreme**, illustrated by Jim Spence, Viking Kestrel, 1985, 58p., Nonfiction, ISBN 0-670-80549-1.

Diana Ross is a popular and well-known singer and movie star. Biographical information includes her personal life as well as her professional one.

DICK
See also Dickie, Richard

Brown, Marcia, **Dick Whittington and His Cat**, illustrated by Marcia Brown, Scribner, 1950, 28p., Picture Book, ISBN 0-684-18998-4.

In this folktale, a young orphan, Dick Whittington, has a very hard time until he purchases the cat, Puss. When Dick sends his cat away on a trading ship, Puss makes her master a wealthy man. 1951 Caldecott Honor book.

DICKIE
See also Dick, Richard

Thayer, Jane, **Puppy Who Wanted a Boy, The**, illustrated by Seymour Fleischman, Morrow, 1958, 48p., Picture Book, LC 58-5317, ISBN 0-688-31631-X.

Dickie is a lonely boy who lives at the Orphans' Home. Petey is a puppy that wants a boy for Christmas and looks everywhere only to find that most boys have their own dog. When Petey sees Dickie, both have a good Christmas. A Reading Rainbow book.

DIDI
See also Desdemona, Dolores, Doretha, Dorothea, Dorothy

Myers, Walter Dean, **Motown and Didi: A Love Story**, Viking Kestrel, 1984, 174p., Fiction, ISBN 0-670-490-628.

Motown and Didi are two loners who live in Harlem and unite in a fight against a local drug dealer, then find themselves falling in love with each other. 1985 Coretta Scott King Award book.

DILAR

Steele, Mary Q., **Journey Outside**, illustrated by Rocco Negri, Viking, 1969, 143p., Fiction, LC 68-18263, ISBN 0-8446-6169-4.

For several generations the Raft People had been traveling to a better place. Young Dilar thinks they travel in circles and he longs to see what else the world offers besides rivers and fish. 1970 Newbery Honor book.

DINAH

Holland, Isabelle, **Dinah and the Green Fat Kingdom**, Harper & Row, 1978, 189p., Fiction, ISBN 0-397-31818-9.

Dinah is a very intelligent and creative girl who has an eating problem. She is teased by her family and classmates and creates her own imaginary land where it is acceptable to be overweight.

DIONIS
See also Dionisio

Snedeker, Caroline, **Downright Dencey**, illustrated by Maginel Wright Barney, Doubleday, 1927, 314p., Fiction, ISBN 0-385-07284-8.

Dionis is one of the Quaker children who live in Nantucket during the early part of the twentieth century. His life revolves around his family, school, friends, and religion. 1928 Newbery Honor book.

DIONISIO
See also Dionis

Rhoads, Dorothy, **Corn Grows Ripe, The**, illustrated by Jean Charlot, Viking, 1956, 88p., Fiction, ISBN 0-670-24168-7.

Dionisio was named for the saint on whose day he was born, but everyone calls him Tigre. The twelve-year-old Mayan boy lives with his family in a small village near the forest. The forest dominates the family's thinking since it provides for their needs and closes out the rest of the world. 1957 Newbery Honor book.

DIRK

DeJong, Meindert, **Wheel on the School, The**, illustrated by Maurice Sendak, Harper & Row, 1954, 298p., Fiction, LC 54-8945, ISBN 0-06-021585-2.

Dirk is one of the six schoolchildren in the fishing village called Shora in Holland. The children learn that when a stork builds a nest on the roof, good luck will follow. 1955 Newbery Award book.

DOBRY

Shannon, Monica, **Dobry**, illustrated by Atanas Katchamakoff, Viking, 1946, 176p., Fiction.

Dobry lives in a mountain village in Bulgaria. A story about his life and the customs of the village. 1935 Newbery Award book.

DOC

Hurd, Thacher, **Mama Don't Allow: Starring Miles and the Swamp Band**, illustrated by Thacher Hurd, Harper & Row, 1984, 40p., Picture Book, LC 83-47703, ISBN 0-06-022689-7; 0-06-022690-0 (lib); 0-06-443078-2 (pbk).

Doc and the Swamp Band have a great time playing at the Alligator Ball, until they discover the dinner menu. 1985 Boston Globe-Horn Book Award. A Reading Rainbow book.

DOLORES
See also Didi, Dorrie, Dotty

Samuels, Barbara, **Duncan and Dolores**, illustrated by Barbara Samuels, Bradbury, 1986, 30p., Picture Book, LC 85-17119, ISBN 0-02-778210-7.

Dolores and Faye see a sign for a cat, Duncan, that needs a home. When Dolores gets the cat and then smothers it with affection and attention, the cat keeps hiding. Dolores begins to think that Duncan likes Faye the best. 1987 Christopher Award. A Reading Rainbow book.

DOMINIC
See also Dominique

Steig, William, **Dominic**, illustrated by William Steig, Farrar, Straus & Giroux, 1972, 146p., Fiction, LC 70-188272, ISBN 0-374-31822-0.

Dominic the dog is restless because there isn't enough happening in his neighborhood. He wants an adventure so Dominic packs his hats and a few other things in a large bandanna and sets off. Soon he meets a witch alligator that knows what will happen to Dominic and gives him advice. Kansas 1975.

DOMINIQUE
See also Dominic

Cameron, Eleanor, **Court of the Stone Children, The**, Dutton, 1973, 191p., Fiction, ISBN 0-525-28350-1.

Two children spend time at the court of stone children at the French Museum in San Francisco. They meet Dominique, a strange girl from the time of Napoleon, who tells them of treason and murder.

DONALD

Montgomery, Rutherford, **Kildee House**, illustrated by Barbara Cooney, Doubleday, 1949, 209p., Fiction, ISBN 0-671-29518-7.

Jerome Kildee lives in an odd house that he built on the mountainside next to a redwood tree. Jerome is a silent man who lives quietly with animals for friends. When there are problems with the animals, Donald and his friend help Jerome find a solution. 1950 Newbery Honor book.

DORETHA
See also Didi, Dorrie, Dotty

Greenfield, Eloise, **Sister**, illustrated by Moneta Barnett, Crowell, 1974, 83p., Fiction, ISBN 0-690-00497-4.

Doretha has kept a diary from the time she was nine years old. At thirteen, she slowly relives her past by reading the diary in hopes that she can avoid the problems that her sister is facing.

DORIS
See also Doretha, Dorothea, Dorothy, Dorrie, Dotty

Hansen, Joyce, **Gift-Giver, The**, Clarion, 1980, 118p., Fiction, ISBN 0-395-29433-9.

Although ten-year-old Doris lives in the ghetto of New York, she has a happy life with a warm family and friends.

DOROTHEA
See also Didi, Dorrie, Dotty

Meltzer, Milton, **Dorothea Lange: Life Through the Camera**, illustrated by Donna Diamond, Viking Kestrel, 1985, 58p., Nonfiction, ISBN 0-670-28047-X.

A biography about Dorothea Lange, a famous woman photographer whose powerful photographs influenced the social consciousness of the United States.

DOROTHY
See also Didi, Doris, Dorrie, Dotty

Baum, L. Frank, **Wonderful Wizard of Oz**, illustrated by W. W. Denslow, Morrow, 1987, 267p., Fiction, ISBN 0-688-06944-4.

When a tornado takes her house, Dorothy finds herself in the magical land of Oz where she has adventures with a lion, a scarecrow, and a tin man, while she searches for the way home.

Carlson, Natalie Savage, **Ann Aurelia and Dorothy, illustrated by Dale Payson**, Harper & Row, 1968, 130p., Fiction, ISBN 0-06-020959-3.

Dorothy becomes friends with Ann Aurelia, a girl who lives in a foster home. The two girls have many neighborhood adventures.

Cole, Joanna, **Magic School Bus Inside the Earth, The**, illustrated by Bruce Degen, Scholastic, 1987, 40p., Picture Book, LC 87-4563, ISBN 0-590-40759-7.

Dorothy and the rest of Ms. Frizzle's class learn firsthand about different kinds of rocks and the formation of the earth when they take a field trip in the magic school bus. A Reading Rainbow book.

DORRIE
See also Dolores, Doretha, Doris, Dorothea, Dorothy

Conford, Ellen, **Me and the Terrible Two**, illustrated by Charles Carroll, Little, Brown, 1974, 117p., Fiction, ISBN 0-316-15303-6.

Dorrie has a difficult time when her best friend moves away and two terrible boys move in next door. Humorous episodes occur as Dorrie adjusts to the neighborhood changes.

DOTTY
See also Dolores, Doretha, Doris, Dorothea, Dorothy

Greene, Constance, **Dotty's Suitcase**, Viking, 1980, 147p., Fiction, ISBN 0-670-28050-X.

Dotty and her two sisters are motherless. They live with their father who is struggling to keep his country store in business during the Depression. Dotty longs to have a suitcase and take trips, and she has a dilemma when she finds a suitcase full of money that robbers have lost.

DOUG

Pevsner, Stella, **Me, My Goat, and My Sister's Wedding**, Clarion, 1985, 180p., Fiction, ISBN 0-89919-305-6.

Doug attempts to control his goat while his sister has a garden wedding, but the goat has a mind of its own and disasters keep happening.

Raskin, Ellen, **Westing Game, The**, Dutton, 1978, 185p., Fiction, LC 77-18866, ISBN 0-525-42320-6.

Doug is one of the sixteen people invited to the reading of the very strange will of the very rich Samuel W. Westing. Doug could become a millionaire, depending on how well he plays the tricky and dangerous Westing Game. 1979 Newbery Award book. 1978 Boston Globe-Horn Book Award. Michigan 1982.

DUEY

Bailey, Pearl, **Duey's Tale**, Harcourt Brace Jovanovich, 1975, 59p., Fiction, ISBN 0-151-265-763.

A maple seedling searches for his own place in life after becoming separated from his mother tree. 1976 Coretta Scott King Award book.

DUFFY

Zemach, Harve, **Duffy and the Devil: A Cornish Tale**, illustrated by Margot Zemach, Farrar, Straus & Giroux, 1973, 40p., Picture Book, ISBN 0-374-318-875.

The devil agrees to do Duffy's spinning and knitting so she can win a carefree life with the squire. Problems arise when it is time for Duffy to guess the devil's name. 1974 Caldecott Award book.

DUNCAN

Samuels, Barbara, **Duncan and Dolores**, illustrated by Barbara Samuels, Bradbury, 1986, 30p., Picture Book, LC 85-17119, ISBN 0-02-778210-7.

Dolores and Faye see a sign for a cat, Duncan, that needs a home. When Dolores gets the cat and then smothers it with affection and attention, the cat keeps hiding. Dolores begins to think that Duncan likes Faye best. 1987 Christopher Award. A Reading Rainbow book.

DUNY

Le Guin, Ursula K., **Wizard of Earthsea, A**, illustrated by Ruth Robbins, Parnassus, 1968, 205p., Fiction, LC 68-21992, ISBN 0-395-27653-5.

Duny's name is taken away from him by a witch when he turns thirteen and he is given a new name. He grows to manhood while attempting to subdue the evil he unleashed on the world as an apprentice to the Master Wizard. 1969 Boston Globe-Horn Book Award.

DURANT

Jackson, C. Paul, **Beginner under the Backboards**, illustrated by Ned Butterfield, Hastings House, 1974, 124p., Fiction, ISBN 0-8038-0762-7.

Durant Salvatore is over six feet four inches tall, very uncoordinated, and only fourteen years old. He lacks confidence and doesn't suspect that he has a talent for basketball.

DWIGHT

Hargrove, Jim, **Dwight D. Eisenhower**, Children's Press, 1987, 100p., Nonfiction, ISBN 0-516-01389-0.

Dwight Eisenhower was one of six boys and was always known to get along well with other people. He attended West Point and became a military leader before being elected president of the United States.

-E-

EARL

Service, Pamela, **Winter of Magic's Return**, Atheneum, 1985, 192p., Fiction, ISBN 0-689-31130-3.

Earl is one of the children who embark on a lengthy quest across a world that has been changed by a 500-year winter brought on by a nuclear holocaust.

EATON

Adler, David A., **Eaton Stanley and the Mind Control Experiments**, illustrated by Joan Drescher, Dutton, 1985, 88p., Fiction, ISBN 0-525-44117-4.

Brian tells the story of his friend Eaton Stanley and their plan to take control of their sixth-grade teacher's mind.

EDDIE
See also Eddy, Edmund, Edward

Frascino, Edward, **Eddie Spaghetti on the Homefront**, Harper & Row, 1983, 114p., Fiction, ISBN 0-06-021895-9.

Eddie Ferrari is too young to work in a war-time factory during World War II so he decides to do what he can to help. He lives in Yonkers, New York, and decides that a hermit might be a spy.

Haywood, Carolyn, **Eddie's Menagerie**, Morrow, 1978, Fiction, ISBN 0-688-32158-5.

Eddie Wilson has many humorous times while working in a pet store. He also rescues a kitten from a young catsnatcher, takes care of a shoplifter, and helps his friend when her cat is poisoned. Utah 1981.

Haywood, Carolyn, **Eddie's Valuable Property**, illustrated by Carolyn Haywood, Morrow, 1975, 192p., Fiction, ISBN 0-688-32014-7.

Eddie and his family are moving. He has to sort through his things to prepare for the move, then he has to meet new people and make new friends. There are several other books about Eddie.

Ish-Kishor, Sulamith, **Our Eddie**, Pantheon, 1969, 183p., Fiction, LC 69-13456, ISBN 0-394-81455-X.

Eddie and his family have many problems because their father, who, although loving, is idealistic and religious and cannot understand the needs of the family. 1970 Newbery Honor book.

Roberts, Willo Davis, **What Could Go Wrong?**, Atheneum, 1989, 167p., Fiction, ISBN 0-689-31438-8.

Eddie and his cousins fly from San Francisco to Seattle and become involved in a mystery filled with suspense.

Yorinks, Arthur, **Hey, Al**, illustrated by Richard Egielski, Farrar, Straus & Giroux, 1986, 28p., Picture Book, LC 86-80955, ISBN 0-374-33060-3.

Al is a janitor and Eddie is his dog. The two live a simple life in a single room and do everything together. They struggle until a mysterious bird offers them a change of fortune. 1987 Caldecott Award book. Kentucky 1988.

EDDY
See also Eddie, Edmund, Edward

Rabinowitz, Ann, **Knight on Horseback**, Macmillan, 1987, 197p., Fiction, ISBN 0-02-775660-2.

After acquiring a small wooden knight, thirteen-year-old Eddy is chased by a mysterious man and transported back in time.

EDITH
See also Meredith

Lindbergh, Anne, **Worry Week**, illustrated by Kathryn Hewitt, Harcourt Brace Jovanovich, 1985, 131p., Fiction, ISBN 0-15-299675-3.

Seven-year-old Edith and her two older sisters make many discoveries when they spend a week by themselves at the family beach cottage in Maine.

EDMUND
See also Eddie, Eddy

Kennedy, John F., **Profiles in Courage**, illustrated by Emil Weiss, Harper & Row, 1955, 164p., Nonfiction, LC 64-17696.

Edmund G. Ross showed political courage under pressure. He is one of the eight statesmen featured in this book. 1964 Jane Addams Award book.

Lewis, C. S., **Lion, the Witch, and the Wardrobe, The**, illustrated by Pauline Baynes, Macmillan, 1950, 154p., Fiction, ISBN 0-02-758110-1.

Edmund and three other children meet a witch, a mighty lion, and the other characters that live in the land of Narnia. This is the first of the seven titles in the Chronicles of Narnia series.

EDUARDO

See also Eddie, Eddy, Edward

Griffiths, Helen, **Last Summer, Spain**, illustrated by Victor Ambrus, Holiday House, 1979, 151p., Fiction, ISBN 0-8234-0361-0.

Eduardo spends several weeks on his father's estate and makes friends with a horse, even though he has never cared much for horses. When the Spanish Civil War breaks out, Eduardo and the horse cross Spain so the boy can be reunited with his mother.

Hurd, Thacher, **Mystery on the Docks**, illustrated by Thacher Hurd, Harper & Row, 1983, 30p., Picture Book, LC 82-48261, ISBN 0-06-022701-X; 0-06-022702-8 (lib).

Eduardo, the famous opera singer, has been kidnapped by Big Al and his gang of tough rats, and put aboard a dark ship. When Ralph, the short-order cook at the Pier 46 diner, is also kidnapped, the two have to figure out how to escape their dangerous situation. A Reading Rainbow book.

EDWARD

See also Eddie, Eddy, Edmund, Eduardo, Ted

Edmonds, Walter D., **Matchlock Gun, The**, illustrated by Paul Lantz, Dodd, Mead, 1941, 50p., Fiction, ISBN 0-396-06369-1.

Edward was left with his mother and sister when his father rode off with the militia. When Indians attack their home, Edward takes action to protect his family using the old Spanish matchlock gun that hangs above the fireplace. 1942 Newbery Award book.

Krensky, Stephen, **Ghostly Business**, Atheneum, 1980, 144p., Fiction, ISBN 0-689-31048-X.

Edward is one of the Wynd children who uses his magic powers to prevent ghosts from taking over houses in Boston.

Seidler, Tor, **Tar Pit**, Farrar, Straus & Giroux, 1987, 153p., Fiction, ISBN 0-374-37383-3.

Edward spends a great deal of time living in a fantasy world where he imagines that an allosaurus lives in the tar pit near his school.

Stolz, Mary, **Dog on Barkham Street, A**, illustrated by Leonard Shortall, Harper & Row, 1960, 184p., Fiction, ISBN 0-06-025841-1.

Edward has several problems. He desperately wants a dog of his own, and his next-door neighbor is a bully. There are other books about these neighbors.

EGAN

Babbitt, Natalie, **Knee-Knock Rise**, illustrated by Natalie Babbitt, Farrar, Straus & Giroux, 1970, 118p., Fiction, LC 79-105622, ISBN 374-3-4257-1.

There is supposedly a fearsome creature that lives at the top of Knee-Knock Rise and the villagers are afraid to go there, so young Egan investigates by himself. 1971 Newbery Honor book.

EGBERT

Lyon, David, **Runaway Duck, The**, illustrated by David Lyon, Lothrop, Lee & Shepard, 1985, 28p., Picture Book, LC 84-5677, ISBN 0-688-04002-0; 0-688-04003-9 (lib).

Egbert, a wooden pull-toy duck, is Sebastian's favorite toy. When Sebastian forgets that he has tied the toy to his father's car, Egbert begins an adventure that takes him to sea. A Reading Rainbow book.

EINSTEIN

Simon, Seymour, **Einstein Anderson: Science Sleuth**, illustrated by Fred Winkowski, Viking, 1980, 73p., Fiction, ISBN 0-14-032098-9.

Einstein Anderson is a young scientific genius who solves mysteries using basic science principles. There are several books about this character and his friends.

ELAINE

Chang, Heidi, **Mary Lewis and the Frogs**, Crown, 1988, 64p., Fiction, ISBN 0-517-56752-0.

Elaine Chow and her Chinese-American family move from San Francisco to Iowa when she is in the third grade. Elaine learns that people are the same everywhere and she is able to learn from a friend just as her family is able to teach their new neighbors.

Rubinstein, Gillian, **Space Demons**, Dial, 1988, 198p., Fiction, ISBN 0-8037-0534-4.

Elaine and her friends are drawn into a new computer game where they experience dangerous situations as they try to get out.

ELANA
See also Alanna, Elena, Ellie

Engdahl, Sylvia Louise, **Enchantress From the Stars**, illustrated by Rodney Shackell, Collier, 1970, 275p., Fiction, ISBN 0-02-043031-0.

Elana is a stowaway on a mission to save a planet from a hostile takeover. 1971 Newbery Honor book.

ELDON

Paulsen, Gary, **Winter Room, The**, Orchard, 1989, 103p., Fiction, LC 89-42541, ISBN 0-531-05839-5; 0-531-08439-6 (lib).

Eldon and his family live on a northern Minnesota farm. Eldon describes the scenes around him and recounts his old Norwegian uncle's tales of an almost mythological logging past. 1990 Newbery Honor book.

ELEANOR
See also Elinor, Ellen, Ellie

Faber, Doris, **Eleanor Roosevelt: First Lady of the World**, illustrated by Donna Ruff, Viking Kestrel, 1985, 58p., Nonfiction, ISBN 0-670-80551-3.

Eleanor Roosevelt was the wife of a president who made a name for herself because of her great respect for all people and her political activities. Biographical information about her childhood and problems in her life as well as her triumphs.

ELENA
See also Alanna, Elana, Ellie

Brenner, Barbara, **Mystery of the Plumed Serpent**, illustrated by Blanche Sims, Knopf, 1981, 188p., Fiction, ISBN 0-394-94531-X.

Elena Garcia and her brother get caught up in a smuggling ring when two sinister characters open a pet store near their home in a run-down part of town.

ELI
See also Elias, Ellie, Elliot, Ellis, Ellsworth

Kirby, Susan, **Culligan Man Can**, Abingdon, 1988, 126p., Fiction, ISBN 0-687-10066-6.

Eli has many problems including being teased by his brothers and letting his rabbit be visited by the neighbor's rabbits.

ELIAS
See also Eli

Wisler, G. Clifton, **Wolf's Tooth**, Lodestar, 1987, 119p., Fiction, ISBN 0-525-67197-8.

Thirteen-year-old Elias lives on the Texas frontier and faces constant hardships. He becomes friends with an Indian boy and learns his own strengths.

ELINOR
See also Eleanor, Ellen, Ellie

Allan, Mabel Esther, **Mills Down Below**, Dodd, Mead, 1980, 205p., Fiction, ISBN 0-396-07926-1.

Elinor Rillsdell lives a lonely life in her family's manor house overlooking the cotton mill owned by her father. Set in pre-World War I England, Elinor becomes more independent as she learns about women's rights.

ELISABETH
See also Beth, Betsy, Betty, Elizabeth, Libby, Lisa, Liz, Liza, Lizzie

Hyman, Trina Schart, **Little Red Riding Hood**, illustrated by Trina Schart Hyman, Holiday House, 1983, 32p., Picture Book, LC 82-7700, ISBN 0-8234-0470-6.

The classic tale by the German Grimm Brothers. On her way to deliver a basket of food to her sick grandmother, Elisabeth encounters a sly wolf. 1984 Caldecott Honor book.

ELIZABETH

See also Beth, Betsy, Betty,
Elisabeth, Libby, Lisa, Liz, Liza, Lizzie

Aliki, **Feelings**, illustrated by Aliki, Greenwillow, 1984, 32p., Picture Book, LC 84-4098, ISBN 0-688-03831-X; 0-688-03832-8 (lib).

Elizabeth is one of the children who is portrayed showing the various emotions that everyone feels: sadness, fear, jealousy, anger, love, and so forth. Poems, dialogs, pictures, and stories. A Reading Rainbow book.

Burnford, Sheila, **Incredible Journey, The**, illustrated by Carl Burger, Little, Brown, 1960, 145p., Fiction, LC 61-5313, ISBN 0-316-11714-5.

John Longridge agrees to care for the three pets of his young friends, Elizabeth and Peter, while they are traveling with their parents for nine months. Bodger, the English bull terrier; Luath, the labrador retriever; and Tao, the Siamese cat, take their own journey, walking and staying together for almost 300 miles as they seek out their family. Kansas 1964. Pacific Northwest 1964. Vermont 1963.

Gleiter, Jan, **Elizabeth Cady Stanton**, illustrated by Rick Whipple, Raintree, 1988, 32p., Nonfiction, ISBN 0-8172-2677-X.

A brief biography about the well-known woman, Elizabeth Cady Stanton, who worked for the rights of women and slaves.

Locker, Thomas, **Sailing With the Wind**, illustrated by Thomas Locker, Dial, 1986, 28p., Picture Book, LC 85-23381, ISBN 0-8037-0311-2; 0-8037-0312-0 (lib).

Elizabeth's uncle works on a ship and travels all over the world. On one visit, he takes Elizabeth on her first sailboat adventure. A Reading Rainbow book.

Lunn, Janet, **Double Spell**, illustrated by A. M. Calder, Puffin, 1968, 134p., Fiction, ISBN 0-88778-023-7.

Elizabeth and her twin sister become involved in a supernatural mystery after they see an unusual doll at an antique store.

Phillips, Ann, **Multiplying Glass**, illustrated by Liz Moyes, Oxford, 1981, 157p., Fiction, ISBN 0-19-271455-4.

Elizabeth and two other children discover an unusual mirror at an antique shop. The mirror shows two fantasy personalities who begin to exhibit sinister behavior.

Wilson, Dorothy Clark, **I Will Be a Doctor! The Story of America's First Woman Physician**, Abingdon, 1983, 160p., Nonfiction, ISBN 0-687-19727-9.

Elizabeth Blackwell came to the United States with her father to help free slaves. She stayed to become the first American woman doctor. This biography gives insight into the difficulties she had to overcome and the determination that she had to reach her goal.

ELLEN

See also Eleanor, Elinor, Ellie

Boutis, Victoria, **Looking Out**, Four Winds, 1988, 139p., Fiction, ISBN 0-02-711830-4.

Ellen Gerson has a big problem with her parents. The year is 1953 and America's anticommunist paranoia is at its height. Ellen's parents are Communists and Ellen is afraid someone will find out. 1989 Jane Addams Award book.

Cleary, Beverly, **Ellen Tibbits**, illustrated by Louis Darling, Morrow, 1951, 160p., Fiction, ISBN 0-688-31264-0.

Ellen Tibbits is in third grade and has a fairly problem-free life. She takes dancing lessons, has braces on her teeth, and wears woolen underwear.

Cleaver, Vera and Bill Cleaver, **Ellen Grae**, illustrated by Ellen Raskin, Lippincott, 1967, 89p., Fiction, ISBN 0-397-30938-4.

Eleven-year-old Ellen has a dilemma when an elderly friend tells her a secret about a crime he committed. There is another book about Ellen Grae.

Erickson, Phoebe, **Double or Nothing**, illustrated by Phoebe Erickson, Harper & Brothers, 1958, 128p., Fiction, LC 58-7762.

Ellen and Jeff Gates want a dog of their own when their parents move them to Vermont. When they find the dog they wanted, he is homeless and hungry, and a twin. Ellen and Jeff know they will have a problem getting their parents' approval to keep Double or Nothing. Vermont 1960.

Irwin, Hadley, **Lilith Summer**, Feminist Press, 1979, 109p., Fiction, ISBN 0-912670-51-7.

Even though she is getting paid, Ellen is not very happy that she has to be a companion to an elderly woman for the summer. As the summer passes, the two becomes friends and Ellen realizes she can learn a great deal from her elderly friend.

Lowry, Lois, **Number the Stars**, Houghton Mifflin, 1989, 137p., Fiction, LC 88-37134, ISBN 0-395-51060-0.

Set in 1943 during the German occupation of Denmark. Ellen Rosen is taken in by her best friend, ten-year-old Annemarie, and her family when all of the Jews in Denmark are being relocated. Annemarie learns to be brave and courageous as she helps to shelter her friend from the Nazis. 1990 National Jewish Book Award. 1990 Newbery Award book. Vermont 1991.

Naylor, Phyllis Reynolds, **Night Cry**, Atheneum, 1984, 154p., Fiction, ISBN 0-689-31017-X.

Thirteen-year-old Ellen has to take care of herself on their farm in Mississippi while her father travels. She has numerous fears and many problems to overcome, including rescuing a kidnap victim. 1985 Edgar Allan Poe Award.

Vivelo, Jackie, **Beagle in Trouble: Super Sleuth II**, Putnam, 1986, 109p., Fiction, ISBN 0-399-21325-2.

Ellen is one of the two partners in the Beagle Detective Agency. The two twelve-year-olds solve crimes using logic and deduction. There are other books about these detectives.

Whitehead, Victoria, **Chimney Witches, The**, illustrated by Linda North, Orchard, 1986, 117p., Fiction, ISBN 0-531-088307-1.

Eight-year-old Ellen discovers and befriends the chimney witches and has an unusual Halloween adventure as she goes with them to attend a Halloween gathering.

ELLIE
See also Eleanor, Elinor,
Ellen, Elma, Elna, Elvira

Singer, Marilyn, **It Can't Hurt Forever**, illustrated by Leigh Grant, Harper & Row, 1978, 186p., Fiction, LC 77-25657, ISBN 0-06-025681-8; 0-06-025682-6 (lib).

Eleven-year-old Ellie Simon has a heart defect. She describes her experiences and the other patients that she meets during twelve days of hospitalization for heart surgery. Minnesota 1983.

ELLIOT
See also Eli

Kalb, Jonah, **Goof That Won the Pennant, The**, illustrated by Sandy Kossin, Houghton Mifflin, 1976, 103p., Fiction, LC 76-21678, ISBN 0-395-24834-5.

Elliot is one of the members of the Blazer's baseball team, a team of oddballs and misfits who do not even try to win. When their coach gives them the idea that winning is more fun than losing, the team decides to try. Indiana 1981.

ELLIS
See also Eli, Ellsworth

Brancato, Robin, **Don't Sit Under the Apple Tree**, Knopf, 1975, 163p., Fiction, ISBN 0-394-93034-7.

Ellis Carpenter lives in the small town of Wissining, Pennsylvania, in 1945. Her family and school activities are told in a first-person account.

ELLSWORTH
See also Eli, Ellis

Brewster, Patience, **Ellsworth and the Cats From Mars**, illustrated by Patience Brewster, Houghton Mifflin/Clarion, 1981, 32p., Fiction, ISBN 0-395-29612-9.

Ellsworth the cat dreams about Martian cats. When he discovers they are real, Ellsworth visits them and has many adventures.

ELMA
See also Ellie

Verheyden-Hilliard, Mary Ellen, **Elma Gonzalez: Scientist With Determination**, illustrated by Marian Menzel, Equity Institute, 1985, 32p., Nonfiction, ISBN 0-932469-01-9.

Elma Gonzalez started out as the child of Mexican-American migrant farm workers. She wanted to attend school and became a scientist as an adult. This brief biography tells of her determination to achieve her goals.

ELMER

Gannett, Ruth Stiles, **My Father's Dragon**, illustrated by Ruth Chrisman Gannett, Random House, 1948, 86p., Fiction, ISBN 0-394-91438-4.

Elmer goes to the South Seas and uses unusual treats to rescue an overworked dragon. 1949 Newbery Honor book.

ELNA
See also Ellie

Noble, Trinka Hakes, **Meanwhile Back at the Ranch**, illustrated by Rony Ross, Dial, 1987, 28p., Picture Book, LC 86-11651, ISBN 0-8037-0353-8; 0-8037-0354-6 (lib).

A bored rancher drives into town while his wife Elna stays at the ranch. There isn't much for the rancher to do in Sleepy Gulch, but back at the ranch amazing things happen to Elna. A Reading Rainbow book.

ELSA

Lindquist, Jennie, **Golden Name Day, The**, illustrated by Garth Williams, Harper & Row, 1955, 248p., Fiction, LC 55-8823, ISBN 0-06-023881-X.

While nine-year-old Nancy is staying with her adopted Swedish grandparents for a year, Elsa and the others try to figure out how she can celebrate a name day since her name is not Swedish. 1956 Newbery Honor book.

ELSIE

DeClements, Barthe, **Nothing's Fair in Fifth Grade**, Viking, 1981, 137p., Fiction, ISBN 0-670-517-410.

Elsie gives the other students in her new fifth-grade class many problems until she finds a friend. California 1986. Georgia 1984. Hawaii 1984. Iowa 1984. Massachusetts 1985. Minnesota 1984. Nebraska 1984. New Mexico 1985. Ohio 1984. Texas 1984. Wisconsin 1984.

ELVIRA
See also Ellie

Nelson, Theresa, **Twenty-Five Cent Miracle, The**, Bradbury, 1986, 214p., Fiction, ISBN 0-02-724370-2.

Eleven-year-old Elvira doesn't have a mother and has to figure out a way to stay with her father who is unemployed.

EMILY

Barth, Edna, **I'm Nobody. Who Are You? The Story of Emily Dickinson**, illustrated by Richard Cuffari, Clarion, 1971, 128p., Nonfiction, ISBN 0-395-28843-6.

The well-known poet, Emily Dickinson, was shy and withdrawn. She was considered to be strange because she chose to live alone with her thoughts and memories. This biography provides information about the poet.

Little, Jean, **Look Through My Window**, illustrated by Joan Sandin, Harper & Row, 1970, 258p., Fiction, ISBN 0-06-023924-7.

Emily is concerned when her family moves into a large old house and takes in a family with four cousins. Her concerns turn to appreciation as she makes new friends and has a satisfying family life.

Wallace, Barbara Brooks, **Peppermints in the Parlor**, Atheneum, 1983, 198p., Fiction, LC 80-12326, ISBN 0-689-30790-X.

Newly orphaned Emily is sent to San Francisco to live with her beloved aunt and uncle. She expectantly enters their once-happy mansion only to find unimaginable horrors. Kansas 1983.

EMMA

Alcock, Vivien, **Stonewalkers**, Delacorte, 1981, 151p., Fiction, ISBN 0-385-29233-3.

Emma is the only one that will believe her friend Poppy when she says that she has made friends with a statue in the garden and that it has come to life. The two girls are captured by a group of statues and find escape nearly impossible.

Brett, Simon, **Three Detectives and the Missing Superstar**, Scribner, 1986, 179p., Fiction, ISBN 0-684-18708-6.

When a rock singer disappears, Emma and her two friends use their detective skills to rescue him.

Carlson, Natalie Savage, **Empty Schoolhouse**, illustrated by John Kaufman, HarperCollins, 1965, 119p., Fiction, ISBN 0-06-020981-X.

Emma tells the story of her family life in Louisiana during the year that her sister attended a parochial school with white children.

Farmer, Penelope, **Summer Birds**, Dell, 1962, 102p., Fiction, ISBN 0-440-47737-9 (pbk).

Emma is one of the English children who is taught to fly the summer that an unusual boy appears. There are other books about Emma.

Fox, Paula, **Village by the Sea, The**, Orchard, 1988, 160p., Fiction, ISBN 0-531-057-887; 0-531-1083-888 (lib).

While her father is in the hospital, ten-year-old Emma is sent to live with her aunt at the beach. Emma has a difficult time until she meets a special friend and they make a sand village. 1989 Boston Globe-Horn Book Award.

MacLachlan, Patricia, **Seven Kisses in a Row**, illustrated by Maria Pia Marrella, Harper & Row, 1983, 56p., Fiction, ISBN 0-06-024084-9.

Seven-year-old Emma and her brother are being cared for by relatives while their parents are at a convention. Emma shares her ideas about childcare with her expectant aunt.

Reit, Seymour, **Behind Rebel Lines: The Incredible Story of Emma Edmonds; Civil War Spy**, Harcourt Brace Jovanovich, 1988, 102p., Nonfiction, ISBN 0-15-200416-5.

During the Civil War, Emma Edmonds became a spy for the Union and took on many disguises to gain information. This biography gives the reasons for her actions.

Stock, Catherine, **Emma's Dragon Hunt**, illustrated by Catherine Stock, Lothrop, Lee & Shepard, 1984, 28p., Picture Book, LC 83-25109, ISBN 0-688-02696-6; 0-688-02698-2 (lib).

When Emma's Grandfather Wong arrives from China to live with her family, he tells Emma all about Chinese dragons. A Reading Rainbow book.

Walter, Mildred Pitts, **Because We Are**, Lothrop, Lee & Shepard, 1983, 192p., Fiction, ISBN 0-688-022-871 (lib).

Emma is a black honor student who is transferred from the integrated school where she has excelled to a segregated school that provides a different type of learning experience. 1984 Coretta Scott King Honor book.

EMMA LOU

Montgomery, Rutherford, **Kildee House**, illustrated by Barbara Cooney, Doubleday, 1949, 209p., Fiction, ISBN 0-671-29518-7.

Jerome Kildee lives in an odd house that he built on the mountainside next to a redwood tree. Jerome is a silent man who lives quietly with animals for friends. When there are problems with the animals, Emma Lou and her friend help Jerome find a solution. 1950 Newbery Honor book.

ENOCH

Sperry, Armstrong, **All Set Sail: A Romance of the Flying Cloud**, illustrated by Armstrong Sperry, Godine, 1984, 175p., Fiction, ISBN 0-87923-523-3.

Enoch Thacher helps to build a clipper ship and then joins the crew to sail it around Cape Horn. A reprint of the 1935 edition. 1936 Newbery Honor book.

ERIC
See also Erick

Roberts, Willo Davis, **Girl with the Silver Eyes, The**, Atheneum, 1982, 181p., Fiction, LC 80-12391, ISBN 0-689-30786-1.

People didn't quite trust ten-year-old Katie because of her strange silver eyes. Eric, Katie, and several other children have paranormal powers. They are able to move things with their minds and understand what animals are thinking. California 1986. Missouri 1983.

ERICK
See also Eric

Kerr, M. E., **Night Kites**, Harper & Row, 1986, 224p., Fiction, ISBN 0-060-232-544 (lib); 0-060-232-536.

Erick is seventeen and has two secrets that he is forced to keep—the identity of his new girlfriend and the reason for his brother's debilitating disease. California 1991.

ERIN
See also Aaron, Aerin

Tapp, Kathy Kennedy, **Smoke from the Chimney**, Macmillan, 1986, 169p., Fiction, ISBN 0-689-50389-X.

Erin and her friend escape into a jungle fantasy after reading the adventures of Tarzan.

ESSIE

Lenski, Lois, **Strawberry Girl**, illustrated by Lois Lenski, Lippincott, 1945, 194p., Fiction, LC 45-7609, ISBN 0-397-30109-X.

The Boyer family with their six children moved near the Slater family's farm in Florida and Essie Slater made a new friend. A regional tale of a family of Florida Crackers who live in the backwoods that includes their speech, customs, folk songs, and superstitions. 1946 Newbery Award book.

ESTABAN
See also Stephan, Steve, Steven

O'Dell, Scott, **King's Fifth, The**, illustrated by Samuel Bryant, Houghton Mifflin, 1966, 264p., Fiction, LC 66-10726, ISBN 0-395-06963-7.

Estaban de Sandoval is a seventeen-year-old Spanish mapmaker. During the years 1540-1541, he is a member of the ill-fated expedition to Cibola, the legendary cities of gold. The story of the expedition, its members, and the effects of greed is told through a series of flashbacks. This book is based on an actual episode in history. 1966 Newbery Honor book.

ESTHER

Hautzig, Esther, **Endless Steppe: Growing up in Siberia, The**, Crowell, 1968, 243p., Nonfiction, LC 68-13582, ISBN 0-690-26371-6.

Esther Rudomin and her family lived happily in Vilna, Poland, until June, 1941, when two Russian soldiers arrested the family. The Rudomins were put in a hot cattle car that traveled across Russia to Siberia, where the family was exiled and became slave laborers in a gypsum mine. The story is based on the author's personal experiences as she was growing up. 1969 Jane Addams Award book.

Rogers, Jean, **Goodbye, My Island**, illustrated by Rie Munoz, Greenwillow, 1983, 85p., Fiction, ISBN 0-688-01965-X.

Twelve-year-old Esther spends her last winter on an island in Alaska's Bering Strait before the Eskimos are relocated. She knows that the way of life on the island will disappear.

ETHAN

Holbrook, Stewart, **America's Ethan Allen**, illustrated by Lynd Ward, Houghton Mifflin, 1949, 95p., Nonfiction, ISBN 0-395-24449-8.

Ethan Allen was an American patriot who led the Green Mountain Boys in the capture of Fort Ticonderoga from the British during the American Revolution. 1950 Caldecott Honor book.

EUNICE

Brittain, Bill, **Wish Giver: Three Tales of Coven Tree, The**, illustrated by Andrew Glass, Harper & Row, 1983, 181p., Fiction, LC 82-48264, ISBN 0-06-020686-1; 0-06-020687-X (lib).

Thaddeus Blinn was a funny little man who appeared from out of nowhere and put his tent by the annual Coven Tree Church Social. He said he had the power to give people exactly what they asked for. Eunice is one of the characters who finds that wishes often have unexpected results when they come true. 1984 Newbery Honor book.

EVA

Andrews, Jan, **Very Last First Time**, illustrated by Ian Wallace, Atheneum, 1985, 30p., Picture Book, LC 85-71606, ISBN 0-689-50388-1.

Eva is a young Inuit living in northern Canada. In the winter, people of her village walk on the bottom of the sea to collect mussels to eat. Eva goes alone for the first time to collect mussels and sees beautiful sights. A Reading Rainbow book.

Baer, Edith, **Frost in the Night**, Pantheon, 1980, 208p., Fiction, ISBN 0-394-94364-3.

Young Eva Bentheim tells the story of her childhood in Germany from 1932 until the election of Hitler as prime minister.

Dickinson, Peter, **Eva**, Delacorte, 1989, 219p., Fiction, ISBN 0-385-29702-5.

When Eva awakes after a serious accident, she discovers that her mind is in the body of a chimpanzee. Set in the future.

EVAN

Kittleman, Laurence, **Canyons Beyond the Sky**, Atheneum, 1985, 196p., Fiction, ISBN 0-689-31138-9.

Twelve-year-old Evan is introduced to archaeology by his father as they dig up artifacts where American Indians had lived over 5,000 years previously. During the dig, Evan has an adventure that takes him to another time.

EVELYN

See also Evelyne

Cleaver, Vera and Bill Cleaver, **Kissimmee Kid**, Lothrop, Lee & Shepard, 1981, 159p., Fiction, ISBN 0-688-51992-X.

Evelyn spends time with her sister and brother-in-law while her parents are on vacation and learns something that causes her great distress.

Walter, Mildred Pitts, **Justin and the Best Biscuits in the World**, illustrated by Catherine Stock, Lothrop, Lee & Shepard, 1986, 122p., Fiction, LC 86-7148, ISBN 0-688-06645-3.

Evelyn is Justin's sister. Justin is tired of his mother and sisters always fussing at him and he is glad to go to his grandfather's ranch for a visit. Justin discovers that cooking and keeping house aren't just women's work. 1987 Coretta Scott King Award.

EVELYNE

See also Evelyn

Carlson, Natalie Savage, **Family Under the Bridge, The**, illustrated by Garth Williams, HarperCollins, 1958, 97p., Fiction, LC 58-5292, ISBN 0-06-020991-7.

Armand, the old hobo, disliked children until Suzy, Paul, and Evelyne moved to his bridge with their mother after being evicted from their apartment. Bridges were the only free shelter in Paris, but Armand didn't think it was the proper place for a family to live. Armand learned that when families stay together they make a home no matter where they live. 1959 Newbery Honor book.

EVERETT

Clifton, Lucille, **Everett Anderson's Friend**, illustrated by Ann Grifalconi, H. Holt, 1976, 25p., Nonfiction, ISBN 0-030-151-619 (lib).

Everett Anderson eagerly awaits the arrival of his new neighbors and is disappointed to find a whole family of girls. Told in rhyme. 1977 Coretta Scott King Honor book.

Clifton, Lucille, **Everett Anderson's Good-Bye**, illustrated by Ann Grifalconi, H. Holt, 1983, 16p., Nonfiction, LC 82-23426, ISBN 0-03-063518-7.

Poetry and illustrations emotionally tell of Everett Anderson's despair over his father's death. The five poems match the five stages of grief: denial, anger, bargaining, depression, and acceptance. 1984 Coretta Scott King Award book.

EZEL

McKissack, Patricia C., **Mirandy and Brother Wind**, illustrated by Jerry Pinkney, Knopf, 1988, 30p., Picture Book, LC 87-349, ISBN 0-394-88765-4; 0-394-98765-9 (lib).

The cakewalk is a dance first introduced in America by slaves. Mirandy is going to her first cakewalk and she wants to catch Brother Wind to help her. She and Ezel dance well with a little help. 1989 Caldecott Honor book. 1989 Coretta Scott King Award book.

EZRA

Holling, Holling Clancy, **Seabird**, illustrated by Holling Clancy Holling, Houghton Mifflin, 1948, 58p., Fiction, ISBN 0-395-18230-1.

In 1832 Ezra Brown carved a gull of ivory and it brought luck to him and to his descendants as they sailed on the high seas. 1949 Newbery Honor book.

Hurwitz, Johanna, **Baseball Fever**, illustrated by Ray Cruz, Morrow, 1981, 128p., Fiction, ISBN 0-688-00711-2.

At nine, Ezra has only one interest and that is baseball. His mother is understanding, but he has to reach a compromise with his European-born father who doesn't understand and thinks baseball is a waste of time.

-F-

FARLEY

Blume, Judy, **Superfudge**, Dutton, 1980, 166p., Fiction, LC 80-10439, ISBN 0-525-40522-4.

Peter Hatcher is not at all happy about the news that there will be a new baby in their house. He worries the new baby will be like his little brother, Farley, known as Fudge, who is a big nuisance. Arizona 1983. California 1983. Colorado 1982. Florida 1985. Georgia 1983. Hawaii 1982. Indiana 1983. Iowa 1983. Nebraska 1983. New Hampshire 1981, 1984, 1985. New Mexico 1984. Ohio 1982. Pacific Northwest 1983. Texas 1982. Utah 1982.

FAYE

Samuels, Barbara, **Duncan and Dolores**, illustrated by Barbara Samuels, Bradbury, 1986, 30p., Picture Book, LC 85-17119, ISBN 0-02-778210-7.

Dolores and Faye see a sign for a cat, Duncan, that needs a home. When Dolores gets the cat and then smothers it with affection and attention, the cat keeps hiding. Dolores begins to think that Duncan likes Faye the best. 1987 Christopher Award. A Reading Rainbow book.

FELICIA

Conford, Ellen, **Felicia the Critic**, illustrated by Arvis Stewart, Little, Brown, 1973, 145p., Fiction, ISBN 0-316-15295-1.

Felicia is a loner and very critical of other people, which gets her into quite a bit of trouble.

FELICITY

Alcock, Vivien, **Mysterious Mr. Ross, The**, Delacorte, 1987, 161p., Fiction, LC 87-5455, ISBN 0-385-29581-2.

Twelve-year old Felicity is saved from drowning on the dangerous seacoast where she lives by the mysterious Mr. Ross. Albert Ross is either an exotic world traveler or a fearsome liar, and he changes the lives of those who seek the truth about him.

FELITA

Mohr, Nicholasa, **Felita**, illustrated by Ray Cruz, Dial, 1979, 112p., Fiction, ISBN 0-8037-3144-2.

Felita's parents are from Puerto Rico. When the family moves to a new neighborhood, they are mistreated and return to their old apartment in a Spanish-speaking neighborhood. There is another book about Felita and her family.

FENTON

Corbett, Scott, **Home Run Trick, The**, illustrated by Paul Galdone, Little, Brown, 1973, 101p., Fiction, LC 72-3478, ISBN 0-316-15693-0.

Fenton and his friend Kerby have problems with their baseball team, the Panthers. The Panthers want to lose an important game with their archrivals when they find out the winners will have to play a girls' team. Mississippi 1976. Missouri 1976.

FERD
See also Ferdinand

McCloskey, Robert, **Time of Wonder**, illustrated by Robert McCloskey, Viking, 1957, 63p., Picture Book, ISBN 0-670-71512-3.

Ferd Clifford, Harry Smith, and Clyde Snowman are a few of the people that live on the island where the children and their parents vacation in the summer. 1958 Caldecott Award book.

FERDINAND
See also Ferd

Leaf, Munro, **Story of Ferdinand, The**, illustrated by Robert Lawson, Viking, 1936, 68p., Picture Book, ISBN 0-670-67424-9.

A young Spanish bull named Ferdinand liked to sit quietly and smell the flowers while the other little bulls ran in the fields bumping their heads together. Ferdinand grew into a large bull and still liked smelling flowers, even after being chosen to fight in the bull ring in Madrid. A Reading Rainbow book.

FERN

White, E. B., **Charlotte's Web**, illustrated by Garth Williams, Harper & Row, 1952, 184p., Fiction, LC 52-9760, ISBN 0-06-026385-7.

Fern saved the runt of the pig litter and named him Wilbur. Wilbur lives in the barn and has a beautiful grey spider for a friend. The spider's name is Charlotte. 1953 Newbery Honor book. Massachusetts 1984. Michigan 1980. Missouri 1980.

FINLEY

Sharmat, Marjorie Weinman, **Nate the Great and the Phony Clue**, illustrated by Marc Simont, Coward-McCann, 1977, 48p., Easy Reader, LC 76-42461, ISBN 0-698-20405-0.

A piece of paper with the letters VITA printed on it appears on Nate's doorstep. The boy detective, Nate the Great, looks for the missing pieces and sees Annie and Finley along the way. A Reading Rainbow book.

FIONA

Keller, Beverly, **Only Fiona**, HarperCollins, 1988, 185p., Fiction, ISBN 0-06-023270-6.

Ten-year-old Fiona has trouble fitting into the new neighborhood. The neighbors all know each other and her creatures cause problems.

FLORA

Raskin, Ellen, **Westing Game, The**, Dutton, 1978, 185p., Fiction, LC 77-18866, ISBN 0-525-42320-6.

Flora is one of the sixteen people invited to the reading of the very strange will of the very rich Samuel W. Westing. She could become a millionaire, depending on how well she plays the tricky and dangerous Westing Game. 1979 Newbery Award book. 1978 Boston Globe-Horn Book Award. Michigan 1982.

FLORENCE

Lexau, Joan M., **Striped Ice Cream**, illustrated by John Wilson, Lippincott, 1968, 95p., Fiction, LC 68-10774, ISBN 0-397-31047-1.

Florence's little sister is resigned to the fact that their mother cannot afford anything special for her birthday, but she does not understand why the family seems to have turned against her, until the big day finally arrives. Arkansas 1971.

Turner, Dorothy, **Florence Nightingale**, illustrated by Richard Hook, Watts, 1986, 32p., Nonfiction, ISBN 0-531-18074-3.

A brief biography about Florence Nightingale, a woman who dedicated her life to others through her career in nursing.

FRAN
See also Frances, Francine, Francis, Francoise, Franny

Sachs, Marilyn, **Bears' House, The**, Dutton, 1987, 76p., Fiction, ISBN 0-525-44286-3.

Fran Ellen is a fourth grader who has many problems. She is bullied by her older sister and her classmates, she worries about her family, and she still sucks her thumb. A bears' house in her classroom offers her a place to relax.

FRANCES
See also Fran, Francine, Francis, Frankie, Franny

Nixon, Joan Lowery, **Family Apart, A**, Bantam, 1987, 176p., Fiction, ISBN 0-553-05432-5.

Frances Kelly and her five siblings leave their widowed mother in New York City as they get aboard the orphan train heading west in 1856. There are other books about the Kelly children. Virginia 1992.

FRANCINE
See also Fran, Frances, Francis, Franny

Sleator, William, **Into the Dream**, illustrated by Ruth Sanderson, Dutton, 1979, ISBN 0-525-32583-2.

Francine and her friend are linked by extrasensory perception and share the same frightening dream where they see a small child and a large glowing object.

FRANCIS
See also Fran, Frances, Francine, Frankie, Franny, Frances

dePaola, Tomie, **Francis, the Poor Man of Assisi**, illustrated by Tomie dePaola, Holiday House, 1982, 48p., Nonfiction, ISBN 0-8234-0435-8.

Francis Di Bernardone was born the son of a rich merchant. He gave up the comfortable lifestyle of his parents to worship Christ by living a simple life. A biography of St. Francis of Assisi.

Myers, Walter Dean, **Fast Sam, Cool Clyde and Stuff**, Viking, 1975, 190p., Fiction, ISBN 0-670-308-749.

When Francis moves to 116th Street he soon makes friends and has a year of unusual experiences. 1976 Coretta Scott King Honor book.

Spier, Peter, **Star-Spangled Banner, The**, illustrated by Peter Spier, Doubleday, 1973, 48p., Nonfiction, LC 73-79712, ISBN 0-385-09458-2; 0-385-07746-7.

Francis Scott Key wrote the poem for The Star-Spangled Banner in 1884. Music was added and it became the American national anthem in 1931. Illustrations of the poem and historical information are included. A Reading Rainbow book.

FRANCOISE
See also Fran, Frances, Francis

Brown, Marcia, **Stone Soup: An Old Tale**, illustrated by Marcia Brown, Scribner, 1947, 40p., Picture Book, ISBN 0-684-92296-7; 0-684-16217-2 (pbk).

Francoise and the other peasants in the village hid their food when they saw three hungry soldiers coming down the road. The soldiers then taught the villagers how to make soup from three stones and soon a village feast was prepared. An old folktale. 1948 Caldecott Honor book.

FRANKIE
See also Frances, Francis

Branscum, Robbie, **For Love of Jody**, illustrated by Allen Davis, Lothrop, Lee & Shepard, 1979, 111p., Fiction, ISBN 0-688-41881-3.

Frankie and her family have a hard life during the Depression. Frankie's father is out of work, there is a drought, her brother is severely retarded, and her mother is expecting another baby.

FRANNY
See also Fran, Frances, Francine, Francis

Greenwald, Sheila, **It All Began with Jane Eyre; Or, the Secret Life of Franny Dillman**, Little, Brown, 1980, 117p., Fiction, ISBN 0-316-32671-2.

Franny Dillman has read the book about Jane Eyre numerous times in her thirteen years. When her mother brings other books home for her to read, Franny decides that she has to be more like the characters in the books with humorous results.

Stolz, Mary, **Noonday Friends**, Harper & Row, 1965, 182p., Fiction, ISBN 0-06-025946-9.

Franny and her twin brother live in New York and their family doesn't have much money. 1966 Newbery Honor book.

FRED
See also Freddy, Frederick, Friedrich

Cox, David, **Bossyboots**, illustrated by David Cox, Crown, 1985, 26p., Picture Book, LC 86-16799, ISBN 0-517-56491-2.

Flash Fred, the famous Australian outlaw, meets his match when he comes up against Abigail as he robs the stage that she is on. Abigail is the bossiest girl in all of Australia. A Reading Rainbow book.

Gibbons, Gail, **Fill It Up! All About Service Stations**, illustrated by Gail Gibbons, Crowell, 1985, 30p., Picture Book, LC 84-45345, ISBN 0-690-04439-9; 0-690-04440-2 (lib).

John and Peggy spend a busy day at their service station. Fred helps with repairs and puts gasoline in the cars. A Reading Rainbow book.

FREDDY
See also Fred, Frederick, Friedrich

Brooks, Walter, **Freddy the Detective**, illustrated by Kurt Wiese, Knopf, 1987, 263p., Fiction, ISBN 0-394-98885-X.

Freddy the pig is a detective living with other animals on a farm. There are other books about Freddy.

FREDERICK
See also Fred, Freddy, Friedrich

Lionni, Leo, **Frederick**, Pantheon, 1967, 40p., Picture Book, ISBN 0-394-91040-0; 0-394-82614-0.

Frederick spends his time daydreaming while the other mice gather food to store for winter. When the cold, dreary days of winter arrive, Frederick cheers his friends with his poems. 1968 Caldecott Honor book.

FRIEDRICH
See also Fred, Freddy, Frederick

Richter, Hans Peter, **Friedrich**, Puffin, 1987, 152p., Fiction, ISBN 0-14-032205-1.

Friedrich was born in Germany in 1925 of Jewish parents. As Hitler rose to power, Friedrich's life changed dramatically.

-G-

GABRIEL

Krumgold, Joseph, **...And Now Miguel**, illustrated by Jean Charlot, Crowell, 1953, 245p., Fiction, LC 53-8415, ISBN 0-690-09118-4.

The Chavez family has raised sheep in New Mexico for centuries. Gabriel is the youngest of the Chavez sons and he is always happy with what he has. His older brother, Miguel, envies him and has a great secret wish that he wants to come true. 1954 Newbery Award book.

GALADRIEL

Paterson, Katherine, **Great Gilly Hopkins, The**, Crowell, 1978, 148p., Fiction, LC 77-27075, ISBN 0-690-03837-2; 0-06-440201-0 (pbk).

Galadriel Hopkins, known as Gilly, has been placed in her third foster home with an almost illiterate foster parent and a freaky foster brother named William. In her short life, Gilly has learned to be tough and she despises her new foster home at first. Slowly, she learns about love and caring. 1979 Newbery Honor book. 1979 Jane Addams Award book. Georgia 1981. Iowa 1981. Kansas 1981. Massachusetts 1981.

GARNET

Enright, Elizabeth, **Thimble Summer**, illustrated by Elizabeth Enright, H. Holt, 1938, 124p., Fiction, LC 66-43350, ISBN 0-03-015686-6.

When Garnet finds a silver thimble in the dried-up creek bed, she thinks it is a talisman. Shortly after, the rains come to end the long drought that the farm has suffered. Rain means the stock and crops will be safe and Garnet's father will have money. 1939 Newbery Award book.

GARRETT

Hickman, Janet, **Stones**, illustrated by Richard Cuffari, Macmillan, 1976, 116p., Fiction, ISBN 0-02-743760-4.

While his father is fighting in France during World War II, Garrett McKay has his own problems with family and neighbors.

GARTH

Rayner, Mary, **Mrs. Pig's Bulk Buy**, illustrated by Mary Rayner, Atheneum, 1981, 30p., Picture Book, LC 80-19875, ISBN 0-689-30831-0.

Garth and his nine brothers and sisters like to put ketchup on everything they eat. Mrs. Pig has a plan to cure the piglets of this habit, which changes their skin from white to pink. A Reading Rainbow book.

GARY

Bell, Thelma Harrington, **Captain Ghost**, illustrated by Corydon Bell, Viking, 1959, 191p., Fiction.

Gary and his friends live in the three new houses on the block near an old-fashioned house that appears empty. When the children turn a tree trunk into a sailing ship, Captain Ghost joins them and helps in solving a mystery. Vermont 1961.

Wallace, Bill, **Trapped in Death Cave**, Holiday House, 1984, 170p., Fiction, ISBN 0-823-405-168.

Gary is convinced that his grandfather did not die a natural death after finding a letter referring to buried treasure. He and a friend set out to find both the treasure and the killer. Utah 1989.

Weiss, Leatie, **My Teacher Sleeps in School**, illustrated by Ellen Weiss, Warne, 1984, 32p., Picture Book, LC 83-10427, ISBN 0-7232-6253-5; 0-14-050559-8.

Gary begins investigating where their teacher really lives when his friend becomes convinced that the teacher must live at school since she always seems to be there. A humorous story with animal characters. Georgia 1987.

GENEVIEVE

Bemelmans, Ludwig, **Madeline's Rescue**, illustrated by Ludwig Bemelmans, Puffin, 1975, 50p., Picture Book, LC 77-2573, ISBN 0-14-050207-6.

When Madeline slips and falls into the Seine River, she is rescued by a brave dog. The dog is named Genevieve and goes to live with Madeline and eleven other girls in an old house in Paris. 1954 Caldecott Award book.

GENNY
See also Jenny, Jinny, Virginia

Greenfield, Eloise, **Talk About a Family**, illustrated by James Calvin, Lippincott, 1978, 60p., Fiction, ISBN 0-397-31789-1.

Genny awaits the return of her brother from the army hoping that he can keep their parents from breaking up.

GEORGE
See also Georgie

Adler, David A., **George Washington, Father of Our Country**, illustrated by Jacqueline Garrick, Holiday House, 1988, 48p., Nonfiction, ISBN 0-8234-0717-9.

George Washington was the first president of the United States. This biography provides information on his youth and the interests that led him to the presidency.

Aliki, **Weed Is a Flower: The Life of George Washington Carver**, Simon & Schuster, 1988, 32p., Nonfiction, ISBN 0-671-66118-3.

George Washington Carver was born a slave but became a famous and world-renowned scientist. This brief biography provides information about this great man.

Carlson, Nancy, **Loudmouth George and the Sixth Grade Bully**, illustrated by Nancy Carlson, Carolrhoda, 1983, 30p., Picture Book, LC 83-7178, ISBN 0-87614-217-X (lib).

After having his lunch taken repeatedly by a bully twice his size, George and his friend Harriet decide to play a trick to teach the bully a lesson. A Reading Rainbow book.

Collier, James Lincoln, **Teddy Bear Habit**, illustrated by Lee Lorenz, Peter Smith, 1967, 177p., Fiction, ISBN 0-8446-6191-0.

Twelve-year-old George always has his teddy bear with him to keep him from failing at things he tries. A humorous story set in New York City.

Fritz, Jean, **George Washington's Breakfast**, illustrated by Paul Galdone, Coward-McCann, 1969, 47p., Fiction, ISBN 0-698-30099-8.

George Allen knows a great deal about George Washington since they share the same first name and the same birthdate. However, George has a difficult time finding out what George Washington ate for breakfast.

Hodges, Margaret, **Saint George and the Dragon**, illustrated by Trina Schart Hyman, Little, Brown, 1984, Picture Book, LC 83-19980, ISBN 0-316-36789-3.

George, the Red Cross Knight, is sent by the Queen of Fairies to rid a dreadful dragon from the kingdom of Princess Una. A retelling of a story from the *Faerie Queene* by Edmund Spenser. 1985 Caldecott Award Book. Pennsylvania 1985.

Joyce, William, **George Shrinks**, illustrated by William Joyce, Harper & Row, 1985, 26p., Picture Book, LC 83-47697, ISBN 0-06-023070-3; 0-06-023071-1 (lib).

George dreamed that he was small, and when he awoke he discovered that it was true. Although he is the size of a mouse, he manages to take care of his baby brother and do all of his chores. A Reading Rainbow book.

Kennedy, John F., **Profiles in Courage**, illustrated by Emil Weiss, Harper & Row, 1955, 164p., Nonfiction, LC 64-17696.

George Norris showed political courage under pressure. He is one of the eight statesmen featured in this book. 1964 Jane Addams Award book.

Meltzer, Milton, **Ain't Gonna Study War No More: The Story of America's Peace Seekers**, Harper & Row, 1985, 282p., Nonfiction, ISBN 0-060-241-993; 0-060-242-000 (lib).

This book presents a history of pacifism and people who have protested against war in the United States from colonial times to the present. George Fox was the leader of the Quaker religion. 1986

Child Study Children's Book Award. 1986 Jane Addams Award.

Mitchell, Barbara, **America, I Hear You: A Story About George Gershwin**, Carolrhoda, 1987, 56p., Nonfiction, ISBN 0-87614-309-5.

A biography of George Gershwin who discovered his musical talent by accident, then went on to write well-known American music.

Mitchell, Barbara, **Click! A Story About George Eastman**, illustrated by Jan Hosking Smith, Carolrhoda, 1986, 56p., Nonfiction, ISBN 0-87614-289-7.

George Eastman's hobby was photography. Photographic equipment was heavy and the supplies were dangerous so George invented the Kodak camera and photographic film. This biography gives information about both the man and the field of photography.

Sufrin, Mark, **George Bush, the Story of the Forty-First President of the United States**, Delacorte, 1989, 107p., Nonfiction, ISBN 0-440-50158-X.

The biography of George Bush and the many political roles that he had before becoming president of the United States.

GEORGIA
See also Georgie

Gherman, Beverly, **Georgia O'Keefe: The Wideness and Wonder of Her World**, Atheneum, 1986, 131p., Nonfiction, ISBN 0-689-31164-8.

Georgia O'Keefe is a well-known artist. This biography tells about her art and her life.

Langton, Jane, **Fledgling, The**, Harper & Row, 1980, 182p., Fiction, LC 79-2008, ISBN 0-06-023-678-7; 0-06-023679-5 (lib).

Georgia Hall is able to jump down twelve steps in two graceful bounds, and she can jump from the porch and float as high as the rooftop. But her fondest wish is to be able to fly, which she is able to do with the help of a mysterious Canada goose. 1981 Newbery Honor book.

GEORGIE
See also George, Georgia

Langton, Jane, **Fragile Flag**, illustrated by Erik Blegvad, Harper & Row, 1984, 275p., Fiction, ISBN 0-06-023699-X.

Nine-year-old Georgie Hall is concerned that the government is going to launch a 'peace missile' into space, so she launches a march on Washington, which grows to include thousands of children.

Lawson, Robert, **Rabbit Hill**, illustrated by Robert Lawson, Viking, 1944, 128p., Fiction, LC 44-8234, ISBN 0-670-58675-7.

There are new folks living in the Big House and Georgie and the other animals of Rabbit Hill wonder if the people will plant a garden and be good providers. 1945 Newbery Award book.

GERALD
See also Jerry

Nesbit, E., **Enchanted Castle**, illustrated by H. R. Millar, Puffin, 1985, 252p., Fiction, ISBN 0-14-035057-8 (pbk).

Gerald is one of the children who spends his summer investigating an enchanted castle and having magical adventures.

Rogers, Jean, **Secret Moose**, illustrated by Jim Fowler, Greenwillow, 1985, 64p., Fiction, ISBN 0-688-042249-X.

Gerald finds a wounded moose near his home in Alaska. He learns all he can about moose in order to help with her healing and is rewarded with a wonderful surprise.

GERALDINE
See also Jerry

Blood, Charles L. and Martin Link, **Goat in the Rug, The**, illustrated by Nancy Winslow Parker, Four Winds, 1976, 30p., Picture Book, LC 80-17315, ISBN 0-590-07763-5.

Geraldine, a goat, and her friend Glee 'Nasbah (Glenmae) live in the Navajo Nation at Indian Rock, Arizona. Glee 'Nasbah is a weaver and Geraldine describes each step of the rug-making process from hair clipping and carding to the dyeing and weaving. Based on a real Navajo weaver. A Reading Rainbow book.

Duder, Tessa, **Jellybean**, Viking Kestrel, 1986, 112p., Fiction, ISBN 0-670-81235-8.

Geraldine lives with her single parent mother who is a musician and much of their time is spent going to rehearsals.

GERTRUDE

Greenwald, Sheila, **Will the Real Gertrude Hollings Please Stand Up?**, Little, Brown, 1983, 162p., Fiction, ISBN 0-316-32707-7.

Gertrude has a learning disability, which has caused her to be labeled a loser. When she spends several weeks with her successful cousin, Gertrude discovers she can teach him something.

GILL
See also Gillespie

Cameron, Eleanor, **Court of the Stone Children, The**, Dutton, 1973, 191p., Fiction, ISBN 0-525-28350-1.

Gill meets a girl who is alone in San Francisco and takes her to the court of stone children at the French Museum. They meet a strange girl from the time of Napoleon and learn of treason and murder.

GILLESPIE
See also Gill

Elkin, Benjamin, **Gillespie and the Guards**, illustrated by James Daugherty, Viking, 1956, 63p., Picture Book.

There were once three brothers who could see better and farther than anyone else in the world and the king made them his guards. When the king offered a prize to anyone who could fool the three guards, a young boy named Gillespie decided to try. 1957 Caldecott Honor book.

GINA
See also Virginia

Skurzynski, Gloria, **Trapped in the Slickrock Canyon**, illustrated by Daniel San Souci, Lothrop, Lee & Shepard, 1984, 123p., Fiction, ISBN 0-688-02688-5.

Gina and her cousin have exciting adventures while hiking through a western canyon. They meet vandals who chase them, and become trapped by a flash flood.

GINGER

Bell, Thelma Harrington, **Captain Ghost**, illustrated by Corydon Bell, Viking, 1959, 191p., Fiction.

Ginger and her friends live in the three new houses near an old-fashioned house that seems to be empty. When the children turn a tree branch into a sailing ship, Captain Ghost joins them and helps in solving a mystery. Vermont 1961.

GLADYS

Robinson, Barbara, **Best Christmas Pageant Ever, The**, illustrated by Judith Gwyn Brown, Harper & Row, 1972, 80p., Fiction, LC 72-76501, ISBN 06-025043-7; 06-025044-5.

Gladys is one of the six Herdman children—kids so awful it is hard to believe they are real. When they decide to participate in the church Christmas pageant, people think it will be the worst one ever. Georgia 1976. Indiana 1978. Minnesota 1982.

GLEE 'NASBAH

Blood, Charles L. and Martin Link, **Goat in the Rug, The**, illustrated by Nancy Winslow Parker, Four Winds, 1976, 30p., Picture Book, LC 80-17315, ISBN 0-590-07763-5.

Glee 'Nasbah is a Navajo Indian weaver who lives in the Navajo Nation at Indian Rock, Arizona, with her goat Geraldine. Geraldine describes each step of the rug-making process from hair clipping and carding to the dyeing and weaving. Based on a real Navajo weaver. A Reading Rainbow book.

GLENDA

Christelow, Eileen, **Robbery at the Diamond Dog Diner, The**, illustrated by Ellen Christelow, Clarion, 1986, 30p., Picture Book, LC 86-2682, ISBN 0-89919-425-7; 0-89919-722-1 (pbk).

Glenda Feathers, the hen, suggests a way that her friend can hide her diamonds from the robbers that are in town. This causes the thieves to capture Glenda with humorous results. A Reading Rainbow book.

Wolkoff, Judie, **In a Pig's Eye**, Bradbury, 1986, 154p., Fiction, ISBN 0-02-793370-9.

In fourth grade, Glenda and her friend have many neighborhood adventures including the publication of a gossipy newspaper and entering their dogs in a dog show.

GLENMAE

Blood, Charles L. and Martin Link, **Goat in the Rug, The**, illustrated by Nancy Winslow Parker, Four Winds, 1976, 30p., Picture Book, LC 80-17315, ISBN 0-590-07763-5.

Glee 'Nasbah (Glenmae) is a Navajo weaver. She and her goat Geraldine live in the Navajo Nation at Indian Rock, Arizona. Geraldine describes each step of the rug-making process from hair clipping and carding to the dyeing and weaving. Based on a real Navajo weaver. A Reading Rainbow book.

GLORIA
See also Glorietta

Haywood, Carolyn, **Eddie's Menagerie**, Morrow, 1978, Fiction, ISBN 0-688-32158-5.

When Gloria's cat is poisoned, her friend Eddie Wilson helps her. Utah 1981.

GLORIETTA
See also Gloria

Fleischman, Sid, **Humbug Mountain**, illustrated by Eric von Schmidt, Little, Brown, 1978, 149p., Fiction, LC 78-9419, ISBN 0-316-28569-2.

Glorietta and her brother, Wiley, live near Humbug Mountain. They have many humorous adventures as they discover a petrified man, their mother's chicken starts a gold rush, and Wiley discovers notorious villains. 1979 Boston Globe-Horn Book Award.

GOLDIE

Goffstein, M. B., **Goldie the Dollmaker**, illustrated by M. B. Goffstein, Farrar, Straus & Giroux, 1969, 55p., Fiction, ISBN 0-374-32739-4.

Goldie is an orphan who lives alone in the forest lovingly carving dolls. When she buys a lamp she cannot afford she comes to realize the joy that her dolls bring to others.

GRACE
See also Gracie

Giff, Patricia Reilly, **Gift of the Pirate Queen, The**, illustrated by Jenny Rutherford, Delacorte, 1982, 164p., Fiction, ISBN 0-385-28339-3.

Grace O'Malley is in sixth grade and has been responsible for the household since her mother's death. Grace is afraid of being replaced when a middle-aged cousin comes from Ireland for an extended visit.

Raskin, Ellen, **Westing Game, The**, Dutton, 1978, 185p., Fiction, LC 77-18866, ISBN 0-525-42320-6.

Grace is one of the sixteen people invited to the reading of the very strange will of the very rich Samuel W. Westing. She could become a millionaire, depending on how she plays the tricky and dangerous Westing Game. 1979 Newbery Award book. 1978 Boston Globe-Horn Book Award. Michigan 1982.

GRACIE
See also Grace

Roberts, Willo Davis, **What Could Go Wrong?**, Atheneum, 1989, 167p., Fiction, ISBN 0-689-31438-8.

Gracie and her cousins fly from San Francisco to Seattle and become involved in a mystery full of suspense.

GREG
See also Gregory

Shura, Mary Francis, **Josie Gambit**, Dodd, Mead, 1986, 160p., Fiction, ISBN 0-396-08810-4.

Greg spends six months with his grandmother and renews a friendship with another boy who plays chess as well as he does. The two boys become involved in a cruel scheme that is set up by a third boy.

Spinelli, Jerry, **Who Put That Hair in My Toothbrush?**, Little, Brown, 1984, 220p., Fiction, ISBN 0-316-80712-5.

Alternating chapters tell each character's point of view as Greg and his younger sister have one problem after another.

GREGORY
See also Greg

Bulla, Clyde Robert, **Chalk Box Kid**, illustrated by Thomas Allen, Random House, 1988, 59p., Easy Reader, ISBN 0-394-99102-8.

There is no room for a garden at Gregory's new house, so he uses his chalk to draw one on a wall.

Sharmat, Mitchell, **Gregory, the Terrible Eater**, illustrated by Jose Aruego and Ariane Dewey, Four Winds, 1980, 28p., Picture Book, LC 85-29290, ISBN 0-02-782250-8.

Gregory the goat is a very picky eater. Instead of eating the usual goat foods like old shoes and tin cans, Gregory likes to eat fruits, vegetables, eggs, and orange juice. A Reading Rainbow book.

GRETA

Sauer, Julia, **Fog Magic**, Viking, 1943, 107p., Fiction, LC 43-14784, ISBN 670-32303-9.

All of her life, Greta has loved the fog surrounding her village in Nova Scotia. When she is ten, she begins to sense that there is something she is looking for in the fog. 1944 Newbery Honor book.

GRETCHEN

Gormley, Beatrice, **Fifth Grade Magic**, illustrated by Emily Arnold McCully, Dutton, 1982, 131p., Fiction, ISBN 0-525-44007-0.

Gretchen loves acting and looks forward to a part in the fifth-grade play. When she does not get a part, Gretchen wished for, and got, a fairy godmother, but things don't work out as the two plan.

GRETEL

Lesser, Rika, **Hansel and Gretel**, illustrated by Paul O. Zelinsky, Dodd, Mead, 1984, 32p., Picture Book, LC 84-8110, ISBN 0-396-08449-4.

Gretel and her brother are the children of a poor woodcutter. While lost in the woods they come across a candy house and a wicked witch who likes to have children for dinner. 1985 Caldecott Honor book.

GUIDO

Haugaard, Erik Christian, **Little Fishes, The**, illustrated by Milton Johnson, Houghton Mifflin, 1967, 215p., Fiction, LC 67-14701, ISBN 0-395-06802-9.

Guido is a twelve-year-old orphan who begs to survive in occupied Italy during World War II. He learns that compassion and understanding will help him survive as he searches for his daily food while witnessing the tragedy of war. 1968 Jane Addams Award book. 1967 Boston Globe-Horn Book Award.

GUS

Fox, Paula, **Stone-Faced Boy**, illustrated by Donald A. Mackay, Bradbury, 1968, 106p., Fiction, ISBN 0-02-735570-5.

Gus is the middle child in a family of five children. He has learned to protect his feelings by neither frowning nor smiling and he thinks that his face has turned to stone.

GUY

Williams, Vera B., **More, More, More Said the Baby**, illustrated by Vera B. Williams, Greenwillow, 1990, 32p., Picture Book, LC 89-2023, ISBN 0-688-09173-3; 0-688-09174-1 (lib).

Little Guy is one of the babies in the three short stories in this book. 1991 Caldecott Honor book.

GWEN
See also Gwendolen, Gwyn

Carris, Joan, **Witch-Cat**, illustrated by Beth Peck, Lippincott, 1984, 154p., Fiction, ISBN 0-397-32068-X.

An experienced witch-cat is supposed to help Gwen recognize her witch powers in present-day Ohio. Their experiences include a trip through time.

GWENDOLEN
See also Gwen, Gwyn

Jones, Diana Wynne, **Charmed Life**, Greenwillow, 1977, 218p., Fiction, ISBN 0-688-84138-4.

Gwendolen is a witch and uses her abilities to work magic. Her sister is unaware that she, too, is a witch. When their parents die, the girls are sent to live in an elegant castle full of witches.

GWYN
See also Gwen, Gwendolen

Nimmo, Jenny, **Snow Spider**, Dutton, 1986, 136p., Fiction, ISBN 0-525-44306-1.

Gwyn receives unusual gifts for his tenth birthday and has to discover if he has inherited the family's magical powers.

Voight, Cynthia, **Jackaroo**, Atheneum, 1985, 291p., Fiction, ISBN 0-689-31123-0.

Set in the Middle Ages, Gwyn is the daughter of an innkeeper who finds the costume of the legendary Jackaroo, a character similar to Robin Hood.

-H-

HADIYA

Walter, Mildred Pitts, **Justin and the Best Biscuits in the World**, illustrated by Catherine Stock, Lothrop, Lee & Shepard, 1986, 122p., Fiction, LC 86-7148, ISBN 0-688-06645-3.

Hadiya is one of Justin's sisters. Justin is tired of his mother and sisters always fussing at him and he is glad to go to his grandfather's ranch for a visit. While there, Justin discovers that cooking and keeping house aren't just women's work. 1987 Coretta Scott King Award book.

HAL

Evans, Hubert, **Son of the Salmon People**, Harbour, 1981, 167p., Fiction, ISBN 0-920080-28-6.

After completing high school, Hal Radigan returns to his Indian home and finds that the small community is being run by a strange and cruel white man. Originally published under the title *Mountain Dog* in 1956.

HALLIE

Beatty, Patricia, **That's One Ornery Orphan**, Morrow, 1980, 222p., Fiction, ISBN 0-688-32227-1.

Hallie is very unhappy at the orphanage where she is sent. Although she is selected to live with three very different families, there are problems at each one. Hallie finally finds happiness with a family that she had been avoiding. Set in Texas in the nineteenth century.

Corcoran, Barbara, **Sasha, My Friend**, illustrated by Richard L. Shell, Atheneum, 1971, 203p., Fiction, LC 69-18968.

Hallie adjusts to an isolated life in Montana with the help of an orphaned wolf pup. Kansas 1972.

HANK
See also Henry

Stahl, Ben, **Blackbeard's Ghost**, illustrated by Ben Stahl, Houghton Mifflin, 1965, 184p., Fiction, LC 65-11022, ISBN 0-395-07115-1.

Hank and J. D. explore the old Boar's Head Tavern as it is being torn down. When they find remnants from long ago, they bring back the ghost of Blackbeard and a witch who had lived in those times. Oklahoma 1969.

HANNAH

Dabcovich, Lydia, **Mrs. Huggins and Her Hen Hannah**, illustrated by Lydia Dabcovich, Dutton, 1985, 22p., Picture Book, LC 85-4406, ISBN 0-525-44203-0.

Mrs. Huggins and her hen Hannah do everything together including the cooking, the cleaning, the washing, and other chores. A Reading Rainbow book.

Schur, Maxine, **Hannah Szenes: A Song of Light**, illustrated by Donna Ruff, Jewish Publication Society, 1986, 106p., Nonfiction, ISBN 0-8276-0251-0.

The true story of Hannah Szenes who escaped the Nazis by going to Israel, then trained to be a spy in Yugoslavia.

Yolen, Jane, **Devil's Arithmetic**, Viking Kestrel, 1988, 170p., Fiction, ISBN 0-670-81027-4.

Thirteen-year-old Hannah is taken back in time to a Polish village in 1942. There she learns about the horrors that were experienced by her grandfather and an aunt during the Holocaust. 1989 National Jewish Book Award.

HANS
See also Hansel

Dodge, Mary Mapes, **Hans Brinker**, illustrated by Cyrus Leroy Baldridge, Grosset & Dunlap, 1945, 314p., Fiction, ISBN 0-448-06011-6.

The classic story of Hans, a young boy in Holland who dreams of winning a pair of silver skates at the skating race.

Greene, Carol, **Hans Christian Andersen: Teller of Tales**, Children's Press, 1986, 128p., Nonfiction, ISBN 0-516-03216-X.

Hans Christian Andersen became a famous author in spite of his lack of both schooling and confidence. His determination helped him to become a major author for the theater and of short stories. A biography about the author, which includes his childhood.

Verne, Jules, **Journey to the Center of the Earth**, Dodd, Mead, 1979, 226p., Fiction, ISBN 0-396-08429-X.

A revised edition of the classic science fiction story. Hans is the guide who takes a group to the center of the earth where they find huge forests, prehistoric monsters, and amazing adventures.

HANSEL
See also Hans

Lesser, Rika, **Hansel and Gretel**, illustrated by Paul O. Zelinsky, Dodd, Mead, 1984, 32p., Picture Book, LC 84-8110, ISBN 0-396-08449-4.

Hansel and his sister are the children of a poor woodcutter. While lost in the woods, they come across a house made of candy and a wicked witch who likes to have children for dinner. 1985 Caldecott Honor book.

HARLEY

Wojciechowska, Maia, **Hey, What's Wrong With This One?**, illustrated by Joan Sandin, Harper & Row, 1969, 72p., Fiction, LC 67-14071, ISBN 0-06-026579-5.

After their mother dies, Harley and his two brothers live with their dad and a succession of housekeepers. Housekeepers keep quitting because of the boys' messes, noise, and pranks. The boys know they need a mother. Georgia 1973.

HAROLD
See also Harry

Howe, Deborah and James Howe, **Bunnicula: A Rabbit Tale of Mystery**, illustrated by Alan Daniel,

Atheneum, 1979, 98p., Fiction, LC 78-11472, ISBN 0-689-30700-4.

Harold, the dog, and Chester, the cat, become concerned about the baby bunny that the Monroe children found at the movie and brought home. The rabbit only sleeps from sunup to sundown and the family finds two fang marks on vegetables that have been drained of their color. Harold and Chester suspect the rabbit is a vampire. Florida 1984. Hawaii 1983. Iowa 1982. Nebraska 1981. New Mexico 1982. Oklahoma 1982. Pacific Northwest 1982. South Carolina 1981. Vermont 1981.

Treece, Henry, **Viking's Dawn**, illustrated by Christine Price, G. Phillips, 1956, 252p., Fiction, ISBN 0-87599-117-3.

Young Harold joins the crew of a great Viking warrior and they set sail to the coasts of Ireland and Scotland. An exciting adventure in which Harold becomes the sole survivor of the journey. There is another book about Harold.

HARRIET

Carlson, Nancy, **Harriet's Recital**, illustrated by Nancy Carlson, Carolrhoda, 1982, 28p., Picture Book, LC 81-18135, ISBN 0-87614-181-5.

Harriet loved her ballet class, but hated the yearly recital and worried constantly about how she might fail. She overcomes her stage fright in this story. A Reading Rainbow book.

Carlson, Nancy, **Loudmouth George and the Sixth-Grade Bully**, illustrated by Nancy Carlson, Carolrhoda, 1983, 30p., Picture Book, LC 83-7178, ISBN 0-87614-217-X (lib).

After having his lunch taken repeatedly by a bully twice his size, George and his friend Harriet decided to play a trick to teach the bully a lesson. A Reading Rainbow book.

Ferris, Jeri, **Go Free or Die**, illustrated by Karen Ritz, Carolrhoda, 1988, 63p., Nonfiction, ISBN 0-87614-317-6.

Harriet Tubman was involved in the underground railroad and led over 300 slaves to freedom. Biographical information tells of her courage and determination to help her people.

Fitzhugh, Louise, **Harriet the Spy**, illustrated by Louise Fitzhugh, Harper & Row, 1964, 298p., Fiction, LC 64-19711, ISBN 0-06-021910-6.

Eleven-year-old Harriet keeps notes on her classmates and neighbors in a secret notebook, but when some of the students read the notebook, they seek revenge. Oklahoma 1967.

Scott, John Anthony, **Woman Against Slavery: The Story of Harriet Beecher Stowe**, Crowell, 1978, 169p., Nonfiction, ISBN 0-690-03844-5.

A biography about Harriet Beecher Stowe that includes information about the times in which she lived and her work to abolish slavery.

Streatfield, Noel, **Skating Shoes**, Dell, 1982, 221p., Fiction, ISBN 0-440-47731-X (pbk).

Nine-year-old Harriet has been told to take skating lessons by her doctor in order to build up her strength. At the skating rink she discovers she has talent and makes a new friend.

Waddell, Martin, **Harriet and the Haunted School**, illustrated by Mark Burgess, Little, Brown, 1985, 84p., Fiction, ISBN 0-316-91623-4.

Eleven-year-old Harriet has a talent for creating mischief. When she kidnaps a circus horse and hides it in a school closet, it is mistaken for a ghost with humorous results.

HARRISON
See also Harry

Hooks, William, **Circle of Fire**, Atheneum/Margaret K. McElderry Book, 1921, 147p., Fiction, ISBN 0-689-50241-9.

Eleven-year-old Harrison Hawkins learns about prejudice when he overhears members of the Ku Klux Klan planning an attack. Set in North Carolina in the mid-1930s.

HARRY
See also Harold, Harrison

Cohen, Barbara, **Carp in the Bathtub**, illustrated by Joan Halpern, Lothrop, Lee & Shepard, 1972, 48p., Fiction, ISBN 0-688-51627-0.

Harry and his sister make friends with the fish that their mother brings home to cook.

Collins, David R., **Harry S. Truman, 33rd President of the United States**, Garrett, 1988, 121p., Nonfiction, ISBN 0-944483-00-3.

Harry S. Truman was a president of the United States. This biography provides information about the man and the events during his presidential years.

Gilden, Mel, **Harry Newberry and the Raiders of the Red Drink**, H. Holt, 1989, 151p., Fiction, ISBN 0-8050-0698-2.

Harry is a fan of comic books. He battles evil with the help of superheroes and thinks his mother may be a superwoman.

King-Smith, Dick, **Harry's Mad**, illustrated by Jill Bennet, Crown, 1984, 123p., Fiction, ISBN 0-517-56254-5.

Ten-year-old Harry receives an African gray parrot from his great uncle's estate. The parrot is intelligent and articulate and the two become friends.

King-Smith, Dick, **Harry's Mad**, Crown, 1987, 123p., Fiction, ISBN 0-517-5625-45.

Harry receives a talking parrot from his great-uncle's estate. The gift is a much more exciting gift than Harry had anticipated. California 1991.

Marney, Dean, **Computer That Ate My Brother, The**, Houghton Mifflin, 1985, 124p., Fiction, ISBN 0-395-37027-2.

Harry discovers that the computer he received for his twelfth birthday has unusual powers after his older brother disappears.

McCloskey, Robert, **Time of Wonder**, illustrated by Robert McCloskey, Viking, 1957, 63p., Picture Book, ISBN 0-670-71512-3.

Harry Smith, Clyde Snowman, and Ferd Clifford are a few of the people that live on the island where the children and their parents vacation in the summer. 1958 Caldecott Award book.

McKinley, Robin, **Blue Sword, The**, Greenwillow, 1982, 272p., Fiction, LC 82-2895, ISBN 0-688-00938-7.

When Harry Crew's father died she left her homeland to travel to Istan, the last outpost of the Homelander empire, to be with her older brother. Harry discovered magic in herself when she was kidnapped by a native king with mysterious powers. 1983 Newbery Honor book.

Selden, George, **Harry Cat's Pet Puppy**, illustrated by Garth Williams, Farrar, Straus & Giroux, 1974, 167p., Fiction, ISBN 0-374-328-560.

Harry Cat and Tucker Mouse try to find a permanent home for a stray puppy that they have found. There is another book about these two friends. Kansas 1977.

HARVEY

Byars, Betsy, **Pinballs, The**, Harper & Row, 1977, 136p., Fiction, LC 76-41518, ISBN 0-06-020917-8; 0-06-020918-6 (lib).

Pinballs don't get to settle where they want to, and neither do foster children. Harvey, Carlie, and Thomas are three lonely children who have been disappointed by their own parents. But under the influence of their foster parents and each other, they decide they really aren't pinballs. Arkansas 1980. California 1980. Georgia 1979. Kansas 1980. Minnesota 1986. Mississippi 1980.

Clifford, Eth, **Harvey's Horrible Snake Disaster**, Houghton Mifflin, 1984, 108p., Fiction, ISBN 0-395-35378-5.

Ten-year-old Harvey has more misadventures than usual when a snake is kidnapped during his cousin Nora's annual visit. Although the two have never been friends, Harvey begins to appreciate Nora.

Cone, Molly, **Amazing Memory of Harvey Bean**, illustrated by Robert MacLean, Houghton Mifflin, 1980, 83p., Fiction, ISBN 0-395-29181-X.

Harvey has a terrible memory. When his parents separate and Harvey goes to live with an unusual couple, he has a wonderful time and learns a way to remember things.

Gilson, Jamie, **Harvey, the Beer Can King**, illustrated by John Wallner, Lothrop, Lee & Shepard, 1978, 127p., Fiction, ISBN 0-688-02382-7.

Harvey thinks he can win the Superkid contest but finds he has many problems in this humorous story of his misadventures. There is another book about Harvey.

HAZEL

Adams, Richard, **Watership Down**, Macmillan, 1972, 429p., Fiction, ISBN 0-02-700030-3.

Hazel is the modest and unassuming leader of a group of rabbits searching for a new location that is safe. Their search includes many adventures before they finally discover Watership Down. California 1977.

Cleaver, Vera and Bill Cleaver, **Hazel Rye**, Lippincott, 1983, 178p., Fiction, ISBN 0-397-31952-5.

Eleven-year-old Hazel wants to be rich, but she doesn't want to have to go to school so she comes up with a money-making scheme that backfires.

HEATHER

Service, Pamela, **Winter of Magic's Return**, Atheneum, 1985, 192p., Fiction, ISBN 0-689-31130-3.

Heather and several other children embark on a quest across a world changed by a 500-year winter brought on by a nuclear holocaust. There is another book about Heather.

Tapp, Kathy Kennedy, **Smoke from the Chimney**, Macmillan, 1986, 169p., Fiction, ISBN 0-689-50389-X.

Heather and her friend escape to a fantasy world after reading the adventures of Tarzan.

Yolen, Jane, **Transfigured Hart**, illustrated by Donna Diamond, Crowell, 1975, 86p., Fiction, ISBN 0-690-00736-1.

Heather and her neighbor see a white hart in the woods, which they become convinced is a unicorn.

HECTOR

Merrill, Jean, **Toothpaste Millionaire, The**, illustrated by Jan Palmer, Houghton Mifflin, 1972, 90p., Fiction, LC 73-22055, ISBN 0-395-18511-4; 0-395-11186-2 (pbk).

Kate tells the story of her friend and classmate, Rufus Mayflower, and how he became a millionaire between sixth and eighth grade. After building up a business, Rufus decided to try something else and sells his business to his friend, Hector. Oklahoma 1977. Vermont 1976.

Wrightson, Patricia, **Little Fear, A**, Atheneum, 1985, 111p., Fiction, LC 83-2784, ISBN 0-689-50291-5.

Mrs. Tucker disliked living in the old people's home so she got herself a dog, Hector, and went to live in a small cottage on a ridge above the swamp flats. Mrs. Tucker is unaware that an ancient gnome also lives in the area and the two have a desperate struggle. 1984 Boston Globe-Horn Book Award.

HEIDI

Mills, Claudia, **After Fifth Grade, the World**, Macmillan, 1989, 125p., Fiction, ISBN 0-02-767041-4.

Ten-year-old Heidi is in fifth grade and knows exactly what she wants, including changing her teacher's rigid ways.

Spyri, Johanna, **Heidi**, illustrated by Ruth Sanderson, Knopf, 1984, 285p., Fiction, ISBN 0-394-53820-X.

The classic story of a young girl who lives happily in the Alps of Switzerland with her grandfather until she is forced to move to the city and become the companion of a crippled girl.

HELEN

DeClements, Barthe, **Sixth Grade Can Really Kill You**, Viking Kestrel, 1985, 146p., Fiction, LC 85-40382, ISBN 0-670-80656-0.

Sixth grade holds some terrible problems for 'bad Helen', the self-proclaimed rowdiest kid in school. If she can't improve her reading skills, Helen is afraid that she will be stuck in the sixth grade forever. New Mexico 1989. New York 1989. Ohio 1989. Pacific Northwest 1988.

Peare, Catherine Owens, **Helen Keller Story, The**, Crowell, 1959, 183p., Nonfiction, LC 59-10979, ISBN 0-690-37520-4.

This biography tells the story of Helen Keller who was born deaf and blind yet as an adult she became an advocate for the blind due to the influence of her teacher. Kansas 1962. Oklahoma 1962.

Sloan, Carolyn, **Helen Keller**, illustrated by Karen Heywood, Hamish Hamilton, 1984, 60p., Nonfiction, ISBN 0-241-11295-8.

The biography of Helen Keller who was unable to hear or see, yet was able to learn and became a spokesperson for the rights of the handicapped.

Taylor, Theodore, **Trouble with Tuck, The**, Doubleday, 1981, 110p., Fiction, ISBN 0-385-17774-7.

When her beloved pet dog begins losing its sight, Helen and her family take unusual measures and locate a guide dog for their pet. Based on a true incident. California 1984.

HELGA

Lindquist, Jennie, **Golden Name Day, The**, illustrated by Garth Williams, Harper & Row, 1955, 248p., Fiction, LC 55-8823, ISBN 0-06-023881-X.

While nine-year-old Nancy is staying with her adopted Swedish grandparents for a year, Helga and the others try to figure out how Nancy can celebrate a name day since her name is not Swedish. 1956 Newbery Honor book.

McSwigan, Marie, **Snow Treasure**, illustrated by Mary Reardon, Dutton, 1942, 179p., Fiction, ISBN 0-525-39556-3.

Helga and other Norwegian children slipped past Nazi soldiers with sleds loaded with gold. The gold was taken twelve miles to a freighter hidden in one of the fiords off Norway's coast. Based on an actual event. In June 1940 the Norwegian freighter reached Baltimore with a cargo of gold worth 9 million dollars. Pacific Northwest 1945.

HENRY
See also Hank

Barrett, Judith, **Cloudy with a Chance of Meatballs**, illustrated by Ron Barrett, Atheneum, 1985, 30p., Picture Book, LC 78-2945, ISBN 0-689-30647-4.

Henry's grandfather tells a tall-tale bedtime story about the town of Chewandswallow where people don't need food stores because it rains soup and juice, snows mashed potatoes, and has hamburger storms. Colorado 1980. Georgia 1984. Nebraska 1982.

Bawden, Nina, **Henry**, illustrated by Joyce Powzyk, Lothrop, Lee & Shepard, 1988, 119p., Fiction, ISBN 0-688-07894-X.

Henry is a baby squirrel that has fallen from his nest. A London family that has been evacuated to the country during World War II tries to raise the young squirrel.

Brittain, Bill, **Wish Giver: Three Tales of Coven Tree, The**, illustrated by Andrew Glass, Harper & Row, 1983, 181p., Fiction, LC 82-48264, ISBN 0-06-020686-1; 0-06-020687-X (lib).

Thaddeus Blinn was a funny little man who appeared from out of nowhere and put his tent by the annual Coven Tree Church Social. He said he had the power to give people exactly what they asked for. Henry is one of the characters who finds that wishes often have unexpected results when they come true. 1984 Newbery Honor book.

Calhoun, Mary, **Cross-Country Cat**, illustrated by Erick Ingraham, Morrow, 1979, 40p., Picture Book, LC 78-31718, ISBN 0-688-22186-6; 0-688-32186-6 (lib).

Henry the cat can walk on his hind legs. When his family goes to their mountain cabin for a weekend, the boy makes a pair of cross-country skis for Henry. The skis come in handy when Henry gets left behind. Colorado 1981. Washington 1982. Wisconsin 1980.

Calhoun, Mary, **Hot-Air Henry**, illustrated by Erick Ingraham, Morrow, 1981, 38p., Picture Book, LC 80-26189, ISBN 0-688-04068-3 (pbk).

Henry is a Siamese cat that wants to fly in a hot-air balloon like the rest of his human family. Taking a chance, he stows away for an exciting flight across the mountains. A Reading Rainbow book.

Cleary, Beverly, **Henry and Ribsy**, illustrated by Louis Darling, Morrow, 1954, 192p., Fiction, LC 54-6402.

Mr. Huggins promises his son, Henry, that he will take him salmon fishing if Henry can keep his dog, Ribsy, from annoying the neighbors. In humorous episodes, Ribsy continuously gets into trouble, and so does Henry. Hawaii 1968. Pacific Northwest 1957. Vermont 1966.

Cleary, Beverly, **Henry and the Paper Route**, illustrated by Louis Darling, Morrow, 1957, 192p., Fiction, LC 57-8562, ISBN 0-688-31380-9.

Humorous events occur when Henry Huggins decides to deliver newspapers and is helped by his neighbor, Ramona Quimby. Pacific Northwest 1960.

Cleary, Beverly, **Henry Huggins**, illustrated by Louis Darling, Morrow, 1950, 155p., Fiction, ISBN 0-688-31385-X.

Henry Huggins finds a stray dog and names him Ribsy. The two have numerous adventures including breeding fish and collecting worms.

Cleary, Beverly, **Ribsy**, illustrated by Louis Darling, Morrow, 1964, 192p., Fiction, LC 64-13263, ISBN 0-688-21662-5.

Ribsy had gotten lost from his owner, Henry Huggins. The city dog has many unpredictable and humorous adventures before he is reunited with Henry. Hawaii 1968. Pacific Northwest 1957. Vermont 1966.

Gillies, John, **Senor Alcalde: A Biography of Henry Cisneros**, Dillon, 1988, 127p., Nonfiction, ISBN 0-87518-374-3.

Henry Cisneros is a Mexican-American who has set high goals for himself and believes that he can reach any goal he sets. He was elected the first Mexican-American mayor of San Antonio, Texas.

This biography provides information about the man and his work.

Mitchell, Barbara, **We'll Race You, Henry: A Story about Henry Ford**, illustrated by Kathy Haubrich, Carolrhoda, 1986, 56p., Nonfiction, ISBN 0-87614-291-9.

Henry Ford was born on a farm and moved to Detroit when he was young. He spent his life inventing and producing automobiles. This biography gives information about the man and his desire to make a better vehicle for mass production.

Robertson, Keith, **Henry Reed, Inc.**, illustrated by Robert McCloskey, Viking, 1958, 239p., Fiction, LC 58-4758, ISBN 0-670-36796-6.

Henry Reed's father is in the diplomatic service and Henry attends the American school in Naples, Italy. Henry is sent to spend the summer with his aunt and uncle in a small New Jersey town to learn about America. He has a summer filled with humorous adventures as he goes into business for himself. Kansas 1961.

Robertson, Keith, **Henry Reed's Baby-Sitting Service**, illustrated by Robert McCloskey, Viking, 1966, 205p., Fiction, LC 66-11908, ISBN 0-670-36825-3.

Henry Reed spends his second summer with his aunt and uncle in Grove's Corner, New Jersey. After surveying the small community to see what type of business to open, Henry decides upon a baby-sitting service with humorous results. Hawaii 1970. Kansas 1969. Pacific Northwest 1969.

Smith, Robert Kimmel, **Chocolate Fever**, illustrated by Gioia Fiammenghi, Putnam, 1972, 93p., Fiction, ISBN 0-399-61224-6.

Henry Green loved chocolate more than anyone in the world until brown spots began popping out all over him and he was diagnosed as having chocolate fever. Massachusetts 1980.

Warner, Gertrude Chandler, **Boxcar Children, The**, illustrated by L. Kate Deal, Whitman, 1950, 154p., Fiction, ISBN 0-8075-0851-9.

Henry and the other three Alden children take refuge in an old boxcar to avoid being sent to live in an institution. This is the first in a series of books about this family.

HERBERT
See also Herbie

Hilton, Suzanne, **World of Young Herbert Hoover, The**, illustrated by Deborah Steins, Walker, 1987, 103p., Nonfiction, ISBN 0-8027-6709-5.

A biography of former President Herbert Hoover, from his difficult childhood through his college years at Stanford University.

HERBIE
See also Herbert

Chapman, Carol, **Herbie's Troubles**, Dutton, 1981, 32p., Picture Book, LC 80-0827, ISBN 0-525-3164-50.

Herbie changes his mind about school when he meets a new boy. California 1985. Georgia 1983.

Kline, Suzy, **Herbie Jones**, illustrated by Richard Williams, Putnam, 1985, 96p., Fiction, LC 84-24915, ISBN 0-399-21183-7.

Third grade has its ups and downs for Herbie Jones and his best friend, Raymond. They get invited to a birthday party for the smartest girl in the class, and they also get into trouble on a class field trip to the museum. Both boys are tired of being in the lowest reading group, and when one gets good grades on spelling tests, he knows he has to help the other. West Virginia 1988.

Kline, Suzy, **Herbie Jones and the Class Gift**, illustrated by Richard Williams, Putnam, 1987, 94p., Fiction, ISBN 0-399-21452-6.

At the end of third grade, Herbie Jones tries to figure out how to earn money so he can help to buy a class gift for the teacher.

HERSCHEL
See also Hershel

Singer, Isaac Bashevis, **Fearsome Inn, The**, illustrated by Nonny Hogrogian, Scribner, 1967, 42p., Fiction, LC 67-23693, ISBN 0-689-70769-X.

All roads lead to the inn and when helpless winter travelers stumble in, they become the victims of the owners, a witch and her husband. Herschel and his companions break the spell cast over the inn and rescue the three girls held captive as servants. 1968 Newbery Honor book.

HERSHEL
See also Herschel

Kimmel, Eric, **Hershel and the Hanukkah Goblins**, illustrated by Trina Schart Hyman, Holiday House, 1989, 32p., Picture Book, ISBN 0-8234-0769-1.

Hershel outwits the goblins that haunt the old synagogue and prevent the villagers from celebrating Hanukkah. 1990 Caldecott Honor book.

HILARY
See also Hillary

Bawden, Nina, **Devil by the Sea**, Lippincott, 1976, 228p., Fiction, ISBN 0-397-31683-6.

Nine-year-old Hilary is convinced that an old man she saw is the Devil and that he was with a friend before the man was murdered.

HILLARY
See also Hilary

Lisle, Janet Taylor, **Afternoon of the Elves**, Orchard, 1980, 122p., Fiction, LC 88-35099, ISBN 0-531-05837-9; 0-531-08437-X (lib).

Nine-year-old Hillary becomes curious about Sara-Kate and the life she leads in the big, gloomy house she shares with her mysterious, silent mother as the two girls work in the miniature village in the backyard, which Sara-Kate says was built by elves. 1990 Newbery Honor book.

HITTY

Field, Rachel, **Hitty: Her First Hundred Years**, illustrated by Dorothy P. Lathrop, Macmillan, 1929, 207p., Fiction, ISBN 0-02-734840-7.

Hitty is an antique wooden doll. As she sits in the window of a New York antique shop, Hitty tells the story of her adventures during her 100 year life. 1930 Newbery Award book.

HOA

Surat, Michele Maria, **Angel Child, Dragon Child**, illustrated by Vo-Dinh Mai, Raintree, 1983, Picture Book, LC 83-8606, ISBN 0-940742-12-8.

As the youngest child, Nguyen Hoa is called Ut. While she attends school in the United States, she is lonely for her mother who is still in Vietnam. One of Ut's classmates suggests holding a special fair to help raise money for transporation for Ut's mother. A Reading Rainbow book.

HOBIE

Gilson, Jamie, **Thirteen Ways to Sink a Sub**, illustrated by Linda Strauss Edwards, Lothrop, Lee & Shepard, 1982, 140p., Fiction, LC 82-141, ISBN 0-688-01304-X.

Hobie Hansen and his friend Nick await the time when their fourth-grade class will have a substitute teacher. When they finally have a substitute, the class has a contest to 'sink' the sub. New Mexico 1986. Ohio 1987. Oklahoma 1985. Pacific Northwest 1985.

HOLLY

Kaufman, Charles, **Frog and the Beanpole**, illustrated by Troy Howell, Lothrop, Lee & Shepard, 1980, 189p., Fiction, ISBN 0-688-41938-0.

Holly is a foster child who feels rejected by life. She becomes friends with an unusual frog and the two run away and join a circus.

Streatfield, Noel, **Theatre Shoes**, Dell, 1985, 288p., Fiction, ISBN 0-440-48791-9 (pbk).

Holly and her siblings are taken in by their grandmother who is a famous actress. The children are enrolled in an acting academy with varying degrees of success. The book is set in 1945 and the children anxiously await the return of their father who is a prisoner of war.

HOMER

McCloskey, Robert, **Homer Price**, illustrated by Robert McCloskey, Viking, 1971, 149p., Fiction, LC 43-16001, ISBN 670-37729-5.

Six humorous stories about Homer Price, his family, and friends. In one episode, Homer and his pet skunk capture four bandits. In another his donut machine goes on the rampage. Pacific Northwest 1947.

Peet, Bill, **Fly Homer Fly**, Houghton Mifflin, 1969, 60p., Fiction, ISBN 0-395-24536-2.

Homer is a pigeon that decides to leave the farm and fly to the city where he makes friends with sparrows and injures himself.

Updike, David, **Autumn Tale, An**, illustrated by Robert Andrew Parker, Pippin Press, 1988, 40p., Fiction, ISBN 0-945912-02-1.

The night before Halloween, Homer puts a large hole in the bottom of a jack-o'-lantern so he can wear it on his head, thus beginning an eerie adventure.

HOPESTILL

Snedeker, Caroline, **Downright Dencey**, illustrated by Maginel Wright Barney, Doubleday, 1927, 314p., Fiction, ISBN 0-385-07284-8.

Hopestill is one of the Quaker children who live in Nantucket during the early part of the twentieth century. Her life revolves around family, school, friends and religion. 1928 Newbery Honor book.

HORACE

MacLachlan, Patricia, **Unclaimed Treasures**, Harper & Row, 1984, 118p., Fiction, ISBN 0-06-024094-6.

Horace looks back to a special summer when he learned about friendship, family, and himself.

HOWARD

Jones, Diana Wynne, **Archer's Goon**, Greenwillow, 1984, 241p., Fiction, ISBN 0-688-02582-X.

In this suspenseful fantasy, thirteen-year-old Howard Sykes discovers some interesting information about his father and the seven wizards who run the town.

Park, Barbara, **Kid in the Red Jacket, The**, Knopf, 1987, 94p., Fiction, ISBN 0-394-98189-8.

Howard is ten years old when his parents decide to move across country. Howard is concerned about going to a new school, and making friends.

HU
See also Hugh

Chrisman, Arthur Bowie, **Shen of the Sea: Chinese Stories for Children**, illustrated by Else Hasselriis, Dutton, 1953, 219p., Fiction, LC 68-13420, ISBN 0-525-39244-0.

Meng Hu is just one of the characters that appears in these sixteen Chinese short stories. 1926 Newbery Award book.

HUGH
See also Hu

Snyder, Zilpha Keatley, **Changing Maze, The**, illustrated by Charles Mikolaycak, Macmillan, 1985, 96p., Fiction, ISBN 0-02-785900-2.

A mysterious story filled with suspense as Hugh searches for his lost pet lamb in the snowy hills and has adventures in the valley.

Sutcliff, Rosemary, **Brother Dusty-Feet**, illustrated by C. Walter Hodges, Oxford, 1979, 231p., Fiction, ISBN 0-19-271444-9.

Set in Elizabethan England, Hugh is an eleven-year-old orphan who runs away from cruel relatives to join a group of strolling actors and finds that he enjoys the freedom of the road.

Van de Wetering, Janwillem, **Hugh Pine and the Good Place**, illustrated by Lynn Munsinger, Houghton Mifflin, 1986, 64p., Fiction, ISBN 0-395-40147-X.

Hugh Pine is a porcupine. He moves to a small deserted island in search of a Good Place, only to find that the peaceful solitude is lonely.

-I-

IAN

Arnosky, Jim, **Gray Boy**, Lothrop, Lee & Shepard, 1988, 82p., Fiction, ISBN 0-688-07345-X.

Ian has been very fond of his pet dog, Gray Boy. When the dog becomes wild, both Ian and Gray Boy have exciting and realistic experiences.

IDA

Burch, Robert, **Ida Early Comes Over the Mountain**, Viking, 1980, 145p., Fiction, ISBN 0-670-39169-7.

Ida Early is tall and thin with stringy hair. When she joins the Sutton family everyone is happy with her cooking and sense of humor, even though other people make fun of Ida. There is another book about Ida Early.

Sendak, Maurice, **Outside Over There**, illustrated by Maurice Sendak, Harper & Row, 1981, 40p., Picture book, ISBN 0-06-025523-4.

While Ida was supposed to be watching her sister, goblins stole the baby girl and Ida had to go searching for her. 1981 Boston Globe-Horn Book Award book. 1982 Caldecott Honor book. 1982 Jane Addams Award book.

Williams, Vera, **Chair for My Mother, A**, illustrated by Vera Williams, Greenwillow, 1982, 32p., Picture Book, LC 81-7010, ISBN 0-688-00914-X; 0-688-00915-8 (lib).

A young girl and her mother save coins in a jar to buy a new chair to replace furniture destroyed in a fire. When there is enough money, her Aunt Ida helps them get the chair. 1983 Boston Globe-Horn Book Award book. 1983 Caldecott Honor book.

IGNACIO

Rohmer, Harriet, **Uncle Nacho's Hat**, illustrated by Veg Resiberg, Children's Book Press, 1989, 32p., Picture Book, LC 88-37090, ISBN 0-89239-043-3.

Uncle Nacho (short for Ignacio) is given a new hat by his niece, Ambrosia. However, he spends so much time worrying about his old hat that he can't enjoy his new one. Adapted from a Nicaraguan folktale, this story is written in both English and Spanish. A Reading Rainbow book.

ILSE

Koehn, Ilse, **Mischling, Second Degree: My Childhood in Nazi Germany**, Greenwillow, 1977, 240p., Nonfiction, ISBN 0-688-801-102; 0-688-84-1104 (lib).

Ilse was a young German girl who became a leader in the Hilter youth, unaware that she had a Jewish background. Based on the author's own experiences. 1978 Jane Addams Honor book. 1978 Boston Globe-Horn Book Award book.

IMOGENE

Robinson, Barbara, **Best Christmas Pageant Ever, The**, illustrated by Judith Gwyn Brown, Harper & Row, 1972, 80p., Fiction, LC 72-76501, ISBN 06-025043-7; 06-025044-5.

Imogene is one of the Herdman children—kids so awful it is hard to believe they are real. When they decide to participate in the church Christmas pageant, people think it will be the worst one ever. Georgia 1976. Indiana 1978. Minnesota 1982.

Small, David, **Imogene's Antlers**, illustrated by David Small, Crown, 1985, 26p., Picture Book, LC 84-12085, ISBN 0-517-55564-6; 0-517-56242-1 (pbk).

Imogene woke up on Thursday morning to discover she had grown a set of antlers on her head. The day was eventful as people tried to help her determine why the antlers grew and how they could be used. A Reading Rainbow book.

INGE

Orgel, Doris, **Devil in Vienna**, Dial, 1978, 246p., Fiction, ISBN 0-8037-1920-5.

Thirteen-year-old Inge is Jewish and forbidden to meet her best friend who is the daughter of a Nazi.

Set in Vienna in 1938 the two friends find ways to continue their friendship and to save Inge's family.

INGRID

Mattingley, Christobel, **Angel with a Mouth-Organ**, illustrated by Astra Lacis, Holiday House, 1986, 32p., Fiction, ISBN 0-8234-0593-1.

As the family decorates their Christmas tree, Ingrid and her brother hear about their mother's childhood as a refugee in war-torn Europe during World War II.

IRENE

Williams, Jay, **Danny Dunn and the Homework Machine**, illustrated by Ezra Jack Keats, McGraw-Hill, 1958, 141p., Fiction, LC 58-10015, ISBN 07-070520-8; 07-070519-4.

Irene has just moved into the neighborhood where Danny Dunn lives. With the assistance of a computer, Danny invents a homework machine that gives the correct answers and can do two papers at one time. Pacific Northwest 1961.

ISAAC

Shulevitz, Uri, **Treasure, The**, illustrated by Uri Shulevitz, Farrar, Straus & Giroux, 1978, 27p., Picture Book, ISBN 0-374-37740-5.

A voice speaks to Isaac three times in his dreams, telling him to go to the city and look for a treasure under the bridge by the royal palace. When Isaac takes the long journey, a surprise awaits him. 1980 Caldecott Honor book.

ISABELLE
See also Izzy

Greene, Constance, **Isabelle the Itch**, illustrated by Emily A. McCully, Viking, 1973, 126p., Fiction, ISBN 0-670-40177-3.

Isabelle has a lot of extra energy, and she learns that when she uses it wisely she can do almost anything she wants. There are other books about Isabelle.

ISADORA
See also Izzy

Pendergraft, Patricia, **Hear the Wind Blow**, Philomel, 1988, 208p., Fiction, ISBN 0-399-21528-X.

Isadora lives in a small town and dreams of another life as she dances like the famous dancer, Isadora Duncan. Her friendships and small-town life are portrayed.

IVAN

Mooser, Steve, **Shadows on the Graveyard Trail**, Dell, 1986, 100p., Fiction, ISBN 0-440-40805-9 (pbk).

Ivan and his mother go in search of his father who had disappeared in this mystery set in the old West.

IVAR

Stong, Phil, **Honk, the Moose**, illustrated by Kurt Wiese, Dodd, Mead, 1955, 80p., Fiction, ISBN 0-396-07358-1.

Ivar and Waino live in the rolling hills of the Iron Range in Minnesota where their parents had moved from Finland. During a very cold winter, the boys find a moose in the stable and the moose refuses to leave. 1936 Newbery Honor book.

IVY

Godden, Rumer, **Story of Holly and Ivy, The**, illustrated by Barbara Cooney, Viking Kestrel, 1985, 31p., Fiction, ISBN 0-670-80622-6.

Ivy is an orphan who gets together with a childless couple and an unsold Christmas doll on Christmas day.

Snyder, Zilpha Keatley, **Changeling, The**, illustrated by Alton Raible, Dell, 1986, 220p., Fiction, ISBN 0-440-41200-5 (pbk).

Ivy Carson develops a close friendship with another girl who is very different than she is. The two girls develop a make-believe world of their own.

Stolz, Mary, **Ivy Larkin**, Dell, 1986, 226p., Fiction, ISBN 0-440-40175-5 (pbk).

Set during the Great Depression, fourteen-year-old Ivy and her family have had to move to increasingly smaller apartments and Ivy has to attend school on a scholarship.

IZZY
See also Isabelle, Isadora

Voight, Cynthia, **Izzy Willy Nilly**, Atheneum, 1986, 258p., Fiction, ISBN 0-689-312-024.

Fifteen-year-old Izzy loses a leg following an automobile accident and he has to face the need to start a new life as an amputee. California 1990.

-J-

JACK
See also Jackie, Jackson, Jacques

Cresswell, Helen, **Ordinary Jack**, Macmillan, 1977, 195p., Fiction, ISBN 0-02-725540-9.

Jack Bagthorpe feels ordinary in an extraordinary family. When Jack's uncle decides to help him, the result is a series of scatterbrained adventures involving the whole family. There are other books about Jack and his family.

Elwell, Peter, **King of the Pipers**, Macmillan, 1984, 32p., Picture Book, ISBN 0-02-733460-0.

In this original fairy tale, Jack the piper is able to turn his misfortunes, including his lack of musical ability, into success.

Fink, Joanne, **Jack, the Seal and the Sea**, illustrated by Gerald Aschenbrenner, Silver Burdett, 1988, 28p., Picture Book, ISBN 0-382-099-850.

Jack sails the seas to fish. He ignores the polluted waters until he receives a message from a sick seal about the problems. A Reading Rainbow book.

Fleischman, Sid, **By the Great Horn Spoon**, illustrated by Eric von Schmidt, Little, Brown, 1963, 193p., Fiction, ISBN 0-316-28577-3.

Jack Flagg is an orphan who stows away on a ship bound for California. He has many humorous adventures as he becomes involved in the 1849 Gold Rush.

Gleiter, Jan, **Jack London**, illustrated by Francis Balistreri, Raintree, 1988, 32p., Nonfiction, ISBN 0-8172-2661-3.

A biography of the famous American writer, Jack London. His life was filled with a variety of jobs and adventures that he used in his adventure stories.

Keele, Luqman and Daniel Pinkwater, **Java Jack**, Crowell, 1980, 152p., Fiction, ISBN 0-690-03996-4.

While visiting his aunt in Missouri, Jack hears that his anthropologist parents have been murdered in Java. When he leaves to find out what has happened, Jack has fantastic adventures including being kidnapped and flying an airplane into a volcano.

Slote, Alfred, **My Trip to Alpha 1**, illustrated by Harold Berson, Lippincott, 1978, 96p., Fiction, ISBN 0-397-31810-3.

Eleven-year-old Jack is able to visit his aunt on another planet through a form of space travel that sends his mind to a substitute body. During the visit, Jack discovers a mystery to be solved. There are other science fiction books about Jack.

Wilder, Laura Ingalls, **On the Banks of Plum Creek**, illustrated by Garth Williams, Harper & Row, 1953, 338p., Fiction, ISBN 0-06-026470-5.

When the Ingalls family moves to Minnesota they take their dog Jack with them. The family lives in a dugout until a new house is built. They face numerous natural disasters including a flood, a blizzard, and grasshoppers. There are other books about this family. 1938 Newbery Honor book.

JACKIE
See also Jack, Jackson, Jacques

Robinson, Jackie, **I Never Had It Made: The Autobiograhy of Jackie Robinson**, Putnam, 1972, 287p., Nonfiction, ISBN 0-399-110-100.

The autobiography of the famous baseball player, Jackie Robinson, who proved that a man should be judged on his skills and character and not on his color. 1973 Coretta Scott King Award.

Scott, Richard, **Jackie Robinson**, Chelsea House, 1987, 111p., Nonfiction, ISBN 0-55546-609-5.

Biographical information about the great baseball player, Jackie Robinson, and the struggles that he had becoming a professional player.

JACKSON
See also Jack, Jackie

Byars, Betsy, **Cracker Jackson**, Viking, 1985, 146p., Fiction, LC 84-24684, ISBN 0-670-80546-7.

Eleven-year-old Jackson Hunter has been given the nickname of Cracker by Alma, his favorite sitter. Alma is in serious trouble and Cracker is unsure what to do to help her. He is afraid to ask his divorced parents for help and his best friend is the class clown. Kansas 1988. South Carolina 1987.

JACOB
See also Jake

Fox, Paula, **Maurice's Room**, illustrated by Ingrid Fetz, Macmillan, 1966, 63p., Fiction, ISBN 0-02-735490-3.

Jacob and his friend Maurice consider the junk they have collected to be valuable and attempt to keep it all despite the protests of Maurice's parents.

Lawson, John, **Spring Rider, The**, Crowell, 1968, 147p., Fiction, LC 68-17079, ISBN 0-690-04785-1.

A legend from the mountains of Virginia about a disappearing rider becomes more than folklore when Jacob encounters a Civil War soldier who takes him on an adventure before the soldier disappears. 1968 Boston Globe-Horn Book Award.

Quackenbush, Robert, **Once Upon a Time: A Story of the Brothers Grimm**, Prentice-Hall, 1985, 36p., Nonfiction, ISBN 0-13-634536-0.

Jacob Grimm and his brother were inseparable from the time they were boys. They lived together, went to school together, and gathered the folk and fairy tales that made them famous. This brief biography provides information on the brothers.

Richler, Mordecai, **Jacob Two-Two and the Hooded Fang**, illustrated by Fritz Wegner, Bantam, 1977, 96p., Fiction, ISBN 0-553-42075-5 (pbk).

A tall tale about six-year-old Jacob who has two of everything including parents, brothers, and sisters. Jacob can never do anything right, and when he is sent to a prison for children he sees 200 other children and meets the Hooded Fang.

JACQUES
See also Jack, Jackie

Westman, Paul, **Jacques Cousteau, Free Flight Undersea,** illustrated by Reg Sandland, Dillon, 1980, 47p., Nonfiction, ISBN 0-87518-188-0.

A biography about Jacques Cousteau, a famous oceanographer who has invented underwater equipment to search the oceans and has documented ocean life.

JAFTA

Lewin, Hugh, **Jafta's Mother**, illustrated by Lisa Kopper, Carolrhoda, 1983, 24p., Picture Book, LC 82-12863, ISBN 0-87614-208-0 (lib).

Jafta is a young boy who lives in an African village. In this book he tells about his mother. There are other books about Jafta and his family. A Reading Rainbow book.

JAKE
See also Jacob

Calvert, Patricia, **Hour of the Wolf**, Scribner, 1983, 147p., Fiction, ISBN 0-684-17961-X.

Jake is challenged by the spirit of a dead friend to enter an international dog sled race, which is 1,000 miles long. Jake has always thought of himself as a loser and has to prove to himself that he has the courage to complete the race.

Jukes, Mavis, **Like Jake and Me**, illustrated by Lloyd Bloom, Knopf, 1984, 30p., Picture Book, LC 83-8380, ISBN 0-394-85608-2; 0-394-95608-7 (lib).

Jake is big, strong, and brave. His stepson, Alex, wants to be just like Jake. When a large, hairy spider crawls into Jake's clothes, Alex finds that

there are some things that even a cowboy is afraid of. 1985 Newbery Honor book.

Mahy, Margaret, **Aliens in the Family**, Scholastic, 1986, 174p., Fiction, ISBN 0-590-40320-6.

Jake meets and tries to protect an extraterrestrial when she visits her father and his new family.

Raskin, Ellen, **Westing Game, The**, Dutton, 1978, 185p., Fiction, LC 77-18866, ISBN 0-525-42320-6.

Jake is one of the sixteen people invited to the reading of the very strange will of the very rich Samuel W. Westing. Jake could become a millionaire, depending on how well he plays the tricky and dangerous Westing Game. 1979 Newbery Award book. 1978 Boston Globe-Horn Book Award. Michigan 1982.

Yolen, Jane, **Commander Toad and the Intergalactic Spy**, illustrated by Bruce Degen, Coward-McCann, 1986, 64p., Easy Reader, LC 85-11018, ISBN 0-698-30747-X; 0-698-20623-1 (pbk).

Commander Toad is the captain of the space ship called Star Warts. Jake Skyjumper is the ship's computer chief. The crew is sent on a dangerous mission to pick up an intergalactic spy. A Reading Rainbow book.

JAMAICA

Havill, Juanita, **Jamaica's Find**, illustrated by Anne Sibley O'Brien, Houghton Mifflin, 1986, 32p., Picture Book, LC 85-14542, ISBN 0-395-39376-0.

Jamaica finds a cuddly, stuffed toy dog at the park and wants to keep it. When she decides to turn the dog in to the lost-and-found shelf, Jamaica meets a new friend named Kristin. A Reading Rainbow book.

JAMAL

Myers, Walter Dean, **Scorpions**, Harper & Row, 1988, 216p., Fiction, LC 85-45815, ISBN 0-06-024364-3; 0-06-024365-1 (lib).

Jamal Hicks is having a hard time at school, at home, and on the streets. His brother had been the leader of the Scorpions, a Harlem gang, until he was jailed and then Jamal reluctantly takes on the role.

Jamal finds that his enemies treat him with respect when he acquires a gun until a tragedy occurs. 1989 Newbery Honor book.

JAMES
See also Jamie, Jim, Jimmie, Jimmy

Clinton, Susan, **James Madison**, Children's Press, 1986, 98p., Nonfiction, ISBN 0-516-01382-3.

The biography of James Madison who served his country for over forty years and became president in 1808.

Dahl, Roald, **James and the Giant Peach: A Children's Story**, illustrated by Nancy Eckholm Burkert, Knopf, 1961, 118p., Fiction, ISBN 0-394-91282-9.

James finds life unhappy when he is sent to live with his aunts after his parents die. A magic potion produces an enormous peach, which becomes his new and exciting home. Massachusetts 1982.

Dickinson, Peter, **Box of Nothing**, Delacorte, 1985, 110p., Fiction, ISBN 0-385-29664-9.

In this fantasy, James becomes involved in parallel universes and is led back in time to the black hole where creation began.

Eager, Edward, **Magic or Not?**, illustrated by N. M. Bodecker, Harcourt Brace Jovanovich, 1985, 190p., Fiction, ISBN 0-15-655121-7 (pbk).

James and his sister have been told that the well by their new house is magical. Although their wishes come true, they are unsure whether it is because of the well.

Fitz-Gerald, Christine Maloney, **James Monroe**, Children's Press, 1987, 100p., Nonfiction, ISBN 0-516-01383-1.

Biographical information about James Monroe, a president of the United States, who was involved in the War of 1812.

Fox, Paula, **How Many Miles to Babylon?**, illustrated by Paul Giovanopoulus, Bradbury, 1967, 117p., Fiction, ISBN 0-02-735590-X.

Ten-year-old James is very lonely. When he runs away from school and hides in a deserted house, three older boys force him to help steal dogs.

Fritz, Jean, **Great Little Madison, The**, Putnam, 1989, 159p., Nonfiction, ISBN 0-399-217-681.

This biography tells about James Madison who started life as a sickly child and went on to become the fourth president of the United States. 1990 Boston Globe-Horn Book Award.

Lillegard, Dee, **James A. Garfield**, Children's Press, 1987, 100p., Nonfiction, ISBN 0-516-01394-7.

James Garfield was the last U.S. president to be born in a log cabin. He lived through the Civil War, Reconstruction, and the Indian Wars. An assassin shot and killed him. This biography tells about his life and the times he lived in.

Lively, Penelope, **Ghost of Thomas Kempe, The**, illustrated by Antony Maitland, Dutton, 1973, 186p., Fiction, ISBN 0-525-30495-9.

When his family moves to a cottage, James meets the ghost of Thomas Kempe, a sorcerer who had lived in the cottage several hundred years earlier. No one will believe James when he says that a ghost is causing pranks.

Newberry, Clare Turlay, **Barkis**, illustrated by Clare Turlay Newberry, Harper & Brothers, 1938, 32p., Picture Book, ISBN 0-06-024421-6.

For his ninth birthday, James receives Barkis, a cocker spaniel. Although James is supposed to share the puppy with his sister, he does not want to since she already has a pet cat. 1939 Caldecott Honor book.

Norton, Mary, **Are All the Giants Dead?**, illustrated by Brian Froud, Harcourt Brace Jovanovich, 1975, 123p., Fiction, ISBN 0-15-203810-8.

James is taken to the land where fairy-tale characters live, and he meets many of his favorite characters and finds out what has happened to them.

Paterson, Katherine, **Come Sing, Jimmy Jo**, Lodestar, 1985, 197p., Fiction, ISBN 0-525-67167-6.

Eleven-year-old James has to get used to being a celebrity when he joins his family's bluegrass group and it becomes popular.

Quackenbush, Robert, **Watt Got You Started, Mr. Fulton? A Story of James Watt and Robert Fulton**, Prentice-Hall, 1982, 39p., Nonfiction, ISBN 0-13-944397-5.

James Watt invented the steam engine that Robert Fulton used in his boats. Biographical information about both men is included in this title.

Raskin, Ellen, **Westing Game, The**, Dutton, 1978, 185p., Fiction, LC 77-18866, ISBN 0-525-42320-6.

James is one of the sixteen people invited to the reading of the very strange will of the very rich Samuel W. Westing. James could become a millionaire, depending on how he plays the tricky and dangerous Westing Game. 1979 Newbery Award book. 1978 Boston Globe-Horn Book Award. Michigan 1982.

Voight, Cynthia, **Dicey's Song**, Atheneum, 1983, 196p., Fiction, LC 82-3882, ISBN 0-689-30944-9.

James Tillerman and his brother and sisters had spent the whole summer looking for their grandmother after their mother abandoned them. Living with their grandmother in her Chesapeake Bay country home is not easy, and old problems and sorrows do not just go away. 1983 Newbery Award book.

JAMIE
See also James

Ames, Mildred, **Cassandra-Jamie**, Scribner, 1985, 135p., Fiction, LC 85-40297, ISBN 0-684-18472-9.

Jamie's mother has been dead for three years and Jamie decides that her father should remarry. She thinks her wonderful English teacher would be the right person for her father, but begins to discover that people are not always as they seem.

Bilson, Geoffrey, **Death Over Montreal**, Kids Can Press, 1982, 109p., Fiction, ISBN 0-919964-45-1.

Set in the middle of the nineteenth century, Jamie Douglas and his family move from Edinburgh, Scotland, to settle in Canada. Bad luck follows the immigrant family but they remain determined.

Caudill, Rebecca, **Certain Small Shepherd, A**, illustrated by William Pene Du Bois, H. Holt, 1965, 48p., Fiction, ISBN 0-03-089755-6.

Jamie had planned on being a shepherd in the Nativity play at church until a snowstorm arrives. Jamie then becomes part of something even more special.

Erwin, Vicki Berger, **Jamie and the Mystery Quilt**, Scholastic, 1987, 151p., Fiction, ISBN 0-590-40122-X (pbk).

Jamie has an exciting and dangerous adventure after finding an old quilt in the attic of the family house.

Konigsburg, Elaine, **From the Mixed-Up Files of Mrs. Basil E. Frankweiler**, illustrated by E. L. Konigsburg, Atheneum, 1980, 162p., Fiction, LC 67-18988, ISBN 0-689-20586-4.

Jamie runs away from home with his sister Claudia. Claudia had planned things out carefully and the two go to live at the Metropolitan Museum of Art. There they find a beautiful statue and a mystery. 1968 Newbery Award book. Kansas 1970.

Krensky, Stephen, **Ghostly Business**, Atheneum, 1980, 144p., Fiction, ISBN 0-689--31048-X.

Jamie is one of the Wynd children who uses her magic powers to try to stop ghosts from taking over houses in Boston.

Mowat, Farley, **Lost in the Barrens**, illustrated by Charles Geer, Little, Brown, 1962, 244p., Fiction, ISBN 0-316-58638-2.

When Jamie moves to the wilderness of northern Canada, he becomes friends with a Cree Indian boy and the two have many adventures.

Smith, Doris Buchanan, **Taste of Blackberries, A**, illustrated by Charles Robinson, Crowell, 1973, 58p., Fiction, LC 72-7558, ISBN 0-690-80512-8; 0-690-80511-X.

Jamie is both special and exasperating. When a harmless prank turns to sudden tragedy, Jamie's best friend is filled with grief and guilt. Georgia 1975.

JAN

See also Jancsi, Janell, Janet, Janetta

McSwigan, Marie, **Snow Treasure**, illustrated by Mary Reardon, Dutton, 1942, 179p., Fiction, ISBN 0-525-39556-3.

Jan and other Norwegian children slipped past Nazi soldiers with sleds loaded with gold. The gold was taken twelve miles to a freighter hidden in one of the fiords off Norway's coast. Based on an actual event. In June 1940 the Norwegian freighter reached Baltimore with a cargo of gold worth 9 million dollars. Pacific Northwest 1945.

Mitchell, Barbara, **Shoes for Everyone: A Story About Jan Matzeliger**, illustrated by Hetty Mitchell, Carolrhoda, 1986, 63p., Nonfiction, ISBN 0-87614-290-0.

The biography of Jan Matzeliger, a shoemaker from Dutch Guiana who came to the United States and made important contributions to the shoe industry through his inventions.

JANCSI

See also Jan

Seredy, Kate, **Good Master, The**, illustrated by Kate Seredy, Viking, 1935, 211p., Fiction, ISBN 0-670-34592-X.

Kate left the city of Budapest to live with her cousin and his family who lived on a ranch on the Hungarian plains, miles from the village. Both children learn a great deal from one another as they share their different lives. 1936 Newbery Honor book.

JANE

See also Janey, Janie

Cleary, Beverly, **Fifteen**, illustrated by Joe Krush and Beth Krush, Morrow, 1956, 254p., Fiction, LC 56-7509, ISBN 0-688-21285-9.

Jane is fifteen years old and a sophomore in high school. When she meets sixteen-year-old Stan, she develops a friendship with him that has its ups and downs. Vermont 1958.

Cooper, Susan, **Over Sea, Under Stone**, Harcourt Brace Jovanovich, 1966, 252p., Fiction, ISBN 0-15-259034-X.

Jane is one of the characters who battles the dark forces of evil while searching for the treasures that will permanently vanquish them.

Eager, Edward, **Magic by the Lake**, illustrated by N. M. Bodecker, Harcourt Brace Jovanovich, 1985, 183p., Fiction, ISBN 0-15-250441-9.

Jane and three other children must tame a magic lake before they can discover its treasure.

Estes, Eleanor, **Middle Moffat, The**, illustrated by Louis Slobodkin, Harcourt Brace Jovanovich, 1942, 317p., Fiction, LC 42-36272, ISBN 0-15-659536-2.

Jane is the middle child in the Moffat family. She has a vivid imagination that leads her into many difficulties. 1943 Newbery Honor book.

Estes, Eleanor, **Moffats, The**, illustrated by Louis Slobodkin, Harcourt Brace Jovanovich, 1941, 290p., Fiction, ISBN 0-15-255095-X.

Jane Moffat and her family are poor but their life is full. There are several other books about the Moffats.

Gathorne-Hardy, Jonathan, **Operation Peeg**, illustrated by Glo Coalson, Lippincott, 1974, 192p., Fiction, ISBN 0-397-31594-5.

Jane and her friend discover two soldiers who have been at a fortress on their island for over thirty years, since World War II. Their discovery involves the girls in an adventure.

Goodall, Jane, **My Life With the Chimpanzees**, Minstrel, 1988, 123p., Nonfiction, ISBN 0-671-66095-0.

Jane Goodall wanted to do animal research. She began working with a famous naturalist who found a way for Jane to study apes, which became her life work. Her biography provides insights into the woman and her work with chimps in the wild.

Lunn, Janet, **Double Spell**, illustrated by A. M. Calder, Puffin, 1968, 134p., Fiction, ISBN 0-88778-023-7.

Jane and her twin sister become involved in a supernatural mystery after seeing an unusual doll in an antique store.

Meigs, Cornelia, **Jane Addams: Pioneer for Social Justice**, Little, Brown, 1970, 274p., Nonfiction, ISBN 0-8368-0144-X.

Jane Addams was born in 1860 and dedicated her life to improving society. This book includes the history of Hull House and the many social reforms that it inspired. 1971 Jane Addams Award book.

Shura, Mary Francis, **Don't Call Me Toad!**, illustrated by Jacqueline Rogers, Putnam, 1987, 124p., Fiction, ISBN 0-399-21706-1.

Eleven-year-old Jane meets a strange new girl who has just moved into town and the two girls become involved in a mystery.

JANELL
See also Jan

Greenfield, Eloise, **Me and Neesie**, illustrated by Moneta Barnett, Crowell, 1975, 33p., Picture Book, LC 74-23078, ISBN 0-690-00714-0; 0-690-00715-9 (lib).

Janell is the only one who can see her best friend Neesie. The two girls laugh and play games together. When Janell begins going to school her relationship with Neesie changes. A Reading Rainbow book.

JANET
See also Jan

Drury, Roger W., **Champion of Merrimack County, The**, illustrated by Fritz Wegner, Little, Brown, 1976, 199p., Fiction, LC 76-6453, ISBN 0-316-19349-6.

Janet Berryfield and her mother are amazed when they see a mouse riding a bicycle around the rim of the bathtub. The mouse is certain that he will win the bike riding championship until he has a disaster while trying a complicated riding trick. A humorous story. Missouri 1979.

JANETTA
See also Jan

Griffith, Helen, **Grandaddy's Place**, illustrated by James Stevenson, Greenwillow, 1987, 40p., Fiction, ISBN 0-688-06254-7.

Janetta is a city child who develops a warm and loving relationship with her grandfather who lives in the country.

JANEY
See also Jane, Janie

Bunting, Eve, **Sixth Grade Sleepover, The**, Harcourt Brace Jovanovich, 1986, 96p., Fiction, ISBN 0-152-753-508.

Janie is worried about going to the sixth-grade all-night sleepover because she doesn't want anyone to know that she is afraid of the dark. She discovers that she isn't the only one that has a secret. Oklahoma 1989.

Gates, Doris, **Blue Willow**, illustrated by Paul Lantz, Viking, 1940, 172p., Fiction, LC 40-32435, ISBN 0-670-17557-9.

Janey Larkin is ten years old and wants to have a real home and be able to go to a regular school. She hopes that the valley her family has come to, which resembles the pattern on her treasured blue willow plate, will be their permanent home. 1941 Newbery Honor book.

JANIE
See also Jane, Janey

Atwater, Richard and Florence, **Mr. Popper's Penguins**, illustrated by Robert Lawson, Little, Brown, 1938, 140p., Fiction, ISBN 0-316-05842-4.

Janie and Bill Popper's father is a housepainter; he is also a dreamer. Mr. Popper is always absent-mindedly dreaming of countries far-away and he regrets that he hasn't traveled, even though he loves his family very much. Mr. Popper's adventures begin when he receives an Air Express package from Antarctica: a package that contains a penguin! 1939 Newbery Honor book. Pacific Northwest 1941.

Little, Jean, **One to Grow On**, illustrated by Jerry Lazare, Little, Brown, 1969, 140p., Fiction, ISBN 0-316-52796-3.

Janie exaggerates and tells lies hoping to get attention and make friends, but she discovers that it is not the way to make real friends.

Pfeffer, Susan Beth, **Kid Power**, illustrated by Leigh Grant, Watts, 1977, 121p., Fiction, ISBN 0-531-00123-7.

When her father offers to pay for half of the cost of a new bicycle, eleven-year-old Janie decides to get a job with humorous results. There is another book about Janie and her family. Oklahoma 1980. Vermont 1979.

JASON

Alexander, Lloyd, **Time Cat**, illustrated by Bill Sokol, Dell, 1963, 191p., Fiction, ISBN 0-440-48677-7.

Jason and his cat travel to nine places and times in history including ancient Egypt, medieval Italy, Incan Peru, Germany in the 1600s, and Massachusetts during the early days of the American Revolution.

Aliki, **Feelings**, illustrated by Aliki, Greenwillow, 1984, 32p., Picture Book, LC 84-4098, ISBN 0-688-03831-X; 0-688-03832-8 (lib).

Jason is one of the children who is portrayed showing the various emotions that everyone feels: sadness, fear, jealousy, anger, love, and so forth. Poems, dialogs, pictures, and stories. A Reading Rainbow book.

Burke, Susan, **Island Bike Business**, illustrated by Betty Greenhatch and Graeme Base, Oxford, 1982, 78p., Fiction, ISBN 0-19-554297-5.

Jason and his friends have dangerous adventures when they attempt to recover missing bicycles.

Ellis, Anne Leo, **Dabble Duck**, illustrated by Sue Truesdell, Harper & Row, 1984, 32p., Picture Book, LC 83-47692, ISBN 0-06-021817-7; 0-06-021818-5 (lib).

Jason keeps a pet duck, named Dabble, in his apartment. Dabble is lonely when Jason is at school so she makes friends with an injured, homeless dog. A Reading Rainbow book.

Hamilton, Virginia, **Bells of Christmas, The**, illustrated by Lambert Davis, Harcourt Brace Jovanovich, 1989, 59p., Fiction, ISBN 0-15-206-450-8.

In 1890 Jason awaits the arrival of his relatives, the Bells, to celebrate Christmas in the Springfield,

Ohio, home where his family has lived for generations. 1990 Coretta Scott King Honor book.

Hutchins, Hazel, **Three and Many Wishes of Jason Reid, The**, illustrated by Julie Tennent, Viking Kestrel, 1988, 87p., Fiction, ISBN 0-670-82155-1.

When Jason encounters an elf, he is given three wishes. For his third wish, he wants more wishes and has to learn the rules of wishes.

Walter, Mildred Pitts, **My Mama Needs Me**, illustrated by Pat Cummings, Lothrop, Lee & Shepard, 1983, 32p., Picture Book, LC 82-12654, ISBN 0-688-01670-7; 0-688-01671-5 (lib).

Jason's mother has just brought his baby sister home from the hospital. Jason wants to be with his friends but stays close by his mother in case she needs him. 1984 Coretta Scott King Award book. A Reading Rainbow book.

JAVAKA

Steptoe, John, **Daddy Is a Monster...Sometimes**, illustrated by John Steptoe, Lippincott, 1980, 30p., Picture Book, LC 77-4464, ISBN 0-397-31762-X; 0-397-31893-6 (lib).

Javaka and his sister, Bweela, have a nice daddy who sometimes seems to turn into a scary monster when the children are too messy or noisy. A Reading Rainbow book.

JAY

Caudill, Rebecca, **Pocketful of Cricket, A**, illustrated by Evaline Ness, H. Holt, 1964, 48p., Picture Book, ISBN 0-913-21-1314.

Jay acquires a pet cricket. When he takes it to school the cricket disturbs the class with its chirping until it becomes the main attraction at show-and-tell. 1965 Caldecott Honor book.

Rawls, Wilson, **Summer of the Monkeys**, Doubleday, 1976, 239p., Fiction, ISBN 0-385-11450-8.

Jay is a fourteen-year-old farm boy in Oklahoma during the 1890s. He is delighted when circus monkeys escape and end up on his farm. California 1981. Kansas 1979. Minnesota 1980. Oklahoma 1979.

JEAN
See also Jeanmarie

Dewey, Ariane, **Laffite the Pirate**, Greenwillow, 1985, 48p., Picture Book, ISBN 0-688-04230-9.

A fictionalized story about Jean Laffite, the pirate, and his exploits during the eighteeenth century along the Gulf coasts of Texas and Louisiana.

Fritz, Jean, **Homesick: My Own Story**, illustrated by Margaret Tomes, Putnam, 1982, 163p., Nonfiction, ISBN 0-399-20933-6.

Based on the author's experiences as an American child growing up in Hankow, China, during the 1920s. 1983 Child Study Children's Book Award. 1983 Christopher Award. 1983 Newbery Honor book. 1983 Jane Addams Award book.

Little, Jean, **Little by Little: A Writer's Education**, Viking Kestrel, 1987, 233p., Nonfiction, ISBN 0-670-81649-3.

An autobiography of the writer, Jean Little. She was born in Taiwan of missionary parents and developed an understanding of handicapped children through her own limited vision.

Meyer, Edith Patterson, **Champions of Peace: Winners of the Nobel Peace Prize**, illustrated by Eric von Schmidt, Little, Brown, 1959, 216p., Nonfiction, LC 59-7355.

Jean Henri Dunant of Switzerland was the founder of the International Red Cross and winner of one of the first Nobel Peace Prizes awarded in 1901. 1960 Jane Addams Award book.

JEANMARIE
See also Jean, Marie

Konigsburg, Elaine, **Up From Jericho Tel**, Atheneum, 1986, 178p., Fiction, ISBN 0-689-31194-X.

Jeanmarie and her friend become invisible occasionally as they search for a stolen necklace.

JED

Bunting, Eve, **Face at the Edge of the World**, Ticknor & Fields, 1985, 192p., Fiction, ISBN 0-899-193-994.

Jed is haunted by the suicide of his best friend, a gifted young black writer, and he decides to pursue the reason that it happened. California 1989.

Garden, Nancy, **Fours Crossing**, Farrar, Straus & Giroux, 1981, 197p., Fiction, ISBN 0-374-32451-4.

Jed and his friend Melissa become involved in dangerous situations as they attempt to solve several mysteries while Melissa is visiting her grandmother in rural New Hampshire. There is another book about the two friends.

JEFF
See also Jeffrey

Asimov, Janet and Isaac Asimov, **Norby and the Mixed-Up Robot**, Beaverbooks, 1983, 96p., Fiction, ISBN 0-8027-6496-7.

Jeff Wells is failing an important subject at the Space Academy. To avoid expulsion, he buys a tutor robot, which leads him and his brother on humorous adventures.

Blume, Judy, **It's Not the End of the World**, Bradbury, 1972, 169p., Fiction, ISBN 0-02-711050-8.

Jeff and his sisters are very upset when their parents decide to get a divorce. Deenie, the older girl, tries to bring their parents together again.

Clifford, Eth, **Just Tell Me When We're Dead**, illustrated by George Hughes, Houghton Mifflin, 1983, 130p., Fiction, LC 83-10865, ISBN 0-395-33071-8.

When Jeff leaves a note that he has gone West, he does not expect his two female cousins to go looking for him, and none of them anticipate the adventures they will have. Oklahoma 1986.

Corbett, Scott, **Trouble with Diamonds, The**, illustrated by Bert Dodson, Dutton, 1985, 96p., Fiction, ISBN 0-525-44190-5.

Jeff becomes involved in a mystery that may include some of the guests at a summer resort with humorous results.

Erickson, Phoebe, **Double or Nothing**, illustrated by Phoebe Erickson, Harper & Brothers, 1958, 128p., Fiction, LC 58-7762.

Jeff and Ellen Gates want a dog of their own when their parents move them to Vermont. When they find the dog they want, he is homeless and hungry, and a twin. Jeff and Ellen know they will have a problem getting their parents' approval to keep Double orNothing. Vermont 1960.

Keith, Harold, **Rifles for Watie**, Crowell, 1957, 332p., Fiction, LC 57-10280, ISBN 0-690-70181-0.

Jeff Busey joined the Union volunteers in 1861 and was probably the only soldier in the West to see the Civil War from both sides and live to tell about it. Jeff learned what it meant to fight in battle and how it felt to always be hungry, dirty, and tired. 1958 Newbery Award book.

Smith, Carole, **Hit-and-Run Connection**, illustrated by Marie DeJohn, Whitman, 1982, 126p., Fiction, ISBN 0-8075-3317-3.

Jeff is determined to find the driver that hit his friend, then left. A chance encounter leads him to believe that the driver is a member of the Chicago White Sox baseball team.

Voight, Cynthia, **Solitary Blue, A**, Atheneum, 1983, 189p., Fiction, LC 83-6007, ISBN 0-689-31008-0.

Jeff Greene was seven when his mother left. He knew it was important to do things just right for his father, the Professor. When his mother reenters Jeff's life, the gap widens between him and his father. 1984 Newbery Honor book.

JEFFREY
See also Jeff

Alexander, Martha, **Move Over, Twerp**, illustrated by Martha Alexander, Dial, 1981, 28p., Picture Book, LC 80-21405, ISBN 0-8037-5814-6.

Jeffrey is excited that he is old enough to ride the school bus. When the big kids call him names and take his seat, he knows he has to solve the problem by himself. Kentucky 1984.

Bosse, Malcolm, **Ganesh**, Crowell, 1981, 192p., Fiction, ISBN 0-690-04103-9.

After growing up in India, Jeffrey is sent to live with his aunt in America where he adapts slowly.

Conford, Ellen, **Revenge of the Incredible Dr. Rancid and His Youthful Assistant, Jeffrey**, Little, Brown, 1980, 119p., Fiction, ISBN 0-316-15288-9.

Jeffrey uses his imagination to fight the school bully and becomes a hero to the class.

Spinelli, Jerry, **Maniac Magee**, Little, Brown, 1990, 184p., Fiction, LC 89-27144, ISBN 0-316-80722-2.

Jeffrey Lionel Magee changed both his name and his life when his parents died. As Maniac Magee he becomes a legend for his athletic abilities and other feats. 1991 Newbery Award book. 1990 Boston Globe-Horn Book Award. Pennsylvania 1991.

JEM
See also Jemima, Jemmy

Lasky, Kathryn, **Jem's Island**, illustrated by Ronald Himler, Scribner, 1982, 56p., Fiction, ISBN 0-684-1724-6.

Jem anticipates a kayak trip with his father similar to the one his father and grandfather had once made. Careful planning prepares them for the trip although, once underway, they get off course.

JEMIMA
See also Jem, Jemmy

Fleming, Ian, **Chitty-Chitty-Bang-Bang: The Magical Car**, illustrated by John Burningham, Random House, 1964, 114p., Fiction, LC 64-21282, ISBN 0-394-81948-9.

Jemima Pott and her twin brother, Jeremy, live with their parents in the woods beside a lake in England. The Potts are an unusual family, and when they buy a car they want an unusual one. They get an old, one-of-a-kind, racing car they call Chitty-Chitty-Bang-Bang that provides amazing adventures. Pacfic Northwest 1967.

Gathorne-Hardy, Jonathan, **Operation Peeg**, illustrated by Glo Coalson, Lippincott, 1974, 192p., Fiction, ISBN 0-397-31594-5.

Jemima and her friend discover two soldiers in a fortress on their island who have been there for over thirty years, since World War II. This discovery involves the girls in an adventure.

JEMMY
See also Jem, Jemima

Fleischman, Sid, **Whipping Boy, The**, illustrated by Peter Sis, Greenwillow, 1986, 90p., Fiction, LC 85-17555, ISBN 0-688-06216-4.

Since it is forbidden to punish the bratty young prince, an orphan named Jemmy is chosen to serve as the whipping boy. The two boys have many adventures when they accidently trade places and become involved in dangerous situations. 1987 Newbery Award book. Arkansas 1989.

JEN
See also Jenna, Jennifer, Jenny, Virginia

Bond, Nancy, **String in the Harp**, Atheneum, 1984, 370p., Fiction, LC 75-28181, ISBN 0-689-50036-8.

After their mother dies, sixteen-year-old Jen and her brother and sister are taken to Wales for a year by their dad. One of the youngsters finds an ancient harp-tuning key that takes him back to the time of the great sixth-century bard, Taliesin. 1977 Newbery Honor book.

JENNA
See also Jen, Jennifer, Virginia

Auch, Mary Jane, **Mom Is Dating Weird Wayne**, Holiday House, 1988, 146p., Fiction, ISBN 0-8234-0720-9.

Jenna's life changes when her father moves out and she thinks that her mother is having a romance with a television weatherman.

JENNIFER
See also Genny, Jen, Jenna, Jenny, Jinny

Adler, David A., **Cam Jansen and the Mystery of the Stolen Diamonds**, illustrated by Susanna Nalti, Viking, 1980, 58p., Fiction, ISBN 0-670-200039-5.

Jennifer Jansen is called Cam. Her photographic memory helps solve the mystery of the hold-up at a jewelry store. There are other books about Cam Jansen.

Anderson, Margaret, **In the Circle of Time**, Knopf, 1979, 181p., Fiction, ISBN 0-394-94029-6.

Jennifer and Robert are fascinated by an unusual circle of stones on a Scottish mountain. The two are projected into the twenty-second century where they find that the glaciers have melted and flooded coastal cities.

Brady, Irene, **Doodlebug**, illustrated by Irene Brady, Houghton Mifflin, 1977, 35p., Fiction, ISBN 0-395-25782-4.

Jennifer buys a small, lame pony at an auction and discovers that he is a prize pony that had been stolen.

Krensky, Stephen, **Ghostly Business**, Atheneum, 1980, 144p., Fiction, ISBN 0-689-31048-X.

Jennifer is one of the Wynd children who uses her magical powers to try to prevent ghosts from taking over Boston houses.

Nixon, Joan Lowery, **Stalker, The**, Delacorte, 1985, 180p., Fiction, ISBN 0-385-2937-63.

Seventeen-year-old Jennifer decides to find the real murderer when her best friend is accused of a crime. California 1989.

Vande Velde, Vivian, **Hidden Magic**, illustrated by Trina Schart Hyman, Crown, 1985, 117p., Fiction, ISBN 0-517-55534-4.

Jennifer is a plain princess who doesn't care about her looks because she has many talents. She battles against an evil witch with the help of a sorcerer.

JENNY
See also Genny, Jen, Jennifer, Jinny, Virginia

Babbitt, Natalie, **Eyes of the Amaryllis**, Farrar, Straus & Giroux, 1977, 127p., Fiction, ISBN 0-374-32241-4.

When Jenny spends three weeks with her grandmother, she is required to search the beach for a sign from her grandfather who had drowned years earlier. The search becomes a deadly game with an exciting climax.

Berger, Melvin, **Germs Make Me Sick!**, illustrated by Marylin Hafner, Crowell, 1985, 32p., Nonfiction, LC 84-45334, ISBN 0-690-04428-3; 0-690-04429-1 (lib).

This science book explains how bacteria and viruses affect the human body and how the body fights them. Jenny is one of the children who is ill. A Reading Rainbow book.

Conford, Ellen, **Jenny Archer**, Little, Brown, 1989, 61p., Easy Reader, ISBN 0-316-15255-2.

Jenny is very creative in completing an autobiography for a class assignment, but discovers creativity and imagination are not always appreciated.

DeClements, Barthe, **Nothing's Fair in Fifth Grade**, Viking, 1981, 137p., Fiction, ISBN 0-670-517-410.

Jenny Sawyer is having a difficult time in fifth grade. She has problems with math, and her teacher is strict and assigns her to be a guide for a new girl who is overweight and steals to buy candy. California 1986. Georgia 1984. Hawaii 1984. Iowa 1984. Massachusetts 1985. Minnesota 1984. Nebraska 1984. New Mexico 1985. Ohio 1984. Texas 1984. Wisconsin 1984.

Eyerly, Jeannette, **Seeing Summer**, Lippincott, 1981, 153p., Fiction, ISBN 0-397-31966-5.

Although Jenny is blind she is able to do most things that sighted children can do. When she is kidnapped she shows how well she can take care of herself.

Kellogg, Steven, **Island of the Skog, The**, illustrated by Steven Kellogg, Dial, 1973, 28p., Picture Book, LC 73-6019, ISBN 0-8037-4122-7.

On National Rodent Day, Jenny and the other mice decide that they are tired of being chased by cats and dogs. They load a ship and sail away to find a peaceful island. After an exhausting voyage, the mice become deserted on an island inhabited by a large-footed skog. A Reading Rainbow book. Michigan 1983.

Mazer, Norma Fox, **Figure of Speech, A**, Dell, 1973, 197p., Fiction, ISBN 0-440-94374-4 (pbk).

Thirteen-year-old Jenny and her elderly grandfather have a special relationship in which honesty and dignity are important.

McCutcheon, Elsie, **Storm Bird**, Farrar, Straus & Giroux, 1987, 176p., Fiction, ISBN 0-374-37269-1.

Twelve-year-old Jenny and her father move from their comfortable home in London to a small fishing village. Jenny hears rumors that are the cause of a crisis that affects them.

Morrison, Dorothy Nafus, **Somebody's Horse**, Atheneum, 1986, 213p., Fiction, ISBN 0-689-31290-3.

Thirteen-year-old Jenny nurses an abandoned horse back to health and enters a local horse show.

Orgel, Doris, **Certain Magic**, Dial, 1975, 176p., Fiction, ISBN 0-8037-5405-1.

Jenny's aunt had been a refugee during World War II. While looking through her aunt's old copybook, Jenny discovers a mystery that she tries to solve when her family goes to London.

Rosen, Lillian, **Just Like Everybody Else**, Harcourt Brace Jovanovich, 1981, 155p., Fiction, ISBN 0-15-241652-8.

At fifteen, Jenny has an accident that leaves her deaf and she discovers the difficulties of trying to fit in with other teenagers.

JEREMIAH
See also Jeremy, Jerimy

Ahlberg, Janet and Allen Ahlberg, **Jeremiah in the Dark Woods**, Viking Kestrel, 1978, 47p., Fiction, ISBN 0-670-40637-6.

Jeremiah Obadiah Jackenary Jones lives in the middle of the Dark Woods in his grandmother's house, which is made of gingerbread and cakes. A comical fairy tale.

JEREMY
See also Jeremiah, Jerimy

Adler, C. S., **Magic of the Glits, The**, Avon, 1979, 90p., Fiction, ISBN 0-380-70403-X (pbk).

During his summer at Cape Cod, Jeremy breaks his leg, and he has to take care of Lynette. He decides that magic is the only way to solve Lynette's problems and tells her stories about the Glits, who were neither human nor fairies. Kansas 1982.

Fleming, Ian, **Chitty-Chitty-Bang-Bang: The Magical Car**, illustrated by John Burningham, Random House, 1964, 114p., Fiction, LC 64-21282, ISBN 0-394-81948-9.

Jeremy and Jemima Pott are twins who live with their parents in the woods beside a lake in England. The Potts are an unusual family, and when they decide to buy a car they want an unusual one. They get an old English racing car named Chitty-Chitty-Bang-Bang and have amazing adventures. Pacific Northwest 1967.

Glenn, Mel, **Squeeze Play**, Clarion, 1989, 135p., Fiction, ISBN 0-89919-859-7.

Jeremy has a very strict teacher in sixth grade. After school he practices baseball and then looks forward to visiting with an elderly friend.

Lasky, Kathryn, **Sugaring Time**, illustrated by Christopher G. Knight, Macmillan, 1983, 58p., Nonfiction, LC 82-23928, ISBN 0-02-751680-6.

Jeremy and his family live on a farm that has a small maple grove. In March, it is time to harvest the sap for maple syrup. Photographs show the family gathering sap and making syrup. 1984 Newbery Honor book.

Little, Jean, **Mama's Going to Buy You a Mockingbird**, Viking Kestrel, 1985, 213p., Fiction, ISBN 0-670-80346-4.

Eleven-year-old Jeremy goes through a difficult time emotionally when he discovers his father has terminal cancer.

JERIMY
See also Jeremiah, Jeremy

Pryor, Bonnie, **Mr. Z and the Time Clock**, Dillon, 1986, 117p., Fiction, ISBN 0-8751-8328-X.

Twelve-year-old Jerimy and his twin sister get involved in a complex fantasy as they travel between the past and the future.

JEROME
See also Jerry

Brooks, Bruce, **Moves Make the Man, The**, Harper & Row, 1984, 280p., Fiction, LC 83-49476, ISBN 0-06-020679-9; 0-06-020698-5 (lib).

Jerome Foxworthy is an excellent student and an excellent basketball player. He is also the first and only black student to integrate the biggest white school in his hometown in North Carolina. He and an emotionally troubled white athlete form a precarious friendship. 1985 Newbery Honor book. 1985 Boston Globe-Horn Book Award.

Montgomery, Rutherford, **Kildee House**, illustrated by Barbara Cooney, Doubleday, 1949, 209p., Fiction, ISBN 0-671-29518-7.

Jerome Kildee lives in an odd house that he built on the mountainside next to a redwood tree. Jerome is a silent man who lives quietly with animals for friends. When there are problems with the animals, the neighbor children help Jerome find a solution. 1950 Newbery Honor book.

JERRY
See also Gerald, Jerome

Bishop, Claire Huchet, **Pancakes—Paris**, illustrated by Georges Schreiber, Viking, 1947, 64p., Fiction, LC 47-2541, ISBN 670-53783-7.

Jerry is an American serviceman who is in France after World War II. He meets a young French boy who lives with his mother and younger sister in a small apartment and who wants to prepare a holiday meal like the one he remembers from before the war. 1947 Newbery Honor book.

Estes, Eleanor, **Ginger Pye**, illustrated by Louis Slobodkin, Harcourt Brace Jovanovich, 1951, 250p., Fiction, LC 51-1446, ISBN 0-15-230930-6.

A mysterious man in a mustard yellow hat and the disappearance of Ginger, their new puppy, bring excitement into the lives of the Pye children. 1952 Newbery Award book.

Hughes, Dean, **Jelly's Circus**, Atheneum, 1986, 153p., Fiction, ISBN 0-689-31217-2.

In this humorous story, Jerry Bean, known as Jelly, convinces his friends that they will make money if they stage a neighborhood circus.

JESS
See also Jessamy, Jesse, Jessica, Jessie

Paterson, Katherine, **Bridge to Terabithia**, illustrated by Donna Diamond, Crowell, 1977, 128p., Fiction, LC 77-02221, ISBN 0-690-135-90.

When Leslie moves into the house near Jess's, he has no idea that they will develop a special friendship. The two create Terabithia, their own secret kingdom in the woods, where they reign as king and queen until a tragedy strikes. 1978 Newbery Award book.

JESSAMY
See also Jess, Jesse

Holland, Isabelle, **Horse Named Peaceable, A**, Lothrop, Lee & Shepard, 1982, 157p., Fiction, ISBN 0-688-00534-9.

Jessamy feels very alone except for her horse. Her mother is dead and her father pays little attention to her. When her horse is sold, Jessamy runs away to rescue it.

JESSE
See also Jess, Jessica, Jessie

Sabin, Francene, **Jesse Owens, Olympic Hero**, illustrated by Hal Frenck, Troll, 1986, 48p., Nonfiction, ISBN 0-8167-0551-8.

Biographical information about the famous track-and-field athlete, Jesse Owens, who won four gold medals in the 1936 Olympics.

JESSICA
See also Jess, Jesse, Jessie

Estern, Anne Graham, **Picolinis**, illustrated by Katherine Coville, Bantam, 1988, 131p., Fiction, ISBN 0-553-15566-0.

Jessica is led into an exciting and dangerous adventure by the miniature circus family that lives in the dollhouse purchased at an auction.

Hahn, Mary Downing, **Daphne's Book**, Clarion, 1983, 177p., Fiction, LC 83-7348, ISBN 0-89919-183-5.

Jessica is not happy to be paired with Daphne for the seventh-grade Write-a-Book contest because the other students think Daphne is strange. A friendship develops between the girls as Jessica gets to know Daphne and discovers the tragic secret that Daphne has been hiding. Kansas 1986.

Root, Phyllis, **Moon Tiger**, illustrated by Ed Young, H. Holt, 1985, 28p., Picture Book, LC 85-7572, ISBN 0-03-000042-4.

Jessica Ellen is sent to bed because she won't read a story to her younger brother. In her room, she imagines a moon tiger that will take her for a ride. A Reading Rainbow book.

Snyder, Zilpha Keatley, **Witches of Worm, The**, illustrated by Alton Raible, Atheneum, 1977, 184p., Fiction, LC 72-75283, ISBN 0-689-30066-2.

Jessica has cared for Worm ever since she first saw the ugly, helpless, newborn kitten. When Worm begins making her do dreadful things against her will, Jessica wonders if Worm is a witch's cat. 1973 Newbery Honor book.

Warner, Gertrude Chandler, **Boxcar Children, The**, illustrated by L. Kate Deal, Whitman, 1950, 154p., Fiction, ISBN 0-8075-0851-9.

Jessica and the other three Alden children move into an old boxcar to avoid being sent to an institution. This is the first in a series of books about this family.

JESSIE
See also Jess, Jessamy, Jesse, Jessica

Fox, Paula, **Slave Dancer, The**, illustrated by Eros Keith, Bradbury, 1973, 176p., Fiction, LC 73-80642, ISBN 0-87888-062-3.

Thirteen-year-old Jessie Bollier lives in New Orleans during the 1840s. He is kidnapped by sailors and taken to a sailing ship that transports slaves. Aboard the ship, Jessie must play his flute while the slaves are forced to dance to the music. 1974 Newbery Award book.

Levinson, Riki, **DinnieAbbieSister-r-r!**, illustrated by Helen Cogancherry, Bradbury, 1987, 89p., Fiction, ISBN 0-02-757380-X.

Set in Brooklyn, Jessie wants to come in first at something but finds it hard with two older brothers.

Sloan, Carolyn, **Sea Child**, Holiday House, 1987, 128p., Fiction, ISBN 0-8234-0723-3.

Jessie has spent ten years in a mysterious place called the Sands. When she visits the mainland she makes contact with a girl who has been expecting her for a long time.

JETHRO

Hunt, Irene, **Across Five Aprils**, Follett, 1964, 223p., Fiction, LC 64-17209, ISBN 0-695-80100-7.

During the Civil War, nine-year-old Jethro has to take care of the family's farm in southern Illinois and finds that there are dangers at home as well as during the battles. 1965 Newbery Honor book.

JILL

Blume, Judy, **Blubber**, Bradbury, 1974, 153p., Fiction, ISBN 0-02-711010-9.

Jill is eleven years old when she and her friends begin tormenting an obese classmate by calling her names and playing mean tricks on her. Jill becomes the next victim when she decides to stick up for the girl. Pacific Northwest 1978.

Lampman, Evelyn, **City Under the Back Steps, The**, illustrated by Honore Valincourt, Doubleday, 1960, 210p., Fiction, LC 60-13539.

After being stung by a strange insect, Jill and her brother find themselves shrinking until they are the size of ants. The two children become pets of the ant queen and have unusual adventures in their own backyard. Vermont 1962.

Oppenheimer, Joan, **Gardine vs. Hanover**, Crowell, 1982, 152p., Fiction, ISBN 0-690-04190-X.

Fifteen-year-old Jill Gardine is not happy that her new stepfather is bringing his children to live with them. Jill and her stepsister almost break up their parents' marriage.

Rodgers, Raboo, **Magnum Fault**, Houghton Mifflin, 1984, 185p., Fiction, ISBN 0-395-34558-8.

Jill and her friend become involved in a serious mystery when Jill's engineer father disappears after an accident that the sheriff claims did not happen.

JIM
See also James, Jimmie, Jimmy

Aaseng, Nathan, **Jim Henson, Muppet Master**, Lerner, 1988, 40p., Nonfiction, ISBN 0-8225-1615-2.

The biography of Jim Henson, the man who created the muppets, including Miss Piggy and Kermit the Frog.

Barracca, Debra and Sal Barracca, **Adventures of Taxi Dog, The**, illustrated by Mark Buehner, Dial, 1990, 32p., Picture Book, LC 89-1056, ISBN 0-8037-0672-3.

Maxi was a dog without a home until Jim, the taxi driver, invited Maxi to live with him. Maxi rides in the taxi with Jim and the two share many adventures as they drive around the city. A Reading Rainbow book.

Christopher, Matt, **Catch That Pass!**, illustrated by Harvey Kidder, Little, Brown, 1969, 130p., Fiction, ISBN 0-316-13932-7.

Jim Nardi fails to catch a pass due to his own fears and causes the team to lose a game. He is able to conquer his fears when he learns that the coach had the same problem.

Gray, Patsey, **Barefoot a Thousand Miles**, Walker, 1984, 92p., Fiction, ISBN 0-8027-6528-9.

Jim leaves his home on the Apache reservation in Arizona to hitchhike to California in search of his dog. On his journey he has numerous adventures including an encounter with a criminal and with the law.

McCall, Edith, **Message from the Mountains**, Walker, 1985, 122p., Fiction, ISBN 0-8027-6582-3.

Set in the frontier in 1826, fifteen-year-old Jim Matthews is unsure what to do when his father does not return from a trip as he had promised.

Santrey, Laurence, **Jim Thorpe, Young Athlete**, illustrated by George Ulrich, Troll, 1983, 48p., Non-fiction, ISBN 0-89375-845-0.

Biographical information about the Native American, Jim Thorpe, and his extraordinary athletic abilities.

Steele, Mary Q., **First of the Penguins, The**, illustrated by Susan Jeffers, Greenwillow, 1973, 154p., Fiction, ISBN 0-688-04801-3.

Thirteen-year-old Jim and his friend began their adventures when they decided to find the first of the penguins.

Stolz, Mary, **Noonday Friends**, Harper & Row, 1965, 182p., Fiction, ISBN 0-06-025946-9.

Jim and his twin sister live in New York City and their family doesn't have much money. 1966 Newbery Honor book.

Zelazny, Roger, **Dark Traveling**, Walker, 1987, 143p., Fiction, ISBN 0-8027-6686-2.

In this science fiction story, Jim and his siblings look through parallel worlds for their father who has disappeared. During their search they discover that war is being waged against their world.

JIMMIE
See also James, Jim, Jimmy

Byars, Betsy, **Good-Bye, Chicken Little**, Harper & Row, 1979, 101p., Fiction, ISBN 0-06-020911-9.

Jimmie feels guilty over the death of his uncle because he could not stop taking a foolish dare.

JIMMY
See also James, Jim, Jimmie

Naylor, Phyllis Reynolds, **One of the Third Grade Thonkers**, illustrated by Waltlern Gaffney-Kessell, Atheneum, 1988, 136p., Fiction, ISBN 0-689-31424-8.

Jimmy Novak and his friends plan on converting a garage into a clubhouse during their summer vacation, but their plans are changed with the arrival of Jimmy's cousin and family emergencies.

Nesbit, E., **Enchanted Castle**, illustrated by H. R. Millar, Puffin, 1985, 252p., Fiction, ISBN 0-14-035057-8 (pbk).

Jimmy is one of the children who spends his summer investigating an enchanted castle and having magical adventures.

Noble, Trinka Hakes, **Day Jimmy's Boa Ate the Wash, The**, illustrated by Steven Kellogg, Dial, 1984, 28p., Picture Book, LC 80-15098, ISBN 0-8037-0094-6.

When a girl tells her mother about the class field trip to the farm, the story becomes more and more interesting because of Jimmy's pet boa constrictor. A Reading Rainbow book.

JINNY
See also Genny, Jennifer, Jenny, Virginia

Walker, David, **Big Ben**, illustrated by Victor Ambrus, Houghton Mifflin, 1969, 134p., Fiction, LC 74-82477, ISBN 0-395-07167-4.

Jinny and her brother acquire Big Ben, a gentle, bumbling St. Bernard puppy. The children discover that living with a fast-growing dog has its hazards as well as joys. Arkansas 1972.

JIRO

Paterson, Katherine, **Master Puppeteer, The**, illustrated by Harv Wells, Crowell, 1975, 179p., Fiction, ISBN 0-690-00913-5.

Jiro is the son of a poor puppetmaker in eighteenth-century Japan. When Jiro runs away from home to become an apprentice at a puppet theater, he has the opportunity to see the social class structure of his country and the unrest that it causes. 1977 Jane Addams Award book.

JO

See also Jo Beth, Jo-Beth, Joe, Mary Jo

Alcott, Louisa M., **Little Women, or Meg, Jo, Beth and Amy**, Little, Brown, 1968, 372p., Fiction, ISBN 0-316-03090-2.

The classic story of four sisters and their family life in New England at the time of the Civil War.

Bawden, Nina, **Rebel on a Rock**, Lippincott, 1978, 158p., Fiction, ISBN 0-397-32140-6.

Jo decides that her stepfather is a spy when the family goes on a vacation abroad, and the family becomes involved in local political problems.

Wrightson, Patricia, **Balyet**, Macmillan, 1989, 129p., Fiction, ISBN 0-689-50468-3.

Fourteen-year-old Jo hides in order to accompany her aboriginal neighbor on a trip, thus provoking a spirit and causing danger. Set in Australia, this story is based on an aboriginal legend.

JO BETH

See also Jo, Jo-Beth

Clifford, Eth, **Just Tell Me When We're Dead**, illustrated by George Hughes, Houghton Mifflin, 1983, 130p., Fiction, LC 83-10865, ISBN 0-395-33071-8.

When their cousin leaves a note that he has gone West, Jo Beth and her older sister decide to go looking for him. None of them expect the adventures they will have. Oklahoma 1986.

JO-BETH

See also Jo, Jo Beth

Clifford, Eth, **Help! I'm a Prisoner in the Library**, Houghton Mifflin, 1979, 96p., Fiction, ISBN 0-590-40605-1.

Jo-Beth and Mary Rose's father forgot to put gas in the car and it runs out of gas in Indianapolis. While their father goes for gas, the two girls go into the Finton Memorial Library for Children. When the lights go out, the girls discover they have been locked into the library for the night during a terrible blizzard. Indiana 1982.

JOAN

Nottridge, Harold, **Joan of Arc**, illustrated by Angus McBride, Bookwright, 1987, 32p., Nonfiction, ISBN 0-531-18177-4.

During the fifteenth century, Joan of Arc led the French people against the British who were taking their lands. Joan believed she was following the directions that she was given when she prayed. Upon her capture, Joan was burned at the stake by the British. She was given sainthood during the twentieth century.

JODY

Erwin, Betty, **Go to the Room of the Eyes**, illustrated by Irene Burns, Little, Brown, 1969, 180p., Fiction, LC 71-77446, ISBN 0-316-24946-7.

When they move into an old house in Seattle, Jody and the other five Evans children discover a strange message left by children who lived there thirty years earlier. The message leads them on a treasure hunt. Vermont 1971.

Van Allsburg, Chris, **Jumanji**, illustrated by Chris Van Allsburg, Houghton Mifflin, 1981, 30p., Picture Book, LC 80-29632, ISBN 0-395-30448-2.

Jody and Peter are bored until they discover an ordinary-looking game board that takes them into a mysterious jungle on an exciting and bizarre adventure. 1982 Caldecott Award book. Kentucky 1983. Washington 1984. West Virginia 1985.

JOE

See also Jo, Joey, Joseph

Boston, Lucy, **Sea Egg**, illustrated by Peter Boston, Harcourt Brace Jovanovich, 1967, 94p., Fiction, ISBN 0-15-271050-7.

Joe and Toby buy an egg-shaped stone while on a seaside holiday. When it hatches, the children discover an unusual playmate and the three have unusual adventures.

DeJong, Meindert, **Along Came a Dog**, illustrated by Maurice Sendak, Harper & Row, 1958, 172p., Fiction, LC 57-9265, ISBN 0-06-021421-X.

Shortly after the big spring ice storm, several unusual things begin to happen. Joe's little red hen becomes different from the other chickens and a big black dog comes searching for a home. A wonderful relationship grows between the two animals, although it takes time for Joe to recognize it. 1959 Newbery Honor book.

Kalb, Jonah, **Goof That Won the Pennant, The**, illustrated by Sandy Kossin, Houghton Mifflin, 1976, 103p., Fiction, LC 76-21678, ISBN 0-395-24834-5.

Joe is one of the members of the Blazer's baseball team, a team of oddballs and misfits who do not even try to win. When their coach gives them the idea that winning is more fun than losing, the team decides to try. Indiana 1981.

Knight, Eric, **Lassie Come Home**, illustrated by Marguerite Kirmse, Holt, Rinehart & Winston, 1940, 248p., Fiction, LC 78-3570, ISBN 0-03-044101-3.

The classic story of the prize collie dog, Lassie, who belonged to a humble household. When hard times fall on her owners, they sell Lassie to a wealthy family several hundred miles away. Lassie heads for her home and Joe, guided only by her instincts. Pacific Northwest 1943.

Latterman, Terry, **Little Joe, a Hopi Indian Boy, Learns a Hopi Indian Secret**, Pussywillow, 1985, 32p., Fiction, ISBN 0-934739-01-3.

Little Joe begins his preparations for adulthood in the Hopi society by first going through a secret ceremony. He learns about his heritage and the responsibilities that go along with becoming an adult.

Rockwell, Thomas, **How to Eat Fried Worms**, illustrated by Emily McCully, Watts, 1973, 115p., Fiction, LC 73-4262, ISBN 0-531-02631-0.

Billy is willing to eat anything and agrees to eat fifteen worms to win a bet. Joe and his other friends watch to see if Billy will really eat them. Arizona 1979. California 1975. Hawaii 1976. Indiana 1977. Iowa 1980. Massachusetts 1976. Missouri 1975. Oklahoma 1976. South Carolina 1976.

Sorensen, Virginia, **Miracles on Maple Hill**, illustrated by Beth Krush and Joe Krush, Harcourt Brace Jovanovich, 1956, 180p., Fiction, LC 56-8358, ISBN 0-15-254558-1.

Joe and Marly have moved with their parents from the city to a small farmhouse on Maple Hill. Marly hopes for miracles—not just the ones that bring sap to the trees to make maple syrup, but one that will help their father recover from his experiences as a prisoner of war. 1957 Newbery Award book.

Steele, Mary Q., **Wish, Come True**, illustrated by Muriel Batherman, Greenwillow, 1979, 115p., Fiction, ISBN 0-688-84230-5.

Joe and his sister think their vacation with their great-aunt will be dull until they find an old metal ring, which they think is magic. Their adventures begin when they search for buried treasure.

Williams, Jay, **Danny Dunn and the Homework Machine**, illustrated by Ezra Jack Keats, McGraw-Hill, 1958, 141p., Fiction, LC 58-10015, ISBN 07-070520-8; 07-070519-4.

Joe is a friend of Danny Dunn. With the assistance of a computer, Danny invents a homework machine that will give the correct answers and write two papers at once. Pacific Northwest 1961.

Williams, Jeanne, **Tame the Wild Stallion**, illustrated by Walle Conoly, Texas Christian University Press, 1985, 181p., Fiction, ISBN 0-87565-002-3.

Set in 1846, Joe Mitchell is a young Texan who is captured by Mexican cowboys. During his year of captivity, Joe learns about people, cultural differences, and the importance of freedom.

JOEL

Bauer, Marion Dane, **On My Honor**, Clarion, 1980, 90p., Fiction, LC 86-2679, ISBN 0-89919-439-7.

Twelve-year-old Joel has given his word to his father that he won't ride his bicycle anywhere except to the park. When his best friend challenges him to a swim in the treacherous Vermillion River, Joel knows they shouldn't because they have been warned never to go near the water there. The consequences of their actions will forever haunt Joel. 1987 Newbery Honor book. Kansas 1989.

Henry, Marguerite, **Justin Morgan Had a Horse**, illustrated by Wesley Dennis, Rand McNally, 1954, 170p., Fiction, LC 54-08903, ISBN 0-528-82255-1.

Joel is involved with the unusual work horse raised in Vermont that becomes the sire of a famous American breed of horses. The horse was known originally as 'Little Bub' but takes the name of his owner, Justin Morgan. 1946 Newbery Honor book.

JOEY
See also Jo, Joe, Joseph

Hicks, Clifford, **Peter Potts Book of World Records**, illustrated by Kathleen Collins Howell, H. Holt, 1987, 101p., Fiction, ISBN 0-8050-0409-2.

Thirteen-year-old Joey and his best friend try many ideas to become world record holders with humorous results.

Hildick, E. W., **Case of the Bashful Bank Robber, The**, illustrated by Liesl Weil, Macmillan, 1987, 138p., Fiction, ISBN 0-02-743870-8.

Joey and his friends solve mysteries from their basement headquarters. There are several other books about this group of friends.

JOHN
See also Johnny, Jonathan, Juan

Barrie, James M., **Peter Pan**, illustrated by Trina Schart Hyman, Scribner, 1980, 183p., Fiction, ISBN 0-684-16611-9.

The classic adventure of John and the other Darling children when they are taken to Never-Neverland by Peter Pan.

Bishop, Claire Huchet, **Pancakes–Paris**, illustrated by Georges Schreiber, Viking, 1947, 64p., Fiction, LC 47-2541, ISBN 670-53783-7.

John is an American serviceman who is in France at the end of World War II. John meets a young French boy who lives with his mother and young sister in a small apartment and who wants to make a special holiday meal like the one he remembers from before the war. 1947 Newbery Honor book.

Brandt, Keith, **John Paul Jones: Hero of the Seas**, illustrated by Susan Swan, Troll, 1983, 48p., Nonfiction, ISBN 0-89375-849-3.

A biography about the American naval hero John Paul Jones and his contributions to the American Revolution.

Burnford, Sheila, **Incredible Journey, The**, illustrated by Carl Burger, Little, Brown, 1960, 145p., Fiction, LC 61-5313, ISBN 0-316-11714-5.

John Longridge agreed to care for the three pets of his young friends, Elizabeth and Peter, while they traveled with their parents for nine months. Bodger, the English bull terrier; Luath, the Labrador retriever; and Tao, the Siamese cat, take their own journey, staying together as they walk over 300 miles seeking their family home. Kansas 1964. Pacific Northwest 1964. Vermont 1963.

Catling, Patrick Skene, **Chocolate Touch, The**, illustrated by Margot Apple, Morrow, 1979, 126p., Fiction, ISBN 0-688-22187-9.

John Midas loves chocolate and his greed causes tremendous problems. After buying a box of chocolates with an unusual coin, everything that John touches turns to chocolate, including his mother. Utah 1983.

Eckert, Alan W., **Incident at Hawk's Hill**, illustrated by John Schoenherr, Little, Brown, 1971, 173p., Fiction, ISBN 0-316-20866-3.

Sixteen-year-old John has a younger brother who is shy and withdrawn. Six-year-old Ben rarely speaks to people but has an amazing ability to communicate with animals. Ben and a badger develop a bond and Ben lives in the badger's burrow for several months. Set on a homestead in the Canadian West prairies in 1870, this book is based on an actual incident. A 1972 Newbery Honor book.

Fritz, Jean, **Will You Sign Here, John Hancock?**, illustrated by Trina Schart Hyman, Coward-McCann, 1976, 47p., Nonfiction, ISBN 0-698-20308-9.

John Henry was the first person to sign the Declaration of Independence. This biography tells about his boyhood and follows him until he became the governor of Massachusetts.

Gibbons, Gail, **Fill It Up! All About Service Stations**, illustrated by Gail Gibbons, Crowell, 1985, 30p., Picture Book, LC 84-45345, ISBN 0-690-04439-9; 0-690-04440-2 (lib).

John and Peggy spend a busy day at their service station. Fred helps with repairs and puts gasoline in the cars. A Reading Rainbow book.

Gleiter, Jan, **John James Audubon**, illustrated by Yoshi Miyaki, Raintree, 1988, 32p., Nonfiction, ISBN 0-8172-2675-3.

John James Audubon was a naturalist who was determined to paint every bird that existed in the young United States. He traveled through forests and down rivers, painting 400 birds in their natural environments. This biography provides information about Audubon and his journeys.

Gretz, Susanna and Alison Sage, **Teddy Bears Cure a Cold**, illustrated by Susanna Gretz and Alison Sage, Four Winds, 1984, 32p., Picture book, LC 84-4015, ISBN 0-590-07949-2.

William the bear feels sick and spends several days in bed while John and the other bears take care of him. A Reading Rainbow book.

Hunt, Mabel Leigh, **Better Known as Johnny Appleseed**, Lippincott, 1950, 212p., Nonfiction, ISBN 0-397-30163-4.

John Chapman was born in Massachusetts during the Revolutionary War. When he was old enough, he headed west, clearing land and planting apple orchards to supply the fruit to the settlers that he knew would soon follow. 1951 Newbery Honor book.

Kellogg, Steven, **Johnny Appleseed**, illustrated by Steven Kellogg, Morrow, 1988, 48p., Nonfiction, ISBN 0-688-06418-3.

John Chapman became known as Johnny Appleseed as he traveled west across the Allegheny Mountains planting apple orchards and living simply. This is a biography about John Chapman.

Kennedy, John F., **Profiles in Courage**, illustrated by Emil Weiss, Harper & Row, 1955, 164p., Nonfiction, LC 64-17696.

Former president John Quincy Adams exhibited political courage under pressure. He is one of the eight statesmen featured in this book. 1964 Addams Award book.

Lillegard, Dee, **John Tyler**, Children's Press, 1987, 100p., Nonfiction, ISBN 0-516-01393-9.

John Tyler became president of the United States after the death of President Harrison. This biography tells about Tyler and his contributions to the country.

MacLachlan, Patricia, **Through Grandpa's Eyes**, illustrated by Deborah Ray, Harper & Row, 1979, 48p., Picture Book, LC 79-2019, ISBN 0-06-024044-X; 0-06-024043-1 (lib).

John loves to go to his grandfather's house. His grandfather is blind and teaches John to see the world in a different way. A Reading Rainbow book.

McNulty, Faith, **Hurricane**, illustrated by Gail Owens, Harper & Row, 1983, 43p., Fiction, ISBN 0-06-024143-8.

John and his parents begin making preparations when they learn that a hurricane is heading toward their New England home.

Morrow, Honore, **On to Oregon**, illustrated by Edward Shenton, Morrow, 1954, 239p., Fiction, ISBN 0-688-21639-0.

Both parents die as the Sager family journeys by wagon train from their home in Missouri to Oregon. Thirteen-year-old John assumes responsibility for his siblings and continues the trip despite hardships.

Paulsen, Gary, **Tracker**, Bradbury, 1984, 90p., Fiction, ISBN 0-02-770220-0.

Thirteen-year-old John has a difficult time accepting the fact that his grandfather is dying of cancer. As he hunts a doe by himself, he gains acceptance of the inevitable.

Ransome, Arthur, **Swallows and Amazons**, illustrated by Arthur Ransome, Cape/Random House, 1981, 351p., Fiction, ISBN 0-224-60631-X.

John Walker and his siblings sail to an island and spend the summer camping by themselves. There are other books about their adventures.

Smith, Kathie Billingslea, **John F. Kennedy**, illustrated by James Seward, Messner, 1987, 24p., Nonfiction, ISBN 0-671-64602-8.

Biographical information about President John F. Kennedy. He was born into a family of wealthy achievers and showed his abilities in the Navy, and later as a member of the House of Representatives.

Tregaskis, Richard, **John F. Kennedy and the PT-109**, Random House, 1962, 192p., Nonfiction, ISBN 0-394-90399-4.

Biographical information about former President John F. Kennedy during World War II. Pacific Northwest 1965.

JOHNNY
See also John, Jonathan, Juan

Bellairs, John, **Curse of the Blue Figurine, The**, Dial, 1983, 200p., Fiction, ISBN 0-8037-1265-0.

Johnny Dixon finds an old black book and a small blue figurine in a church. When he takes them home, he is plunged into a horrifying ghost story. There are several other books about Johnny and his adventures.

Branscum, Robbie, **Adventures of Johnny May**, illustrated by Deborah Howland, Harper & Row, 1984, 87p., Fiction, ISBN 0-06-020615-2.

Set in the hills of Arkansas, Johnny May shoots a deer to take to her hungry grandparents on Christmas.

Brenner, Barbara, **Wagon Wheels**, illustrated by Don Bolognese, Harper & Row, 1978, 64p., Easy Reader, LC 76-21391, ISBN 0-06-020668-3; 0-06-020669-1 (lib).

Johnny, Willie, Little Brother, and their parents left Kentucky in 1878 to go west as pioneers. After their mother dies, the men build a dugout where they stay for a winter and where the three boys wait while their father searches for new land. Based on the true story of a family that traveled to Kansas to take advantage of free land offered through the Homestead Act. A Reading Rainbow book.

Forbes, Esther, **Johnny Tremain**, illustrated by Lynd Ward, Houghton Mifflin, 1943, 256p., Fiction, ISBN 0-395-06766-9.

This book is set in Boston in 1773. Johnny Tremain is a bright, talented fourteen-year-old apprentice to a silversmith. When molten lead burns Johnny's hand it becomes useless and he becomes a dispatch rider. Johnny meets Boston patriots and becomes involved in events leading to the Boston Tea Party and the Battle of Lexington. 1944 Newbery Award book.

Sawyer, Ruth, **Journey Cake, Ho!**, illustrated by Robert McCloskey, Viking, 1953, 45p., Picture Book, ISBN .

When Johnny leaves the farm due to hard times, his journey cake leads him on many chases that result in a farmyard full of animals. 1954 Caldecott Honor book.

Ward, Lynd, **Biggest Bear, The**, illustrated by Lynd Ward, Houghton Mifflin, 1952, 84p., Picture Book, LC 52-8730, ISBN 0-395-14806-5.

Little Johnny goes hunting in the woods near his farm for the largest bear he can find. He returns with a very small bear cub. The cub grows and grows and gets into more and more mischief until Johnny has to find a solution. 1953 Caldecott Award book.

JONAH

Heide, Florence Parry, **Banana Twist**, Holiday House, 1978, 111p., Fiction, ISBN 0-8234-034-3.

Jonah Krock loves both sweets and television. He becomes friends with his neighbor who is determined to become Jonah's friend, and the boys have some humorous times until Jonah realizes his friend has beat him out of something important. Arkansas 1981.

Honeycutt, Natalie, **All New Jonah Twist**, Bradbury, 1986, 110p., Fiction, ISBN 0-02-744840-1.

In third grade, Jonah decides he will change himself to be the person that everyone wants him to be with humorous results. There is another book about Jonah.

Hutton, Warwick, **Jonah and the Great Fish**, illustrated by Warwick Hutton, Atheneum, 1983, 32p., Picture Book, ISBN 0-689-502-834.

A retelling of the biblical story of Jonah, a man who was swallowed by a large fish and emerged to tell the tale. 1984 Boston Globe-Horn Book Award book.

JONATHAN
See also John, Johnny, Juan

Avi, **Fighting Ground**, illustrated by Ellen Thompson, Lippincott, 1984, 151p., Fiction, ISBN 0-397-320-736; 0-397-320-744 (lib).

When Jonathan is thirteen he goes to fight in the Revolutionary War. He learns that there are wars within people as well as between people. 1985 Scott O'Dell Award.

Bach, Richard, **Jonathan Livingston Seagull**, illustrated by Russell Munson, Macmillan, 1970, 93p., Fiction, LC 75-119617, ISBN 0-380-01286-3.

Jonathan is not an ordinary seagull. He spends so much time perfecting his flying that he does not have time to get food, and the other gulls ostracize him for being different. Hawaii 1974.

Beatty, Patricia, **Jonathan Down Under**, Morrow, 1982, 219p., Fiction, ISBN 0-688-01467-4.

In the 1850s, Jonathan and his father move to Australia in hopes of striking it rich after they are unable to find gold in California. They experience a lot of hard luck, and Jonathan is left to survive on his own when his father dies in a cave-in.

Dalgliesh, Alice, **Bears on Hemlock Mountain, The**, illustrated by Helen Sewell, Scribner, 1952, 68p., Fiction, ISBN 0-684-19169-5.

Eight-year-old Jonathan and his family live in a farmhouse at the foot of a hill known as Hemlock Mountain. When he is sent alone to go over Hemlock Mountain to borrow a large iron cooking pot, Jonathan has to convince himself that there are no bears there. 1953 Newbery Honor book.

de Angeli, Marguerite, **Yonie Wondernose**, illustrated by Marguerite de Angeli, Doubleday, 1944, 38p., Fiction, ISBN 0-385-07573-1.

Seven-year-old Jonathan is a young Amish boy who lives on a Pennsylania Dutch farm. He is called 'Yonie Wondernose' by his father because he is so curious. 1945 Caldecott Honor book.

Gates, Doris, **Little Vic**, illustrated by Kate Seredy, Viking, 1951, 160p., Fiction, LC 51-13558, ISBN 0-670-43435-3.

The son of a famous race horse, an undersized colt has the potential to be a winner but no one recognizes it except for Jonathan, the stable boy. Jonathan trains to become a jockey and wins the right to ride his favorite horse to victory. Kansas 1954.

Houghton, Eric, **Steps Out of Time**, Lothrop, Lee & Shepard, 1980, 128p., Fiction, ISBN 0-688-41970-4.

Jonathan and his father have moved to a new home. As Jonathan returns home from school during a mist, he discovers an unusual family that has come with the mist. A time fantasy in which Jonathan moves ahead in time and experiences events that happen to his relatives of the future.

Lasky, Kathryn, **Sugaring Time**, illustrated by Christopher G. Knight, Macmillan, 1983, 58p., Nonfiction, LC 82-23928, ISBN 0-02-751680-6.

Jonathan and his family live on a farm that has a small maple grove. In March, it is time to harvest the sap for maple syrup. Photographs show the family gathering sap and making syrup. 1984 Newbery Honor book.

Lindgren, Astrid, **Brothers Lionheart**, illustrated by J. K. Lambert, Penguin, 1975, 183p., Fiction, ISBN 0-14-031955-7.

Jonathan knows that his little brother doesn't have long to live, so he tells him of a fantasy land where the two can be together and fight the forces of evil.

Service, Pamela, **Stinker from Space**, Scribner, 1988, 83p., Fiction, ISBN 0-684-18910-0.

Jonathan is one of the children who befriends an alien who has taken on the body of a skunk until he can find a way to return to his own planet.

JOSEPH
See also Jo, Joe, Joey

Freedman, Russell, **Indian Chiefs**, Holiday House, 1987, 151p., Nonfiction, ISBN 0-8234-0625-3.

Joseph was the famous chief of the Nez Perce Indian tribe. He is one of the six American Indian chiefs who are covered in this title.

JOSH
See also Joshua

Fleischman, Sid, **McBroom Tells the Truth**, illustrated by Walter Lorraine, Little, Brown, 1981, 42p., Fiction, ISBN 0-316-28550-1.

In this tall tale, Josh McBroom and his family have hilarious adventures when they buy a New England farm that can produce four crops a year. There are other books about the McBroom family.

Holland, Barbara, **Prisoners at the Kitchen Table**, Clarion, 1979, 121p., Fiction, LC 79-11730, ISBN 0-395-28969-6.

Polly Conover is showing Josh Blake her new fishing pole when a couple stop their car and say that they are relatives of Polly's. They invite Polly and Josh to their home, and the next day the children realize they have been kidnapped. It is scary, lonely, and boring until Josh comes up with a plan. Pacific Northwest 1983. South Carolina 1983.

Zirpoli, Jane, **Roots in the Outfield**, Houghton Mifflin, 1988, 149p., Fiction, ISBN 0-395-45184-1.

Josh is taunted by the members of the baseball team because of his fear of the ball. When he goes to live with his father and stepmother, Josh is able to meet his favorite baseball player.

JOSHUA
See also Josh

Clifford, Eth, **Remembering Box**, illustrated by Donna Diamond, Houghton Mifflin, 1985, 70p., Fiction, ISBN 0-395-38476-1.

Nine-year-old Joshua and his grandmother have a special relationship and she shares her memories when he stays with her.

Levoy, Myron, **Magic Hat of Mortimer Wintergreen, The**, HarperCollins, 1988, 211p., Fiction, ISBN 0-06-023842-9.

A melodramatic and humorous story set in 1893. Thirteen-year-old Joshua and his younger sister meet a famous magician as they escape from their wicked aunt.

JUAN
See also John, Johnny, Jonathan

Cameron, Ann, **Most Beautiful Place in the World, The**, illustrated by Thomas B. Allen, Knopf, 1988, 57p., Fiction, LC 88-532, ISBN 0-394-89463-4; 0-394-99463-9 (lib).

Juan has grown up living with his grandmother in a small Central American town. When he is seven years old he knows the value of hard work, the joy of learning, and the location of the most beautiful place on earth. 1989 Jane Addams Award book.

de Trevino, Elizabeth Borton, **I, Juan de Pareja**, Farrar, Straus & Giroux, 1965, 180p., Fiction, LC 65-19330, ISBN 0-374-33531-1.

Juan de Pareja was born into slavery early in the seventeenth century in Seville, Spain. He became the slave of the painter Velasquez and the two became companions and friends. Juan was given his freedom and learned to paint. Several of Juan's paintings hang in European museums today. Based on factual historical information. 1966 Newbery Award book.

Politi, Leo, **Song of the Swallows**, illustrated by Leo Politi, Scribner, 1949, 32p., Picture Book, ISBN 0-684-92309-2.

Juan lives near the village of Capistrano where old Julian is the bell ringer for the beautiful Mission. When the swallows leave Capistrano for the season, Juan prepares for their return. 1950 Caldecott Award book.

JUDSON

Evarts, Hal G., **Bigfoot**, Scribner, 1973, 190p., Fiction, LC 73-1329, ISBN 684-13388-1.

Judson Reed, better known as Dingo, had heard and laughed at the stories about Bigfoot. After being hired as a camping guide by a famous professor, Dingo finds himself involved in a search for the Bigfoot that has been going to their camp. Arkansas 1976.

JUDY

Lee, Betsy, **Judy Blume's Story**, Dillon, 1981, 112p., Nonfiction, ISBN 0-87518-209-7.

A biography about the popular author, Judy Blume. The book includes numerous photographs.

JULES

Quackenbush, Robert, **Who Said There's No Man on the Moon?**, Prentice-Hall, 1985, 36p., Nonfiction, ISBN 0-13-958430-7.

Jules Verne was a writer of science stories. This biography gives information about the writer and his interest in science.

JULIA

See also Julie

Cameron, Eleanor, **Room Made of Windows, A**, illustrated by Trina Schart Hyman, Little, Brown, 1971, 271p., Fiction, LC 77-140479, ISBN 0-316-12523-7.

Julia loves unusual words and wants to be a writer like her father who died before he had anything published. Julia and her brother live with their mother in a large old house with interesting neighbors, and Julia doesn't want her mother to remarry because Julia would have to move away from her special room. 1971 Boston Globe-Horn Book Award.

Cameron, Eleanor, **That Julia Redfern**, illustrated by Gail Owens, Dutton, 1982, 133p., Fiction, ISBN 0-525-44015-1.

Julia Redfern has a lively imagination and an independent spirit. When her father dies, she helps her family through the difficult times. There are several other books about Julia.

Conrad, Pam, **My Daniel**, Harper & Row, 1989, 140p., Fiction, ISBN 0-06-021313-2.

Grandmother Julia visits New York and takes her grandchildren to the Museum of Natural History. When they view the dinosaur displays, she tells about her youthful years in Nebraska along with information about the skeletel remains.

JULIAN

See also Julie

Cameron, Ann, **Julian's Glorious Summer**, illustrated by Dora Leder, Random House, 1987, 62p., Easy Reader, ISBN 0-394-99117-6.

Julian is afraid of falling so he plans ways to avoid having to learn to ride a bicycle, including working in the house and in the garden. There are other books about Julian and his family.

Enright, Elizabeth, **Gone-Away Lake**, illustrated by Beth Krush and Joe Krush, Harcourt Brace Jovanovich, 1957, 192p., Fiction, LC 57-7172, ISBN 0-15-636460-3.

Julian and his cousin, Portia, make three interesting discoveries in the woods around their new summer home. They find a Latin inscription, a swamp that had once been a lake, and two fascinating people who live in the old summer houses that were thought to be deserted. When the vine-covered Villa Caprice is uncovered, it reveals its secrets of fifty years. 1958 Newbery Honor book.

O'Dell, Scott, **Captive, The**, Houghton Mifflin, 1979, 210p., Fiction, ISBN 0-395-27811-2.

Sixteen-year-old Julian is a Spaniard who is shipwrecked on a desert island during the early 1500s. He is forced to impersonate a Mayan god in order to survive. This is the first volume of a trilogy.

Politi, Leo, **Song of the Swallows**, illustrated by Leo Politi, Scribner, 1949, 32p., Picture Book, ISBN 0-684-92309-2.

Old Julian is the bell ringer for the beautiful Capistrano Mission. Juan lives near the village of Capistrano, and when the swallows leave for the season he prepares for their return. 1950 Caldecott Award book.

JULIE
See also Julia, Julian, Juliette, Julius

George, Jean Craighead, **Julie of the Wolves**, illustrated by John Schoenherr, Harper & Row, 1972, 170p., Fiction, ISBN 0-06-021944-0.

The story of the young Eskimo girl Miyax is told in three parts. The first and third tell of her amazing journey across miles of Arctic tundra. Traveling alone, she is befriended by wolves. The short midsection is a flashback about her decision to take this trip. This adventure story of survival and courage also tells of the conflicts between primitive and modern life-styles. 1973 Newbery Award book.

Hunt, Irene, **Up a Road Slowly**, Berkeley, 1966, 192p., Fiction, ISBN 0-425-10003-0.

When her mother dies, Julie goes to live with her very strict aunt and learns a great deal about growing up. When her father remarries and she can return home, Julie decides to stay with her aunt. 1967 Newbery Award book.

Pryor, Bonnie, **Mr. Z and the Time Clock**, Dillon, 1986, 117p., Fiction, ISBN 0-8751-8328-X.

Twelve-year-old Julie and her twin brother become involved in a complex fantasy as they travel between the past and the future.

JULIETTE
See also Julie

Kudlinski, Kathleen V., **Juliette Gordon Low: America's First Girl Scout**, illustrated by Sheila Hamanaka, Viking Kestrel, 1988, 55p., Nonfiction, ISBN 0-670-82208-6.

Biographical information about the founder of the American Girl Scouts and how she decided to start the organization.

JULIUS
See also Julie

Clymer, Eleanor, **Luke Was There**, Dell, 1973, 72p., Fiction, ISBN 0-440-40139-9.

Julius runs away from the children's shelter but is helped by the counselor that works there.

JUNE

Holl, Kristi, **Just Like a Real Family**, Atheneum, 1983, 122p., Fiction, ISBN 0-689-30970-8.

The sixth-grade class project involves visits to a retirement home, and June becomes friends with an elderly man who is able to help her with family problems.

JUNIOR

Hamilton, Virginia, **Planet of Junior Brown, The**, Macmillan, 1971, 210p., Fiction, ISBN 0-02-742510-X.

Junior Brown is one of the unusual characters in this book. Junior is a musical prodigy who weighs 300 pounds. He and his friends play hooky from school and when they are caught their private world is destroyed. 1972 Newbery Honor book.

JUNIUS

Hamilton, Virginia, **Junius Over Far**, Harper & Row, 1985, 277p., Fiction, ISBN 0-06-022195-X; 0-06-022194-1.

Fourteen-year-old Junius is interested in learning about his lost heritage and wants to follow his grandfather when he returns to his home island in the Caribbean. 1986 Coretta Scott King Honor book.

JUSTICE

Hamilton, Virginia, **Justice and Her Brothers**, Greenwillow, 1978, 217p., Fiction, LC 78-54684, ISBN 0-688-80182-X.

While school is out for the summer, eleven-year-old Justice is left with her older, twin brothers while their parents work. The brothers are able to communicate telepathically, which causes unusual situations. 1979 Coretta Scott King Honor book.

JUSTIN

Collier, James Lincoln and Christopher Collier, **Winter Hero**, Four Winds, 1978, 152p., Fiction, ISBN 0-02-722990-4.

During the Revolutionary War, Justin wants to be a hero like his brother. He becomes a spy and then a member of the troops in Shay's Rebellion.

Ellerby, Leona, **King Tut's Game Board**, Lerner, 1980, 120p., Fiction, ISBN 0-8225-0765-X.

Justin makes friends with a mysterious boy while he is on vacation with his parents in Egypt. The two boys explore museums and monuments, and Justin finds that his friend knows a great deal about Egyptian history. At the end of one of their trips, the boys discover an incredible secret.

Henry, Marguerite, **Justin Morgan Had a Horse**, illustrated by Wesley Dennis, Rand McNally, 1954, 170p., Fiction, LC 54-08903, ISBN 0-528-82255-1.

An unusual work horse raised in Vermont becomes the sire of a famous American breed of horses and takes the name of his owner, Justin Morgan. 1946 Newbery Honor book.

Lasker, Joe, **Tournament of Knights**, Crowell, 1986, 32p., Fiction, ISBN 0-690-04542-5.

Set in the Middle Ages, Justin is a young knight preparing for his first tournament when he is challenged by an older knight.

Pendergraft, Patricia, **Miracle at Clement's Pond**, Philomel, 1987, 199p., Fiction, ISBN 0-399-21438-0.

Justin and his friends find a baby near the pond. They cause problems in their small town when they leave the baby on a porch.

Skurzynski, Gloria, **Trapped in the Slickrock Canyon**, illustrated by Daniel San Souci, Lothrop, Lee & Shepard, 1984, 123p., Fiction, ISBN 0-688-02688-5.

Justin and his cousin have exciting adventures while they are hiking in a western canyon. They encounter vandals who chase them and become entrapped by a flash flood.

Walter, Mildred Pitts, **Justin and the Best Biscuits in the World**, illustrated by Catherine Stock, Lothrop, Lee & Shepard, 1986, 122p., Fiction, LC 86-7148, ISBN 0-688-06645-3.

Justin's mother and sisters are always fussing at him so he is glad to go to his grandfather's ranch for a visit. Justin discovers that cooking and keeping house aren't just women's work. 1987 Coretta Scott King Award book.

JUT

Carris, Joan, **When the Boys Ran the House**, illustrated by Carol Newsom, Lippincott, 1982, 150p., Fiction, ISBN 0-397-32020-5.

Jut's father is in Europe on business and his mother is ill, so Jut becomes the head of the household and assumes responsibility for his three younger brothers. Near disastrous results occur as bees invade the kitchen and the youngest brother eats a goldfish in this humorous story. Indiana 1986.

-K-

KALA

Luenn, Nancy, **Arctic Unicorn**, Atheneum, 1986, 167p., Fiction, ISBN 0-689-31278-4.

Thirteen-year-old Kala lives in a remote Eskimo village. She finds that her life is disrupted by the appearance of a young hunter and the beginnings of supernatural powers.

KARANA

O'Dell, Scott, **Island of the Blue Dolphins**, Houghton Mifflin, 1960, 184p., Fiction, LC 60-5213, ISBN 0-395-06962-0.

The island of San Nicholas lies off the coast of California. In the early 1800s, an Indian girl missed the ship that took the rest of her people off the island. For the next eighteen years, Karana lived alone on this desolate spot with a ferocious pack of wild dogs, limited food, and loneliness. Her contentment came from self-reliance and her acceptance of her fate.

Based on a historical incident. 1961 Newbery Award book. Hawaii 1964. Kansas 1963.

KAREN
See also Karin

Blume, Judy, **It's Not the End of the World**, Bradbury, 1972, 169p., Fiction, ISBN 0-02-711050-8.

Twelve-year-old Karen, her brother, and sister are very upset when their parents plan on getting a divorce. The older sister tries to bring their parents back together again.

Duncan, Lois, **Third Eye**, Little, Brown, 1984, 220p., Fiction, ISBN 0-316-19553-7.

Karen is concerned about her unusual psychic powers until she learns how to use them to help the police in locating missing children. Indiana 1987.

Hurwitz, Johanna, **Tough-Luck Karen**, illustrated by Diane de Groat, Morrow, 1982, 156p., Fiction, ISBN 0-688-01485-2.

Thirteen-year-old Karen thinks she is unlucky since she has had problems with school and with making friends since her family moved to New Jersey.

Service, Pamela, **Stinker from Space**, Scribner, 1988, 83p., Fiction, ISBN 0-684-18910-0.

Karen is one of the children who befriends an alien who has taken on the body of a skunk until he can return to his own planet.

KARIN
See also Karen

Koplinka, Charlotte, **Silkies, a Novel of the Shetlands**, Erickson, 1978, 148p., Fiction, ISBN 0-8397-7810-4.

Karin lives in the Shetland Islands where her father is a fisherman. Karin discovers that her mother had come from the seal people when her father was lost in a storm.

Rosenberg, Maxine B., **Being Adopted**, illustrated by George Ancona, Lothrop, Lee & Shepard, 1984, 44p., Nonfiction, LC 83-17522, ISBN 0-688-02672-9; 0-688-02673-7 (lib).

Eight-year-old Karin was born in Korea and adopted by an American family. She and two other children tell about their experiences as adopted members of families who have different cultural and racial roots than they do. A Reading Rainbow book.

KARL
See also Carl

Lindgren, Astrid, **Brothers Lionheart**, illustrated by J. K. Lambert, Penguin, 1975, 183p., Fiction, ISBN 0-14-031955-7.

Karl knows that he won't live long, so his older brother tells him of a special land where the two can be together and battle evil.

KATE
See also Catherine, Katherine, Kathleen, Katie, Katy, Sara-Kate

Alcock, Vivien, **Cuckoo Sisters**, Delacorte, 1986, 160p., Fiction, ISBN 0-385-29467-0.

Eleven-year-old Kate has a big surprise when a teenager dressed in punk style comes to the house and declares that she is the family's long-missing older daughter.

Bawden, Nina, **Squib**, illustrated by Hank Blaustein, Lothrop, Lee & Shepard, 1982, 159p., Fiction, ISBN 0-688-01299-X.

Kate is obsessed with the idea that a little boy she sees is her little brother who had drowned in a tragic accident.

Briggs, Katharine, **Kate Crackernuts**, Greenwillow, 1979, 223p., Fiction, ISBN 0-688-80240-0.

Two girls named Kate grow up and secretly become friends in seventeenth-century Scotland. The mother of one Kate is a witch and causes problems when she marries the father of the other Kate.

Byars, Betsy, **Computer Nut, The**, Viking, 1984, 153p., Fiction, LC 84-0327, ISBN 0-670-2354-82.

Ten-year-old Kate uses her computer to communicate with someone who says he is from outer space and will visit the Earth. Arkansas 1987.

Clymer, Eleanor, **Spider, the Cave, and the Pottery**, illustrated by Ingrid Fetz, Dell, 1971, 66p., Fiction, ISBN 0-440-40166-6 (pbk).

Kate visits her Hopi grandmother and learns to make bowls from the clay that she finds in a cave.

Greene, Constance, **Beat the Turtle Drum**, illustrated by Donna Diamond, Viking, 1976, 119p., Fiction, ISBN 0-670-15241-1.

Thirteen-year-old Kate loves her younger sister who wants to rent a horse for a week. When the younger girl's wish comes true, everyone's life is forever changed.

Hooks, William, **Pioneer Cat**, illustrated by Charles Robinson, Random House, 1988, 63p., Easy Reader, ISBN 0-394-92038-4.

Nine-year-old Kate wonders how she can keep her cat a secret as the family travels by wagon train from Missouri to Oregon.

Merrill, Jean, **Toothpaste Millionaire, The**, illustrated by Jan Palmer, Houghton Mifflin, 1921, 90p., Fiction, LC 73-22055, ISBN 0-395-18511-4; 0-395-11186-2 (pbk).

Kate tells the story of her friend and classmate, Rufus Mayflower, and how he became a millionaire between sixth and eighth grade. After building up a business, Rufus decided to try something else and sold his business to his friend, Hector. Oklahoma 1977. Vermont 1976.

O'Neal, Zibby, **In Summer Light**, Viking Kestrel, 1985, p., Fiction, ISBN 0-670-80-7842.

Kate spends a difficult summer with her overbearing father who is an artist. She learns to develop her own goals with the assistance of an attractive young man that she meets. 1986 Boston Globe-Horn Book Award.

Pearce, A. Philippa, **Way to Sattin Shore, The**, illustrated by Charlotte Voake, Greenwillow, 1983, 182p., Fiction, ISBN 0-688-02319-3.

Kate's father died ten years earlier, on the day that she was born. As Kate attempts to learn the truth about his death, she discovers a mystery.

Pope, Elizabeth Marie, **Perilous Gard, The**, illustrated by Richard Cuffari, Houghton Mifflin, 1974, 280p., Fiction, ISBN 0-395-185-122.

In 1558, Kate Sutton is imprisoned in a remote castle called Elvenwood. While there, she becomes involved in a series of events that lead her to an underground labyrinth that holds the last of the druids practicing their magic. 1975 Newbery Honor book.

Pople, Maureen, **Other Side of the Family**, H. Holt, 1986, 167p., Fiction, ISBN 0-8050-0758-X.

At fifteen, Kate Tucker is sent to live with an eccentric grandmother in order to avoid the fighting of World War II.

Seredy, Kate, **Good Master, The**, illustrated by Kate Seredy, Viking, 1935, 211p., Fiction, ISBN 0-670-34592-X.

Jancsi and his family live on a ranch on the Hungarian plain, miles from the village. When his cousin comes from the city of Budapest to live with the family, both children learn a great deal from one another. 1936 Newbery Honor book.

Service, Pamela, **Vision Quest**, Atheneum, 1989, 141p., Fiction, ISBN 0-689-31498-1.

Kate Elliot distrusts the world after the loss of her father and a move to the Nevada desert. When she finds two mysterious stones, she becomes involved with an ancient Indian shaman and an adventure with a new friend.

Wetterer, Margaret, **Kate Shelley and the Midnight Express**, illustrated by Karen Rite, Carolrhoda, 1990, 48p., Easy Reader, ISBN 0-876-144-253.

Fifteen-year-old Kate Shelley risks her life during a storm to prevent a train wreck. A Reading Rainbow book.

KATHERINE
See also Catherine, Cathy, Kate, Kathy, Katie, Katy, Kay

Eager, Edward, **Magic by the Lake**, illustrated by N. M. Bodecker, Harcourt Brace Jovanovich, 1985, 183p., Fiction, ISBN 0-15-250441-9.

Katherine and three other children have to tame a magic lake before they can discover its treasures.

KATHLEEN
See also Kate, Kathy, Katie, Katy, Kay

Clymer, Eleanor, **My Mother Is the Smartest Woman in the World**, illustrated by Nancy Kincade, Atheneum, 1982, 86p., Fiction, ISBN 0-689-30916-3.

Kathleen encourages her mother to run for mayor and the family becomes involved in an exciting campaign.

Jones, Diana Wynne, **Dogsbody**, Greenwillow, 1977, 256p., Fiction, ISBN 0-688-08191-6.

Kathleen befriends a small outer space puppy banished to Earth.

KATHY
See also Catherine, Cathy, Kate, Katherine, Kathleen, Katie, Katy, Kay

Clark, Margaret Goff, **Who Stole Kathy Young?**, Dodd, Mead, 1980, 191p., Fiction, ISBN 0-396-07888-5.

When Kathy is kidnapped, her friend sees it happen and works with the sheriff to help find Kathy in an exciting mystery.

Kellogg, Steven, **Best Friends**, illustrated by Steven Kellogg, Dial, 1986, 30p., Picture Book, LC 85-15971, ISBN 0-8037-0099-7; 0-8037-0101-2 (lib).

Kathy and Louise are best friends and do everything together. When Louise goes away for the summer, Kathy feels lonely and mad until a new neighbor and his dog move into the house next door. A Reading Rainbow book.

Wells, Rosemary, **When No One Was Looking**, Dial, 1980, 218p., Fiction, ISBN 0-8037-9855-5.

Kathy is a talented and obsessive young tennis player who has the ability to reach the nationals if she can control her temper. When the body of her rival is found in the club swimming pool, the mystery of her death causes Kathy to look at her own ambitions.

KATIE
See also Catherine, Cathy, Kate, Katherine, Kathleen, Kathy, Katy, Kay

Calhoun, Mary, **Katie John**, illustrated by Paul Frame, Harper & Row, 1960, 134p., Fiction, ISBN 0-06-020951-8.

Katie John and her family move into a house that they have inherited, which a friend says is haunted. There are several other books about Katie John.

Erwin, Betty, **Go to the Room of the Eyes**, illustrated by Irene Burns, Little, Brown, 1969, 180p., Fiction, LC 71-77446, ISBN 0-316-24946-7.

When they move into an old house in Seattle, Katie and the other five Evans children discover a strange message left by children who lived there thirty years earlier. The message leads the children on a treasure hunt. Vermont 1971.

Kehret, Peg, **Deadly Stranger**, Dodd, Mead, 1987, 174p., Fiction, ISBN 0-396-09039-7.

Twelve-year-old Katie has started going to a new school and almost immediately becomes involved in a hit-and-run accident and the kidnapping of her new friend.

McDonnell, Christine, **Count Me In**, Viking Kestrel, 1986, 173p., Fiction, ISBN 0-670-80417-7.

Thirteen-year-old Katie has a difficult time adjusting to her new stepfather and to the news that her mother is pregnant.

Roberts, Willo Davis, **Girl with the Silver Eyes, The**, Atheneum, 1982, 181p., Fiction, LC 80-12391, ISBN 0-689-30786-1.

People didn't quite trust Katie because of her strange silver eyes, but there was something even stranger about her. Katie had paranormal powers; she could move things with her mind and could understand what animals were thinking. Katie discovers that there are three other children like her. California 1986. Missouri 1983.

Wright, Betty Ren, **Ghosts Beneath Our Feet**, Holiday House, 1984, 137p., Fiction, ISBN 0-8234-0538-9.

While spending the summer in an old house in a deserted Wisconsin mining town, Katie and her family encounter a ghost that warns them of impending danger.

KATY
See also Catherine, Cathy, Kate,
Katherine, Kathleen, Kathy, Katie, Kay

Boutis, Victoria, **Katy Did It**, illustrated by Gail Owens, Greenwillow, 1982, 96p., Fiction, ISBN 0-688-00688-4.

Eight-year-old Katy is unsure of her abilities when she and her father go on a backpacking trip.

Milhous, Katherine, **Egg Tree, The**, illustrated by Katherine Milhous, Scribner, 1950, 30p., Picture Book, ISBN 0-684-12716-4.

On Easter morning Katy and her brother Carl search for colored eggs. Katy finds beautiful decorated eggs in the closet and their grandmother shows them how to decorate more eggs and how to make an egg tree. 1951 Caldecott Award book.

Van Allsburg, Chris, **Stranger, The**, illustrated by Chris Van Allsburg, Houghton Mifflin, 1986, 32p., Picture Book, ISBN 0-395-42331-7.

Katy Bailey's father hit a stranger on the road near their farm and took the man home. The stranger didn't talk, didn't tire, and amazing things happened each year in the autumn after he left. Kentucky 1990.

KAY
See also Catherine, Cathy,
Katherine, Kathleen, Kathy, Katie, Katy

Melling, O. R., **Singing Stone, The**, Viking Kestrel, 1986, 206p., Fiction, ISBN 0-670-80817-2.

Kay Warrick is drawn into a fantasy world when she travels to Ireland alone to follow a mysterious guest.

KEILL

Hill, Douglas, **Galactic Warlord**, Dell, 1987, 126p., Fiction, ISBN 0-440-92787-0 (pbk).

Keill Randor is a Legionary who sets out to avenge the destruction of his home planet. A story of interplanetary good and evil. There is another book about Keill.

KEITH

Cleary, Beverly, **Mouse and the Motorcycle, The**, illustrated by Louis Darling, Morrow, 1965, 158p., Fiction, LC 65-20956, ISBN 0-688-31698-0.

When Keith played with his toy motorcycle, he was unaware that he was being watched enviously by a young mouse named Ralph. Ralph attempts to ride the motorcyle and finds an unexpected career and an unusual friend. Hawaii 1969. Kansas 1968. New Hampshire 1983. Pacific Northwest 1968.

KELLY

Auch, Mary Jane, **Glass Slippers Give You Blisters**, Holiday House, 1989, 169p., Fiction, ISBN 0-8234-0752-7.

Kelly is determined to get involved in junior high school by being the star of a school play. She finds that her daydreams do not work out the way that she had hoped.

Gondosch, Linda, **Who Needs a Bratty Brother?**, illustrated by Helen Cogancherry, Lodestar, 1985, 112p., Fiction, ISBN 0-525-67170-6.

Eleven-year-old Kelly McCoy tries numerous ideas to get rid of her bratty younger brother who puts worms in her cup and leaves a dried mouse tail in her book. Kentucky 1988.

Hahn, Mary Downing, **December Stillness**, Clarion, 1988, 179p., Fiction, LC 88-2572, ISBN 0-89919-758-2.

Kelly decides to focus on the homeless for a social studies paper on contemporary issues. As she gets to know a homeless Vietnam veteran, she tries to help him and learns that the reasons for people's behavior are very complicated. 1989 Child Study

Children's Book Award. 1989 Jane Addams Honor Book. California 1991.

KEN

Knowles, Anne, **Halcyon Island**, Harper & Row, 1980, 120p., Fiction, ISBN 0-06-023203-X.

Ken is afraid of water and refuses to learn to swim despite his father's taunting as they vacation near the river.

Major, Kevin, **Hold Fast**, Dell, 1978, 170p., Fiction, ISBN 0-440-93756-6 (pbk).

After their parents die in an automobile wreck, Ken and his younger brother are sent to live with different relatives. Ken rebels against his strict uncle and decides to run away.

KENDRA

Danziger, Paula, **Remember Me to Harold Square**, Delacorte, 1987, 139p., Fiction, ISBN 0-385-29610-X.

Kendra and her brother explore New York City with a visitor from Iowa.

KERBY
See also Kirby

Corbett, Scott, **Home Run Trick, The**, illustrated by Paul Galdone, Little, Brown, 1973, 101p., Fiction, LC 72-3478, ISBN 0-316-15693-0.

Kerby and his friend Fenton have problems with their baseball team, the Panthers. The Panthers want to lose an important game with their archrivals when they find out the winners will have to play a girl's team. Mississippi 1976. Missouri 1976.

KERRI
See also Carey, Carrie

Roberts, Willo Davis, **Girl with the Silver Eyes, The**, Atheneum, 1982, 181p., Fiction, LC 80-12391, ISBN 0-689-30786-1.

Kerri, Katie, and several other children have paranormal powers. They are able to move things with their minds and understand what animals are thinking. California 1986. Mississippi 1983.

KEVIN

Skurzynski, Gloria, **Lost in the Devil's Desert**, illustrated by Joseph M. Scrofani, Lothrop, Lee & Shepard, 1982, 96p., Fiction, LC 81-13667, ISBN 0-688-00898-4.

Eleven-year-old Kevin Hoffman had gone with his family to visit an elderly relative in a small Utah town near the desert. Kevin accidentally becomes involved with two escaped convicts who dump Kevin in the desert where they leave him to die. Kevin is alone and lost with only his wits to help him survive his desert ordeal. Utah 1984.

Talbot, Charlene Joy, **Orphan for Nebraska**, Atheneum, 1979, 208p., Fiction, ISBN 0-689-30698-9.

In 1872 Kevin arrives from Ireland to discover his only relative is in jail. He goes West and works for the editor of a small newspaper in Nebraska. Based on an actual episode.

KI-PAT

Aardema, Verna, **Bringing the Rain to Kapiti Plain**, illustrated by Beatriz Vidal, Dial, 1981, 26p., Picture Book, LC 80-25886, ISBN 0-8037-0904-8.

When the African rains come late to the Kapiti Plain, the grass becomes brown and the cows hungry. As Ki-pat watches his herd, he has an idea on how to get the dark clouds to rain down. Adapted from an old Kenyan tale. A Reading Rainbow book.

KIB

Bates, Betty, **Thatcher Payne-in-the-Neck**, illustrated by Linda Strauss Edwards, Holiday House, 1985, 130p., Fiction, ISBN 0-8234-0584-2.

Kib and Thatcher are friends who plot to get their widowed parents together and then realize that being brother and sister could ruin their friendship.

KIM

Means, Florence Crannell, **Moved-Outers, The**, illustrated by Helen Blair, Houghton Mifflin, 1945, 154p., Fiction, LC 45-2267, ISBN 0-395-06933-5.

Kim Ohara and his family were Japanese-Americans living in California. On December 7, 1941, their lives were changed forever. On that day the Japanese attacked Pearl Harbor. Mr. Ohara was taken into custody by the FBI and Kim, his sister, and his mother, were moved to a Relocation Camp. 1946 Newbery Honor book.

KIP

Brett, Jan, **First Dog, The**, illustrated by Jan Brett, Harcourt Brace Jovanovich, 1988, 32p., Picture Book, LC 88-2224, ISBN 0-15-227650-5.

Kip the cave boy lives in Paleolithic times. He and Paleowolf face danger and hunger as they journey. When they decide to join forces and help one another, Paleowolf becomes the first dog. A Reading Rainbow book.

KIRBY
See also Kerby

Duncan, Lois, **Gift of Magic**, illustrated by Arvis Stewart, Little, Brown, 1971, 183p., Fiction, ISBN 0-316-19545-6.

Kirby and his siblings each have a special gift, but his gift of dance is not one that Kirby wants.

KIRSTEN

Shaw, Janet, **Meet Kirsten: An American Girl**, illustrated by Renee Graef, Pleasant Company, 1986, 61p., Fiction, ISBN 0-937295-00-0.

Nine-year-old Kirsten Larson and her family immigrate from Sweden to a Minnesota farm in 1854. There are several books about Kirsten and her new life.

KIT

Gleiter, Jan, **Kit Carson**, illustrated by Rick Whipple, Raintree, 1987, 32p., Nonfiction, ISBN 0-8172-2650-8.

Kit Carson wanted to hunt and trap from the time he was a boy. He went West and learned the languages and ways of the Indians, which made him

valuable as a frontier scout. This is a biography about Kit Carson and his deeds.

Roos, Stephen, **Fair-Weather Friends**, illustrated by Dee deRosa, Atheneum, 1987, 115p., Fiction, ISBN 0-689-31297-0.

When they meet at their summer homes, twelve-year-old Kit and her friend find that their friendship has changed as they have matured.

Speare, Elizabeth George, **Witch of Blackbird Pond, The**, Houghton Mifflin, 1958, 249p., Fiction, ISBN 0-395-07114-3.

Set in colonial times, Kit visits Connecticut from her home in Barbados and avoids a witch-hunt, although she is friendly with a witch. 1959 Newbery Award book.

KONDI

Williams, Karen Lynn, **Galimoto**, illustrated by Catherine Stock, Lothrop, Lee & Shepard, 1990, 25p., Picture Book, LC 89-2258, ISBN 0-688-08789-2; 0-688-08790-6.

A galimoto is a type of push toy that children in Malawi, Africa, make. Kondi's older brother laughs at him when Kondi says that he is going to make his own galimoto. A Reading Rainbow book.

KRISTI
See also Kristy

Hahn, Mary Downing, **Doll in the Garden: A Ghost Story**, Clarion, 1989, 160p., Fiction, ISBN 0-899-198-481.

An antique doll that Kristi and her friend find buried in a garden leads the girls to an eerie adventure. By going through the hedge, the girls enter the ghostly world of an earlier time. Virginia 1992.

KRISTIN

Havill, Juanita, **Jamaica's Find**, illustrated by Anne Sibley O'Brien, Houghton Mifflin, 1986, 32p., Picture Book, LC 85-14542, ISBN 00-395-39376-0.

Kristin loses her cuddly, stuffed toy dog at the park. When she goes to the lost-and-found shelf, she meets Jamaica, the girl who found the toy, and finds both her dog and a friend. A Reading Rainbow book.

KRISTY

See also Kristi

Martin, Ann, **Kristy's Great Idea**, Scholastic, 1986, 153p., Fiction, ISBN 0-590-41985-4 (pbk).

Kristy encourages her friends to join her in forming a babysitter's club. There are numerous books about Kristy and her friends.

-L-

LACHIE

Leodhas, Sorche Nic, **Always Room for One More**, illustrated by Nonny Hogrogrian, Holt, Rinehart & Winston, 1965, 24p., Picture Book, LC 65-12881, ISBN 0-8050-0331-2.

Lachie Maclachlan and his wife have ten children, yet their house always had room for one more person. Based on an old Scottish folk song. 1966 Caldecott Award book.

LACY

Beatty, Patricia, **Lacy Makes a Match**, Morrow, 1979, 222p., Fiction, ISBN 0-688-22200-5.

Lacy was left on the Bingham's doorstep at Coyote Mountain, California, and at thirteen, she is curious about who she is. Lacy has many chores and plots to marry off the three older brothers to relieve her duties. Set in the late 1800s.

LANGSTON

Rollins, Charlemae, **Black Troubadour: Langston Hughes**, Rand McNally, 1970, 143p., Nonfiction.

A biography of Langston Hughes, a famous black American writer of poems, stories, novels, and plays. 1971 Coretta Scott King Award book.

LARRY

Asimov, Isaac, **Key Word, and Other Mysteries**, illustrated by Rod Burke, Avon, 1977, 54p., Fiction, ISBN 0-380-43224-2 (pbk).

Larry helps his detective-father solve four mysteries using thoughtful analysis.

Miles, Betty, **Secret Life of the Underwear Champ, The**, Knopf, 1981, 117p., Fiction, ISBN 0-394-845-633 (pbk); 0-394-945-638 (lib).

When ten-year-old Larry is asked to appear in a television commercial, he doesn't realize until later what he will be advertising. Georgia 1986. Mississippi 1984. Missouri 1984.

LAURA

See also Laurie

Bunting, Eve, **Happy Funeral**, illustrated by Vo-Dinh Mai, Harper & Row, 1982, 38p., Fiction, ISBN 0-06-020893-7.

When her grandfather dies, Laura's Chinese-American family has ceremonies to honor him, including a procession through Chinatown.

Eager, Edward, **Magic or Not?**, illustrated by N. M. Bodecker, Harcourt Brace Jovanovich, 1985, 190p., Fiction, ISBN 0-15-655121-7.

Laura and her brother have been told that the well by their new house is magical. Although their wishes come true, they are unsure whether it is because of the well.

Giff, Patricia Reilly, **Laura Ingalls Wilder: Growing Up in the Little House**, illustrated by Eileen McKeating, Viking Kestrel, 1987, 56p., Nonfiction, ISBN 0-670-81072-X.

Laura Ingalls Wilder began writing the 'Little House' books when she was sixty-five years old to tell about her childhood. This biography provides information about this popular author and includes her adult life.

Hahn, Mary Downing, **Time of the Witch, The**, Clarion, 1982, 171p., Fiction, ISBN 0-89919-1150.

While staying with her sister for the summer, Laura meets an old woman who offers to use witchcraft to help bring Laura's separated parents back together.

Sargent, Sarah, **Watermusic**, Clarion, 1986, 120p., Fiction, ISBN 0-89919-436-2.

Thirteen-year-old Laura has a very unusual part-time job; she plays a flute for a large, batlike creature. In this science fiction story, Laura is led into an imaginative adventure as one odd creature leads her to the next until she encounters a totally different being.

Wilder, Laura Ingalls, **Farmer Boy**, illustrated by Garth Williams, Harper & Row, 1953, 371p., Fiction, ISBN 0-06-026421-7.

Laura and her family move from their log cabin in Wisconsin to the prairies of Kansas, while Almanzo Wilder is growing up on a farm in New York. The lives of these families will intertwine in later books in this popular series.

Wilder, Laura Ingalls, **Little House in the Big Woods**, illustrated by Garth Williams, Harper & Row, 1953, 237p., Fiction, ISBN 0-06-026431-4.

This is the first of the nine books about Laura Wilder and her family. Set in 1870, the Wilders move from New York State to Wisconsin and live in a small house.

Wilder, Laura Ingalls, **Little Town on the Prairie**, illustrated by Garth Williams, Harper & Row, 1953, 304p., Fiction, ISBN 0-06-026450-0.

In this book about the Ingalls family, Laura gets into trouble at school but finally becomes a certified school teacher. There are other books about this family. 1942 Newbery Honor book.

Wilder, Laura Ingalls, **These Happy Golden Years**, illustrated by Garth Williams, Harper & Row, 1953, 288p., Fiction, ISBN 0-06-026480-2.

Laura Ingalls begins teaching and she is courted by Almanzo Wilder in this book in the popular series about the Ingalls family. 1944 Newbery Honor book.

LAURIE
See also Laura

Christopher, John, **When the Tripods Came**, Dutton, 1988, 151p., Fiction, ISBN 0-525-44397-5.

Fourteen-year-old Laurie tells about the arrival of the alien Tripods and their gradual control of the earth. Part of the Tripod series.

Duncan, Lois, **Stranger with My Face**, Little, Brown, 1981, 250p., Fiction, ISBN 0-316-19551-0.

Seventeen-year-old Laurie Stratton lives at Cliff House on the northern tip of Brighton Island. She senses that someone is spying on her and possibly impersonating her. When she discovers what is actually happening, it is more unbelievable than she had imagined. California 1984. Indiana 1986. Massachusetts 1983.

Pfeffer, Susan Beth, **Dear Dad, Love Laurie**, Scholastic, 1989, 120p., Fiction, ISBN 0-590-41681-2.

Laurie's parents are divorced and she writes her dad a weekly letter telling him about her sixth-grade year, relationships, and activities.

Roberts, Willo Davis, **Don't Hurt Laurie!**, illustrated by Ruth Sanderson, Atheneum, 1981, 166p., Ficiton, LC 76-46569, ISBN 0-689-30571-0.

Laurie spends a lot of time in hospitals with injuries caused by her mother. The family moves frequently so no one will suspect the child abuse, and it is difficult for Laurie to find someone to help her. Georgia 1982. Indiana 1980.

LEAH

Cohen, Barbara, **Carp in the Bathtub**, illustrated by Joan Halpern, Lothrop, Lee & Shepard, 1972, 48p., Fiction, ISBN 0-688-51627-0.

Leah and her brother befriend the carp that their mother has brought home to cook.

LEIBEL

Singer, Isaac Bashevis, **Fearsome Inn, The**, illustrated by Nonny Hogrogrian, Scribner, 1967, 42p., Fiction, LC 67-23693, ISBN 0-689-70769-X.

All roads lead to the inn and when helpless winter travelers stumble in, they become victims of the owners, a witch and her husband. Leibel and his companions break the spell cast over the inn and rescue the three girls held captive as servants. 1968 Newbery Honor book.

LEIGH
See also Li

Cleary, Beverly, **Dear Mr. Henshaw**, illustrated by Paul O. Zelinsky, Morrow, 1983, 134p., Fiction, LC 83-5372, ISBN 0-688-02405-X; 0-688-02406-8 (lib).

Leigh has been a fan of writer Boyd Henshaw for four years. When Leigh's teacher assigns a letter-writing project to students to ask questions of authors, Leigh writes to Mr. Henshaw. He tells about his many family and personal problems and receives surprising answers from Mr. Henshaw. 1984 Christopher Medal. 1984 Newbery Award book. Oklahoma 1986. Vermont 1985.

LEILA
See also Lila

Muskopf, Elizabeth, **Revenge of Jeremiah Plum, The**, illustrated by David Christiana, H. Holt, 1987, 212p., Fiction, ISBN 0-8050-0203-0.

Leila and her friend become involved in an old mystery when a ghost refuses to rest until his murder is solved.

LELAND

Brittain, Bill, **Wish Giver: Three Tales of Coven Tree, The**, illustrated by Andrew Glass, Harper & Row, 1983, 181p., Fiction, LC 82-48264, ISBN 0-06-020686-1; 0-06-020687-X (lib).

Thaddeus Blinn was a funny little man who appeared from out of nowhere and put his tent by the annual Coven Tree Church Social. He said he had the power to give people exactly what they asked for. Leland is one of the characters who finds that wishes often have unexpected results when they come true. 1984 Newbery Honor book.

LENA
See also Lina

Haskins, James, **Lena Horne**, Coward, 1983, 160p., Nonfiction, LC 83-15411, ISBN 0-698-20586-3.

This biography of the singer, Lena Horne, tells of her personal life, her career, and her political activism. 1984 Coretta Scott King Honor book.

LENNIE
See also Lenny

Byars, Betsy, **TV Kid**, illustrated by Richard Cuffari, Viking, 1976, 123p., Fiction, ISBN 0-670-73331-8.

Lennie's preoccupation with television due to boredom and loneliness cause him to fail in school. He has many misadventures near the motel that his mother runs.

LENNY
See also Lennie

Conford, Ellen, **Lenny Kandell, Smart Aleck**, illustrated by Walter Gaffney-Kessell, Little, Brown, 1983, 120p., Fiction, ISBN 0-316-15313-3.

Eleven-year-old Lenny is constantly practicing his stand-up comedy routine to the annoyance of his family and friends.

Gilson, Jamie, **Dial Leroi Rupert, DJ**, illustrated by John Wallner, Lothrop, Lee & Shepard, 1979, 126p., Fiction, ISBN 0-688-51888-5.

Lenny is a sixth-grade boy who gets into a great deal of mischief with his two friends. The boys get into trouble with adults and finally meet a disc jockey who helps them.

LENORA
See also Lenore

Brittain, Bill, **Wish Giver: Three Tales of Coven Tree, The**, illustrated by Andrew Glass, Harper & Row, 1983, 181p., Fiction, LC 82-48264, ISBN 0-06-020686-1; 0-06-020687-X (lib).

Thaddeus Blinn was a funny little man who appeared from out of nowhere and put his tent by the annual Coven Tree Church Social. He said he had the power to give people exactly what they asked for. Lenora is one of the characters who finds that wishes often have unexpected results when they come true. 1984 Newbery Honor book.

LENORE
See also Lenora

Thurber, James, **Many Moons**, illustrated by Louis Slobodkin, Harcourt Brace Jovanovich, 1943, 45p., Picture Book, ISBN 0-15-251873-8.

Lenore is a ten-year-old princess who lives in a kingdom by the sea. When she becomes ill she wants to have the moon to enable her to become well again. 1944 Caldecott Award book.

LEO
See also Leonard

McDonnell, Christine, **Toad Food and Measle Soup**, illustrated by Diane de Groat, Dial, 1982, 109p., Fiction, ISBN 0-8037-8488-0.

Five humorous short stories about Leo and his family, including his mother's vegetarian cooking.

Meltzer, Milton, **Ain't Gonna Study War No More: The Study of America's Peace Seekers**, Harper & Row, 1985, 282p., Nonfiction, ISBN 0-060-241-993; 0-060-242-000 (lib).

This book presents a history of pacifism and those who have protested against war. The Russian novelist Leo Tolstoy was a pacifist and resisted using force for any reason. 1986 Jane Addams Award book.

LEON

Raskin, Ellen, **Mysterious Disappearance of Leon (I Mean Noel), The**, illustrated by Ellen Raskin, Dutton, 1980, 160p., Fiction, ISBN 0-525-35540-5.

Leon Carillon is seven years old when he is married to protect the family's business interests. Leon is immediately sent off to boarding school, and his young bride spends the next twenty years looking for him in this humorous mystery.

LEONA

Havill, Juanita, **It Always Happens to Leona**, illustrated by Emily McCully, Crown, 1989, 88p., Fiction, ISBN 0-517-57227-3.

Leona is the middle child, and she is certain that the only time she gets attention is when there is trouble and she is blamed.

LEONARD
See also Leo

Pinkwater, D. Manus, **Alan Mendelsohn, the Boy from Mars**, Dutton, 1979, 248p., Fiction, ISBN 0-525-25360-2.

Leonard was not popular in school but made a friend with the new student. The two boys buy a mind control system and have a series of humorous adventures through time and space.

LEROI
See also Leroy

Gilson, Jamie, **Dial Leroi Rupert, DJ**, illustrated by John Wallner, Lothrop, Lee & Shepard, 1979, 126p., Fiction, ISBN 0-688-51888-5.

Leroi Rupert is a disc jockey who helps three sixth-grade boys solve their problems when they get into trouble with adults because of their constant mischief.

LEROY
See also Leroi

Robinson, Barbara, **Best Christmas Pageant Ever, The**, illustrated by Judith Gwyn Brown, Harper & Row, 1972, 80p., Fiction, LC 72-76501, ISBN 06-025043-7; 06-025044-5.

Leroy is one of the Herdman children—kids so awful it is hard to believe they are real. When they decide to participate in the church Christmas pageant, people think it will be the worst one ever. Georgia 1976. Indiana 1978. Minnesota 1982.

Sobol, Donald, **Encyclopedia Brown Keeps the Peace**, illustrated by Leonard Shortall, Dutton, 1969, 96p., Fiction, ISBN 0-525-67208-7.

As Leroy 'Encyclopedia' Brown solves ten detective cases with his knowledge, the reader is challenged to solve them also. There are numerous other books about this character. Pacific Northwest 1972.

LESLIE

Paterson, Katherine, **Bridge to Terabithia**, illustrated by Donna Diamond, Crowell, 1977, 128p., Fiction, LC 77-02221, ISBN 0-690-135-90.

When Leslie moves into the house near Jess's, she has no idea that they will develop a special friendship. The two create Terabithia, their own secret kingdom in the woods, where they reign as king and queen until a tragedy strikes. 1978 Newbery Award book.

LEVI

Hamilton, Virginia, **Justice and Her Brothers**, Greenwillow, 1978, 217p., Fiction, LC 78-54684, ISBN 0-688-80182-X.

Levi and his twin brother are thirteen years old and able to communicate telepathically. While their parents work during the summer, the two boys watch their younger sister. 1979 Coretta Scott King Honor book.

Van Steenwyk, Elizabeth, **Levi Strauss: The Blue Jeans Man**, Walker, 1988, 96p., Nonfiction, ISBN 0-8027-6795-8.

Levi Strauss was born in Germany and came to the United States as a trader. This biography includes information on his development of sturdy work clothes for miners during the Gold Rush.

LEWIS
See also Lou, Louie, Louis, Luigi

Bellairs, John, **House With a Clock In Its Walls**, illustrated by Edward Gorey, Dial, 1973, 179p., Fiction, ISBN 0-8037-3823-4.

Lewis lives with an aunt who adopted him when his parents died. He discovers that his uncle and a neighbor are wizards, and that a magic doomsday clock is hidden in the walls of the house. There are other books about Lewis and his adventures.

Fox, Paula, **Likely Place**, illustrated by Edward Ardizzone, Macmillan, 1967, 57p., Fiction, ISBN 0-02-735761-9.

Nine-year-old Lewis is imaginative but his parents think he is a problem. When Lewis is left to spend a week with a babysitter he befriends an elderly man and discovers they have much in common.

LI
See also Leigh

Leaf, Margaret, **Eyes of the Dragon, The**, illustrated by Ed Young, Lothrop, Lee & Shepard, 1987, 32p., Picture Book, ISBN 0-68806-1559; 0-68806-1567.

Li is a young boy who watched an artist paint a wondrous dragon on the wall surrounding his small village. The artist left off the dragon's eyes, and the villagers discovered why when they demanded that the eyes be added. California 1990.

LIANG

Demi, **Liang and the Magic Paintbrush**, illustrated by Demi, H. Holt, 1980, 30p., Picture Book, LC 80-11351, ISBN 0-03-056289-9.

Liang is a boy who lives in China and wants to paint but he is too poor to buy a paintbrush. An old man gives him a magic paintbrush and everything that Liang paints magically comes to life. Liang has to use his wits when the greedy king wants the paintbrush. A Reading Rainbow book.

LIBBY
See also Elisabeth, Elizabeth

Jarrow, Gail, **If Phyllis Were Here**, Houghton Mifflin, 1987, 132p., Fiction, ISBN 0-395-43667-2.

Eleven-year-old Libby goes through difficult times when her grandmother leaves and moves to Florida. The older woman had taken care of Libby and understands her.

Pitt, Nancy, **Beyond the High White Wall**, Scribner, 1986, 135p., Fiction, ISBN 0-684-18663-2.

Set at the beginning of the twentieth century in Russia, Libby sees a murder in the family cornfield and her family decides to emigrate to America. Based on an actual event.

Woolley, Catherine, **Libby Shadows a Lady**, illustrated by Don Almquist, Morrow, 1974, 191p., Fiction, ISBN 0-688-31787-1.

While spending a week with her aunt in New York City, Libby becomes involved in a mystery and thwarts an attempted kidnapping.

LILA
See also Leila

Alexander, Sue, **Lila on the Landing**, illustrated by Ellen Eagle, Clarion, 1987, 55p., Fiction, ISBN 0-89919-340-4.

Lila is an imaginative but very clumsy girl. She is always left out of group games, but eventually her friends join her in the quiet games that she creates.

McMullan, Kate, **Great Ideas of Lila Fenwick**, illustrated by Diane de Groat, Dial, 1986, 118p., Fiction, ISBN 0-8037-0317-1.

Five humorous episodes about Lila Fenwick and her fifth-grade classroom. There is another book about Lila.

LILIE
See also Lillian, Lily

Ish-Kishor, Sulamith, **Our Eddie**, Pantheon, 1969, 183p., Fiction, LC 69-13456, ISBN 0-394-81455-X.

Lilie and Eddie relate the difficulties their family suffers because of their father who, although loving, is religious and idealistic and doesn't understand the needs of the family. 1970 Newbery Honor book.

LILLIAN
See also Lilie, Lily

Corcoran, Barbara, **Private War of Lillian Adams, The**, Atheneum, 1989, 162p., Fiction, ISBN 0-689-31443-4.

Set in 1917, Lillian is overly concerned with spies in a humorous, yet serious, story.

Gish, Lillian, **Actor's Life for Me! As Told to Selma G. Lanes**, illustrated by Patricia Henderson Lincoln, Viking Kestrel, 1987, 73p., Nonfiction, ISBN 0-670-80416-9.

Lillian Gish became an actress in the early 1900s as a way to support her mother and sister. This biography tells about the actress and early theater and film.

LILY
See also Lilie, Lillian

Fox, Paula, **Lily and the Lost Boy**, Orchard, 1987, 149p., Fiction, ISBN 0-531-08320-9.

Eleven-year-old Lily Corey and her family are visiting on a Greek island. When Jack, the 'lost boy' appears, trouble begins and Lily's relationship with her older brother is threatened.

Hest, Amy, **Pete and Lily**, Clarion/Ticknor & Fields, 1986, 112p., Fiction, ISBN 0-89919-354-4.

Twelve-year-old Lily and her best friend are concerned about the romance that is developing between their single parents.

Shreve, Susan, **Lily and the Runaway Baby**, illustrated by Sue Truesdell, Random House, 1987, 62p., Fiction, ISBN 0-394-99104-4.

Lily is a third grader who feels neglected by her family, so she takes her baby sister and runs away from home.

Yolen, Jane, **Commander Toad and the Planet of the Grapes**, illustrated by Bruce Degen, Coward-McCann, 1982, 64p., Easy Reader, ISBN 0-698-30736-4; 0-698-20540-5 (pbk).

Commander Toad and his crew explore hopper space on the ship Star Warts. Lieutenant Lily is in charge of the engine room. When the crew lands on a planet of giant grapes, Lily's allergies make her sneeze. A Reading Rainbow book.

LINA
See also Lena

DeJong, Meindert, **Wheel on the School, The**, illustrated by Maurice Sendak, Harper & Row, 1954, 298p., Fiction, LC 54-8945, ISBN 0-06-021585-2.

Lina is the only girl among the six school-children that live in the fishing village called Shora in Holland. The children learn that when a stork builds a nest on the roof there will be good luck. 1955 Newbery Award book.

LINCOLN

Mason, Theodore K., **Two Against the Ice: Amundsen and Ellsworth**, Dodd, Mead, 1982, 192p., Nonfiction, ISBN 0-396-08092-8.

Lincoln Ellsworth and his best friend wanted to explore the Arctic from the time they were boys. Their childhoods and early experiences helped to provide the stamina they needed for the expedition that they took as adults. Biographical information about Lincoln from his childhood through the famous expedition.

LINDA

See also Lucinda, Melinda, Orlinda

Clymer, Eleanor, **We Lived in the Almont**, Dell, 1970, 87p., Fiction, ISBN 0-440-40144-5.

Linda's father works as the superintendent at the Almont Apartments. Linda meets many of the residents and makes a special friend.

Jordan, June, **New Life: New Room**, illustrated by Ray Cruz, Crowell, 1975, 52p., Fiction, ISBN 0-690-00212-2.

Linda and her family have a problem trying to fit a new baby into their already crowded two-bedroom apartment.

LINDY

See also Lucinda, Melinda, Orlinda

Amoss, Berthe, **Mockingbird Song, The**, Harper & Row, 1988, 123p., Fiction, ISBN 0-06-020061-8; 0-06-020062-6 (lib).

Eleven-year-old Lindy is unable to get along with her new stepmother so she goes to live with the elderly lady that lives next door. She returns after the birth of a baby sister.

McGraw, Eloise Jarvis, **Money Room**, Atheneum, 1981, 182p., Fiction, ISBN 0-689-50208-7.

Lindy, her mother, and brother move to the farm they have inherited and begin searching for the Money Room they have heard about as a way to supplement their income.

LISA

See also Elisabeth, Elizabeth, Liza

Burchard, Peter, **Sea Change**, Farrar, Straus & Giroux, 1984, 117p., Fiction, ISBN 0-374-36460-5.

Stories about Lisa, Alice, and Ann, who are daughter, mother, and grandmother. The stories tell how the family members deal with problems, and with each other.

Kastner, Erich, **Lisa and Lottie**, illustrated by Victoria de Larrea, Avon, 1982, 136p., Fiction, ISBN 0-380-57117-X (pbk).

While at summer camp, Lisa meets her twin sister who she did not know existed, and the two girls switch homes without telling their parents. Translated from the German.

LITTLE GOPHER

dePaola, Tomie, **Legend of the Indian Paintbrush, The**, illustrated by Tomie dePaola, Putnam, 1988, 38p., Picture Book, LC 87-20160, ISBN 0-399-21534-4.

The young Indian boy, Little Gopher, was smaller than the other boys and he couldn't keep up with them as they wrestled and played. Little Gopher had a Dream-Vision that revealed he would become important to his people through his paintings and that he could capture the colors of the sunset. A Reading Rainbow book.

LITTLE WOLF

Baker, Olaf, **Where the Buffaloes Begin**, illustrated by Stephen Gammell, Warne, 1981, 46p., Picture Book, LC 80-23319, ISBN 0-7232-195-4.

After hearing a legend told by the tribe's oldest member, Little Wolf, an Indian boy, courageously seeks a sacred lake so he can witness the beginning of buffaloes. 1982 Caldecott Honor book.

LIVVIE
See also Olive, Olivia

Davis, Jenny, **Sex Education: A Novel**, Orchard, 1988, 150p., Fiction, ISBN 0-531-05756-9.

Livvie Sinclair met David in their ninth-grade biology class, and they immediately became close friends and worked on their term project together. The tragedy that ends their relationship is retold by Livvie. Pacific Northwest 1991.

LIZ
See also Elisabeth, Elizabeth, Liza, Lizzie

Wallace, Bill, **Ferret in the Bedroom, Lizards in the Fridge**, Holiday House, 1986, 132p., Fiction, ISBN 0-8234-0600-8.

Twelve-year-old Liz has a houseful of unusual animals due to her zoologist father. The unpredictable behavior of the animals causes confusion when friends visit. South Carolina 1989.

Wilson, Eric, **Vampires of Ottawa**, Collins, 1984, 120p., Fiction, ISBN 0-00-222858-0.

Liz attempts to solve a mystery that involves vampires and a wealthy Canadian family. There are other books about Liz Austen.

LIZA
See also Elisabeth, Elizabeth, Lisa, Liz

Baker, Barbara, **Third Grade Is Terrible**, illustrated by Roni Shepard, Dutton, 1989, 106p., Fiction, ISBN 0-525-44425-4.

Liza is certain that the school year will be terrible when she is separated from her best friend and moved to a class with a very strict teacher.

Hughes, Monica, **Ring-Rise, Ring-Set**, Watts, 1982, 129p., Fiction, ISBN 0-531-04433-5.

Liza is determined to be a part of a scientific expedition that sets out to keep another Ice Age from occurring. Set in the future, Liza lives with a primitive culture when she is found by them.

Martin, Ann, **With You and Without You**, Holiday House, 1986, 179p., Fiction, ISBN 0-8234-0601-6.

Twelve-year-old Liza O'Hara has many changes to cope with when her father becomes ill and dies.

Mayer, Mercer, **Liza Lou and the Yeller Belly Swamp**, illustrated by Mercer Mayer, Parent's Magazine Press, 1976, 46p., Picture Book, ISBN 0-819-3080-13.

Liza Lou is able to outwit the witches, devils, and other haunts in the Yeller Belly Swamp with her quick thinking. California 1983.

LIZZIE
See also Elisabeth, Elizabeth, Liz

Ross, Rhea Beth, **Bet's On, Lizzie Bingman!**, Houghton Mifflin, 1988, 186p., Fiction, ISBN 0-395-44472-1.

Set in 1914, fourteen-year-old Lizzie finds her brother's patronizing attitude towards women to be frustrating and she decides to prove her independence.

LOLLY

Marshall, Edward, **Three by the Sea**, illustrated by James Marshall, Dial, 1981, 48p., Easy Reader, LC 80-26097, ISBN 0-8037-8671-9 (pbk); 0-8037-8687-5 (lib).

Lolly, Spider, and Sam are three friends who have a picnic at the beach. After lunch they decide to share their favorite stories. Lolly reads a story from her reader and the boys decide they can tell better ones. A Reading Rainbow book.

LONNY

Benchley, Nathaniel, **Feldman Fieldmouse, a Fable**, illustrated by Hilary Knight, Harper & Row, 1971, 96p., Fiction, ISBN 0-06-020484-2.

Lonny Stebbens saves a baby mouse from the exterminators. The mouse lives contentedly in a cage until his Uncle Feldman arrives to teach him about the natural world.

LORNA

Service, Pamela, **Reluctant God, The**, Atheneum, 1988, 211p., Fiction, ISBN 0-689-31404-3.

Lorna makes a new friend who has been entombed for 4,000 years, and the two become involved in an adventure filled with mystery. A time travel fantasy.

LORRAINE

Moore, Emily, **Something to Count On**, Dutton, 1980, 103p., Fiction, ISBN 0-525-39595-4.

Ten-year-old Lorraine is constantly in trouble at school and wishes that her divorced parents were different. Set in the Bronx in New York.

LOTTIE

Kastner, Erich, **Lisa and Lottie**, illustrated by Victoria de Larrea, Avon, 1982, 136p., Fiction, ISBN 0-380-57117-X.

While at summer camp, Lottie meets her twin sister who she did not know existed, and the two girls decide to switch families. Translated from the German.

LOU
See also Lewis, Louanne, Louie, Louis, Louisa, Louise, Luigi

Brandt, Keith, **Lou Gehrig, Pride of the Yankees**, illustrated by John Lawn, Troll, 1986, 46p., Nonfiction, ISBN 0-8167-0549-6.

The famous baseball player, Lou Gehrig, became interested in the sport when he was five years old. He was a baseball star on his high school and college teams and later became a well-known player for the New York Yankees.

LOUANNE
See also Lou

Carlson, Nancy, **Louanne Pig in Making the Team**, illustrated by Nancy Carlson, Carolrhoda, 1985, 28p., Picture Book, LC 85-3775, ISBN 0-87614-281-1 (lib).

Louanne Pig plans to try out for cheerleading and her friend, Arnie, plans to try out for football. They practice together and when they get to try-outs, something surprising happens. A Reading Rainbow book.

LOUIE
See also Lewis, Lou, Louis, Luigi

Keats, Ezra Jack, **Regards to the Man in the Moon**, illustrated by Ezra Jack Keats, Four Winds, 1981, 32p., Picture Book, LC 81-848, ISBN 0-590-07820-8.

When his friends laugh at Louie and call his stepfather a junk man, Louie and his parents use their imaginations, an old bathtub, and other junkyard treasures to allow Louie and his friends to travel through space. A Reading Rainbow book.

Stevenson, James, **'Could Be Worse!'**, illustrated by James Stevenson, Greenwillow, 1977, 30p., Picture Book, LC 76-28534, ISBN 0-688-80075-0; 0-688-84075-2 (lib).

Louie's grandpa and his house are always the same. Grandpa even says the same things. One morning Grandpa says something different, and a story with many adventures begins. A Reading Rainbow book.

Stevenson, James, **What's Under My Bed**, illustrated by James Stevenson, Greenwillow, 1983, 30p., Picture Book, LC 83-1454, ISBN 0-688-02325-8; 0-688-02327-4 (lib).

When Louie and his sister Mary Ann spend the night at grandpa's house, they have trouble sleeping until he tells them a story of his own childhood when he was scared at bedtime. A Reading Rainbow book.

LOUIS
See also Lewis, Lou, Louie, Luigi

Gretz, Susanna and Alison Sage, **Teddy Bears Cure a Cold**, illustrated by Susanna Gretz and Alison Sage, Four Winds, 1984, 32p., Picture Book, LC 84-4015, ISBN 0-590-07949-2.

William the bear feels sick and spends several days in bed while Louis and the other bears take care of him. A Reading Rainbow book.

Iverson, Genie, **Louis Armstrong**, illustrated by Kevin Brooks, Crowell, 1976, 32p., Nonfiction, ISBN 0-690-01127-X.

A biography about Louis Armstrong whose ability to play the trumpet made him one of the greatest of all jazz musicians.

Keeler, Stephen, **Louis Braille**, illustrated by Richard Hook, Bookwright, 1986, 32p., Nonfiction, ISBN 0-531-18071-9.

Louis Braille became blind as a child after accidentally injuring his eye. He spent his life developing a way for blind people to be able to read. This brief biography provides an insight into the man and his work.

Provenson, Alice and Martin Provenson, **Glorious Flight: Across the Channel with Louis Bleriot, The**, illustrated by Alice Provenson and Martin Provenson, Viking, 1983, 39p., Picture Book, LC 82-7034, ISBN 0-670-34259-9.

Louis Bleriot was taking his family for a drive on a morning in 1901 when he saw a machine flying through the air. From then on the Frenchman was obsessed with flying. In 1909 he took a daring flight across the English Channel. Based on factual information. 1984 Caldecott Award book.

Sabin, Francene, **Louis Pasteur, Young Scientist**, illustrated by Susan Swan, Troll, 1983, 48p., Nonfiction, ISBN 0-89375-853-1.

A biography of Louis Pasteur, the French microbiologist who discovered pasteurization, rabies, and several vaccines.

White, E. B., **Trumpet of the Swan, The**, illustrated by Edward Frascino, Harper & Row, 1970, 210p., Fiction, LC 72-112484, ISBN 06-026397-0.

Louis is a Trumpeter Swan that lacks a voice, yet is determined to become a Trumpeter. Sam Beaver is a boy who loves all wild things. Sam befriends Louis and takes him to school where Louis learns to read and write. Indiana 1975. Kansas 1973. Oklahoma 1973.

Yorinks, Arthur, **Louis the Fish**, illustrated by Richard Egielski, Farrar, Straus & Giroux, 1980, 28p., Picture Book, LC 80-16855, ISBN 0-374-34658-5.

Louis becomes a butcher because his grandfather and father had been butchers, but he is not a happy man because he doesn't like meat. When Louis changes into a salmon, he becomes a happy fish. A Reading Rainbow book.

LOUISA
See also Lou

McSwigan, Marie, **Snow Treasure**, illustrated by Mary Reardon, Dutton, 1942, 179p., Fiction, ISBN 0-525-39556-3.

Louisa and other Norwegian children slipped past Nazi soldiers with sleds loaded with gold. The gold was taken twelve miles to a freighter hidden in one of the fiords off Norway's coast. Based on an actual event. In June 1940 the Norwegian freighter reached Baltimore with a cargo of gold worth 9 million dollars. Pacific Northwest 1945.

Meigs, Cornelia, **Invincible Louisa**, illustrated with photographs, Little, Brown, 1961, 195p., Nonfiction, LC 68-21174, ISBN 0-316-56590-3.

A biography about the eventful life of Louisa May Alcott, the author. She was raised in an intellectually stimulating family and used her family members as models for the characters in her books. 1934 Newbery Award book.

LOUISE
See also Lou

Benjamin, Carol Lea, **Wicked Stepdog**, Crowell, 1982, 119p., Fiction, ISBN 0-690-04171-3.

Twelve-year-old Louise lives with her father, and when he remarries the household becomes quite different. Louise is given an added chore with the addition of her stepmother's dog, but the chore becomes a pleasure when she discovers a boy who also walks a dog.

Brown, Marcia, **Stone Soup: An Old Tale**, illustrated by Marcia Brown, Scribner, 1947, 40p., Picture Book, ISBN 0-684-92296-7; 0-6844-16217-2 (pbk).

Louise and the other peasants hid their food when they saw three hungry soldiers coming down the road. The soldiers then taught the villagers how to make soup from three stones and soon a village feast was prepared. An old folktale. 1948 Caldecott Honor book.

Greaves, Margaret, **Cat's Magic**, Harper & Row, 1981, 183p., Fiction, ISBN 0-022123-2.

Louise Higgs is orphaned and sent to live with an aunt on an isolated farm. Louise discovers a magical cat and goes on trips through time where she has exciting adventures.

Kellogg, Steven, **Best Friends**, illustrated by Steven Kellogg, Dial, 1986, 30p., Picture Book, LC 85-15971, ISBN 0-8037-0099-7; 0-8037-0101-2 (lib).

Louise and Kathy are best friends and do everything together. When Louise goes away for the summer, Kathy feels lonely and mad until the new neighbor and his dog move into the house next door. A Reading Rainbow book.

Lowry, Lois, **Us and Uncle Fraud**, Houghton Mifflin, 1984, 148p., Fiction, ISBN 0-395-36633-X.

Eleven-year-old Louise and her brother become involved in a series of adventures as they attempt to learn the truth about their eccentric uncle.

Paterson, Katherine, **Jacob Have I Loved**, Crowell, 1980, 244p., Fiction, LC 80-668, ISBN 0-690-04078-4; 0-690-04079-2 (lib); 0-06-440368-6 (pbk).

Louise reveals how she has felt that her twin sister, Caroline, has robbed her of everything: her hopes for schooling, her friends, her mother, and even her name. Alone and unsure, Louise finally begins to find her own identity. 1981 Newbery Award book.

Ungerer, Tomi, **Crictor**, illustrated by Tomi Ungerer, Harper & Row, 1958, 32p., Picture Book, LC 58-5288, ISBN 0-06-026180-3.

Madame Louise Bodot taught school in a peaceful French village. For her birthday she received an O-shaped box from her son containing a pet boa constrictor who she named Crictor. A Reading Rainbow book.

LUCAS
See also Luke

Aiken, Joan, **Midnight Is a Place**, Viking, 1974, 287p., Fiction, LC 74-760, ISBN 0-670-47483-5.

Fourteen-year-old Lucas lives a lonely and monotonous life in the house of his unpleasant guardian. The unexpected arrival of an unusual little French girl begins a series of events that completely changes his life. Set in nineteenth-century England.

Hurwitz, Johanna, **Class Clown**, illustrated by Sheila Hamanaka, Morrow, 1987, 98p., Fiction, LC 86-23624, ISBN 0-688-06723-9.

Lucas Cott is one of the smartest and most rambunctious students in the third-grade class. He doesn't mean to be the class clown and he tries to behave, yet he still causes the unexpected to occur. Kentucky 1989. South Carolina 1990. West Virginia 1989.

LUCCA

Lessac, Frane, **My Little Island**, illustrated by Frane Lessac, Lippincott, 1984, 38p., Picture Book, LC 84-48355, ISBN 0-397-32114-7; 0-397-32115-5 (lib).

A young boy visits the Caribbean island where he was born, taking his best friend Lucca. The two boys visit family, go swimming, diving, and more. A Reading Rainbow book.

LUCIE
See also Lucinda, Lucy

Hewitt, Marsha and Claire Mackay, **One Proud Summer**, Women's Educational Press, 1981, 159p., Fiction, ISBN 0-88961-048-7.

After her father dies, thirteen-year-old Lucie goes to work with her mother in a textile mill in a small Canadian town. The working conditions are terrible and the workers strike. Based on an actual historical incident.

LUCINDA
See also Cindy, Linda, Lindy, Lucie, Lucy

Karl, Jean, **Beloved Benjamin Is Waiting**, Dutton, 1978, 150p., Fiction, ISBN 0-525-26372-1.

Lucinda lives in fear because of her parents' fighting and neighborhood gangs. While hiding in an old house near a cemetery, she confides in a statue of a boy who died in 1889 and becomes involved in a science fiction adventure.

Sawyer, Ruth, **Roller Skates**, illustrated by Valenti Angelo, Dial, 1969, 192p., Fiction, ISBN 0-440-47499-X (pbk).

Lucinda has a privileged childhood in New York in the late 1800s. When her parents go on a lengthy trip to Europe, Lucinda stays with elderly friends and spends her time roller skating around the city, seeing sights, and making friends. 1937 Newbery Award book.

LUCIUS

Kennedy, John F., **Profiles in Courage**, illustrated by Emil Weiss, Harper & Row, 1955, 164p., Nonfiction, LC 64-17696.

Lucius Q. C. Lamar showed political courage under pressure. He is one of the eight statesmen featured in this book. 1964 Jane Addams Award book.

LUCY
See also Lucie, Lucinda

Feldman, Alan, **Lucy Mastermind**, illustrated by Irene Trivas, Dutton, 1985, 115p., Fiction, ISBN 0-525-44155-7.

Eleven-year-old Lucy has many ways to avoid schoolwork and to stay in trouble in this humorous book.

Lewis, C. S., **Lion, the Witch, and the Wardrobe, The**, illustrated by Pauline Baynes, Macmillan, 1950, 154p., Fiction, ISBN 0-02-758110-1.

Lucy and three other children meet a witch, a mighty lion, and other characters that live in the land of Narnia. This is the first of the seven titles in the Chronicles of Narnia series.

Logan, Carolyn, **Power of the Rellard, The**, Angus & Robertson, 1986, 231p., Fiction, ISBN 0-207-15367-1.

Lucy and her siblings discover that a toy theater they play with is quite unusual. Lucy finds she has a special power and must protect her family from evil forces trying to take the power from her.

Shreve, Susan, **Lucy Forever and Miss Rosetree, Shrinks**, Holt, 1987, 121p., Fiction, ISBN 0-805-003-401.

Lucy and her friend Rosie are in sixth grade and operate Shrinks Inc., a psychiatric practice. While trying to help a small deaf girl who has severe problems, the two girls find themselves in tremendous danger. 1988 Edgar Allan Poe Award.

Stevens, Carla, **Trouble for Lucy**, illustrated by Ronald Himler, Clarion, 1979, 80p., Fiction, ISBN 0-89919-523-7.

While traveling by wagon train to Oregon in 1843, Lucy's puppy causes constant problems.

LUIGI
See also Lewis, Lou, Louie, Louis

Burke, Susan, **Island Bike Business**, illustrated by Betty Greenhatch and Graeme Base, Oxford, 1982, 78p., Fiction, ISBN 0-19-554297-5.

Luigi and his friends have dangerous adventures when they attempt to recover missing bicycles.

LUKE
See also Lucas

Clymer, Eleanor, **Luke Was There**, Dell, 1973, 72p., Fiction, ISBN 0-440-40139-9 (pbk).

Luke is a counselor for the children at the shelter where he works. He is able to help one youngster when the boy really needs Luke.

Taylor, Theodore, **Trouble with Tuck, The**, Doubleday, 1981, 110p., Fiction, ISBN 0-385-17774-7.

When their pet dog begins to lose its eyesight, Luke and his family take unusual measures and get a guide dog for their pet. Based on a true incident. California 1984.

Wallace, Bill, **Beauty**, Holiday House, 1988, 177p., Fiction, LC 88-6422, ISBN 0-8234-0715-2.

Luke's parents have separated and he and his mother have moved to his grandpa's farm. Luke is unhappy but finds comfort in riding and caring for a horse named Beauty. Kansas 1991. Oklahoma 1991.

LULU

Brown, Laurene Krasny and Marc Brown, **Visiting the Art Museum**, illustrated by Laurene Krasny Brown and Marc Brown, Dutton, 1986, 32p., Nonfiction, LC 85-32552, ISBN 0-525-44233-2.

A family goes to an art museum where they see examples of various art styles, from primitive art to works by twentieth-century pop artists such as Roy Lichtenstein. One of the children takes Lulu, her toy robot, on the outing. A Reading Rainbow book.

LUPITA

Beatty, Patricia, **Lupita Mañana**, Morrow, 1981, 192p., Fiction, ISBN 0-688-003-583; 0-688-003-591 (lib).

Thirteen-year-old Lupita enters California illegally to find work in order to help her poverty-stricken family. She constantly worries about being caught. 1982 Jane Addams Honor book.

LUTHER

Peck, Robert Newton, **Soup**, illustrated by Charles Gehm, Knopf, 1974, 96p., Fiction, ISBN 0-394-82700-7; 0-394-92700-1 (lib).

Luther Wesley Vinson is known as Soup. He and his best friend have numerous adventures and misadventures during their third-grade year as they grow up in a small Vermont town. Michigan 1984.

Peck, Robert Newton, **Soup for President**, illustrated by Ted Lewin, Knopf, 1978, 107p., Fiction, ISBN 0-394-93675-2.

Luther is also known as Soup. When he runs for class president he has his best friend manage his campaign. There are numerous other books about Soup. Mississippi 1981. Missouri 1981.

Quackenbush, Robert, **Here a Plant, There a Plant, Everywhere a Plant, Plant: A Story of Luther Burbank**, Prentice-Hall, 1982, 36p., Nonfiction, ISBN 0-13-387266.

Luther Burbank's experiments with the grafting and crossbreeding of plants to create better vegetables is told in cartoonlike illustrations.

LYDIA

McDonnell, Christine, **Just for the Summer**, illustrated by Diane de Groat, Viking Kestrel, 1987, 117p., Fiction, ISBN 0-670-80059-7.

Lydia learns a great deal about herself and has interesting experiences while spending the summer with her favorite aunts.

LYNDON

Devaney, John, **Lyndon Baines Johnson: President**, Walker, 1986, 122p., Nonfiction, ISBN 0-8027-6639-0.

Lyndon Baines Johnson became president of the United States after the assassination of John F. Kennedy. This biography explores the childhood experiences that influenced Johnson.

LYNN
See also Marilyn, Melinda,

Paige, David, **Day in the Life of a Marine Biologist, A**, illustrated by Robert Ruhlin, Troll, 1981, 32p., Nonfiction, LC 80-54097, ISBN 0-89375-446-3; 0-89375-447-1 (pbk).

A day in the life of Lynn Walter who works as a marine biologist for an oceanographic institute. Color photographs show Lynn at work as she studies ocean life. A Reading Rainbow book.

-M-

MADELINE

Bemelmans, Ludwig, **Madeline's Rescue**, illustrated by Ludwig Bemelmans, Puffin, 1975, 50p., Picture Book, LC 77-2573, ISBN 0-14-050207-6.

A young French girl named Madeline slipped and fell into the Seine River. The dog that rescued her was taken to live with Madeline and eleven other girls in an old house in Paris. There are other books about Madeline. 1954 Caldecott Award book.

MADGE

Walsh, Jill Paton, **Unleaving**, Farrar, Straus & Giroux, 1976, 145p., Fiction, LC 76-8857, ISBN 0-374-38042-2.

Madge inherits her grandmother's home at the beach and decides to rent it to a philosophy professor and his students for the summer. There is an earlier book about Madge. 1976 Boston Globe-Horn Book Award.

MAFATU

Sperry, Armstrong, **Call It Courage**, illustrated by Armstrong Sperry, Macmillan, 1940, 95p., Fiction, ISBN 0-02-786030-2.

The young Polynesian boy, Mafatu, was afraid of the sea and avoided it. The villagers branded him a coward even though he was the son of the Great Chief. Determined to conquer his fear or be conquered, Mafatu set off in a canoe with only his little dog and a pet albatross for company. 1941 Newbery Award book.

MAGGIE

See also Margaret, Marguerite

Alter, Judy, **Maggie and a Horse Named Devildust**, Texas Monthly Press, 1989, 159p., Fiction, ISBN 0-936650-08-7.

Maggie wants to tame a wild horse and be a trick rider in a 'Wild West' show but her mother has other plans for her. Set in Texas at the turn of the century.

Bates, Betty, **Great Male Conspiracy**, Holiday House, 1986, 167p., Fiction, ISBN 0-8234-0629-6.

Maggie rejects all men, including her father and male classmates, because of both real and imagined attitudes and actions.

Byars, Betsy, **Not-Just-Anybody Family, The**, illustrated by Jacqueline Rogers, Delacorte, 1986, 149p., Fiction, ISBN 0-440-50211-X.

Maggie and Vern Blossom try to straighten out their family's affairs when their grandfather is jailed for disturbing the peace and their brother breaks both his legs. There are other books about the Blossoms.

Cassedy, Sylvia, **Behind the Attic Wall**, Crowell, 1983, 315p., Fiction, ISBN 0-690-04337-6.

Maggie has lived in numerous boarding schools and foster homes. Finally she is sent to live with her great aunts in their old mansion. Maggie hears mysterious sounds and finds a locked door that leads to a hidden room with unusual dolls in it.

Clymer, Eleanor, **Get-Away Car, The**, Dutton, 1978, 149p., Fiction, ISBN 0-525-30470-3.

Maggie lives with her grandmother. The two decide to run away when an aunt tries to send grandmother to a nursing home. The trip includes several adventures and a mystery. Oklahoma 1981.

Field, Rachel, **Calico Bush**, illustrated by Allen Lewis, Macmillan, 1966, 201p., Fiction, ISBN 0-02-734610-2.

Marguerite Ledoux is called Maggie by the English family to whom she is bound-out in colonial America. Maggie saves the family from an Indian attack with her quick thinking. 1932 Newbery Honor book.

Sharmat, Marjorie Weinman, **Getting Something on Maggie Marmelstein**, illustrated by Ben Shecter, Harper & Row, 1971, 101p., Fiction, ISBN 0-06-025552-8.

A humorous story about Maggie Marmelstein and her archenemy, Thad Smith. There are several other books about Maggie.

MALCOLM

Gessner, Lynne, **Malcolm Yucca Seed**, illustrated by William Sauts Back, Harvey, 1977, 63p., Fiction, ISBN 0-8178-5632-3-X.

Malcolm is a young Navajo boy who wants a Navajo name but knows he must earn it. He has the opportunity when a bad storm destroys the family corral.

Konigsburg, Elaine, **Up From Jericho Tel**, Atheneum, 1986, 178p., Fiction, ISBN 0-689-31194-X.

Eleven-year-old Malcolm and his friend find themselves invisible on occasion as they search for a stolen necklace.

MALLORY

Alexander, Lloyd, **Wizard in the Tree**, illustrated by Laszlo Kubinyi, Dutton, 1975, 137p., Fiction, ISBN 0-525-43128-4.

While hunting for mushrooms in the forest, Mallory finds a tattered old wizard caught in a tree that has been cut down. The two have several adventures before the wizard leaves to join the other magic folks.

MANOLO

Wojciechowska, Maia, **Shadow of a Bull**, illustrated by Alvin Smith, Atheneum, 1976, 165p., Fiction, LC 64-12563, ISBN 0-689-30042-5.

Manolo Olivar is the son of a famous bullfighter and everyone expects him to grow up to be a bullfighter, too. Even though Manolo looks like his father, he knows that he is not brave like his father and thinks of himself as a coward. 1965 Newbery Award book.

MARC

See also Marco, Marcos, Marcus, Mark

Bober, Natalie S., **Marc Chagall: Painter of Dreams**, illustrated by Vera Rosenberry, Jewish Publication Society, 1991, 124p., Nonfiction, LC 91-25463, ISBN 0-8276-0379-7.

The famous painter Marc Chagall had wanted to paint from the time he was a boy growing up in a small Hasidic Jewish village in Russia. He was able to continue his art until his death at age ninety-seven. This book includes biographical information and photographs of his paintings.

MARCO

See also Marc, Mark

Greene, Carol, **Marco Polo: Voyager to the Orient**, Children's Press, 1987, 108p., Non-Fiction, ISBN 0-516-03229-1.

Marco Polo was a famous explorer of the Middle East, India, and the Far East. This biography includes historical information about the thirteenth century.

Marzollo, Jean, **Soccer Sam**, illustrated by Blanche Sims, Random House, 1987, 48p., Easy Reader, LC 86-47533, ISBN 0-394-88406-X; 0-394-98406-4 (lib).

Marco has come from Mexico to spend a year living with his cousin Sam. Marco speaks limited English and doesn't know how to play basketball, but he is a success at teaching the second graders how to play soccer. A Reading Rainbow book.

MARCOS

See also Marc, Mark

Seuss, Dr., **McElligot's Pool**, illustrated by Dr. Seuss, Random House, 1947, 52p., Picture Book, ISBN 0-394-80083-4; 0-394-90083-9 (lib).

A farmer laughs at Marcos for fishing in the small McElligot's Pool. However, Marcos imagines all types and sizes of fish that may be there and keeps on fishing. 1948 Caldecott Honor book. Pacific Northwest 1950.

MARCUS
See also Marc, Mark

Bunting, Eve, **Is Anybody There?**, Lippincott, 1988, 170p., Fiction, ISBN 0-397-32303-4.

Thirteen-year-old Marcus lives with his widowed mother. When small items begin disappearing from the house, Marcus decides to solve the mystery on his own. South Carolina 1991.

Lowry, Lois, **Us and Uncle Fraud**, Houghton Mifflin, 1984, 148p., Fiction, ISBN 0-395-36633-X.

Marcus and his sister have a series of adventures as they attempt to learn the truth about their eccentric uncle.

MARCY

Danziger, Paula, **Cat Ate My Gymsuit, The**, Delacorte, 1974, 147p., Fiction, LC 74-8898, ISBN 0-440-01612-6; 0-440-01696-7 (lib).

Marcy Lewis has many problems and deep feelings of insecurity. When her unconventional junior high school English teacher is fired, Marcy courageously campaigns for her favorite teacher. Marcy's values cost her quite a bit at both home and school, and she has to decide whether her values are worth the price. Hawaii 1981. Massachusetts 1979.

Danziger, Paula, **There's a Bat in Bunk Five**, Delacorte, 1980, 150p., Fiction, ISBN 0-4400-86-051; 0-4400-8606-X (lib).

Fourteen-year-old Marcy is on her own for the first time when she works as a counselor at an arts camp. California 1984.

MARGARET
See also Maggie, Marguerite, Meg, Peggy

Blume, Judy, **Are You There God? It's Me, Margaret**, Bradbury, 1970, 149p., Fiction, LC 79-122741, ISBN 0-87888-022-4.

Margaret Simon is almost twelve years old and she talks to God a lot about the problems of growing up. Hawaii 1975. Indiana 1976. New Hampshire 1980.

Faber, Doris, **Margaret Thatcher: Britain's 'Iron Lady'**, illustrated by Robert Masheris, Viking Kestrel, 1985, 57p., Nonfiction, ISBN 0-670-80785-0.

Biographical information about Margaret Thatcher, who grew up as the daughter of a grocer and became the first female prime minister of Great Britain.

L'Engle, Madeleine, **Wrinkle in Time, A**, Dell, 1962, 211p., Fiction, ISBN 0-440-498-58.

On a dark and stormy night, Margaret Murray, her little brother, and their mother go down to the kitchen for a midnight snack. An unearthly stranger arrives and the children are taken through a wrinkle in time as they become involved in a search for their scientist father. 1963 Newbery Award book. Oklahoma 1965.

Nixon, Joan Lowery, **Maggie, Too**, Harcourt Brace Jovanovich, 1985, 101p., Fiction, ISBN 0-15-250350-1.

Twelve-year-old Margaret learns about her famous father and about herself when she becomes friends with her grandmother. There is another book about Margaret.

Rabe, Berniece, **Margaret's Moves**, illustrated by Julie Downing, Dutton, 1986, 105p., Fiction, ISBN 0-525-44271-5.

Nine-year-old Margaret uses a wheelchair and wants a new one that is faster and more flexible, but her parents think there are other things more important.

Saunders, Susan, **Margaret Mead: The World Was Her Family**, illustrated by Ted Lewin, Viking Kestrel, 1987, 58p., Nonfiction, ISBN 0-670-81051-7.

A biography of the famous anthropologist, Margaret Mead, and her contributions to the field that she spent her life studying.

Smith, Alison, **Trap of Gold**, Dodd, Mead, 1985, 176p., Fiction, ISBN 0-0-396-08721-3.

Thirteen-year-old Margaret has an exciting and suspense-filled adventure that involves a gold nugget, an abandoned gold mine, and a frightening stranger.

MARGO
See also Margot

Rabe, Berniece, **Rehearsal for the Bigtime**, Watts, 1988, 144p., Fiction, ISBN 0-531-10504-0.

Margo begins playing the clarinet and forms a musical group determined to make it to the top.

MARGOT
See also Margo

Hurwitz, Johanna, **Law of Gravity, The**, illustrated by Ingrid Fetz, Morrow, 1978, 192p., Fiction, ISBN 0-688-32142-9.

Margot's friends are going to be gone, so Margot decides to spend her summer trying to get her mother to go downstairs since she never leaves their sixth-story walkup apartment. Set in New York, this is a story about a happy family and neighborhood adventures.

MARGUERITE
See also Maggie, Margaret, Meg

Field, Rachel, **Calico Bush**, illustrated by Allen Lewis, Macmillan, 1966, 201p., Fiction, ISBN 0-02-734610-2.

Marguerite Lidoux is called Maggie by the English family to whom she is bound-out in colonial America. Maggie saves the family from an Indian attack with her quick thinking. 1932 Newbery Honor book.

MARI
See also Marilyn, Mary

Donnelly, Elfie, **Offbeat Friends**, Crown, 1982, 119p., Fiction, ISBN 0-517-54617-5.

Mari develops an unusual friendship with an elderly woman who lives at the mental hospital. When her friend runs away, Mari decides to help her.

MARIA
See also Marie

Ets, Marie Hall and Aurora Labastida, **Nine Days to Christmas**, illustrated by Marie Hall Ets, Viking, 1959, 48p., Picture Book, LC 59-16438, ISBN 670-51350-4.

Maria is the servant of a family planning their younger daughter's first posada, a special Christmas party held nine days before Christmas. At the party, the young girl finds she has a very special pinata. 1960 Caldecott Award book.

MARIE
See also Jeanmarie, Maria

Brown, Marcia, **Stone Soup: An Old Tale**, illustrated by Marcia Brown, Scribner, 1947, 40p., Picture Book, ISBN 0-684-92296-7; 0-684-16217-2 (pbk).

Marie and the other peasants hid their food when they saw three hungry soldiers coming down the road. The soldiers then taught the villagers how to make a soup from three stones and soon a village feast was prepared. An old folktale. 1948 Caldecott Honor book.

Greene, Carol, **Marie Curie: Pioneer Physicist**, Children's Press, 1984, 112p., Nonfiction, ISBN 0-516-03203-8.

Marie Curie was a famous chemist at a time when few women studied science. She was also dedicated to her family. This biography gives information about the woman and the times she lived in.

Hamerstrom, Frances, **Adventure of the Stone Man**, illustrated by William Kimber, Crossing, 1977, 103p., Fiction, ISBN 0-912278-89-7.

Marie and her brother find a cave in the mountain near their home in France, which they make their secret place. They find traces of primitive people in their cave and have other exciting experiences.

MARILYN
See also Lynn, Mari, Mary

Cleary, Beverly, **Socks**, illustrated by Beatrice Darwin, Morrow, 1973, 156p., Fiction, ISBN 0-440-48256-9 (pbk).

Marilyn and Bill Bricker are a young couple who buy Socks, a kitten with white paws. Socks is taken to the Bricker's home where he is petted, pampered, and loved. When the Bricker's have a baby, Socks is no longer the center of attention and problems begin. Kansas 1976.

MARIO

Rubinstein, Gillian, **Space Demons**, Dial, 1988, 198p., Fiction, ISBN 0-8037-0534-4.

Mario and his friends are drawn into a new computer game where they experience dangerous situations as they attempt to get out.

MARION

Holbrook, Stewart, **Swamp Fox of the Revolution, The**, illustrated by Ernest Richardson, Random House, 1959, 180p., Nonfiction.

Marion Francis was an American general during the Revolutionary War who organized a guerilla band to fight the British in South Carolina. Pacific Northwest 1962.

MARK
See also Marc, Marco, Marcos, Marcus

Eager, Edward, **Magic by the Lake**, illustrated by N. M. Bodecker, Harcourt Brace Jovanovich, 1985, 183p., Fiction, ISBN 0-15-250441-9.

Mark and three other children must tame a magic lake before they can discover its treasure.

Hermes, Patricia, **Who Will Take Care of Me?**, Harcourt Brace Jovanovich, 1983, 99p., Fiction, ISBN 0-15-296265-4.

When their grandmother dies, twelve-year-old Mark runs away with his retarded brother because he fears they will be separated and his brother put in an institution.

Morey, Walt, **Gentle Ben**, illustrated by John Schoenherr, Dutton, 1965, 191p., Fiction, ISBN 0-525-30429-0.

Mark Anderson is a frail, sensitive thirteen-year-old boy growing up on the outskirts of an Alaskan fishing village. In an exciting adventure, he befriends the huge five-year-old bear, Ben, who has been ignored and half starved by a man who found him as a cub. Dutton Jr. Animal Book Award. Oklahoma 1968.

Streatfield, Noel, **Theatre Shoes**, Dell, 1985, 288p., Fiction, ISBN 0-440-48791-9 (pbk).

Mark and his siblings are taken in by their grandmother who is a famous actress. The children are enrolled at an acting academy with varying degrees of success. The book is set in 1945 and the children anxiously await the return of their father who is a prisoner of war.

Warren, Mary Phraner, **Haunted Kitchen, The**, illustrated by Len Epstein, Westminster, 1976, 124p., Fiction, ISBN 0-664-32584-X.

Mark and his family move to a new house in Portland, Oregon, and begin hearing strange noises that they think is a ghost.

Yep, Laurence, **Mark Twain Murders**, Four Winds, 1982, 152p., Fiction, ISBN 0-02-793670-8.

An exciting mystery set in San Francisco in 1864. Mark Twain is a reporter who becomes involved with a teenager whose stepfather has been murdered. The two uncover a plot by spies as they investigate the murder and put their own lives in danger.

MARLEE
See also Marly

Harris, Mark Jonathan, **With a Wave of the Wand**, Lothrop, Lee & Shepard, 1980, 191p., Fiction, ISBN 0-688-41941-0.

As a fifth grader, Marlee is going through a very difficult time in her life. Her parents have separated and she has had to move with her mother and brother to Venice, California.

MARLEEN

Perl, Lila, **Marleen, the Horror Queen**, Clarion, 1985, 164p., Fiction, ISBN 0-89919-368-4.

Thirteen-year-old Marleen has problems with her self-image, particularly when she compares herself with her mother who is a bodybuilder.

MARLY
See also Marlee

Sorensen, Virginia, **Miracles on Maple Hill**, illustrated by Beth Krush and Joe Krush, Harcourt Brace Jovanovich, 1956, 180p., Fiction, LC 56-8358, ISBN 0-15-254558-1.

Marly and Joe moved with their parents from the city to a small farmhouse on Maple Hill. Marly hopes for miracles—not just the ones that bring sap to the trees to make maple syrup, but one that will help their father recover from his experiences as a prisoner of war. 1957 Newbery Award book.

MARSHA

Fenner, Carol, **Skates of Uncle Richard**, illustrated by Ati Forberg, Random House, 1978, 46p., Fiction, ISBN 0-394-93553-5.

Marsha dreams of being an ice-skating champion but finds she is clumsy with the skates that she receives for Christmas. Her uncle helps her with her skating. 1979 Coretta Scott King Award book.

MARSHALL

Scioscia, Mary, **Bicycle Rider**, illustrated by Ed Young, Harper & Row, 1983, 38p., Nonfiction, ISBN 0-06-025223-5.

Marshall Taylor is a little known black sports hero who won the ten-mile bicycle race in Indianapolis, Indiana.

Snyder, Zilpha Keatley, **Egypt Game, The**, illustrated by Alton Raible, Atheneum, 1967, 215p., Fiction, LC 67-2717, ISBN 0-689-30006-9; 0-689-70297-3.

Marshall Ross spends a lot of time with his older sister Melanie who is eleven. When April Hall moves into their apartment building to live with her grandmother, the children become interested in ancient Egypt and begin playing the Egypt Game. The game continues until a murder takes place in their neighborhood. 1968 Newbery Honor book.

MARTHA

Caines, Jeannette, **Just Us Women**, illustrated by Pat Cummings, Harper & Row, 1982, 32p., Picture Book, LC 81-48655, ISBN 0-06-020941-0; 0-06-020942-0 (lib).

A young girl and her Aunt Martha plan a special car trip to North Carolina. As the two of them travel in Aunt Martha's new car, they can stop whenever they want. A Reading Rainbow book.

Eager, Edward, **Magic by the Lake**, illustrated by N. M. Bodecker, Harcourt Brace Jovanovich, 1985, 183p., Fiction, ISBN 0-15-250441-9.

Martha and three other children must tame a magic lake before they can discover its treasures.

Herlihy, Dirlie, **Ludie's Song**, Dial, 1988, 212p., Fiction, ISBN 0-8037-0533-6.

During the early 1950s, thirteen-year-old Martha Armstrong visits her aunt and uncle in rural Georgia. Martha makes friends with a young black woman and questions racial assumptions.

Sauer, Julia, **Light at Tern Rock, The**, illustrated by Georges Schreiber, Viking, 1951, 63p., Fiction.

Ronnie and his Aunt Martha agree to spend two weeks at the lighthouse on Tern Rock to relieve the lighthouse keeper. When he doesn't return, they have to spend Christmas and it becomes a very special day. 1952 Newbery Honor book.

Snyder, Zilpha Keatley, **Changeling, The**, illustrated by Alton Raible, Dell, 1986, 220p., Fiction, ISBN 0-440-41200-5 (pbk).

Martha develops a close friendship with a girl who is very different than she is and the two create their own make-believe world.

Walter, Mildred Pitts, **Trouble's Child**, Lothrop, Lee & Shepard, 1985, 157p., Fiction, ISBN 0-688-042-147 (lib).

Martha lives on an island off the Louisiana coast with her grandmother who is a midwife. Martha wants to leave the island to go to high school to gain new skills and information. 1986 Coretta Scott King Honor book.

MARTIN
See also Marty

Adler, David A., **Martin Luther King Jr.: Free at Last**, illustrated by Robert Casilla, Holiday House, 1986, 48p., Nonfiction, ISBN 0-82340-618-0.

A biography of the famous civil rights activist Martin Luther King, Jr., who was assassinated for his beliefs.

Hargrove, Jim, **Martin Van Buren**, Children's Press, 1987, 100p., Nonfiction, ISBN 0-516-01391-2.

Martin Van Buren was a president of the United States. This biography gives information on both his strengths and weaknesses.

King-Smith, Dick, **Martin's Mice**, illustrated by Jez Alborough, Crown, 1988, 122p., Fiction, ISBN 0-517-57113-7.

Martin the cat doesn't want to catch and eat mice, so he makes a pet out of one of the mice.

Patterson, Lillie, **Martin Luther King, Jr. and the Freedom Movement**, Facts on File, 1989, 178p., Nonfiction, ISBN 0-8160-1605-4.

A biography of the Baptist minister, Martin Luther King, Jr., and the leadership role he took in the civil rights movement of the 1960s. 1990 Coretta Scott King Honor book.

Pryor, Bonnie, **Vinegar Pancakes and Vanishing Cream**, illustrated by Gail Owens, Morrow, 1987, 118p., Fiction, ISBN 0-688-06728-X.

Martin Snodgrass compares himself to his siblings and finds himself lacking, so he decides to become famous in this humorous family story.

MARTY
See also Martin

Aaron, Chester, **Duchess**, Lippincott, 1982, 182p., Fiction, ISBN 0-397-31948-7.

Because of his many problems, thirteen-year-old Marty is sent to his uncle's sheep ranch. At the ranch he is given the responsibility of training a border collie puppy that he has found.

MARV
See also Marvin

Nichols, Joan Kane, **All but the Right Folks**, Stemmer House, 1985, 100p., Fiction, ISBN 0-88045-065-7.

Marv lives in San Francisco with his father. He becomes confused when he discovers that he will be spending the summer in New York City with a white grandmother that he didn't know about.

MARVIN
See also Marv

Geller, Mark, **My Life in the 7th Grade**, Harper & Row, 1986, 121p., Fiction, ISBN 0-06-021982-3.

Marvin Berman learns about friendship and how to make up his own mind while he is in seventh grade.

Glass, Franklin, **Marvin and Tige**, St. Martin's Press, 1977, 232p., Fiction, ISBN 0-312-51783-1.

Marvin Stewart is a former advertising executive who has dropped out of the rat race and is all alone. He meets Tige Jackson, age eleven, who is also alone and the two develop an unusual friendship. 1978 Coretta Scott King Award.

Van Leeuwen, Jean, **Great Christmas Kidnapping Caper, The**, illustrated by Steven Kellogg, Dial, 1975, 133p., Fiction, ISBN 0-8037-5416-7.

Marvin and his mice friends move into a dollhouse in the toy department of a large store where the Santa Claus leaves food for them. When Santa is kidnapped, the mice go in search of him. There are other books about Marvin and his gang. Kansas 1978. South Carolina 1979.

MARY

See also Mari, Marilyn, Mary Ann,
Mary Anne, Mary Jo, Mary Rose, Rosemary

Burnett, Frances Hodgson, **Secret Garden, The**, illustrated by Shirley Hughes, Viking Kestrel, 1988, 256p., Fiction, ISBN 0-670-82571-9.

After her parents die in India, Mary Lenox is sent to live in a grand but gloomy house in England. Her lonely life changes with the help of a handicapped boy, a young villager, and a secret garden.

Butler, Beverly, **My Sister's Keeper**, Dodd, Mead, 1980, 221p., Fiction, ISBN 0-396-07803-6.

Set in 1871, Mary James goes to help her sister in the woods of Wisconsin and experiences a forest fire.

Cassedy, Sylvia, **M. E. and Morton**, Crowell, 1987, 312p., Fiction, ISBN 0-690-04562-X.

Mary Ella has a mildly retarded brother, a weak father, and an overly concerned mother. An unusual girl that moves into the neighborhood becomes a friend with near disastrous results.

Cleaver, Vera and Bill Cleaver, **Where the Lilies Bloom**, illustrated by Jim Spanfeller, Lippincott, 1969, 174p., Fiction, ISBN 0-397-31111-7.

Mary Call is responsible for taking care of the younger children after her father dies. This story is set in Appalachia. There is another book about Mary when she is older.

Greenfield, Eloise, **Mary McCleod Bethune**, illustrated by Jerry Pinkney, Crowell, 1977, 32p., Nonfiction, LC 76-11522, ISBN 0-690-01129-6.

A biography of Mary McCleod Bethune. As a small child, Mary wanted to learn to read since no one else in her large family of sixteen children could. There were no schools for black children in the countryside of South Carolina until she was eleven. When she finally got her education she became a teacher, then started her own school for black students. 1978 Coretta Scott King Honor book.

Meltzer, Milton, **Mary McCleod Bethune: Voice of Black Hope**, illustrated by Stephen Marchesi, Viking Kestrel, 1987, 58p., Nonfiction, ISBN 0-670-80744-3.

Mary McCleod Bethune was a black woman who wanted to help educate black children and won the support of many people. This biography provides information about her background and her deeds.

Nixon, Joan Lowery, **Dark and Deadly Pool, The**, Delacorte, 1987, 179p., Fiction, ISBN 0-385-295-855.

Mary Elizabeth's sixteenth summer is more exciting than she had anticipated. While working at an expensive health club, a mysterious event ends in murder. Indiana 1990.

Ryan, Mary C., **Frankie's Run**, Little, Brown, 1987, 160p., Fiction, ISBN 0-316-76370-5.

Mary decides to organize a fund-raiser to help finance a library program that her younger brother enjoys. Although things go wrong, Mary learns a lot and has the support of her large family.

Travres, P. L., **Mary Poppins**, illustrated by Mary Shepard, Harcourt Brace Jovanovich, 1981, 206p., Fiction, ISBN 0-15-252408-8.

The ever-popular story of the magical Mary Poppins who is blown into the household of the Banks family to care for their children. There are several other titles about Mary Poppins. Hawaii 1965.

Wilder, Laura Ingalls, **By the Shores of Silver Lake**, illustrated by Garth Williams, Harper & Row, 1953, 290p., Fiction, ISBN 0-06-026416-0.

The Ingalls family didn't do well in Plum Creek, Minnesota, so Pa went west to the Dakota Territory and the family became the first settlers in a new town. When the family catches scarlet fever, Mary becomes blind. There are other books about this family. 1940 Newbery Honor book. Pacific Northwest 1942.

Wilder, Laura Ingalls, **On the Banks of Plum Creek**, illustrated by Garth Williams, Harper & Row, 1953, 338p., Fiction, ISBN 0-06-026470-5.

Mary Ingalls and her family move to Minnesota and live in a dugout until they can build a new house. This pioneer family faces many misfortunes including a flood, a blizzard, and grasshoppers. There are other books about this family. 1938 Newbery Honor book.

MARY ANN
See also Ann, Mary, Mary Anne

Aliki, **Digging Up Dinosaurs**, illustrated by Aliki, Crowell, 1981, 32p., Picture Book, LC 85-42979, ISBN 0-690-04714-2; 0-690-04716-9 (lib).

Mary Ann Mantrell found the first dinosaur fossils in England in 1822. In 1841, Dr. Richard Owen named the giant reptiles Dinosauria. The book includes this and other true information about dinosaur bones including where they are found and how museum exhibits are put together. A Reading Rainbow book.

Stevenson, James, **'Could Be Worse!'**, illustrated by James Stevenson, Greenwillow, 1977, 30p., Picture Book, LC 76-28534, ISBN 0-688-80075-0; 0-688-84075-2 (lib).

Mary Ann's grandpa and his house are always the same. Grandpa even says the same things. One morning Grandpa says something different and a story with many adventures begins. A Reading Rainbow book.

Stevenson, James, **What's Under My Bed?**, illustrated by James Stevenson, Greenwillow, 1983, 30p., Picture Book, LC 83-1454, ISBN 0-688-02325-8; 0-688-02327-4 (lib).

Mary Ann and her brother Louie spend the night at grandpa's house, and they have trouble sleeping, until he tells them a story about his childhood when he was scared at bedtime. A Reading Rainbow book.

MARY ANNE
See also Anne, Mary, Mary Ann

Martin, Ann, **Kristy's Great Idea**, Scholastic, 1986, 153p., Fiction, ISBN 0-590-41985-4 (pbk).

Mary Anne and her friends decide to form a babysitting club. There are numerous books about this group of friends.

MARY JO
See also Jo, Mary

Udry, Janice May, **Mary Jo's Grandmother**, illustrated by Eleanor Mill, Whitman, 1970, 32p., Picture Book, ISBN 0-807-549-843.

Mary Jo has to get help to their remote farm when her grandmother is injured in a fall. 1971 Coretta Scott King Honor book.

MARY ROSE
See also Mary, Rose

Clifford, Eth, **Help! I'm a Prisoner in the Library**, Houghton Mifflin, 1979, 96p., Fiction, ISBN 0-590-40605-1.

Mary Rose and Jo-Beth's father forgot to put gas in the car. When the car runs out of gas in Indianapolis, their father goes to get gas and the girls go into the Finton Memorial Library for Children. When the lights go out, the girls discover they have been locked in the library for the night during a terrible blizzard. Indiana 1982.

Clifford, Eth, **Just Tell Me When We're Dead**, illustrated by George Hughes, Houghton Mifflin, 1983, 130p., Fiction, LC 83-10865, ISBN 0-395-33071-8.

When their cousin leaves a note that he has gone West, Mary Rose and her younger sister decide to go looking for him. None of them expect the adventures that they will have. Oklahoma 1986.

Sachs, Marilyn, **Truth about Mary Rose, The**, illustrated by Louis Glanzman, Scholastic, 1987, 159p., Fiction, ISBN 0-590-40402-4.

Mary Rose Ramirez enjoys hearing the stories about the family member that she has been named for. As she hears more and more family stories, she realizes that various family members differ in their perceptions of the first Mary Rose.

MATILDA
See also May

Dahl, Roald, **Matilda**, illustrated by Quentin Blake, Viking Kestrel, 1988, 240p., Fiction, ISBN 0-670-82439-9.

Matilda is a very bright little girl who manages to resolve the problems at her school through her intellectual and psychic abilities. Utah 1991.

Nesbit, E., **Cockatoucan**, illustrated by Elroy Hughes, Dial, 1988, 30p., Fiction, ISBN 0-8037-0474-7.

Matilda and her nursemaid get on a carriage that takes them to a fantastic village.

MATT
See also Matthew, Matthias

Bunting, Eve, **Ghost Children**, Ticknor & Fields, 1989, 163p., Fiction, ISBN 0-89919-843-0.

Matt and his younger sister are orphans who are sent to live with their aunt. Matt becomes involved in a mystery concerning life-sized dolls belonging to the aunt.

Gault, William Campbell, **Wild Willie, Wide Receiver**, Dutton, 1974, 147p., Fiction, ISBN 0-525-42788-0.

Coach Matt Tulley has problems with his new super-athlete as the Chicago Miners fight their way to the Super Bowl.

Speare, Elizabeth George, **Sign of the Beaver, The**, Houghton Mifflin, 1983, 135p., Fiction, LC 83-118, ISBN 0-395-33890-5.

During the early 1700s, thirteen-year-old Matt was left alone to guard his family's newly built wilderness cabin while his father went to get the rest of the family. Matt learned new survival methods from Attean, a proud young Indian. Matt also began to appreciate the Beaver Clan's way of life, their heritage and the problems the Indians faced as their wilderness home became settled. 1984 Child Study Children's Book Award. 1984 Christopher Award. 1984 Newbery Honor book. 1984 Scott O'Dell Award.

Turner, Ann, **Dakota Dugout**, illustrated by Ronald Himler, Macmillan, 1985, 28p., Picture Book, LC 85-3084, ISBN 0-02-789700-1.

A woman tells her granddaughter what it was like when she was a new bride and went to live with her husband, Matt, in a sod house that he had built on the Dakota prairie. Life was hard and lonely during those years, yet she missed them later in life. A Reading Rainbow book.

MATTHEW
See also Matt, Matthias

Blumberg, Rhoda, **Commodore Perry in the Land of the Shogun**, illustrated with photographs, Lothrop, Lee & Shepard, 1985, 144p., Nonfiction, LC 84-21800, ISBN 0-688-03723-2.

Commodore Matthew Perry was sent by American President Fillmore in 1853 to request that the Emperor of Japan allow Japanese harbors be opened to American ships. Perry's role in opening Japan's closed society to world trade was one of history's most significant diplomatic achievements. 1986 Newbery Honor book. 1985 Boston Globe-Horn Book Award. 1986 Golden Kite Award.

Ferris, Jeri, **Arctic Explorer: The Story of Matthew Henson**, Carolrhoda, 1989, 80p., Nonfiction, ISBN 0-8761-370-2.

Matthew Henson was a black explorer who co-discovered the North Pole. This biography tells of the struggles, hardships, and determination that were required to reach the North Pole.

Houston, James, **Frozen Fire: A Tale of Courage**, illustrated by James Houston, Atheneum/Margaret K. McElderry Book, 1977, 149p., Fiction, ISBN 0-689-50083-1.

Matthew Morgan flies with his father to the Canadian Arctic where his father is searching for copper. Matthew and an Eskimo friend survive tremendous hardships when they search for Matthew's father after they are lost in a storm. Based on a true story. There are other books about Matthew.

Wiseman, David, **Jeremy Visick**, Houghton Mifflin, 1981, 170p., Fiction, ISBN 0-395-30449-0.

When Matthew discovers an old tombstone in Cornwall, England, he is taken back into the 1800s and a coal mine where a disaster occurred.

MATTHIAS
See also Matt, Matthew

Jacques, Brian, **Redwall**, illustrated by Gary Chalk, Philomel, 1986, 351p., Fiction, ISBN 0-399-21424-0.

Matthias becomes an unexpected hero when the animals of Redwall Abbey are forced into battle with an evil rat and his band.

MAUDE
See also Maudie

Lexau, Joan M., **Striped Ice Cream**, illustrated by John Wilson, Lippincott, 1968, 95p., Fiction, LC 68-10774, ISBN 0-397-31047-1.

Maude's little sister is resigned to the fact that their mother cannot afford anything special for her birthday, but she does not understand why the whole family seems to have turned against her, until the big day finally arrives. Arkansas 1971.

MAUDIE
See also Maude

Naylor, Phyllis Reynolds and Lura Schield Reynolds, **Maudie in the Middle**, illustrated by Gwyn Brown, Atheneum, 1988, 161p., Fiction, ISBN 0-689-31395-0.

Maudie lives on an Iowa farm in the early 1900s. As the middle child in a large family, she feels unappreciated and unnoticed and tries to get her family's attention.

MAUREEN

Chase, Mary, **Wicked Pigeon Ladies in the Garden**, illustrated by Don Bolognese, Peter Smith, 1968, 115p., Fiction, ISBN 0-8446-6192-9.

Maureen Swanson is disobedient and willful. When she sneaks into the old Messerman Place, she is transported back in time and learns that the Messerman daughters had been changed into pigeons because they were unkind.

Henry, Marguerite, **Misty of Chincoteague**, illustrated by Wesley Dennis, Rand McNally, 1947, 175p., Fiction, LC 47-11404, ISBN 0-02-743622-5.

Maureen and Paul's determination to own a Chincoteague pony is greatly increased when the Phantom and her colt are among those rounded up for the yearly auction. Based on actual events that happened on the island of Chincoteague. 1948 Newbery Honor book.

Henry, Marguerite, **Sea Star: Orphan of Chincoteague**, illustrated by Wesley Dennis, Rand McNally, 1949, 174p., Fiction, LC 49-11474, ISBN 0-02-743627-6.

Maureen and Paul rescue a wild colt. The colt is raised by a mare that has lost her colt. Pacific Northwest 1952.

MAURICE

Fox, Paula, **Maurice's Room**, illustrated by Ingrid Fetz, Macmillan, 1966, 63p., Fiction, ISBN 0-02-735490-3.

Eight-year-old Maurice has filled his room with all of the valuable junk that he has collected, much to his parents' dissatisfaction.

MAX
See also Maximillian

Demuth, Patricia Brennan, **Max, the Bad-Talking Parrot**, illustrated by Bo Zaunders, Dodd, Mead, 1986, 32p., Picture Book, ISBN 0-396-087-671.

A misunderstanding causes a strain in the friendship between Max the parrot and Mrs. Goosebump, until a burglary brings an unexpected benefit. Georgia 1989.

Isadora, Rachel, **Max**, illustrated by Rachel Isadora, Macmillan, 1976, 32p., Picture Book, LC 76-9088, ISBN 0-02-747450-7.

Max is a great baseball player. He finds that his sister's dancing class is a good way to warm up for his Saturday game. A Reading Rainbow book.

Rice, Eve, **Remarkable Return of Winston Potter Crisply, The**, Greenwillow, 1976, 185p., Fiction, ISBN 0-688-84145-7.

Young Max and his sister are suspicious of their older brother's activities and suspect him of being a spy. A humorous family story.

Sendak, Maurice, **Where the Wild Things Are**, illustrated by Maurice Sendak, Harper & Row, 1963, 40p., Picture Book, ISBN 0-06-025493-9.

Max gets into so much mischief that he is sent to bed without dinner. A forest begins growing in his room and Max goes to join the wild things. 1964 Caldecott Award book. A Reading Rainbow book.

MAXIMILLIAN
See also Max

Konigsburg, Elaine, **Journey to an 800 Number**, Atheneum, 1982, 138p., Fiction, ISBN 0-689-30901-5.

When his mother remarries, Maximillian goes to stay with his father for awhile. His father has a camel, which he takes to conventions, and Maximillian has the opportunity to meet several unusual characters.

MAY
See also Matilda, Maybeth

Erwin, Betty, **Go to the Room of the Eyes**, illustrated by Irene Burns, Little, Brown, 1969, 180p., Fiction, LC 71-77446, ISBN 0-316-24946-7.

When they move into an old house in Seattle May and the other five Evans children discover a strange message left by children who lived there thirty years earlier. The message leads them on a treasure hunt. Vermont 1971.

Khalsa, Dayal Kaur, **I Want a Dog**, illustrated by Dayal Kaur Khalsa, Potter, 1987, 22p., Picture Book, LC 86-30329, ISBN 0-517-56532-3.

May wants a pet dog more than anything but her parents tell her she cannot have one until she is able to take care of it. So May pretends a roller skate is a dog and she takes it everywhere on a leash. A Reading Rainbow book.

Singer, Marilyn, **It Can't Hurt Forever**, illustrated by Leigh Grant, Harper & Row, 1978, 186p., Fiction, LC 77-25657, ISBN 0-06-025681-8; 0-06-025682-6 (lib).

May is one of the other patients who eleven-year-old Ellie Simon meets when she goes into the hospital for heart surgery. Minnesota 1983.

MAYBETH
See also Beth, May

Voight, Cynthia, **Dicey's Song**, Atheneum, 1983, 196p., Fiction, LC 82-3882, ISBN 0-689-30944-9.

Maybeth Tillerman and her brothers and sister had spent the whole summer looking for their grandmother after their mother abandoned them. Living with grandma in her Chesapeake Bay country home is not easy, and old problems and sorrows do not go away easily. 1983 Newbery Award book.

MAYO

Hamilton, Virginia, **M. C. Higgins, the Great**, Macmillan, 1974, 278p., Fiction, LC 72-92439, ISBN 0-02-742480-4.

Mayo Cornelius Higgins and his family live in the Ohio hills. Due to strip mining, a slag heap moves closer and closer to the their house and M. C. is torn between trying to get his family away and fighting for the home that they love. 1975 Newbery Award-book. 1974 Boston Globe-Horn Book Award.

MAZIE

Veglahn, Nancy, **Fellowship of the Seven Stars**, Abingdon, 1981, 175p., Fiction, ISBN 0-687-12927-3.

Mazie turns to the loving support of a cult when her family life becomes unbearable; however, she sees that not all is right within the loving cult group either.

MEAGAN
See also Meg, Megan, Megin

Polese, Carolyn, **Promise Not to Tell**, illustrated by Jennifer Barrett, Human Sciences Press, 1985, 72p., Fiction, ISBN 0-89885-239-0.

Eleven-year-old Meagan is molested by her riding instructor and she is afraid to tell anyone. 1986 Christopher Award.

MEG
See also Margaret, Meagan, Megan, Megin

Alcott, Louisa M., **Little Women, or Meg, Jo, Beth and Amy**, Little, Brown, 1968, 372p., Fiction, ISBN 0-316-03090-2.

The classic story of four sisters and their family life in New England at the time of the Civil War.

L'Engle, Madeleine, **Swiftly Tilting Planet, A**, Farrar, Straus & Giroux, 1978, 278p., Fiction, LC 78-9648, ISBN 0-374-37362-0.

A companion volume to *A Wrinkle in Time*. Charles Wallace, the youngest Murray, travels through time and space in a battle against an evil dictator who would destroy the entire universe. His sister, Meg, goes with him in spirit by entering his thoughts and emotions. 1980 Jane Addams Award book.

L'Engle, Madeleine, **Wrinkle in Time, A**, Dell, 1962, 211p., Fiction, ISBN 0-440-498-58.

On a dark and stormy night, Margaret Murray, known as Meg, her little brother, and their mother go down to the kitchen for a midnight snack. An unearthly stranger arrives and the children are taken through a wrinkle in time as they search for their missing scientist father. 1963 Newbery Award book. Oklahoma 1965.

Lowry, Lois, **Summer to Die, A**, illustrated by Jenni Oliver, Houghton Mifflin, 1977, 154p., Fiction, ISBN 0-395-25338-1.

Although Meg loves her beautiful sister, she is also jealous of her until she discovers that her sister is dying. California 1981. Massachusetts 1981.

Wright, Betty Ren, **Ghost in the Window**, Holiday House, 1987, 152p., Fiction, ISBN 0-82340-661-X.

Fourteen-year-old Meg has time to sort through her feelings about her parents' divorce when she goes to visit her father in a north woods town. She also becomes involved in a mystery and uses her ESP to help solve it.

MEGAN
See also Meagan, Meg, Megin

Hall, Lynn, **Megan's Mare**, Scribner, 1983, 56p., Fiction, ISBN 0-684-17874-5.

Eleven-year-old Megan receives a message from a thoroughbred pony by ESP, which begins an unusual friendship.

Roberts, Willo Davis, **Megan's Island**, Atheneum, 1988, 187p., Fiction, ISBN 0-689-31397-7.

Eleven-year-old Megan and her mother move frequently with little warning. When a detective appears, Megan is certain that her family is involved in a mystery. 1989 Edgar Allan Poe Award.

Steele, Mary Q., **Wish, Come True**, illustrated by Muriel Batherman, Greenwillow, 1979, 115p., Fiction, ISBN 0-688-84230-5.

Megan and her brother think their vacation with their great-aunt will be dull until they find an old metal ring, which they think is magical. Their adventures begin when they search for buried treasure.

MEGIN
See also Meagan, Meg, Megan

Spinelli, Jerry, **Who Put That Hair in My Toothbrush?**, Little, Brown, 1984, 220p., Fiction, ISBN 0-316-80712-5.

Alternating chapters tell each character's point of view as Megin and her older brother quarrel about everything.

MEI LI

Handforth, Thomas, **Mei Li**, illustrated by Thomas Handforth, Doubleday, 1938, 48p., Picture Book, ISBN 0-385-07401-8.

Mei Li and her brother live in Peiping, China. They are hoping that their three lucky pennies and three lucky marbles will be enough to go to the New Year Fair in the city. 1939 Caldecott Award book.

MEL
See also Melanie, Melinda, Melissa, Melvin

Gibbons, Gail, **Sunken Treasure**, illustrated by Gail Gibbons, Crowell, 1988, 32p., Nonfiction, LC 87-30114, ISBN 0-690-04734-7; 0-690-04736-3 (lib).

Mel Fisher has a lengthy search for the lost treasure ship, the Atocha, which was a Spanish galleon that sunk off the Florida coast in 1622. Includes information on other famous treasure hunts and the history of diving. A Reading Rainbow book.

MELANIE
See also Mel, Melinda, Melissa, Melvin

Conford, Ellen, **Hail, Hail Camp Timberwood**, illustrated by Gail Owens, Little, Brown, 1978, 151p., Fiction, ISBN 0-316-15291-9.

Melanie is an only child, so she is sent to camp for two months to learn to develop relationships with other children. California 1982. Pacific Northwest 1981.

Snyder, Zilpha Keatley, **Egypt Game, The**, illustrated by Alton Raible, Atheneum, 1967, 215p., Fiction, LC 67-2717, ISBN 0-689-30006-9; 0-689-70297-3.

Melanie Ross, age eleven, and her younger brother, Marshall, became friends with April Hall when she moved into their apartment building to live with her grandmother. The children became interested in ancient Egypt and play the Egypt Game until there is a murder in their neighborhood. 1968 Newbery Honor book.

MELINDA
See also Linda, Lindy, Mel

Beatty, Patricia, **Melinda Takes a Hand**, Morrow, 1983, 196p., Fiction, ISBN 0-688-02422-X.

Set in 1893, thirteen-year-old Melinda gets into many humorous adventures in the small frontier Colorado town where she lives.

Gates, Doris, **Morgan for Melinda**, Viking, 1980, 189p., Fiction, ISBN 0-670-48932-8.

Melinda is terrified of horses but forces herself to learn to ride them to satisfy her father. She has an elderly friend who helps her learn to conquer her fears. Set in California's Monterey peninsula. There is another book about Melinda.

MELISSA
See also Mel

Garden, Nancy, **Fours Crossing**, Farrar, Straus & Giroux, 1981, 197p., Fiction, ISBN 0-374-32451-4.

Thirteen-year-old Melissa and her friend have dangerous adventures as they try to solve several mysteries while Melissa is visiting her grandmother in rural New Hampshire. There is another book about Melissa and her friend, Jed.

Singer, Marilyn, **It Can't Hurt Forever**, illustrated by Leigh Grant, Harper & Row, 1978, 186p., Fiction, LC 77-25657, ISBN 0-06-025681-8; 0-06-025682-6 (lib).

Melissa is one of the other patients who eleven-year-old Ellie Simon meets when she goes to the hospital for heart surgery. Minnesota 1983.

MELVIN
See also Mel

Kessler, Leonard, **Old Turtle's Baseball Stories**, illustrated by Leonard Kessler, Greenwillow, 1982, 55p., Easy Reader, LC 81-6390, ISBN 0-688-00723-6; 0-688-00724-4 (lib).

In the summer, Old Turtle and his friends play baseball and in the winter they tell baseball stories. Old Turtle tells a story about Melvin Moose, the greatest hitter, and the game that he started called Mooseball. A Reading Rainbow book.

MEREDITH
See also Edith

Sorenson, Jody, **Secret Letters of Mama Cat, The**, Walker, 1988, 122p., Fiction, ISBN 0-8027-6791-5.

Twelve-year-old Meredith has quite a few major problems in her life. The family has moved; her grandmother has died; and her deaf sister is going away to school.

MICHAEL
See also Miguel, Mike

Barrie, James M., **Peter Pan**, illustrated by Trina Schart Hyman, Scribner, 1980, 183p., Fiction, ISBN 0-684-16611-9.

The classic adventure of Michael and the other Darling children when they are taken to Never-Neverland by Peter Pan.

Bell, Thelma Harrington, **Captain Ghost**, illustrated by Corydon Bell, Viking, 1959, 191p., Fiction.

Michael and his friends live in the three new houses near an old-fashioned house that seems to be empty. When the children turn a tree trunk into a sailing ship, Captain Ghost joins them and helps in solving a mystery. Vermont 1961.

Brenner, Barbara, **Mystery of the Plumed Serpent**, illustrated by Blanche Sims, Random House, 1981, 188p., Fiction, ISBN 0-394-94531-X.

Michael Garcia and his sister find themselves caught up in a smuggling ring when sinister characters open a pet store near their home in a run-down part of town.

Christopher, Matt, **Great Quarterback Switch**, illustrated by Eric Jon Nones, Little, Brown, 1984, 97p., Fiction, ISBN 0-316-13903-3.

Although he is in a wheelchair, Matt continues to play football by sending telepathic messages to his brother.

Curtis, Philip, **Invasion of the Brain Sharpeners**, illustrated by Tony Ross, Knopf, 1981, 117p., Fiction, ISBN 0-394-94676-6.

When a space machine filled with aliens arrives at school to help sharpen students' brains, Michael is the only one who recognizes the dangers.

Donnelly, Elfie, **So Long, Grandpa**, Crown, 1981, 92p., Fiction, ISBN 0-517-54423-7.

Michael goes through many emotions, including anger and guilt, when he finds out that his beloved grandfather is dying of cancer.

Gordon, Shirley, **Boy Who Wanted a Family**, illustrated by Charles Robinson, Harper & Row, 1980, 89p., Fiction, ISBN 0-06-022052-X.

Michael is an orphan who has lived in many different foster homes. His only wish is to have family of his own.

Hahn, Mary Downing, **Wait Till Helen Comes: A Ghost Story**, Clarion, 1986, 184p., Fiction, LC 86-2648, ISBN 0-89919-453-2.

Michael and Molly aren't happy about moving into a converted church in the country with their mother, stepfather, and spooky stepsister, Heather. Heather is unpleasant and hard to get along with, but, when she becomes obsessed with a small tombstone and a ghost, Michael and Molly realize that they have to save her. Indiana 1989. Pacific Northwest 1989. Texas 1989. Utah 1988. Vermont 1988.

Mathis, Sharon Bell, **Hundred-Penny Box, The**, illustrated by Leo Dillon and Diane Dillon, Viking, 1975, 47p., Fiction, ISBN 0-670-38787-8.

When Michael's elderly relative comes to live with his family, she brings along a box with one 100 pennies in it, one penny for each year of her age. She uses the pennies to tell the stories of her life. 1976 Newbery Honor book.

McCleery, William, **Wolf Story**, illustrated by Warren Chappell, Shoe String, 1988, 82p., Fiction, ISBN 0-208-02191-4.

Five-year-old Michael becomes part of a bedtime story that his father tells him about a wolf and a hen.

McSwigan, Marie, **Snow Treasure**, illustrated by Mary Reardon, Dutton, 1942, 179p., Fiction, ISBN 0-525-39556-3.

Michael and other Norwegian children slipped past Nazi soldiers with sleds loaded with gold. The gold was taken twelve miles to a freighter hidden in one of the fiords of Norway's coast. Based on an actual event. In June 1940, the Norwegian freighter reached Baltimore with a cargo of gold worth 9 million dollars. Pacific Northwest 1945.

MICK
See also Mickey

McCaffrey, Mary, **My Brother Ange**, illustrated by Denise Saldutti, Crowell, 1982, 86p., Fiction, ISBN 0-690-04195-0.

Eleven-year-old Mick Tooley is irritated by his younger brother and finds life boring in the London flat that they share with their mother. When an accident happens, Mick discovers the importance of his family.

MICKEY
See also Mick

Sendak, Maurice, **In the Night Kitchen**, illustrated by Maurice Sendak, Harper & Row, 1970, 40p., Picture Book, ISBN 0-06-025-489-0.

Mickey has a dream-fantasy in which he helps three bakers get milk for their cake batter. 1971 Caldecott Honor book.

MIGUEL
See also Michael, Mike

Krumgold, Joseph, **...And Now Miguel**, illustrated by Jean Charlot, Crowell, 1953, 245p., Fiction, LC 53-8415, ISBN 0-690-09118-4.

The Chavez family has raised sheep in New Mexico for centuries. Miguel Chavez envies his two brothers who are always happy. The older brother can always get what he wants and the younger brother is happy with whatever he has. Miguel thinks it is hard being in the middle and having a great secret wish. 1954 Newbery Award book.

MIKE
See also Michael, Miguel

Carrick, Carol, **Some Friend**, illustrated by Donald Carrick, Clarion, 1979, 112p., Fiction, ISBN 0-395-28966-1.

Mike decides that he has to take a stand with his best friend who is bossy and always manages to get his own way.

Christopher, Matt, **Dog That Stole Football Plays**, illustrated by Bill Ogden, Little, Brown, 1980, 144p., Fiction, ISBN 0-316-13978-5.

Mike buys a dog when he discovers they can read each other's minds. The dog is able to help Mike's football team win games by giving Mike information about the other team's plans. Just before an important game, the dog becomes ill and the team is on their own.

Garden, Nancy, **Prisoner of Vampires**, illustrated by Michele Chessare, Farrar, Straus & Giroux, 1984, 213p., Fiction, ISBN 0-374-36129-0.

When Mike's friend Alexander is researching a class project, he meets a vampire and the two boys decide they have to stop the vampire as sinister events begin to happen. A suspenseful and scary story set in Cambridge, Massachusetts.

Nye, Peter, **Storm**, Watts, 1982, 92p., Fiction, ISBN 0-531-04425-4.

Sixteen-year-old Mike Denton gets himself into more and more trouble as he runs away from a prank and finds himself involved with a cocaine smuggler.

MILDRED

Norton, Mary, **Are All the Giants Dead?**, illustrated by Brian Froud, Harcourt Brace Jovanovich, 1975, 123p., Fiction, ISBN 0-15-203810-8.

Mildred and a friend go to a magical land where fairy-tale characters live, and they find out what has become of their favorite characters.

MILES

Hurd, Thacher, **Mama Don't Allow: Starring Miles and the Swamp Band**, illustrated by Thacher Hurd, Harper & Row, 1984, 40p., Picture Book, LC 83-47703, ISBN 0-06-022689-7; 0-06-022690-0 (lib); 0-06-443078-2 (pbk).

Miles and the Swamp Band have a great time playing at the Alligator Ball until they discover the dinner menu. 1985 Boston Globe-Horn Book Award. A Reading Rainbow book.

MILO

Juster, Norton, **Phantom Tollbooth, The**, illustrated by Jules Feiffer, Random House, 1961, 255p., Fiction, ISBN 0-394-81500-9.

Milo is quite lazy and bored until he is given a magical tollbooth that takes him to a fantastic land filled with amazing adventures.

Manes, Stephen, **Be a Perfect Person in Just Three Days**, Clarion, 1982, 76p., Fiction, ISBN 0-89919-0642.

Milo is tired of his family problems and those at school, so he locates a library book that promises to help him become perfect in just three days. Arkansas 1985. California 1988. Georgia 1987.

MINERVA

Mackay, Claire, **Minerva Program**, James Lorimer, 1984, 1984p., Fiction, ISBN 0-88862-717-3.

Minerva Wright has been banned from using the school computers. Assisted by her brother and friends, Minerva uses the computer to solve a mystery.

MIRANDA
See also Miranda

Greenwald, Sheila, **Secret in Miranda's Closet, The**, Dell, 1989, 138p., Fiction, ISBN 0-440-40128-3 (pbk).

Miranda cannot compare to her mother who is glamorous and very feminine. When Miranda spends a weekend in an old house, she discovers a rare doll in the attic. Miranda's life and attitude begin to change as she creates a world for the doll, and for herself.

Hughes, Frieda, **Getting Rid of Aunt Edna**, illustrated by Ed Levine, Harper & Row, 1986, 74p., Fiction, ISBN 0-06-022637-4.

Miranda is an apprentice witch who has been given the task of getting Aunt Edna to leave since the older witch's spells always have problems and don't work correctly.

Tusa, Tricia, **Miranda**, illustrated by Tricia Tusa, Macmillan, 1985, 26p., Picture Book, LC 84-21764, ISBN 0-02-789520-3.

Miranda loves to play the piano. Her family, piano teacher, and classmates all enjoy her playing until Miranda discovers boogie-woogie music. A Reading Rainbow book.

Worth, Valerie, **Gypsy Gold**, Farrar, Straus & Giroux, 1983, 175p., Fiction, ISBN 0-374-32828-5.

Sixteen-year-old Miranda runs away from her family and a forced engagement to an older man. She joins a band of gypsies and finds peace and a supportive group of people.

MIRANDY
See also Miranda

McKissack, Patricia C., **Mirandy and Brother Wind**, illustrated by Jerry Pinkney, Knopf, 1988, 30p., Picture Book, LC 87-349, ISBN 0-394-88765-4; 0-394-98765-9 (lib).

The cakewalk is a dance first introduced in America by slaves. Mirandy is going to her first cakewalk and she wants to catch Brother Wind to help her. 1989 Caldecott Honor book. 1989 Coretta Scott King Award book.

MIRIAM

Speare, Elizabeth George, **Calico Captive**, illustrated by W. T. Mars, Houghton Mifflin, 1957, 274p., Fiction, ISBN 0-395-07112-7.

Miriam Willard is captured by Indians after attending her first dance. This story is based on a diary kept in 1754 by an actual captive.

MITCH
See also Mitchell

Gilson, Jamie, **Can't Catch Me, I'm the Ginger-bread Man**, Lothrop, Lee & Shepard, 1981, 188p., Fiction, ISBN 0-688-00436-9.

In this humorous story, Mitch hopes to win a national baking contest with his gingerbread recipe. When his parents' health food store burns down, Mitch thinks his chances of attending the contest are gone.

Gilson, Jamie, **Dial Leroi Rupert, DJ**, illustrated by John Wallner, Lothrop, Lee & Shepard, 1979, 126p., Fiction, ISBN 0-688-51888-5.

Mitch and two of his sixth-grade friends get into a great deal of mischief and find themselves in trouble with adults who don't see the humor in what the boys are doing.

MITCHELL
See also Mitch

Sharmat, Marjorie Weinman, **Mitchell Is Moving**, illustrated by Jose Aruego and Ariane Dewey, Macmillan, 1978, 47p., Easy Reader, LC 78-6816, ISBN 0-02-782410-1.

After living in the same house for sixty years, Mitchell the dinosaur decides he is tired of being in the same place and decides to move. His neighbor Margo tries to stop him, but Mitchell leaves and discovers that new isn't necessarily better. A Reading Rainbow book.

MIYAX

George, Jean Craighead, **Julie of the Wolves**, illustrated by John Schoenherr, Harper & Row, 1972, 170p., Fiction, ISBN 0-06-021944-0.

The story of the young Eskimo girl Miyax is told in three parts. The first and third tell of her amazing journey across miles of Arctic tundra. Traveling alone, she is befriended by wolves. The short midsection is a flashback about her decision to take this trip. This adventure story of survival and courage also tells of the conflicts between primitive and modern life-styles. 1973 Newbery Award book.

MOHANDAS

Yolen, Jane, **Children of the Wolf**, Viking, 1984, 136p., Fiction, ISBN 0-670-21763-8.

Mohandas is an orphan who lives in an orphanage in India. He befriends two young girls who have been raised by wolves and are hated by the other children.

MOLLIE
See also Molly

Weiss, Leatie, **My Teacher Sleeps in School**, illustrated by Ellen Weiss, Warne, 1984, 32p., Picture Book, LC 83-10427, ISBN 0-7232-6253-5; 0-14-050559-8.

Mollie the elephant thinks that the classroom teacher must live at school since she always seems to be in the classroom. The other students soon begin investigating to discover whether it is true in this humorous story. Georgia 1987.

MOLLY
See also Mollie

Cohen, Barbara, **Molly's Pilgrim**, illustrated by Michael J. Deraney, Lothrop, Lee & Shepard, 1983, 30p., Picture Book, LC 83-797, ISBN 0-688-02103-4; 0-688-02104-2 (lib).

Molly is a Russian immigrant and her classmates laugh at her because of her imperfect speech. At Thanksgiving, each student makes a pilgrim doll for the school display. Molly is embarrassed when her mother dresses the doll as she herself was dressed before leaving Russia to seek religious freedom. A Reading Rainbow book.

Gleiter, Jan, **Molly Pitcher**, illustrated by Charles Shaw, Raintree, 1987, 32p., Nonfiction, ISBN 0-8172-2652-4.

Molly Pitcher followed her husband when he went to fight with the American army in 1778, and found herself involved in the fighting. This biography includes illustrations of the battleground that she fought on.

Hahn, Mary Downing, **Wait Till Helen Comes: A Ghost Story**, Clarion, 1986, 184p., Fiction, LC 86-2648, ISBN 0-89919-453-2.

Molly and Michael aren't happy about moving into a converted church in the country with their mother, stepfather, and spooky stepsister, Heather. Heather is unpleasant and hard to get along with. However, when Heather becomes obsessed with a small tombstone and a ghost, Molly and Michael realize that they have to save her. Indiana 1989. Pacific Northwest 1989. Texas 1989. Utah 1988. Vermont 1988.

Thompson, Jean, **Ghost Horse of the Palisades, The**, illustrated by Stephen Marchesi, Morrow, 1986, 101p., Fiction, ISBN 0-688-06145-1.

Molly's father wants to capture the wild stallion that has taken their new mare. Molly hopes that her widowed father will become interested in her teacher.

Willard, Nancy, **Firebrat**, illustrated by David Wiesner, Knopf, 1988, 120p., Fiction, ISBN 0-394-99008-0.

Molly is not eager to spend the summer with an eccentric grandmother in New York City, but her attitude changes as she makes a friend and has a fantastic adventure when they discover the Crystal Empire.

MOMO

Rankin, Louise, **Daughter of the Mountains**, illustrated by Kurt Wiese, Viking, 1948, 191p., Fiction, ISBN 0-671-29517-9.

Momo and her family live near a monastery in Tibet. Momo wants a particular dog for her own and she has many adventures as she travels to fulfill her desire. 1949 Newbery Honor book.

MONA

Raskin, Ellen, **Figgs and Phantoms**, Dutton, 1974, 152p., Fiction, ISBN 0-525-29680-8.

Mona Figg is a member of an unusual family that has fantastic personalities and adventures. 1974 Newbery Honor book.

MONTY

Platt, Kin, **Brogg's Brain**, Lippincott, 1981, 124p., Fiction, ISBN 0-397-31946-0.

Monty Davis runs track in high school but has little motivation to win despite his father who was a track star.

MOON SHADOW

Yep, Laurence, **Dragonwings**, Harper & Row, 1975, 248p., Fiction, LC 74-2625, ISBN 06-026737-2; 06-026738-0.

Moon Shadow was eight when he sailed from China to join his father in San Francisco's Chinatown. His father had a fabulous dream to build a flying machine. Inspired by a factual account from 1909. 1976 Newbery Honor book. 1976 Jane Addams Honor book.

MORGAN

Corbett, Scott, **Deadly Hoax**, Dutton, 1981, 86p., Fiction, ISBN 0-525-28585-7.

Morgan and his best friend become involved with aliens from outer space who want to destroy an atomic power plant.

MOTT

Wojciechowska, Maia, **Hey, What's Wrong With This One?**, illustrated by Joan Sandin, Harper & Row, 1969, 72p., Fiction, LC 67-14071, ISBN 0-06-026579-5.

After their mother dies, Mott and his two brothers live with their dad and a succession of housekeepers. Housekeepers keep quitting because of the boys' messes, noise, and pranks. The boys know they need a mother. Georgia 1973.

-N-

NAN
See also Nancy

Norton, Andre, **Red Hart Magic**, illustrated by Donna Diamond, Crowell, 1976, 179p., Fiction, ISBN 0-690-01147-4.

Nan and her stepbrother don't consider themselves to be family until they are transported back to the seventeenth century and have adventures together.

NANCY
See also Nan

Duncan, Lois, **Gift of Magic**, illustrated by Arvis Stewart, Little, Brown, 1971, 183p., Fiction, ISBN 0-316-19545-6.

Nancy and her siblings each have a special gift, which was predicted by their grandmother. Nancy's gift is one of magic.

Lindquist, Jennie, **Golden Name Day, The**, illustrated by Garth Williams, Harper & Row, 1955, 248p., Fiction, LC 55-8823, ISBN 0-06-023881-X.

While nine-year-old Nancy is staying with her adopted Swedish grandparents for a year, everyone tries to figure out how she can celebrate a name day since her name is not Swedish. 1956 Newbery Honor book.

Thacker, Nola, **Summer Stories**, illustrated by William Low, Lippincott, 1988, 150p., Fiction, ISBN 0-397-32288-7.

Ten-year-old Nancy Wilson spends her summers visiting her cousins, and they have quiet days together.

Verheyden-Hilliard, Mary Ellen, **Engineer From the Comanche Nation**, illustrated by Marian Wenzel, Equity Institute, 1985, 32p., Nonfiction, ISBN 0-932469-10-8.

Nancy Wallace is a Comanche Indian. She excelled in academics and sports in high school and went on to become an engineer. This brief biography tells of her determination to achieve her goals.

NAOMI

Levoy, Myron, **Alan and Naomi**, Harper & Row, 1977, 192p., Fiction, LC 76-41522, ISBN 0-06-023799-6; 0-06-023800-3 (lib).

Set in New York in the 1940s, Alan tries to befriend Naomi, a girl traumatized by Nazi brutality in France. 1978 Jane Addams Honor book.

NAT
See also Nate, Nathaniel

Latham, Jean Lee, **Carry on Mr. Bowditch**, illustrated by John O'Hara Cosgrave II, Houghton Mifflin, 1955, 249p., Nonfiction, LC 55-5219, ISBN 0-395-06881-9.

As a child, Nat Bowditch loved both mathematics and the sea. His father had lost his ship in 1771 and the family had to move to Salem, but Nat kept thinking of ships and the sea and how his mathematics could help sailors. 1956 Newbery Award book.

NATE
See also Nat, Nathaniel

Butterworth, Oliver, **Enormous Egg**, Little, Brown, 1956, 188p., Fiction, ISBN 0-316-11904-0.

Twelve-year-old Nate Twitchell is astonished when a large egg hatches into a Triceratops.

Ellerby, Leona, **King Tut's Game Board**, Lerner, 1980, 120p., Fiction, ISBN 0-8225-0765-X.

Nate is a mysterious boy who knows a great deal about Egyptian history. He becomes friends with a boy on vacation and takes him to see the famous Egyptian sights before Nate's identity is revealed.

Sharmat, Marjorie Weinman, **Nate the Great and the Sticky Case**, illustrated by Marc Simont, Coward-McCann, 1978, 48p., Easy Reader, LC 77-17011, ISBN 0-698-20629-0.

Nate the Great and his dog Sludge solve the mystery of a missing dinosaur stamp for Nate's friend, Claude. These characters appear in other Nate the Great books. A Reading Rainbow book.

NATHANIEL
See also Nat, Nate

Greenfield, Eloise, **Nathaniel Talking**, illustrated by Jan Spivey Gilchrist, Writers and Readers, 1988, 30p., Nonfiction, ISBN 0-86316-200-2.

Poetry from Nathaniel. 1990 Coretta Scott King Honor book.

Smith, Robert Kimmel, **Jelly Belly**, Delacorte, 1981, 155p., Fiction, ISBN 0-440-44207-9.

Nathaniel Robbins is called Ned by his family since that is what he called bread when he was small. It is hard for the eleven-year-old Ned to stop eating and he keeps growing wider. His parents send him to a summer diet camp where he and his bunkmates have 'cheating' adventures. Hawaii 1985. Indiana 1984. Pacific Northwest 1984. South Carolina 1984.

NED

Fox, Paula, **One-Eyed Cat**, Bradbury, 1984, 216p., Fiction, LC 84-10964, ISBN 0-02-735540-3.

Ned had received an air rifle for his eleventh birthday. When his father hid the rifle in the attic, Ned found it and shot it just once aiming at a shadow. When a one-eyed cat appears, Ned feels quilty and assumes responsibility for his actions. 1985 Child Study Children's Book Award. 1985 Christopher Award. 1985 Newbery Honor book.

Konigsburg, Elaine, **Throwing Shadows**, Atheneum, 1979, 151p., Fiction, ISBN 0-689-30714-4.

The story of Ned as he hunts for sharks teeth is one of the five stories in this book.

Smith, Robert Kimmel, **Jelly Belly**, Delacorte, 1981, 155p., Fiction, ISBN 0-440-44207-9.

Nathaniel Robbins has been called Ned by his family ever since he was tiny and called bread by that name. It is hard for eleven-year-old Ned to stop eating and he keeps growing wider. His parents send him to summer diet camp where he and his bunk-mates have 'cheating' adventures. Hawaii 1985. In-diana 1984. Pacific Northwest 1984. South Carolina 1984.

NEESIE

Greenfield, Eloise, **Me and Neesie**, illustrated by Moneta Barnett, Crowell, 1975, 33p., Picture Book, LC 74-23078, ISBN 0-690-00714-0; 0-690-00715-9 (lib).

Neesie and Janell are best friends who laugh and play games together. Janell is the only one who can see Neesie, and when she begins going to school their relationship changes. A Reading Rainbow book.

NEIL

Christopher, John, **Empty World**, Dutton, 1978, 134p., Fiction, ISBN 0-525-29250-0.

Neil lives in a small English village with his grandparents after his parents die. Neil learns about survival as a plague sweeps across Europe killing the population.

NELDA
See also Nell

Edwards, Pat, **Nelda**, Houghton Mifflin, 1987, 161p., Fiction, ISBN 0-395-43021-6.

Nelda dreams of movie stars and wealth during the Great Depression but realizes that her migrant family is really the most important part of her life.

NELL
See also Nelda

Newberry, Clare Turlay, **Barkis**, illustrated by Clare Turlay Newberry, Harper & Brothers, 1938, 32p., Picture Book, ISBN 0-06-024421-6.

For his ninth birthday, James receives Barkis, a cocker spaniel. Although he is supposed to share the puppy with his sister, Nell, James does not want to since Nell already has a pet cat. 1939 Caldecott Honor book.

NELSON

Hawes, Louise, **Nelson Malone Meets the Man from Mush-Nut**, illustrated by Bert Dodson, Lodestar, 1986, 116p., Fiction, ISBN 0-525-67181-1.

Ten-year-old Nelson has humorous adventures that begin when he takes a magical snake belonging to his piano teacher to the pet day at school.

NICHOLAS
See also Nick, Nicky, Nicolas

Fleischman, Paul, **Graven Images: Three Stories**, illustrated by Andrew Glass, Harper & Row, 1982, 85p., Fiction, LC 81-48649, ISBN 0-06-021906-8; 0-06-021907-6 (lib).

Nicholas is an apprentice cobbler. He is one of the characters that appears in three short stories about chiseled figures—a wooden boy, a copper saint, and a marble statue—and their effect on people. 1983 Newbery Honor book.

NICK
Nicholas, Nicky, Nicolas, Nicole

Gilson, Jamie, **Thirteen Ways to Sink a Sub**, illustrated by Linda Strauss Edwards, Lothrop, Lee & Shepard, 1982, 140p., Fiction, LC 82-141, ISBN 0-688-01304-X.

Nick and his friend, Hobie Hansen, await the time when their fourth grade will have a substitute teacher. When they finally get a substitute, the class has a contest to 'sink' the sub. New Mexico 1986. Ohio 1987. Oklahoma 1985. Pacific Northwest 1985.

Wibberley, Leonard, **Crime of Martin Coverly, The**, Farrar, Straus & Giroux, 1980, 167p., Fiction, ISBN 0-374-31656-2.

Fifteen-year-old Nick Ormsby discovers he has an ancestor who was a famous pirate. Nick is drawn into the past and sails with his ancestor's pirate crew. When the crew is captured by the British and sentenced to hang for piracy, Nick returns with questions about the present.

NICKY
See also Nicholas, Nick, Nicolas, Nicole

Jones, McClure, **Fix-Up Service**, Putnam, 1985, 152p., Fiction, ISBN 0-399-21132-2.

Nicky Russell is in the ninth grade and finds herself running a dating service business.

NICOLAS
See also Nicholas, Nick, Nicky

Lionni, Leo, **Nicolas, Where Have You Been?**, illustrated by Leo Lionni, Knopf, 1987, 32p., Picture Book, ISBN 0-394-883-705; 0-394-983-70-X (lib).

When his misadventures change to adventures, Nicolas, a young mouse, learns that all birds are not enemies as he thought they were. 1988 Jane Addams Honor Book.

MacLachlan, Patricia, **Unclaimed Treasures**, Harper & Row, 1984, 118p., Fiction, ISBN 0-06-024094-6.

Nicolas looks back to a special summer when he learned about friendship, family, and himself.

NICOLE
See also Nick, Nicky

Sachs, Marilyn, **Pocket Full of Seeds, A**, illustrated by Ben Stahl, Doubleday, 1973, 137p., Fiction, ISBN 0-385-06091-2.

Nicole Nieman lived in France at the time of the German occupation. When she returns from an overnight visit with a friend, she discovers that her family has been taken by the Nazis and that her life is in danger. Based on an actual event. 1974 Jane Addams Honor Book.

NILDA

Mohr, Nicholasa, **Nilda**, illustrated by Nicholosa Mohr, Harper & Row, 1973, 292p., Fiction, LC 73-8046, ISBN 06-024331-7; 06-024332-5.

Ten-year-old Nilda Ramirez lives in the neighborhood known as El Barrio—Spanish Harlem, New York City. She watches the secure world of her childhood slowly change. Set in the 1940s. 1974 Jane Addams Award book.

NINA

See also Christina

Cameron, Eleanor, **Court of the Stone Children, The**, Dutton, 1973, 191p., Fiction, ISBN 0-525-28350-1.

Nina is alone in San Francisco until she meets Gill, and he introduces her to the court of stone children at the French Museum. There they meet a strange girl from the time of Napoleon and learn of treason and murder.

Ehrlich, Amy, **Where It Stops, Nobody Knows**, Dial, 1988, 212p., Fiction, ISBN 0-803-705-751.

Nina and her mother are constantly moving and Nina wonders if they will ever be able to stop hiding. Vermont 1990.

Pevsner, Stella, **Smart Kid Like You, A**, Seabury, 1975, 216p., Fiction, ISBN 0-816-431-388.

Nina slowly begins accepting her parent's divorce only to discover that her father is marrying her seventh-grade math teacher. Vermont 1977.

NOAH

Emberley, Barbara, **One Wide River to Cross**, illustrated by Ed Emberley, Prentice-Hall, 1966, 32p., Picture Book.

A brief text from an American folk song is illustrated to tell the story of the animals as they board Noah's ark. 1967 Caldecott Honor book.

Ferris, Jeri, **What Do You Mean? A Story about Noah Webster**, illustrated by Steve Michaels, Carolrhoda, 1988, 63p., Nonfiction, ISBN 0-87614-330-3.

A biography about Noah Webster, the famous compiler of dictionaries, and his interest in learning.

Spier, Peter, **Noah's Ark**, illustrated by Peter Spier, Doubleday, 1977, 42p., Picture Book, LC 76-43630, ISBN 0-385-09473-6; 0-035-12730-8.

The biblical story of Noah and the ark that he built. When a great flood comes, all types of creatures arrive in pairs from all over to climb aboard and escape the flood. 1978 Caldecott Award book. 1982 Jane Addams Award book.

NOEL

Bawden, Nina, **Kept in the Dark**, Lothrop, Lee & Shepard, 1982, 160p., Fiction, ISBN 0-688-00900-X.

Noel and his siblings have many adjustments to make when they are left with grandparents that they do not know. Life becomes frightening when a stranger appears.

NORA

Clifford, Eth, **Harvey's Horrible Snake Disaster**, Houghton Mifflin, 1984, 108p., Fiction, ISBN 0-395-35378-5.

Ten-year-old Harvey has more misadventures than usual when a snake is kidnapped during his cousin Nora's annual visit. Although the two have never been friends, Harvey begins to appreciate Nora.

Hurwitz, Johanna, **Busybody Nora**, illustrated by Susan Jeschke, Morrow, 1976, 64p., Fiction, ISBN 0-688-32057-0.

Six-year-old Nora lives with her family in a large apartment building. She thinks she should be friends with all 200 people in the building.

Hurwitz, Johanna, **Nora and Mrs. Mind-Your-Own-Business**, illustrated by Susan Jeschke, Morrow, 1977, 64p., Fiction, ISBN 0-688-22097-5.

Nora is in the first grade. When she and her younger brother get a new babysitter, they have to figure out how to make her a friend.

NYASHA

Steptoe, John, **Mufaro's Beautiful Daughters: An African Tale**, illustrated by John Steptoe, Lothrop, Lee & Shepard, 1987, 30p., Picture Book, LC 84-7158, ISBN 0-688-04045-4; 0-688-04046-2 (lib).

Mufaro lived in an African village with his two beautiful daughters. Nyasha was as kind as she was beautiful, while Manyara was almost always ill-tempered. When the Great King looked for a wife, Manyara was determined to be chosen. 1987 Boston Globe-Horn Book Award. 1988 Caldecott Honor book. A Reading Rainbow book.

-O-

OBADIAH
See also Obidiah

Turkle, Brinton, **Thy Friend, Obadiah**, illustrated by Brinton Turkle, Viking, 1969, 37p., Picture Book, ISBN 0-670-71229-9.

Obadiah is a young Quaker boy who is befriended by a seagull and has difficulty accepting the unusual friendship. There are other books about this character. 1970 Caldecott Honor book.

OBIDIAH
See also Obadiah

Hansen, Joyce, **Which Way Freedom?**, Walker, 1986, 120p., Fiction, LC 85-29547, ISBN 0-8027-6636-6 (lib); 0-8027-6623-4.

Obidiah had been a slave before joining the Sixth U.S. Artillery of Colored Troops during the Civil War. He still feels like a slave and has difficult adjustments to make as he seeks personal freedom. The story is based on actual historical events. 1987 Coretta Scott King Honor book.

OLGA

Bond, Michael, **Complete Adventures of Olga da Polga**, illustrated by Hans Helweg, Delacorte, 1983, 511p., Fiction, ISBN 0-440-00981-2.

Olga is a guinea pig that gets into numerous humorous adventures.

OLIVE
See also Livvie

Jeschke, Susan, **Perfect the Pig**, illustrated by Susan Jeschke, H. Holt, 1980, 38p., Picture Book, LC 80-39998, ISBN 0-03-058622-4.

A tiny pig wants wings to take him away from his unloving family. When his wish is magically granted, he flies away and lands on the windowsill of Olive, an artist. Olive thinks he is a Perfect Pig, and the two become great friends until Perfect is stolen by a greedy street entertainer. A Reading Rainbow book.

OLIVER
See also Ollie

Enright, Elizabeth, **Saturdays, The**, Dell, 1987, 175p., Fiction, ISBN 0-440-47615-1.

Randy lives with his three siblings and their father. They devise a scheme where they can take turns on Saturdays to spend their allowances on the pleasures and adventures to be found in their hometown of New York City during the 1940s.

Fleischman, Sid, **Ghost in the Noonday Sun**, illustrated by Peter Sis, Greenwillow, 1965, 131p., Fiction, ISBN 0-688-081-9.

Oliver Finch is kidnapped by pirates to help locate a treasure. Oliver has many humorous adventures on the high seas as he outwits the pirates.

Henry, Joanne Landers, **Log Cabin in the Woods: A True Story about a Pioneer Boy**, illustrated by Joyce Audy Zarins, Four Winds, 1988, 60p., Nonfiction, ISBN 0-02-743670-5.

Oliver Johnson was an Indiana pioneer. This biography tells about his life when he was eleven years old and his family was turning woodlands into a farm.

Judson, Clara Ingram, **Mr. Justice Holmes**, illustrated by Robert Todd, Follett, 1956, 192p., Nonfiction, LC 85-0919.

Oliver Wendell Homes was a famous justice on the Supreme Court. This biography tells about his early education, his years in the military, his study of law, and his career. 1957 Newbery Honor book.

Newberry, Clare Turlay, **Marshmallow**, illustrated by Clare Turlay Newberry, Harper & Brothers, 1942, 24p., Picture Book, ISBN 0-06-024460-7.

Oliver is a middle-aged tabby cat that lives in an apartment in Manhattan. He is an indoor cat and does not know that the world is full of other animals until he meets a baby bunny named Marshmallow. 1943 Caldecott Honor Book.

Sharmat, Marjorie Weinman, **Nate the Great Stalks Stupidweed**, illustrated by Marc Simont, Coward-McCann, 1986, 48p., Easy Reader, LC 85-30161, ISBN 0-698-20626-6.

Rosamond picks weeds that nobody wants and finds homes for them at an adopt-a-weed sale, complete with certificates of ownership. Oliver buys a weed and then loses it, giving Nate the Great, boy detective, a case to solve. A Reading Rainbow book.

Steiner, Barbara, **Oliver Dibbs and the Dinosaur Cause**, illustrated by Eileen Christelow, Four Winds, 1986, 156p., Fiction, ISBN 0-02-787880-5.

When the fifth-grade class studies dinosaurs, Olive Dibbs decides that the Stegasaurus should be the state fossil with humorous results.

OLIVIA
See also Livvie

Brittain, Bill, **Wish Giver: Three Tales of Coven Tree, The**, illustrated by Andrew Glass, Harper & Row, 1983, 181p., Fiction, LC 82-48264, ISBN 0-06-020686-1; 0-06-020687-X (lib).

Thaddeus Blinn was a funny little man who appeared from out of nowhere and put his tent by the annual Coven Tree Church Social. He said he had the power to give people exactly what they asked for. Olivia is one of the characters who finds that wishes often have unexpected results when they come true. 1984 Newbery Honor book.

Perl, Lila, **Dumb Like Me, Olivia Potts**, Clarion, 1976, 181p., Fiction, ISBN 0-395-28870-3.

Olivia is tired of being compared to her brilliant siblings and decides it's easier to be dumb. When she and a friend get involved in solving a mystery, she has to use her own special talents.

OLLIE
See also Oliver

Robinson, Barbara, **Best Christmas Pageant Ever, The**, illustrated by Judith Gwyn Brown, Harper & Row, 1972, 80p., Fiction, LC 72-76501, ISBN 06-025043-7; 06-025044-5.

Ollie is one of the six Herdman children—kids so awful it is hard to believe they are real. When they decide to participate in the church Christmas pageant, people think it will be the worst one ever. Georgia 1976. Indiana 1978. Minnesota 1982.

OMRI

Banks, Lynn Reid, **Indian in the Cupboard, The**, illustrated by Brock Cole, Doubleday, 1980, 181p., Fiction, LC 79-6533, ISBN 0-385-17051-3; 0-385-17060-2 (lib).

Omri receives a plastic Indian for his ninth birthday from his friend Patrick. He also received gifts of an old bathroom cupboard and a jewelry box key to lock the cupboard with. Omri keeps the Indian in the cupboard and soon finds himself involved in an adventure when the tiny Indian comes to life. California 1985. Pacific Northwest 1984.

OPIE

Clifford, Eth, **Rocking Chair Rebellion**, Houghton Mifflin, 1978, 147p., Fiction, ISBN 0-395-27163-0.

Opie Cross becomes involved with the patients at a home for the elderly and causes the old people to have a rebellion.

Fleischman, Sid, **Ghost on Saturday Night, The**, illustrated by Eric von Schmidt, Little, Brown, 1974, 57p., Fiction, LC 73-1475, ISBN 0-316-28583-8.

Opie's aunt said that she would buy him a horse when he had earned enough money for a good saddle. So, Opie goes into the fog business. His humorous adventures running errands in the fog include catching a ghost and a bank robber. Arkansas 1977. Indiana 1979. Mississippi 1977. Missouri 1976.

ORLINDA
See also Linda, Lindy

McKissack, Patricia C., **Mirandy and Brother Wind**, illustrated by Jerry Pinkney, Knopf, 1988, 30p., Picture Book, LC 87-349, ISBN 0-394-88765-4; 0-394-98765-9 (lib).

The cakewalk is a dance first introduced in America by slaves. Mirandy is going to her first cakewalk and she wants to catch Brother Wind to help her. Her friend, Orlinda, is also going to the dance. 1989 Caldecott Honor book. 1989 Coretta Scott King Award book.

ORVILLE

Graeber, Charlotte Towner, **Grey Cloud**, illustrated by Lloyd Bloom, Four Winds, 1979, 124p., Fiction, ISBN 0-02-736910-2.

Orville is a lonely, withdrawn boy who raises pigeons. When a new boy moves to the country, the two boys become friends after experiencing many mishaps together.

Kline, Suzy, **ORP**, Putnam, 1989, 94p., Fiction, ISBN 0-399-21639-1.

Orville Rudemeyer Pygenski, Jr., hates his name and forms a club where he meets a group of people who feel the same way about their names.

OSA

Grifalconi, Ann, **Village of Round and Square Houses**, illustrated by Ann Grifalconi, Little, Brown, 1986, 32p., Picture Book, LC 85-24150, ISBN 0-316-32862-6 (lib).

Osa is a young African girl who lives in a village on the side of a volcano. Her grandmother explains why the men live in square houses and the women live in round ones. 1987 Caldecott Award book.

OSCAR

Manes, Stephen, **That Game from Outer Space: The First Strange Thing That Happened to Oscar Noodleman**, illustrated by Tony Auth, Dutton, 1983, 57p., Fiction, ISBN 0-525-44056-9.

Oscar discovers an unusual video machine in the arcade and finds out that it is really a spaceship filled with aliens who need his help.

Park, Barbara, **Operation: Dump the Chump**, Knopf, 1982, 113p., Fiction, LC 81-8147, ISBN 0-394-94976-5 (lib); 0-394-84976-0.

Eleven-year-old Oscar Winkle has a pesty little brother who is always humiliating him. Oscar finally decides he has to get rid of the pest for a whole summer in this humorous story. Indiana 1985.

OTIS

Cleary, Beverly, **Otis Spofford**, illustrated by Louis Darling, Morrow, 1953, 191p., Fiction, ISBN 0-688-31720-0.

Otis Spofford gets into constant mischief but meets his match when he cuts a girl's hair.

McGinnis, Lila, **Ghost Upstairs**, illustrated by Amy Rowen, Hastings House, 1982, 119p., Fiction, ISBN 0-8038-9286-1.

Otis White is a lively young ghost who moves into the bedroom of a young boy after his mansion is demolished. Otis is curious and gets his new roommate into many humorous situations.

Raskin, Ellen, **Westing Game, The**, Dutton, 1978, 185p., Fiction, LC 77-18866, ISBN 0-525-42320-6.

Otis is one of the sixteen people invited to the reading of the very strange will of the very rich Samuel W. Westing. Otis could become a millionaire, depending on how he plays the tricky and dangerous Westing Game. 1979 Newbery Award book. 1978 Boston Globe-Horn Book Award. Michigan 1982.

-P-

PABLO

Lewis, Thomas P., **Hill of Fire**, illustrated by Joan Sandin, Harper & Row, 1971, 63p., Easy Reader, LC 70-121802, ISBN 0-06-023803-8.

Pablo's father is a farmer in a small village in Mexico. He is an unhappy man because nothing ever happens in the village. Then one day while he and Pablo are plowing, the earth begins to open and pour smoke and fire from the ground as a volcano is born. Based on a factual episode. A Reading Rainbow book.

PADDY

Goodall, John S., **Adventures of Paddy Pork, The**, illustrated by John S. Goodall, Harcourt Brace Jovanovich, 1968, 60p., Picture Book, ISBN 0-15-201589-1.

A young pig, Paddy Pork, sees a circus wagon go by and becomes involved in an adventure in this wordless picture book. 1969 Boston Globe-Horn Book Award.

PAOTZE

Young, Ed, **Lon Po Po: A Red-Riding Hood Story from China**, illustrated by Ed Young, Philomel, 1989, 30p., Picture Book, LC 88-15222, ISBN 0-399-21619-7.

Paotze lives with her two sisters and mother in the countryside of northern China. When their mother goes to visit their grandmother, a wolf visits the children and claims to be their grandmother. 1990 Caldecott Award book.

PARKER

Domke, Todd, **Grounded**, Knopf, 1982, 186p., Fiction, ISBN 0-394-85163-3.

Parker and his friends produce a play to raise money with humorous results.

PAT
See also Patricia, Patrick, Pattie, Patty

Crompton, Annie Eliot, **Rain-Cloud Pony**, illustrated by Paul Frame, Bantam, 1977, 127p., Fiction, ISBN 0-553-15066-9 (pbk).

Pat Dunfield loves horses but her parents can't afford to buy her one. Pat allows herself to mislead the parents of a friend and makes several discoveries about money and friendship.

Perez, N. A., **Breaker**, Houghton Mifflin, 1988, 206p., Fiction, ISBN 0-395-45537-5.

After his father dies in a mining accident in 1902, young Pat MacFarlane has to fight to make his way in the world.

PATRICIA
See also Pat, Pattie, Patty

Hest, Amy, **Pete and Lily**, Clarion/Ticknor & Fields, 1986, 112p., Fiction, ISBN 0-89919-354-4.

Twelve-year-old Patricia and her best friend, Lily, worry about the romance that is developing between their single parents.

PATRICK
See also Pat

Banks, Lynn Reid, **Indian in the Cupboard, The**, illustrated by Brock Cole, Doubleday, 1980, 181p., Fiction, LC 79-6533, ISBN 0-385-17051-3; 0-385-17060-2.

Patrick gave his friend, Omri, a plastic Indian for his ninth birthday. Omri also received an old bathroom cupboard and a jewelry box key to lock the cupboard with. Omri keeps the Indian in the cupboard and soon finds himself involved in an adventure when the tiny Indian comes to life. California 1985. Pacific Northwest 1984.

Carrick, Carol, **What Happened to Patrick's Dinosaur?**, illustrated by Donald Carrick, Clarion, 1986, 32p., Picture Book, ISBN 0-89919-4060.

Patrick loves dinosaurs and develops an imaginary reason for their extinction. California 1989.

dePaola, Tomie, **Patrick: Patron Saint of Ireland**, Holiday House, 1992, 32p., Nonfiction, LC 91-19417, ISBN 0-8234-0924-4.

Patrick was born into a noble British family. As a young boy he was kidnapped by bandits and taken to Ireland where he was sold as a slave. Later he became a bishop and established the first church in Ireland, converting thousands of people to Christianity before his death in 461. After his death he was made a saint. This is a biography in picture book format.

Fritz, Jean, **Where Was Patrick Henry on the 29th of May?**, illustrated by Margot Tomes, Coward-McCann, 1975, 47p., Nonfiction, ISBN 0-698-20307-0.

Patrick Henry was a famous American statesman who made many contributions during the Revolutionary War.

PATTIE
See also Pat, Patricia, Patty

Greenfield, Eloise and Lessie Jones Little, **Childtimes: A Three-Generation Memoir**, illustrated by Jerry Pinkney, Crowell, 1979, 160p., Nonfiction, ISBN 0-690-03875-5.

The memoirs of three generations of black women—grandmother, mother, and daughter—who grew up between 1850-1950. 1980 Coretta Scott King Honor book.

Paton Walsh, Jill, **Green Book, The**, illustrated by Lloyd Bloom, Farrar, Straus & Giroux, 1982, 74p., Fiction, ISBN 0-374-32778-5.

As the Earth dies, a select group flees to another planet. Pattie is the youngest colonist and enjoys the new experiences that are provided.

PATTY
See also Pat, Patricia, Pattie

Greene, Bette, **Summer of My German Soldier**, Dial, 1973, 230p., Fiction, ISBN 0-8037-8321-3.

During World War II, twelve-year-old Patty Bergen makes friends with a German prisoner of war who is interned near her home in Arkansas. When he escapes, Patty hides him and has to pay a high price. Massachusetts 1980.

PAUL

Brown, Marcia, **Stone Soup: An Old Tale**, illustrated by Marcia Brown, Scribner, 1947, 40p., Picture Book, ISBN 0-684-92296-7; 0-684-16217-2 (pbk).

Paul and the other peasants hid their food when they saw three hungry soldiers coming down the road. The soldiers then taught the villagers how to make a soup from three stones and soon a village feast was prepared. An old folktale. 1948 Caldecott Honor book.

Carlson, Natalie Savage, **Family Under the Bridge, The**, illustrated by Garth Williams, HarperCollins, 1958, 97p., Fiction, LC 58-5292, ISBN 0-06-020991-7.

Armand, the old hobo, disliked children until Suzy, Paul, and Evelyne moved to his bridge with their mother after being evicted from their apartment. Bridges were the only free shelter in Paris, but Armand didn't think it was the proper place for a family to live. Armand learned that when families stick together they make a home no matter where they live. 1959 Newbery Honor book.

Fox, Paula, **Lily and the Lost Boy**, Orchard, 1987, 149p., Fiction, ISBN 0-531-08320-9.

Paul Corey and his family are spending time on a Greek island. Paul's relationship with his sister is threatened when Jack, the 'lost boy', appears.

Fritz, Jean, **And Then What Happened, Paul Revere?**, illustrated by Margot Tomes, Coward-McCann, 1973, 45p., Nonfiction, ISBN 0-698-20274-0.

This biography about the famous American, Paul Revere, gives background on his work as a silversmith as well as telling about his famous ride during the American Revolution.

Greene, Constance, **Unmaking of Rabbit**, Viking, 1972, 125p., Fiction, ISBN 0-670-74136-1.

Eleven-year-old Paul lives with his grandmother although he wants to live with his mother in the city. A shy and lonely boy, his friends call him Rabbit.

Greenfield, Eloise, **Paul Robeson**, Crowell, 1975, 32p., Nonfiction, ISBN 0-690-00660-8.

A biography of Paul Robeson, a black man who became a famous singer, actor, and spokesman for equal rights. 1976 Jane Addams Honor book.

Henry, Marguerite, **Misty of Chincoteague**, illustrated by Wesley Dennis, Rand McNally, 1947, 175p., Fiction, LC 47-11404, ISBN 0-02-743622-5.

Paul and Maureen's determination to own a Chincoteague pony is greatly increased when the Phantom and her colt are among those rounded up for the yearly auction. Based on actual events that happened on the island of Chincoteague. 1948 Newbery Honor book.

Henry, Marguerite, **Sea Star: Orphan of Chincoteaque**, illustrated by Wesley Dennis, Rand McNally, 1949, 174p., Fiction, LC 49-11474, ISBN 0-02-743627-6.

Maureen and Paul rescue a wild colt. The colt is then raised by a mare who has lost her colt. Pacific Northwest 1952.

Kellogg, Steven, **Paul Bunyan**, illustrated by Steven Kellogg, Morrow, 1984, 38p., Picture Book, LC 83-26684, ISBN 0-688-03849-2; 0-688-03850-6 (lib).

A tall tale about the huge logger, Paul Bunyan, and his great ox, Babe. Paul was the largest and strongest baby ever born in Maine. He grew and grew until his family decided to move to the wilderness so Paul would have more room. As a young man, Paul decided to move West where he became a famous lumberjack. A Reading Rainbow book.

Myers, Walter Dean, **Young Landlords, The**, Viking, 1979, 197p., Fiction, LC 79-13264, ISBN 0-670-79454-6.

Fifteen-year-old Paul becomes a landlord when he and his friends acquire a run-down Harlem tenement. 1980 Coretta Scott King Award book.

Norton, Mary, **Bed-Knob and Broomstick**, illustrated by Erik Blegvad, Harcourt Brace Jovanovich, 1957, 189p., Fiction, ISBN 0-15-611500-X.

Paul Wilson and his siblings meet a woman who is studying to be a witch. The children are given magical powers and have unusual adventures.

Rounds, Glen, **Morning the Sun Refused to Rise, an Original Paul Bunyan Tale, The**, Holiday House, 1984, 48p., Fiction, ISBN 0-8234-0514-1.

A humorous tall tale that takes Paul Bunyan to Sweden to assist in defrosting the axles on the North and South Poles.

Schlee, Ann, **Vandal**, Crown, 1981, 188p., Fiction, ISBN 0-517-54424-5.

Set in an England of the future where the population obeys the orders of a machine and has no memory due to an evening drink that dulls them. Paul becomes associated with people who do remember and he becomes more and more rebellious.

Sleator, William, **Into the Dream**, illustrated by Ruth Sanderson, Dutton, 1979, 1979p., Fiction, ISBN 0-525-32583-2.

Paul and his friend are linked by extrasensory perception and share the same frightening dream where they see a small child and a large glowing object.

Slote, Alfred, **Hang Tough, Paul Mather**, Lippincott, 1973, 156p., Fiction, ISBN 0-397-31451-5.

Ten-year-old Paul has leukemia. He loves to pitch and sneaks out of the hospital to play with his baseball team.

Viereck, Phillip, **Summer I Was Lost, The**, illustrated by Ellen Viereck, John Day Company, 1965, 158p., Fiction, LC 65-13735, ISBN 0-381-99659-X.

School had not gone well and Paul was thinking of himself as a loser. When he goes to summer camp, Paul gets lost on an overnight hike. In order to stay alive he has to use his hidden strengths and find himself. Vermont 1967.

PEARL

De Veaux, Alexis, **Enchanted Hair Tale, An**, illustrated by Cheryl Hanna, Harper & Row, 1987, 42p., Picture Book, LC 85-45824, ISBN 0-06-021623-9; 0-06-021624-7 (lib).

Pearl Poet travels with the circus. When the son of a friend runs away from home for the day because he is tired of being ridiculed for his wild, strange-looking hair, Pearl helps him accept and enjoy both his hair and himself. 1988 Coretta Scott King Honor book. A Reading Rainbow book.

Hamilton, Virginia, **Magical Adventures of Pretty Pearl, The**, Harper & Row, 1983, 311p., Fiction, LC 82-48629, ISBN 0-06-022187-9; 0-06-022186-0 (lib).

Pretty Pearl and her brother leave their home on a mountain peak in Africa to follow the slave ships to Georgia. Pearl has many godlike powers that she wants to use. 1984 Coretta Scott King Award book.

Steig, William, **Amazing Bone, The**, illustrated by William Steig, Farrar, Straus & Giroux, 1976, 28p., Picture Book, LC 76-26479, ISBN 0-374-302448-0.

One beautiful spring day, Pearl, the young pig, becomes acquainted with a talking bone, which had once belonged to a witch. On the way to Pearl's home, the two encounter several mishaps including a fox that wants Pearl to be his dinner. A Reading Rainbow book.

PEDRO

Krumgold, Joseph, **...And Now Miguel**, illustrated by Jean Charlot, Crowell, 1953, 245p., Fiction, LC 53-8415, ISBN 0-690-09118-4.

The Chavez family has raised sheep in New Mexico for centuries. Pedro is the oldest of the Chavez boys and he is able to get what he wants. His younger brother, Miguel, is envious of Pedro and has a great secret wish that he wants to come true. 1954 Newbery Award book.

PEGGY
See also Margaret

Balian, Lorna, **Sweet Touch, The**, Abingdon, 1976, 40p., Fiction, ISBN 0-687-407-737.

Peggy conjures up a genie with her plastic ring. But the genie is a beginner and can only grant one wish, which he doesn't know how to stop. Colorado 1978. Georgia 1978.

Gibbons, Gail, **Fill It Up! All About Service Stations**, illustrated by Gail Gibbons, Crowell, 1985, 30p., Picture Book, LC 84-45345, ISBN 0-690-04439-9; 0-690-04440-2 (lib).

Peggy and John spend a busy day at their service station. Fred helps with repairs and puts gasoline in the cars. A Reading Rainbow book.

Wiseman, David, **Adam's Common**, Houghton Mifflin, 1984, 175p., Fiction, ISBN 0-395-35976-7.

Peggy Donovan is an American who becomes involved in English history as she travels back in time to the nineteenth century.

PENELOPE
See also Penny

Uttley, Alison, **Traveler in Time**, illustrated by Phyllis Bray, Faber & Faber, 1981, 331p., Fiction, ISBN 0-571-06182-6.

While staying with a great aunt at their ancestral farmhouse, Penelope discovers she is able to go back in time to the sixteenth century when Mary, Queen of Scots, was imprisoned.

PENNY
See also Penelope

De Regniers, Beatrice Schenk, **Penny**, illustrated by Betsy Lewin, Lothrop, Lee & Shepard, 1966, 59p., Fiction, ISBN 0-688-06265-2.

A fantasy about Penny, a very tiny child who is raised in a human home.

Haywood, Carolyn, **Penny and Peter**, illustrated by Carolyn Haywood, Harcourt Brace Jovanovich, 1946, 160p., Fiction, ISBN 0-15-260467-7.

Penny is an adopted child and when she is seven the family adopts a little boy named Peter. There are other books about Penny and her family.

Tilly, Nancy, **Golden Girl**, Farrar, Straus & Giroux, 1985, 216p., Fiction, ISBN 0-374-32694-0.

Set in a town on the North Carolina coast, thirteen-year-old Penny struggles with the problems typical of junior high school and friends.

PERRY

Krensky, Stephen, **Ghostly Business**, Atheneum, 1980, 144p., Fiction, ISBN 0-689-31048-X.

Perry is one of the Wynd children who use their magical powers to try to prevent ghosts from taking over Boston houses.

PETE

See also Peter, Petey

Cone, Molly, **Mishmash**, illustrated by Leonard Shortall, Houghton Mifflin, 1962, 114p., Fiction, ISBN 0-395-06711-1.

Pete gets a dog when his family moves to a new house. The dog is always getting into trouble and causes many humorous moments. There are other books about this dog and his owner.

dePaola, Tomie, **Bill and Pete Go Down the Nile**, illustrated by Tomie dePaola, Putnam, 1987, 28p., Picture Book, LC 86-12258, ISBN 0-399-21395-3.

When Pete the bird and his crocodile friend, Bill, begin the new school year, they wonder what they will learn. On an exciting class trip to a Cairo museum they encounter a jewel thief. A Reading Rainbow book.

Howe, Deborah and James Howe, **Bunnicula: A Rabbit Tale of Mystery**, illustrated by Alan Daniel, Atheneum, 1979, 98p., Fiction, LC 78-11472, ISBN 0-689-30700-4.

The Monroe children, Pete and Toby, find a baby bunny and take it home. The rabbit only sleeps from sunup to sundown and the family finds two fang marks on vegetables that have been drained of their color. Harold, the dog, and Chester, the cat, become concerned that the rabbit is a vampire. Florida 1984. Hawaii 1983. Iowa 1982. Nebraska 1981. New Mexico 1982. Oklahoma 1982. Pacific Northwest 1982. South Carolina 1981. Vermont 1981.

Rylant, Cynthia, **Fine White Dust, A**, Bradbury, 1986, 106p., Fiction, LC 86-1003, ISBN 0-02-777240-3.

Thirteen-year-old Pete mows lawns and hangs out with his best friend, Rufus, in the summer. The visit of a traveling preacher to their small North Carolina town gives Pete a chance to reconcile his own deeply held religious beliefs with those of his family and friends. 1987 Newbery Honor book.

Smith, Robert Kimmel, **War with Grandpa, The**, illustrated by Richard Lauter, Delacorte, 1984, 141p., Fiction, ISBN 0-3895-2931-27; 385-2931-43 (lib).

Pete decides to declare war on his grandfather because he doesn't want to give up his room when the elderly man moves in with the family. California 1990. Georgia 1989. Indiana 1987. Kansas 1987. Pacific Northwest 1987. South Carolina 1986. Vermont 1986.

PETER

See also Pete, Petey

Barrie, James M., **Peter Pan**, illustrated by Trina Schart Hyman, Scribner, 1980, 183p., Fiction, ISBN 0-684-16611-9.

The classic adventures of Peter Pan, a boy who chose not to grow up. He lives in Never-Neverland where there are pirates and Indians and other boys.

Blume, Judy, **Superfudge**, Dutton, 1980, 166p., Fiction, LC 80-10439, ISBN 0-525-40522-4.

Peter Hatcher is not at all happy about the news that there will be a new baby in their house. He worries that the new baby will be like his little brother, Farley, better known as Fudge, who is a big nuisance. Arizona 1983. California 1983. Colorado 1982. Florida 1985. Georgia 1983. Hawaii 1982. Indiana 1983. Iowa 1983. Nebraska 1983. New Hampshire 1981, 1984, 1985. New Mexico 1984.

Ohio 1982. Pacific Northwest 1983. Texas 1982. Utah 1982.

Blume, Judy, **Tales of a Fourth Grade Nothing**, illustrated by Roy Doty, Dutton, 1972, 120p., Fiction, LC 70-179050, ISBN 0-525-40720-0.

Peter Hatcher is in fourth grade and he has a problem, his little brother, Fudge. Peter finds his brother more and more difficult in this humorous story. Arizona 1977. Arkansas 1975. Georgia 1977. Maine 1983. Massachusetts 1977, 1983. New Hampshire 1982. Oklahoma 1975. Pacific Northwest 1975. South Carolina 1977.

Bolton, Elizabeth, **Ghost in the House**, illustrated by Ray Burns, Troll, 1985, 48p., Easy Reader, ISBN 0-8167-0418-X.

After being accused of losing them, Peter looks for the ghost responsible for the numerous items missing from the house.

Bond, Nancy, **String in the Harp**, Atheneum, 1984, 370p., Fiction, LC 75-28181, ISBN 0-689-50036-8.

After their mother dies, twelve-year-old Peter and his two sisters are taken to Wales for a year by their dad. One of the youngsters finds an ancient harp-tuning key that takes him back to the time of the great sixth-century bard, Taliesin. 1977 Newbery Honor book.

Burnford, Sheila, **Incredible Journey, The**, illustrated by Carl Burger, Little, Brown, 1960, 145p., Fiction, LC 61-5313, ISBN 0-316-11714-5.

While Peter and his sister Elizabeth travel with their parents for nine months, their adult friend, John Longridge, agrees to take care of their three pets. Bodger, the English bull terrier; Luath, the Labrador retriever; and Tao, the Siamese cat, take their own journey, walking and staying together for almost 300 miles to seek out their family. Kansas 1964. Pacific Northwest. Vermont 1963.

Estern, Anne Graham, **Picolinis**, illustrated by Katherine Coville, Bantam, 1988, 131p., Fiction, ISBN 0-553-15566-0 (pbk).

Peter is led into an adventure by a miniature family of circus performers living in the dollhouse that has been purchased at an auction.

Haywood, Carolyn, **Penny and Peter**, illustrated by Carolyn Haywood, Harcourt Brace Jovanovich, 1946, 160p., Fiction, ISBN 0-15-2600467-7.

Peter is adopted by a family when their adopted daughter is seven. There is another book about Peter and Penny.

Henry, Marguerite, **San Domingo: The Medicine Hat Stallion**, illustrated by Robert Lougheed, Rand McNally, 1972, 230p., Fiction, ISBN 0-528-82443-0.

Peter Lundy was very fond of his horse. When his father sold the stallion, Peter left home and became a rider for the Pony Express. His many adventures finally lead him to his stallion. Set in the Nebraska Territory in the mid-1800s.

Hicks, Clifford, **Peter Potts Book of World Records**, illustrated by Kathleen Collins Howell, H. Holt, 1987, 101p., Fiction, ISBN 0-8050-0409-2.

Thirteen-year-old Peter and his best friend try many ideas to become world record holders with humorous results.

Keats, Ezra Jack, **Goggles**, illustrated by Ezra Jack Keats, Macmillan, 1969, 32p., Picture Book, LC 70-78081, ISBN 0-02-749590-6.

Peter and his friend have to outsmart the neighborhood bullies before they can enjoy playing with the motorcycle goggles that they have found. 1970 Caldecott Honor book.

Keats, Ezra Jack, **Peter's Chair**, illustrated by Ezra Jack Keats, Harper & Row, 1967, 32p., Picture Book, LC 67-4816, ISBN 0-06-023112-2.

Peter is upset when his parents paint his old crib and high chair for his new baby sister. Peter decides to run away with his dog, Willie, taking his special chair before it can be painted. A Reading Rainbow book.

Keats, Ezra Jack, **Snowy Day, The**, illustrated by Ezra Jack Keats, Viking, 1962, 30p., Picture Book, LC 62-15441, ISBN 0-670-65400-0.

Peter woke up to find that snow had fallen during the night. He dressed in his snowsuit and went outside to play in the snow, making snow tracks, a snowman, and a snow angel. 1963 Caldecott Award book. A Reading Rainbow book.

Lewis, C. S., **Lion, the Witch, and the Wardrobe, The**, illustrated by Pauline Baynes, Macmillan, 1950, 154p., Fiction, ISBN 0-02-758110-1.

Peter and three other children meet a witch, a mighty lion, and the other characters that live in the land of Narnia. This is one of the seven titles in the Chronicles of Narnia series.

Lorimer, Janet, **Mystery of the Missing Treasure, The**, Scholastic, 1987, 103p., Fiction, ISBN 0-590-40490-3 (pbk).

Twelve-year-old Peter learns that a treasure is supposed to be buried on the property of his family's new house. While searching for the treasure, he becomes involved in time travel.

Mattingley, Christobel, **Angel with a Mouth-Organ**, illustrated by Astra Lacis, Holiday House, 1984, 32p., Fiction, ISBN 0-8234-0593-1.

As the family decorates their Christmas tree, Peter and his sister hear about their mother's childhood as a refugee in war-torn Europe during World War II.

McSwain, Marie, **Snow Treasure**, illustrated by Mary Reardon, Dutton, 1942, 179p., Fiction, ISBN 0-525-39556-3.

Peter and other Norwegian children slipped sleds loaded with gold past Nazi soldiers. The gold was taken twelve miles to a freighter hidden in one of the fiords off Norway's coast. Based on an actual event. In June 1940 the Norwegian freighter reached Baltimore with a cargo of gold worth 9 million dollars. Pacific Northwest 1945.

Morey, Walt, **Canyon Winter**, Dutton, 1977, 202p., Fiction, ISBN 0-525-27410-3.

Peter is the only survivor of a plane crash in the Rocky Mountains and has to make his way through rough terrain to return to civilization.

Nesbit, E., **Railway Children**, illustrated by C. E. Brock, Puffin, 1988, 240p., Fiction, ISBN 0-14-035005-5.

When their father leaves, Peter and the rest of his family move from London to a tiny cottage in the country where the railroad becomes an important part of their lives.

Quackenbush, Robert, **Old Silver Leg Takes Over: A Story of Peter Stuyvesant**, Prentice-Hall, 1986, 36p., Nonfiction, ISBN 0-13-633934-4.

During colonial times, Peter Stuyvesant was the governor of New Amsterdam (New York). This biography tells how he turned a frontier town into a well-known city.

Shura, Mary Francis, **Search for Grissi**, illustrated by Ted Lewis, Dodd, Mead, 1985, 126p., Fiction, ISBN 0-396-08584-9.

Eleven-year-old Peter and his family have moved to Brooklyn, New York, from Peoria, Illinois. While searching for his sister's lost cat, Peter gets to know his new home better.

Sutcliff, Rosemary, **Flame-Colored Taffeta**, Farrar, Straus & Giroux, 1986, 129p., Fiction, ISBN 0-374-32344-5.

Set in eighteenth-century England, young Peter and a friend rescue a wounded man and become involved in spying and smuggling.

Van Allsburg, Chris, **Jumanji**, illustrated by Chris Van Allsburg, Houghton Mifflin, 1981, 30p., Picture Book, LC 80-29632, ISBN 0-395-30448-2.

Peter and Jody were bored until they discovered an ordinary-looking game board that takes them into a mysterious jungle on an exciting and bizarre adventure. 1982 Caldecott Award book. Kentucky 1983. Washington 1984. West Virginia 1985.

PETEY
See also Pete, Peter

Dunn, Marylois and Ardath Mayhar, **Absolutely Perfect Horse**, Harper & Row, 1983, 186p., Fiction, ISBN 0-06-021774-X.

Petey and his family have many changes to adjust to when their father returns from the military. The horse that his sister buys seems to be a loser but turns into a winner when it saves their cattle from a wild dog pack.

Thayer, Jane, **Puppy Who Wanted a Boy, The**, illustrated by Seymour Fleischman, Morrow, 1958, 48p., Picture Book, LC 58-5317, ISBN 0-688-31631-X.

Petey the puppy wanted a boy for Christmas. He looked and looked but the boys all had their own dogs. As Petey walks by the Orphans' Home, he sees a boy named Dickie who looks lonely. Petey's Christmas wish comes true in an unexpected manner. A Reading Rainbow book.

PHIL
See also Philip, Phillip

Cole, Joanna, **Magic School Bus Inside the Earth, The**, illustrated by Bruce Degen, Scholastic, 1987, 40p., Picture Book, LC 87-4563, ISBN 0-590-40759-7.

Phil and the rest of Ms. Frizzle's class learn firsthand about different kinds of rocks and the formation of the earth when they take a field trip in the magic school bus. A Reading Rainbow book.

Shyer, Marlene Fanta, **Grandpa Ritz and the Luscious Lovelies**, Scribner, 1985, 170p., Fiction, ISBN 0-684-18408-7.

Twelve-year-old Phil lives with his grandfather to keep the elderly man company after he becomes widowed. Phil learns a lot about how grief can affect people as they get older.

PHILIP
See also Phil, Phillip

Bawden, Nina, **Robbers**, Lothrop, Lee & Shepard, 1979, 155p., Fiction, ISBN 0-688-51902-4.

When his father remarries, Philip is taken away from the safety of his grandmother's castle to a new and adventurous life in London.

Hawes, Charles Boardman, **Dark Frigate, The**, illustrated by Warren Chappell, Little, Brown, 1971, 246p., Fiction, LC 77-117023, ISBN 0-316-35096-6.

Young Philip Marsham sets sail on the frigate Rose of Dawn, which is seized in midocean by twelve men who have been taken from a wreck. Philip is forced to join these pirates in their murderous expeditions until all are captured and face hanging on Execution Dock. 1924 Newbery Award book.

Sullivan, Mary, **Earthquake 2099**, Dutton, 1982, 119p., Fiction, ISBN 0-525-66761-X.

Set in the future, eleven-year-old Philip has always lived in a controlled environment until his family moves to the wilderness area. When an earthquake separates him from his family, his cousin's knowledge of survival saves their lives.

Taylor, Theodore, **Cay, The**, Doubleday, 1969, 137p., Fiction, ISBN 0-385-07906-0.

During World War II, the ship that Philip and his mother are on is torpedoed. Philip is blinded and marooned on a small island. There he is befriended by an old West Indian sailor who teaches Philip a great deal.

PHILLIP
See also Phil, Philip

Konigsburg, Elaine, **Throwing Shadows**, Atheneum, 1979, 151p., Fiction, ISBN 0-689-30714-4.

The story of Phillip as he records the life story of an old woman is one of the five short stories in this book.

PHOEBE

Danziger, Paula, **Divorce Express**, Delacorte, 1982, 148p., Fiction, ISBN 0-440-92062-0.

Fourteen-year-old Phoebe is not happy with the adjustments that she has had to make since her parents' divorce. She meets another girl on the bus that she takes each weekend as she travels from one parent to the other, and the girls help one another with their problems.

Fleischman, Paul, **Phoebe Danger, Detective, in the Case of the Two-Minute Cough**, illustrated by Margot Apple, Houghton Mifflin, 1983, 58p., Fiction, ISBN 0-395-33226-5.

Phoebe and a friend open a detective agency. Their first case involves locating a valuable bottle of cough medicine that has been taken.

Roos, Stephen, **And the Winner Is...**, illustrated by Dee deRosa, Atheneum, 1989, 113p., Fiction, ISBN 0-689-31300-4.

Phoebe Wilson doesn't want her friends to know that her family's financial situation has changed drastically, and she does everything she can, which only causes her one problem after another.

Roos, Stephen, **Fair-Weather Friends**, illustrated by Dee deRosa, Atheneum, 1988, 123p., Fiction, ISBN 0-689-31301-2.

When they meet at their summer homes, Phoebe and her friend find that their friendship has changed as they have matured.

Shore, Laura Jan, **Sacred Moon Tree, The**, Bradbury, 1986, 209p., Fiction, ISBN 0-02-782790-9.

Twelve-year-old Phoebe disguises herself as a boy in order to travel behind enemy lines during the Civil War to help a friend try to rescue his brother from a Confederate prison.

PHYLLIS

Nesbit, E., **Railway Children**, illustrated by C. E. Brock, Puffin, 1988, 240p., Fiction, ISBN 0-14-035005-5.

When their father leaves, Phyllis and the rest of the family move from London to a tiny cottage in the country where the railroad becomes important to them.

PIER

DeJong, Meindert, **Wheel on the School, The**, illustrated by Maurice Sendak, Harper & Row, 1954, 298p., Fiction, LC 54-8945, ISBN 0-06-02158-2.

Pier is one of the six schoolchildren in the fishing village named Shora in Holland. Pier and the other children learn that when a stork builds a nest on the roof there will be good luck. 1955 Newbery Award book.

PIERRE

Hamerstrom, Frances, **Adventure of the Stone Man**, illustrated by William Kimber, Crossing, 1977, 103p., Fiction, ISBN 0-912278-89-7.

Pierre and his sister find a cave in the mountains near their home in France and make it their secret place. They find traces of prehistoric people and have other interesting experiences.

PIPPI

Lindgren, Astrid, **Pippi Longstocking**, illustrated by Louis Glanzman, Viking, 1963, 158p., Fiction, ISBN 0-670-55745-5.

Nine-year-old Pippi lives by herself without any adults to supervise her. She is full of mischief and fun. There are several books about Pippi.

PIRI

Siegal, Aranka, **Upon the Head of the Goat: A Childhood in Hungary, 1939-1944**, Farrar, Straus & Giroux, 1981, 214p., Fiction, LC 81-12642, ISBN 0-374-38059-7.

Nine-year-old Piri was visiting her grandmother's farm in the Ukraine in 1939. When the war began Piri could not get back home to Hungary. When she returned to her family a year later she found many changes. Based on the author's childhood experiences in Hungary as she and her family survived five years of Hitler's rule. 1982 Newbery Honor book. 1982 Boston Globe-Horn Book Award.

POINSETTIA

Bond, Felicia, **Poinsettia and Her Family**, illustrated by Felicia Bond, Crowell, 1981, 32p., Picture Book, LC 81-43035, ISBN 0-690-04144-6; 0-690-04145-4 (lib).

Poinsettia Pig is tired of her six messy, noisy brothers and sisters. They always seem to be in the way in the fine old house that they share with their parents. When her parents accidentally leave Poinsettia alone, she is at first happy, but then begins to miss her family. A Reading Rainbow book.

McKissack, Patricia C., **Mirandy and Brother Wind**, illustrated by Jerry Pinkney, Knopf, 1988, 30p., Picture Book, LC 98-349, ISBN 0-394-88765-4; 0-394-98765-9 (lib).

The cakewalk is a dance first introduced in America by slaves. Mirandy is going to her first cakewalk and she wants to catch Brother Wind to help her, so she asks Poinsettia for advice. 1989 Caldecott Honor book. 1989 Coretta Scott King Award book.

POLLY

Brittain, Bill, **Wish Giver: Three Tales of Coven Tree, The**, illustrated by Andrew Glass, Harper & Row, 1983, 181p., Fiction, LC 82-48264, ISBN 0-06-020686-1; 0-06-020687-X (lib).

Thaddeus Blinn was a funny little man who appeared from out of nowhere and put his tent by the annual Coven Tree Church Social. He said he had the power to give people exactly what they asked for. Polly is one of the characters who finds that wishes often have unexpected results when they come true. 1984 Newbery Honor book.

Cresswell, Helen, **Secret World of Polly Flint, The**, illustrated by Shirley Felts, Macmillan, 1982, 176p., Fiction, ISBN 0-02-725400-3.

Polly is very imaginative and sees things that others cannot see. One May Day, she travels through time to rescue four inhabitants of a lost village who are trapped in the wrong time.

Holland, Barbara, **Prisoners at the Kitchen Table**, Clarion, 1979, 121p., Fiction, LC 79-11730, ISBN 0-395-28969-6.

Polly Conover is showing Josh Blake her new fishing rod when a couple stop their car and say that they are relatives of Polly's. They invite the two children to their home, and the next day Polly and Josh realize they have been kidnapped. It is scary, lonely, and boring until Josh comes up with a plan. Pacific Northwest 1983. South Carolina 1983.

Sidney, Margaret, **Five Little Peppers and How They Grew**, illustrated by William Sharp, Grosset & Dunlap, 1948, 310p., Fiction, ISBN 0-448-06008-6.

A classic story from the late 1800s about a widow who struggles to raise her five children. Polly is the eldest of these lively children.

POPPY

Alcock, Vivien, **Stonewalkers**, Delacorte, 1981, 151p., Fiction, ISBN 0-385-29233-3.

When Poppy makes friends with a statue in the garden and sees it come to life, her friend Emma is the only one that believes her. The two girls are captured by a group of statues and find escape nearly impossible.

PORTIA

Enright, Elizabeth, **Gone-Away Lake**, illustrated by Beth Krush and Joe Krush, Harcourt Brace Jovanovich, 1957, 192p., Fiction, LC 57-7172, ISBN 0-15-231649-3.

Portia and her cousin, Julian, make three interesting discoveries in the woods around their summer home. They find a Latin inscription, a swamp that had once been a lake, and two fascinating people who live in the summer houses that were thought to be deserted. When the vine-covered Villa Caprice is uncovered, it reveals its secrets of fifty years. 1958 Newbery Honor book.

Stewart, Ruth Ann, **Portia: The Life of Portia Washington Pittman, the Daughter of Booker T. Washington**, Doubleday, 1977, 154p., Nonfiction, ISBN 0-385-053-290.

A biography about Portia Washington, who was born in 1883 to a father who was a famous black scientist. 1978 Coretta Scott King Honor book.

PRISCILLA

Leverich, Kathleen, **Best Enemies**, illustrated by Susan Condie Lamb, Greenwillow, 1989, 79p., Fiction, ISBN 0-688-08316-1.

Priscilla makes a new friend on the first day of school and discovers that the only thing worse than having the girl for an enemy is having her for a friend.

-Q-

QUANG

Huynh, Quang Nhuong, **Land I Lost: Adventures of a Boy in Vietnam, The**, illustrated by Vo-Dinh Mai, Harper & Row, 1982, 115p., Nonfiction, LC 80-8437, ISBN 0-06-024592-1; 0-06-024593-X.

Autobiographical reminiscences of the author's boyhood which he spent in the highlands of Vietnam. Kansas 1985.

QUEENIE

Burch, Robert, **Queenie Peavy**, illustrated by Jerry Lazare, Viking, 1966, 159p., Fiction, LC 66-15649, ISBN 0-670-58422-3.

Thirteen-year-old Queenie is taunted by her classmates because her father is in prison. She causes a lot of problems until she discovers something important about her father and about herself. 1967 Jane Addams Award book. Georgia 1971.

QUENTIN

Brittain, Bill, **All the Money in the World**, illustrated by Charles Robinson, Harper & Row, 1979, 150p., Fiction, ISBN 0-06-020676-4.

Quentin Stowe wants more money than his father can give him. When he accidentally catches a leprechaun, Quentin is given three wishes. His wish for money creates disasters for the world. Arkansas 1982.

-R-

RACHEL

Duncan, Lois, **Summer of Fear**, Little, Brown, 1976, 217p., Fiction, LC 76-8264, ISBN 0-316-19548-0.

Rachel knows that she should feel sorry for her seventeen-year-old cousin, Julia, since Julia's parents have recently died. Instead, Rachel feels uncomfortable around Julia, and her dog fears and hates Julia. California 1983. New Mexico 1983. Vermont 1978.

Mazer, Norma Fox, **After the Rain**, Morrow, 1987, 290p., Fiction, LC 86-33270, ISBN 0-688-06867-7.

Fifteen-year-old Rachel is impatient with her grandfather since he is not an easy man to love. When she discovers that her grandfather has cancer, Rachel gets to know him better than ever before as he becomes the most important person in her life. 1988 Newbery Honor book.

Rodda, Emily, **Pigs Are Flying! The**, illustrated by Noela Young, Greenwillow, 1986, 137p., Fiction, ISBN 0-688-08130-4.

Rachel is bored and wishes that something interesting would happen, when she finds herself on a unicorn in another world.

Wells, Rosemary, **Fog Comes on Little Pig Feet, The**, illustrated by Rosemary Wells, Dial, 1972, 128p., Fiction, ISBN 0-8037-2636-8.

Rachel is not happy at the boarding school her parents send her to because there is little time for privacy and doing the things she wants to do. When she tries to protect a runaway, the school becomes even more unpleasant.

Whelan, Gloria, **Silver**, illustrated by Stephen Marchesi, Random House, 1988, 58p., Fiction, ISBN 0-394-99611-9.

Ten-year-old Rachel is an Alaskan girl who wants to be a sled dog racer like her father. She has an adventure trying to find her huskie puppy when he is kidnapped by a wolf mother and taken to her den.

RAFE

Mayne, William, **Drift**, Delacorte, 1986, 166p., Fiction, ISBN 0-385-29446-8.

Set in pioneer days, Rafe Johnson and an Indian girl have to survive a fierce winter in the wilderness. The book gives two accounts of the adventure, one from the point of view of Rafe and the other from the girl.

RALPH

Cleary, Beverly, **Mouse and the Motorcycle, The**, illustrated by Louis Darling, Morrow, 1965, 158p., Fiction, LC 65-20956, ISBN 0-688-31698-0.

A young mouse named Ralph is envious of the toy motorcycle that the boy, Keith, is playing with. When Ralph attempts to ride the motorcycle, he finds an unexpected career, and an unusual friend. Hawaii 1969. Kansas 1968. New Hampshire 1983. Pacific Northwest 1968.

Cleary, Beverly, **Ralph S. Mouse**, illustrated by Paul O. Zelinsky, Morrow, 1982, 160p., Fiction, LC 82-3516, ISBN 0-688-01452-6; 0-688-01455-0 (lib).

Ryan Bramble is one of the few human beings that can understand Ralph, the little brown mouse. Ryan takes Ralph to school and the classroom experiences are humorous, yet upsetting to a defenseless, intelligent mouse. 1983 Golden Kite Award. Iowa 1985. West Virginia 1987.

Cleary, Beverly, **Runaway Ralph**, illustrated by Louis Darling, Morrow, 1970, 175p., Fiction, LC 77-95786, ISBN 0-688-21701-X.

Ralph, the small brown mouse, runs away to a summer camp on his little motorcycle. Instead of finding freedom and lots of sandwich crumbs, Ralph is caught and placed in a cage. Other characters include a grouchy hamster, a villainous cat, and numerous human campers. Arkansas 1973. Hawaii 1972.

Hurd, Thacher, **Mystery on the Docks**, illustrated by Thacher Hurd, Harper & Row, 1983, 30p., Picture Book, LC 82-48261, ISBN 0-06-022701-X; 0-06-022702-8 (lib).

Ralph, the short-order cook at the Pier 46 diner, is kidnapped by Big Al and his gang of tough rats. Aboard a dark ship, Ralph discovers his favorite opera singer, Eduardo, who has also been kidnapped. The two have to figure out how to escape their dangerous situation. A Reading Rainbow book.

Meyer, Edith Patterson, **Champions of Peace: Winners of the Nobel Peace Prize**, illustrated by Eric von Schmidt, Little, Brown, 1959, 216p., Nonfiction, LC 59-7355.

Dr. Ralph Bunche was the first American black man to win the Nobel Peace Prize. He received his award in 1952. 1960 Jane Addams Award book.

Robinson, Barbara, **Best Christmas Pageant Ever, The**, illustrated by Judith Gwyn Brown, Harper & Row, 1972, 80p., Fiction, LC 72-76501, ISBN 06-025043-7; 06-025044-5.

Ralph is one of the six Herdman children—kids so awful it is hard to believe they are real. When they decide to participate in the church Christmas pageant, people think it will be the worst one ever. Georgia 1976. Indiana 1978. Minnesota 1982.

RAMAN

Arora, Shirley L., **What Then, Raman?**, illustrated by Hans Guggenheim, Follett, 1960, 176p., Fiction, LC 60-13357, ISBN 0-695-49275-6.

Raman, the woodcutter's son, is the first person in his family and in his village in India to go to school. Raman is one of the best readers in the school and one of the worst in arithmetic. Raman learns that his reading skills give him a great responsibility in both his family and in his village since he is the only person that can read. 1961 Jane Addams Award book.

RAMON

O'Dell, Scott, **Black Pearl, The**, illustrated by Milton Johnson, Houghton Mifflin, 1967, 140p., Fiction, LC 67-23311, ISBN 0-395-06961-0.

Ramon Salazar grew up with the knowledge that he would someday join his father searching for pearls in the waters of Baja California. When Ramon is sixteen he learns about pearling and finds the great pearl. He also gains two enemies: one of his father's divers and the sea monster, Manta Diablo. 1968 Newbery Honor book.

RAMONA

Cleary, Beverly, **Ramona and Her Father**, illustrated by Alan Tiegreen, Morrow, 1977, 186p., Fiction, LC 77-1614, ISBN 0-688-22114-9; 0-688-32114-3 (lib).

During her second-grade year, Ramona's father unexpectedly loses his job and the whole Quimby family has their routine upset. 1978 Newbery Honor book. Hawaii 1979. New Mexico 1981. Texas 1981. Utah 1980.

Cleary, Beverly, **Ramona and Her Mother**, illustrated by Alan Tiegreen, Morrow, 1979, 207p., Fiction, ISBN 0-688-32195-X.

Mrs. Quimby is seen from seven-year-old Ramona's point of view. Ramona realizes that her mother loves her even though Mrs. Quimby is often tired and harassed. 1981 Jane Addams Award book. Pacific Northwest 1980.

Cleary, Beverly, **Ramona Quimby, Age 8**, illustrated by Alan Tiegreen, Morrow, 1981, 190p., Fiction, LC 80-28425, ISBN 0-688-00477-6; 0-688-00478-4 (lib).

Ramona Quimby has started third grade. Her low point is reached the day she throws up in class, and the teacher has the other students hold their noses and file into the hall. The humorous ups and downs of Ramona and her family continue. 1982 Newbery Honor book. Arkansas 1984. Michigan 1984. Ohio 1985.

Cleary, Beverly, **Ramona the Brave**, illustrated by Alan Tiegreen, Morrow, 1975, 190p., Fiction, LC 74-16494, ISBN 0-688-22015-0; 0-688-32015-5 (lib).

Ramona Quimby enters the first grade feeling very grown-up. She quickly learns that her teacher is perplexed by students who are different and Ramona cannot help being different. Humorous episodes occur as Ramona learns more about herself and her surroundings. Missouri 1978.

Cleary, Beverly, **Ramona the Pest**, illustrated by Louis Darling, Morrow, 1968, 192p., Fiction, ISBN 0-688-31721-9.

Ramona Quimby has started kindergarten and her curiosity leads her to become a kindergarten dropout. Georgia 1970. Hawaii 1971. Oklahoma 1971. Pacific Northwest 1971.

Scott, Elaine, **Ramona: Behind the Scenes of a Television Show**, illustrated by Margaret Miller, Morrow, 1988, 88p., Nonfiction, LC 87-33313, ISBN 0-688-06818-9; 0-688-06819-7 (lib).

Numerous black-and-white photographs show the making of the ten-part television series about Beverly Cleary's famous character, Ramona Quimby. Included are the way a book is adapted to become a script, auditions, filming, and editing. A Reading Rainbow book.

RANDY

Kessler, Leonard, **Old Turtle's Baseball Stories**, illustrated by Leonard Kessler, Greenwillow, 1982, 55p., Easy Reader, LC 81-6390, ISBN 0-688-00723-6; 0-688-00724-4 (lib).

In the summer, Old Turtle and his friends play baseball and in the winter they tell baseball stories. Old Turtle tells a story about the greatest base stealer, Randy Squirrel. A Reading Rainbow book.

RAY
See also Raymond

Mathis, Sharon Bell, **Ray Charles**, Crowell, 1973, 31p., Nonfiction, ISBN 0-690-670-656; 0-690-670-664 (lib).

A biography about the famous black musician, Ray Charles, who became famous despite his blindness. 1974 Coretta Scott King Award book.

RAYMOND
See also Ray

Geller, Mark, **Raymond**, Harper & Row, 1988, 89p., Fiction, ISBN 0-06-022207-7.

Thirteen-year-old Raymond and his mother are the victims of abuse by his father. Raymond is desperate and concerned for his mother.

Kline, Suzy, **Herbie Jones**, illustrated by Richard Williams, Putnam, 1985, 96p., Fiction, LC 84-24915, ISBN 0-399-21183-7.

Third grade has its ups and downs for Raymond and his best friend, Herbie Jones. They are invited to a birthday party for the smartest girl in the class, and they get into trouble on the class field trip to the museum. Both boys are tired of being in the lowest reading group, and when one begins doing well on his spelling papers, he knows he has to help the other. West Virginia 1988.

Stevenson, Drew, **Case of the Horrible Swamp Monster, The**, illustrated by Susan Swan, Dodd, Mead, 1984, 95p., Fiction, ISBN 0-396-08466-4.

Raymond and his sixth-grade friends film a monster movie at a swamp and find something unexpected on their developed film that creates an exciting mystery.

Stevenson, Drew, **Case of the Wandering Werewolf, The**, illustrated by Linda Winchester, Dodd, Mead, 1987, 128p., Fiction, ISBN 0-396-09154-7.

Raymond and his friends become involved in a mystery when they decide to find out what a werewolf is doing in their woods.

REBECCA
See also Becky

Gordon, Sheila, **Middle of Somewhere: A Story of South Africa, The**, Orchard, 1990, 154p., Fiction, ISBN 0-531-059-081.

Nine-year-old Rebecca and her family are threatened with being forced from their South African village for black people to a distant and desolate development to make room for a new suburb for white people. 1991 Jane Addams Honor Book.

Lexau, Joan M., **Striped Ice Cream**, illustrated by John Wilson, Lippincott, 1968, 95p., Fiction, LC 68-10774, ISBN 0-397-31046-3.

Seven-year-old Rebecca is resigned to the fact that her mother cannot afford anything special for her birthday, but she does not understand why her older sisters and brother seem to turn against her, until the big day finally arrives. Arkansas 1971.

Rosenberg, Maxine B., **Being Adopted**, illustrated by George Ancona, Lothrop, Lee & Shepard, 1984, 44p., Nonfiction, LC 83-17522, ISBN 0-688-02672-9; 0-688-02673-7 (lib).

Seven-year-old Rebecca and two other children tell about their experiences as adopted members of families who have different racial and cultural roots than they do. A Reading Rainbow book.

Sachs, Marilyn, **Fourteen**, Dutton, 1983, 116p., Fiction, ISBN 0-525-44044-5.

When Rebecca is fourteen years old, a new boy moves into her apartment building and the two become friends. Rebecca worries that her mother will use her personal experiences in the children's books that she writes so Rebecca keeps her first romance a secret.

Wiggin, Kate Douglas, **Rebecca of Sunnybrook Farm**, Dell, 1986, 240p., Fiction, ISBN 0-440-47533-3 (pbk).

The classic story of a young girl who lived life to the fullest in a tiny community in Maine over one hundred years ago.

RENEE

Roth-Hano, Renee, **Touch Wood: A Girlhood in Occupied France**, Four Winds, 1988, 297p., Fiction, ISBN 0-02-777340-X.

Renee is nine years old when her Jewish family seeks safety in exile in France during World War II. Based on actual experiences.

RETTA

Byars, Betsy, **Night Swimmers, The**, illustrated by Troy Howell, Delacorte, 1980, 131p., Fiction, LC 79-53597, ISBN 0-440-06261-6; 0-440-06262-4 (lib).

Since their mother died, Retta has been in charge of taking care of her two younger brothers while their father performs as a country-western singer. Retta feeds her brothers, buys their clothes, and finds a swimming pool where they can go swimming at night. 1981 Jane Addams Award book.

RHODA

Schotter, Roni, **Rhoda, Straight and True**, Lothrop, Lee & Shepard, 1986, 181p., Fiction, ISBN 0-688-06157-5.

Twelve-year-old Rhoda has an accident while playing in a dangerous spot in Brooklyn. She is rescued by one of the Mancy kids who are considered undesirable by the rest of the neighborhood. As Rhoda gets to know the Mancy family she learns to admire them. Set in the early 1950s.

RHONDY

Greenfield, Eloise, **Grandmama's Joy**, illustrated by Carole Byard, Philomel, 1980, 32p., Picture Book, LC 79-11403, ISBN 0-399-21064-4.

Grandmother has taken care of Rhondy ever since the girl was a baby. On a beautiful day her grandmother is sad, and Rhondy tries to cheer her up by reminding her of the really important things in life. 1981 Coretta Scott King Honor book. A Reading Rainbow book.

RICHARD
See also Dick, Dickie, Richie, Rickey, Ricky

Aliki, **Digging Up Dinosaurs**, illustrated by Aliki, Crowell, 1981, 32p., Picture Book, LC 85-42979, ISBN 0-690-04714-2; 0-690-04716-9 (lib).

Mary Ann Mantell found the first dinosaur fossils in England in 1822. In 1841, Dr. Richard Owen named the giant reptiles Dinosauria. This book includes this and other true information about dinosaur bones including where they are found and how museum exhibits are put together. A Reading Rainbow book.

Asimov, Isaac, **It's Such a Beautiful Day**, Creative Education, 1985, 63p., Fiction, ISBN 0-88682-008-1.

Richard Henshaw is forced to find another way to school when the transport door fails to open. Set in the future, Richard rediscovers the joys of the natural world.

Etra, Jonathan and Stephanie Spinner, **Aliens for Breakfast**, illustrated by Steve Bjorkman, Random House, 1988, 62p., Fiction, ISBN 0-394-92093-7; 0-394-82093-2.

Richard finds an intergalactic agent in his cereal box and joins him in a fight to save the Earth from the Dranes, one of whom is pretending to be a student in Richard's class. Texas 1991.

Hargrove, Jim, **Richard M. Nixon: The Thirty-Seventh President**, Children's Press, 1985, 128p., Nonfiction, ISBN 0-516-03212-7.

Richard Nixon was a president of the United States. This biography covers his youth and his political career.

Pevsner, Stella, **Keep Stompin' Till the Music Stops**, Clarion, 1977, 136p., Fiction, ISBN 0-395-28875-4.

Richard and his extended family visit their grandfather in Illinois to get the elderly man to move to a senior citizen home in Florida. However, grandfather doesn't want to go and enlists the aid of the children to help him.

Yolen, Jane, **Transfigured Hart**, illustrated by Donna Diamond, Crowell, 1975, 86p., Fiction, ISBN 0-690-00736-1.

While recovering from a serious illness, Richard sees a white hart in a neighboring wood. He and a neighbor girl are convinced it is a unicorn and try to save it from hunters.

RICHIE
See also Richard

Myers, Walter Dean, **Fallen Angels**, Scholastic, 1988, 336p., Fiction, ISBN 0-590-409-425.

After graduating from a Harlem high school, seventeen-year-old Richie Perry enlists in the Army and spends a devastating year on active duty in Vietnam. 1989 Coretta Scott King Award book.

RICKEY
See also Richard, Ricky

Wartski, Maureen Crane, **Lake Is on Fire, The**, Westminster, 1981, 131p., Fiction, ISBN 0-664-32687-0.

Fifteen-year-old Rickey has been blinded in an accident and refuses sympathy. When he accepts an invitation to visit a mountain cabin, he and his dog are caught in a forest fire and have to figure out how to escape.

RICKY
See also Richard, Rickey

McMahan, Ian, **Lost Forest**, Macmillan, 1985, 113p., Fiction, ISBN 0-02-765570-9.

Ricky searches for his mother, a wildlife photographer who has disappeared on a field trip, using a vast computer system and an electronic friend.

Wallace, Bill, **Dog Called Kitty, A**, Holiday House, 1980, 153p., Fiction, LC 80-16293, ISBN 0-8234-0376-9.

Ricky has been afraid of dogs ever since he was attacked as a baby by a mad dog. When a small, motherless, hungry puppy shows up at the farm, Ricky resists the animal but soon a relationship of trust develops between the two of them. Nebraska 1985. Oklahoma 1983. Texas 1983.

RINGO

King, Clive, **Me and My Million**, Crowell, 1979, 180p., Fiction, ISBN 0-690-03972-7.

Ringo has dyslexia and when his brother tries to involve him in a robbery, he takes the wrong bus and becomes involved with a gang of real criminals. A humorous story set in London.

RINKO

Uchida, Yoshiko, **Jar of Dreams, A**, Atheneum, 1981, 131p., Fiction, ISBN 0-689-50210-9.

As a Japanese-American living in California in the 1930s, Rinko is aware of the prejudices against the Japanese and she wants to be a real American. There are several other books about Rinko.

ROALD

Dahl, Roald, **Boy: Tales of a Childhood**, Farrar, Straus & Giroux, 1984, 160p., Nonfiction, ISBN 0-374-37374-4.

The popular English children's author tells about his boyhood escapades and his first job in this autobiography.

Mason, Theodore K., **Two Against the Ice: Amundsen and Ellsworth**, Dodd, Mead, 1982, 192p., Nonfiction, ISBN 0-396-08092-8.

Roald Amundsen and his best friend were determined to explore the Arctic from the time they were boys. Their childhoods and early experiences helped to provide the stamina needed for the expedition they went on as adults. Biographical information about Roald from his childhood through the famous expedition.

ROB
See also Robbie, Robby, Robert, Roberto

Roberts, Willo Davis, **View from the Cherry Tree, The**, Atheneum, 1975, 181p., Fiction, ISBN 0-689-30483-8.

Rob enjoys watching people and events from his seat in the cherry tree, until he sees a murder and no one will believe him.

ROBBIE
See also Rob, Robby, Robert, Roberto

Hunter, Mollie, **Stranger Came Ashore; a Story of Suspense, A**, Harper & Row, 1975, 163p., Fiction, ISBN 0-06-022652-8.

When a stranger comes to their house in the Shetland Islands during a storm, young Robbie realizes that the stranger is the evil Master of the Seal Folk. Robbie must have help to use ancient magic to return the evil one to his kingdom under the sea.

ROBBY
See also Rob, Robbie, Robert, Roberto

Slote, Alfred, **Moving In**, Lippincott, 1988, 167p., Fiction, ISBN 0-397-32262-3.

Eleven-year-old Robby has had numerous challenges since his mother died. His biggest challenge is trying to keep his father from remarrying. There is another book about Robby.

ROBERT
See also Bob, Bobby, Rob, Robbie, Roberto

Anderson, Margaret, **In the Circle of Time**, Knopf, 1979, 181p., Fiction, ISBN 0-394-94029-6.

Robert and Jennifer are fascinated by an unusual circle of stones on a Scottish mountain. The two are projected into the twenty-second century where they find that the glaciers have melted and flooded coastal cities.

Bains, Rae, **Robert E. Lee, Brave Leader**, illustrated by Dick Smolinski, Troll, 1986, 43p., Nonfiction, ISBN 0-8167-0545-3.

Robert E. Lee was a famous general during the American Civil War. This biography covers his childhood and the struggles he faced as a young man.

Fisher, Lois, **Radio Robert**, Dodd, Mead, 1985, 128p., Fiction, ISBN 0-396-08503-2.

Robert becomes a celebrity with his radio ad-libs. He has to come to terms with his feelings about family and friends. There is another book about Robert.

Gretz, Susanna and Alison Sage, **Teddy Bears Cure a Cold**, illustrated by Susanna Gretz and Alison Sage, Four Winds, 1984, 32p., Picture Book, LC 84-4015, ISBN 0-590-07949-2.

William the bear feels sick and spends several days in bed while Robert and the other bears take care of him. A Reading Rainbow book.

Kennedy, John F., **Profiles in Courage**, illustrated by Emil Weiss, Harper & Row, 1955, 164p., Nonfiction, LC 64-17696.

Robert A. Taft showed political courage under pressure. He is one of the eight statesmen featured in this book. 1964 Jane Addams Award book.

Lawson, Robert, **They Were Strong and Good**, illustrated by Robert Lawson, Viking, 1940, 64p., Fiction, ISBN 0-670-69949-7.

This is the story of the author's mother and father and their mothers and fathers. Like most people that helped to make America a great nation, they were not famous, but they were strong and good, and worked hard, and had families. 1941 Caldecott Award book.

Levy, Elizabeth, **Dracula Is a Pain in the Neck**, illustrated by Mordicai Gerstein, Harper & Row, 1983, 74p., Fiction, ISBN 0-06-023823-2.

When he goes to summer camp, Robert insists on taking his Dracula doll and pillow and finds they cause him problems in this mystery.

Nesbit, E., **Five Children and It**, illustrated by H. R. Miller, Ernest Benn, 1957, 223p., Fiction, ISBN 0-8277-2137-4.

Robert is one of the five children who discovers a very furry and unusual creature while playing in a gravel pit. The creature has the ability to grant wishes, and the children have many magical adventures that are continued in other books.

Park, Barbara, **Operation: Dump the Chump**, Knopf, 1982, 113p., Fiction, LC 81-8147, ISBN 0-394-94976-5 (lib); 0-394-84976-0.

Robert Winkle is seven and a half and constantly humiliates his older brother, Oscar. Oscar finally decides he has to get rid of the pest for the summer in this humorous story. Indiana 1985.

Peck, Robert Newton, **Day No Pigs Would Die, A**, Knopf, 1973, 150p., Fiction, ISBN 0-394-48235-2.

In the rural Vermont of 1920, a twelve-year-old Shaker boy, Robert, receives the first thing he has ever wanted and owned, a pet pig, which he names Pinky. The pig becomes more of a friend than a pet and as Pinky grows to maturity, so does Robert. When times turn hard Robert is forced into making difficult decisions and assuming adult responsibilities. Colorado 1977.

Peck, Robert Newton, **Soup**, illustrated by Charles Gehm, Knopf, 1974, 96p., Fiction, ISBN 0-394-82700-7; 0-394-92700-1 (lib).

The adventures and misadventures of Robert and his friend Soup when they are in third grade in a small Vermont town. Michigan 1984.

Peck, Robert Newton, **Soup for President**, illustrated by Ted Lewin, Knopf, 1978, 107p., Fiction, ISBN 0-394-93675-2.

Robert manages his friend's campaign for class president at school in the small Vermont town they live in. There are numerous books about these two friends. Mississippi 1981. Missouri 1981.

Quackenbush, Robert, **Watt Got You Started, Mr. Fulton? A Story of James Watt and Robert Fulton**, Prentice-Hall, 1982, 39p., Nonfiction, ISBN 0-13-944397-5.

James Watt invented the steam engine that Robert Fulton used in the boats he designed. Biographical information is included about both men in this title.

ROBERTA
See also Bobby

Nesbit, E., **Railway Children**, illustrated by C. E. Brock, Puffin, 1988, 240p., Fiction, ISBN 0-14-035005-5 (pbk).

When their father leaves, Roberta and the rest of her family move to a tiny cottage in the country where the railroad becomes an important part of their lives.

ROBERTO
See also Bob, Bobby, Rob, Robbie, Robby, Robert

Walker, Paul Robert, **Pride of Puerto Rico: The Life of Roberto Clemente**, Harcourt Brace Jovanovich, 1988, 136p., Nonfiction, ISBN 0-15-200562-5.

Roberto Clemente was born in Puerto Rico and wanted to play baseball from childhood. He became a well-known ball player and died a hero. This biography tells about his childhood, his career, and his humanitarian actions.

ROBIN

Corbin, William, **Golden Mare**, illustrated by Pers Crowell, Coward-McCann, 1955, 122p., Fiction, LC 55-6891, ISBN 698-20054-3.

Magic, the golden palomino mare, is fortunate to have Robin Daveen to look after her since no one else sees her beauty. Robin is lucky to have Magic because he feels strong and unafraid when he rides her. The two have many adventures until a difficult decision has to be reached. Pacific Northwest 1958.

de Angeli, Marguerite, **Door in the Wall, The**, Doubleday, 1949, 121p., Fiction, ISBN 0-385-07283-X.

Set in medieval London, ten-year-old Robin is left alone by his parents due to the plague. When he is stricken with an illness, he is unable to walk. 1950 Newbery Award book.

McKinley, Robin, **Outlaws of Sherwood**, Greenwillow, 1988, 282p., Fiction, ISBN 0-688-07178-3.

The legendary folk hero, Robin Hood, lives in Sherwood Forest with a group of loyal followers.

Phillips, Ann, **Multiplying Glass**, illustrated by Liz Moyes, Oxford, 1981, 157p., Fiction, ISBN 0-19-271455-4.

Robin and two other children discover an unusual mirror at an antique shop. The mirror shows two fantasy personalities who begin to exhibit sinister behavior.

ROGER

Kalb, Jonah, **Goof That Won the Pennant, The**, illustrated by Sandy Kossin, Houghton Mifflin, 1976, 103p., Fiction, LC 76-21678, ISBN 0-395-24834-5.

Roger is one of the members of the Blazer's baseball team, a team of oddballs and misfits who do not even try to win. When their coach gives them the idea that winning is more fun than losing, the team decides to try. Indiana 1981.

Ransome, Arthur, **Swallows and Amazons**, illustrated by Arthur Ransome, Cape/Random House, 1981, 351p., Fiction, ISBN 0-224-60631-X.

Roger Walker and his siblings sail to an island and spend the summer camping by themselves. There are other books about the adventures of this family.

Skurzynski, Gloria, **Minstrel in the Tower**, illustrated by Julek Heller, Random House, 1988, 60p., Fiction, ISBN 0-394-99598-8.

Set in medieval times, Roger and his sister are kidnapped and held captive in a tower when they set out to find their uncle.

RON
See also Ronald, Ronnie

Christopher, Matt, **Dirt Bike Racer**, illustrated by Barry Bomzer, Little, Brown, 1979, 149p., Fiction, ISBN 0-316-13977-7.

Ron decides to repair a small dirt bike that he finds. He meets an old man who had once been a racer and who assists Ron in many ways.

RONALD
See also Ron, Ronnie

Behrens, June, **Ronald Reagan—An All American**, Children's Press, 1981, 31p., Nonfiction, ISBN 0-516-03565-7.

A biography about former American President Ronald Reagan. Included are his Illinois childhood, his experiences in Hollywood as an actor, and his political life.

RONNIE
See alsl Ron, Ronald, Veronica

Sauer, Julia, **Light at Tern Rock, The**, illustrated by Georges Schreiber, Viking, 1951, 63p., Fiction.

Ronnie and his Aunt Martha agree to spend two weeks at the lighthouse on Tern Rock to relieve the lighthouse keeper. When he doesn't return, they have to spend Christmas there and it becomes a very special day. 1952 Newbery Honor book.

ROSA
See also Rosamond, Rose, Rosie, Rosy

Bellairs, John, **Letter, the Witch, and the Ring, The**, illustrated by Richard Egielski, Dial, 1976, 188p., Fiction, LC 75-28968, ISBN 0-8037-4740-3; 0-8037-4741-1 (lib).

This is the third book of the trilogy that includes *The House With a Clock in Its Walls* and *The Figure in the Shadows*. Rosa Rita sets off on a summer trip with her neighbor, Mrs. Zimmerman, who is a genuine witch. As the two attempt to discover the meaning of a strange deathbed letter, their trip becomes a nightmare and they are drawn into a dark world of occult mysteries. Utah 1981.

Williams, Vera B., **Music, Music for Everyone**, illustrated by Vera B. Williams, Greenwillow, 1984, 31p., Picture Book, LC 83-14196, ISBN 0-688-02604-4; 0-688-02603-6 (lib).

When her grandma is ill, Rosa and her friends attempt to earn money by playing music in order to fill the empty money jar. 1985 Jane Addams Honor book.

ROSAMOND
See also Rosa, Rose, Rosie, Rosy

Sharmat, Marjorie Weinman, **Nate the Great Stalks Stupidweed**, illustrated by Marc Simont, Coward-McCann, 1986, 48p., Easy Reader, LC 85-30161, ISBN 0-698-20626-6.

Rosamond picks weeds that nobody wants and finds homes for them at an adopt-a-weed sale, complete with certificates of ownership. Oliver buys a weed and then loses it, giving Nate the Great, boy detective, a case to solve. A Reading Rainbow book.

ROSE
See also Mary Rose, Rosa, Rosamond, Rosemary, Rosie, Rosy

Lunn, Janet, **Root Cellar, The**, Scribner, 1983, 229p., Fiction, ISBN 0-684-178-559.

Twelve-year-old Rose is an orphan sent to live with unknown relatives on a Canadian farm. In the root cellar, she makes friends with people who had lived on the farm more than a hundred years prior. California 1988.

Souci, Robert D., **Talking Eggs, The**, illustrated by Jerry Pinkney, Dial, 1989, 30p., Picture Book, LC 88-33469, ISBN 0-8037-0619-7; 0-8037-0620-0 (lib).

A Creole folktale about two very different sisters. Rose is spoiled and lazy while Blanche is sweet and works hard. Rose is their mother's favorite and Blanche is forced to do all of the work. When Blanche meets an old witch-woman she enters a wondrous world that changes her life. 1990 Caldecott Honor book. 1990 Coretta Scott King Honor book.

ROSEMARY
See also Mary, Rose, Rosie

Bolton, Carole, **Good-Bye Year**, Lodestar, 1982, 186p., Fiction, ISBN 0-525-66787-3.

After seeing a famous movie, thirteen-year-old Rosemary dreams of becoming a movie star. Reality sets in when her musician father informs the family they must move and a boy she once knew moves back to town.

ROSIE
See also Rosa, Rosamond,
Rose, Rosemary, Rosy

Brenner, Barbara, **Year In the Life of Rosie Bernard**, Harper & Row, 1983, 84p., Fiction, ISBN 0-06-020657-8.

Rosie Bernard goes to live with her grandparents and numerous relatives when her mother dies. Rosie's father is an actor and when he decides to remarry, Rosie decides she has to do something. Set in Brooklyn in the 1930s.

Hammer, Charles, **Me, the Beef, and the Bum**, Farrar, Straus & Giroux, 1984, 215p., Fiction, ISBN 0-374-34903-7.

Rosie runs away from home with her prize steer and is led to a hide-out by a bum. While hiding out, Rosie takes time to think about her father and the death of her mother.

Harris, Robie, **Rosie's Double Dare**, illustrated by Tony DeLuna, Knopf, 1980, 111p., Fiction, ISBN 0-394-94459-3.

Rosie wants to play on her brother's baseball team when a vacancy occurs. She also wants special rules, and the team makes a request that causes a predicament for Rosie.

Rappaport, Doreen, **Trouble at the Mines**, illustrated by Joan Sandin, Crowell, 1987, 96p., Fiction, ISBN 0-690-044-461 (lib); 0-690-044-453.

Rosie Wilson is the daughter of a coal miner in Pennsylvania. Set in 1899, Rosie tells the story of a famous strike and the woman known as Mother Jones. Based on an actual event. 1988 Jane Addams Honor book.

Voight, Cynthia, **Stories about Rosie**, illustrated by Dennis Kendrick, Atheneum, 1986, 47p., Fiction, ISBN 0-689-31296-2.

Humorous stories about Rosie the spaniel and her family.

ROSY
See also Rosa, Rosamond,
Rose, Rosemary, Rosie

Greenwald, Sheila, **Give Us a Great Big Smile, Rosy Cole**, illustrated by Sheila Greenwald, Little, Brown, 1981, 76p., Fiction, ISBN 0-316-32672-0.

Rosy is not very enthusiastic about her tenth birthday, just as she isn't very enthusiastic about her violin lessons. There is another book about Rosy and her family.

ROWENA

Brittain, Bill, **Wish Giver: Three Tales of Coven Tree, The**, illustrated by Andrew Glass, Harper & Row, 1983, 181p., Fiction, LC 82-48264, ISBN 0-06-020686-1; 0-06-020687-X (lib).

Thaddeus Blinn was a funny little man who appeared from out of nowhere and put his tent by the annual Coven Tree Church Social. He said he had the power to give people exactly what they asked for. Rowena is one of the characters who finds that wishes often have unexpected results when they come true. 1984 Newbery Honor book.

ROXANNE

Hall, Lynn, **Leaving, The**, Scribner, 1980, 116p., Fiction, ISBN 0-684-167-166.

Many family changes occur when Roxanne decides to leave her parent's farm to move to the city. 1981 Boston Globe-Horn Book Award.

Warren, Cathy, **Roxanne Bookman: Live at Five!**, Bradbury, 1988, 100p., Fiction, ISBN 0-02-792492-0.

Ten-year-old Roxanne finds it challenging to be a member of a family of winners. During a three-week period she has many problems including losing the championship baseball game for her team and almost losing her best friend.

ROY

Brown, Laurene Krasny and Marc Brown, **Visiting the Art Museum**, illustrated by Laurene Krasny Brown and Marc Brown, Dutton, 1986, 32p., Nonfiction, LC 85-32552, ISBN 0-525-44233-2.

A family goes to an art museum where they see examples of various art styles, from primitive art to works by twentieth-century pop artists such as Roy Lichtenstein. A Reading Rainbow book.

Van Raven, Pieter, **Time of Troubles, A**, Scribner/Macmillan, 1990, 180p., Fiction, ISBN 0-684-19212-8.

Roy Purdy's father gets out of prison in the Chesapeake Bay area and the two go cross-country to California to look for work. At fourteen, Roy grows up quickly as he sees the poverty of the Depression and the cruel exploitation of desperate people. 1991 Scott O'Dell Award.

RUDY

Baylor, Byrd, **Hawk, I'm Your Brother**, illustrated by Peter Parnall, Scribner, 1976, 48p., Fiction, ISBN 0-684-14571-5.

Rudy Soto is a young Indian boy who steals a baby redtail hawk hoping that he can learn to fly if he makes the hawk his brother. 1977 Caldecott Honor book.

Jordan, June, **New Life: New Room**, illustrated by Ray Cruz, Crowell, 1975, 52p., Fiction, ISBN 0-690-00212-2.

Rudy and his family have a problem trying to fit a new baby into their already crowded two-bedroom apartment.

RUFUS

Estes, Eleanor, **Rufus M.**, illustrated by Louis Slobodkin, Harcourt Brace Jovanovich, 1943, 320p., Fiction, LC 88-35813, ISBN 0-15-2694-153.

Seven-year-old Rufus is the youngest child in the Moffat family. When the family has financial problems, he attempts to rescue them. 1944 Newbery Honor book.

Merrill, Jean, **Toothpaste Millionaire, The**, illustrated by Jan Palmer, Houghton Mifflin, 1972, 90p., Fiction, LC 73-22055, ISBN 0-395-18511-4; 0-395-11186-2 (pbk).

Kate tells the story of her friend and classmate, Rufus Mayflower, and how he became a millionaire between sixth and eighth grade. After building up his toothpaste business, Rufus decided to try something else and sold his business to his friend, Hector. Oklahoma 1977. Vermont 1976.

Rylant, Cynthia, **Fine White Dust, A**, Bradbury, 1986, 106p., Fiction, LC 86-1003, ISBN 0-02-777240-3.

Rufus and thirteen-year-old Pete are best friends who live in a small North Carolina town. When a traveling preacher comes to town, Pete is given a chance to reconcile his own deeply held religious beliefs with those of his friends. 1987 Newbery Honor book.

RUSS
See also Russel, Russell

Ellis, Melvin, **Flight of the White Wolf**, Scholastic, 1970, 208p., Fiction, ISBN 0-590-42053-4 (pbk).

Russ takes flight with Gray, an adult wolf, to avoid the people wanting to kill the wolf. Oklahoma 1974. Vermont 1972.

Meltzer, Milton, **Ain't Gonna Study War No More: The Story of America's Peace Seekers**, Harper & Row, 1985, 282p., Nonfiction, ISBN 0-060-241-993; 0-060-242-000 (lib).

Russ Ford refused to register for the draft and is one of those featured for war resistance in the United States. This book also presents a history of pacifism from colonial times to the present. 1986 Child Study children's Book Award. 1986 Jane Addams Award book.

RUSSEL
See also Russ, Russell

Paulsen, Gary, **Dogsong**, Bradbury, 1985, 171p., Fiction, LC 84-20443, ISBN 0-02-770180-8.

Russel Susskit is a fourteen-year-old Eskimo boy. After being taught by the blind old man, Oogruk, and listening to his songs and stories of journeys, Russel harnesses Oogruk's dogs for a dog run across his country. Russel takes a 1,400 mile journey by dogsled across ice, tundra, and mountains. 1986 Newbery Honor book.

RUSSELL
See also Russ, Russel

Cade-Edwards, Eileen, **Squirrel in My Tea Cup!**, Borealis Press, 1981, 38p., Fiction, ISBN 0-88887-037-X.

After Russell buys a small squirrel from a classmate, he and his family discover it is not easy to raise an outdoor creature inside.

Coville, Bruce, **Monster's Ring, The**, illustrated by Katherine Coville, Pantheon, 1982, 87p., Fiction, LC 82-3436, ISBN 0-394-85320-2; 0-394-95320-7 (lib).

Russell is usually a timid boy. On Halloween night he is eager to frighten the school bully, so Russell acquires a magic ring and the power to change himself into a hideous monster. Pacific Northwest 1985. South Carolina 1985.

Hurwitz, Johanna, **Russell Sprouts**, illustrated by Lillian Hoban, Morrow, 1987, 68p., Fiction, ISBN 0-688-07166-X.

Six-year-old Russell is in first grade and has a good year both at school and with his family. There is another book about Russell.

Wright, Betty Ren, **Christina's Ghost**, Holiday House, 1985, 105p., Fiction, LC 85-42880, ISBN 0-8234-0581-8.

Christina had looked forward to spending part of her summer with her grandmother but becomes miserable when she has to stay with her grumpy uncle in a spooky, isolated Victorian house. Her summer changes when she sees the ghostly figure of Russell Charles, a small sad boy, and feels an evil presence in the attic. Georgia 1988. Indiana 1989. Oklahoma 1988. Texas 1988.

RUTH
See also Ruthie

Serraillier, Ian, **Silver Sword**, illustrated by C. Walter Hodges, Phillips, 1959, 187p., Fiction, ISBN 0-87599-104-1.

Ruth is one of three children who fend for themselves for five years in the defeated city of Warsaw after their parents are taken away to a prison and a concentration camp. The children have extraordinary adventures as they go across Germany and into Switzerland.

RUTHIE
See also Ruth

Etchemendy, Nancy, **Stranger From the Stars**, illustrated by Teje Etchemendy, Avon, 1983, 150p., Fiction, ISBN 0-380-83568-1 (pbk).

Twelve-year-old Ruthie discovers that a stranger setting up a camp in a nearby canyon is from another world.

RYAN

Cleary, Beverly, **Ralph S. Mouse**, illustrated by Paul O. Zelinsky, Morrow, 1982, 160p., Fiction, LC 82-3516, ISBN 0-688-01452-6; 0-688-01455-0 (lib).

Ryan Bramble is one of the few human beings that can understand Ralph, the little brown mouse. Ryan takes Ralph to school and the classroom experiences are humorous, yet upsetting to a defenseless, intelligent mouse. 1983 Golden Kite Award. Iowa 1985. West Virginia 1987.

-S-

SAL

See also Sally, Salvador

McCloskey, Robert, **Blueberries for Sal**, illustrated by Robert McCloskey, Viking, 1948, 54p., Picture Book, ISBN 0-670-17591-9.

While eating blueberries, Little Sal and a bear cub both lose their mothers and they almost end up with each other's mother. 1949 Caldecott Honor book.

McCloskey, Robert, **One Morning in Maine**, illustrated by Robert McCloskey, Viking, 1952, 64p., Picture Book, ISBN 0-670-52627-4.

It is a big day for Sal when she discovers that she has a loose tooth and gets to make a trip to the grocery store on the mainland. 1953 Caldecott Honor book.

SALA

Calders, Pere, **Brush**, illustrated by Carme Sole Vendrell, Kane/Miller, 1986, 24p., Picture Book, LC 85-23873, ISBN 0-916291-05-7.

Sala's puppy was given away and the boy knew he needed another pet. Sala finally tied a rope to a large brush and pretended it was a dog with amazing results. A Reading Rainbow book.

SALLY

See also Sal

Blacknall, Carolyn, **Sally Ride: America's First Woman in Space**, Dillon, 1984, 78p., Nonfiction, ISBN 0-87518-260-7.

This biography gives information about Sally Ride as she was growing up and how her interests and education helped her to become the first woman astronaut.

SALVADOR

See also Sal

Ets, Marie Hall and Aurora Labastida, **Nine Days to Christmas**, illustrated by Marie Hall Ets, Viking, 1959, 48p., Picture Book, LC 59-16438, ISBN 670-51350-4.

Salvador helps his younger sister keep track of the days until her first posada, a special Christmas party held nine days before Christmas. At the posada, his sister discovers she has a very special pinata. 1960 Caldecott Award book.

SAM

See also Samantha, Sammy, Samuel

Brittain, Bill, **Wish Giver: Three Tales of Coven Tree, The**, illustrated by Andrew Glass, Harper & Row, 1983, 181p., Fiction, LC 82-48264, ISBN 0-06-020686-1; 0-06-020687-X (lib).

Thaddeus Blinn was a funny little man who appeared from out of nowhere and put his tent by the annual Coven Tree Church Social. He said he had the power to give people exactly what they asked for. Sam is one of the characters who finds that wishes often have unexpected results when they come true. 1984 Newbery Honor book.

Cohen, Barbara, **Thank You, Jackie Robinson**, illustrated by Richard Cuffari, Lothrop, Lee & Shepard, 1974, 125p., Fiction, ISBN 0-688-07909-1.

Sam becomes friends with the cook at his mother's inn and the two share talk about their favorite subject, baseball.

Ernst, Lisa Campbell, **Sam Johnson and the Blue Ribbon Quilt**, illustrated by Lisa Campbell Ernst, Lothrop, Lee & Shepard, 1983, 32p., Picture Book, LC 82-9980, ISBN 0-688-01516-6; 0-688-01517-4 (lib).

Sam Johnson discovers that he enjoys patchwork and wants to join his wife's quilting club. When the ladies laugh at him, the men begin to sew their own quilt. A Reading Rainbow book.

Fritz, Jean, **Make Way for Sam Houston**, illustrated by Elise Primavera, Putnam, 1986, 109p., Nonfiction, ISBN 0-399-21303-1.

Sam Houston had a fascinating life before he became governor of Texas. He was an advocate for the Indians, an officer in the Army, a lawyer, and he played an important role in the history of Texas.

Fritz, Jean, **Why Don't You Get a Horse, Sam Adams?**, illustrated by Trina Schart Hyman, Coward-McCann, 1974, 47p., Nonfiction, ISBN 0-698-20292-9.

When Sam Adams left Massachusetts for Philadelphia in 1774 to attend the Philadelphia Convention as a representative, it was his first journey. His clothes were so shabby that his friends provided him with new clothes, and he had to learn to ride a horse. Other biographical information is included.

George, Jean Craighead, **My Side of the Mountain**, illustrated by Jean Craighead George, Dutton, 1959, 178p., Fiction, ISBN 0-525-35530-8.

Young Sam Gribley spends a winter alone on a mountain in the Catskills relying on his wits to survive.

Gilson, Jamie, **Do Bananas Chew Gum?**, Lothrop, Lee & Shepard, 1980, 158p., Fiction, LC 80-11414, ISBN 0-688-41960-7; 0-688-51960-1 (lib).

When he moves to a new town, Sam hopes to keep his poor reading and writing abilities from the rest of the sixth graders. Sam feels stupid until others help him learn that something can be done about his problem. Arkansas 1983.

Gipson, Fred, **Savage Sam**, illustrated by Carl Burger, Harper & Row, 1962, 214p., Fiction, ISBN 0-06-011561-0.

The dog, Savage Sam, becomes a hero when he helps three children who have been kidnapped by a tribe of Apache Indians.

Gould, Deborah, **Grandpa's Slide Show**, illustrated by Cheryl Harness, Lothrop, Lee & Shepard, 1987, 32p., Fiction, ISBN 0-688-06973-8.

Sam's grandfather had given slide shows many times when he was alive. After his grandfather's death, Sam gave a slide show to help the family with their grief.

Keats, Ezra Jack, **Apt. 3**, illustrated by Ezra Jack Keats, Macmillan, 1971, 34p., Picture Book, LC 78-123135, ISBN 0-02-749510-8.

Sam and his younger brother Ben could hear someone playing a harmonica in their apartment building. When they search for the source of the music, they find a new friend. A Reading Rainbow book.

Kennedy, John F., **Profiles in Courage**, illustrated by Emil Weiss, Harper & Row, 1955, 164p., Nonfiction, LC 64-17696.

Sam Houston showed political courage under pressure. He is one of the eight statesmen featured in this book. 1964 Jane Addams Award book.

Levy, Elizabeth, **Dracula Is a Pain in the Neck**, illustrated by Mordicai Gerstein, Harper & Row, 1983, 74p., Fiction, ISBN 0-06-023823-2.

Sam told his younger brother not to take his Dracula doll and pillow to summer camp because they would cause trouble. The younger brother takes them anyway and Sam is proven to be right in this mystery.

Lowry, Lois, **All about Sam**, illustrated by Diane de Groat, Houghton Mifflin, 1988, 135p., Fiction, ISBN 0-395-4866-29.

Sam Krupnik is Anastasia's little brother. This book tells about his birth and goes through his mischievous toddlerhood. Arkansas 1991.

Marshall, Edward, **Three by the Sea**, illustrated by James Marshall, Dial, 1981, 48p., Easy Reader, LC 80-26097, ISBN 0-8037-8671-9 (pbk); 0-8037-8687-5 (lib).

Lolly, Spider, and Sam are three friends who have a picnic at the beach. After lunch they decide to share their favorite stories. Lolly reads a story from her reader and the boys decide they can tell better ones. A Reading Rainbow book.

Marzollo, Jean, **Soccer Sam**, illustrated by Blanche Sims, Random House, 1987, 48p., Easy Reader, LC 86-47533, ISBN 0-394-88406-X; 0-394-98406-4 (lib).

Sam's cousin Marco has come from Mexico to visit Sam and his family for a year. Marco speaks limited English and doesn't know how to play basketball, but he is a success at teaching the second graders how to play soccer. A Reading Rainbow book.

Ness, Evaline, **Sam, Bangs and Moonshine**, illustrated by Evaline Ness, H. Holt, 1966, 36p., Picture Book, LC 66-10113, ISBN 03-059805-2; 03-059810-9.

Samantha is the daughter of a fisherman who is always called Sam. She has the bad habit of lying because she has trouble telling the difference between real and moonshine. Her moonshine causes problems for her friend Thomas who does whatever Sam asks. 1967 Caldecott Award book.

Shub, Elizabeth, **Cutlass in the Snow**, illustrated by Rachel Isadora, Greenwillow, 1986, 46p., Fiction, ISBN 0-688-05928-7.

In 1797, blinking lights lead Sam and his grandfather to buried treasure on the deserted Fire Island. Based on an actual historical event.

White, E. B., **Trumpet of the Swan, The**, illustrated by Edward Frascino, Harper & Row, 1970, 210p., Fiction, LC 72-112484, ISBN 06-026397-0.

Sam Beaver is a boy who loves all wild things. He befriends Louis the Trumpeter Swan who lacks a voice. Louis is determined to become a trumpeter, and Sam takes him to school where the swan learns to read and write. Indiana 1975. Kansas 1973. Oklahoma 1973.

Williams, Jay, **Magic Grandfather, The**, illustrated by Gail Owens, Four Winds, 1979, 149p., Fiction, ISBN 0-02-793100-5.

Sam discovers that his grandfather is an enchanter and when he accidentally gets sent into another world, Sam and his cousin have to look through the magic books to find a way to bring him back.

Williams, Vera B., **Three Days on a River in a Red Canoe**, illustrated by Vera B. Williams, Greenwillow, 1981, 30p., Picture Book, LC 80-23893, ISBN 0-688-80307-5; 0-688-84307-7.

Sam, his cousin, and their mothers buy a used red canoe and take a three-day river trip. They learn to paddle the canoe, put up a tent, build a fire and cook out-of-doors during their adventure. A Reading Rainbow book.

SAMANTHA
See also Sam, Sammy

Ness, Evaline, **Sam, Bangs and Moonshine**, illustrated by Evaline Ness, H. Holt, 1966, 36p., Picture Book, LC 66-10113, ISBN 03-059805-2; 03-059810-9.

Samantha is the daughter of a fisherman who is always called Sam. She has the bad habit of lying because she has trouble telling the difference between real and moonshine. Her moonshine causes problems for her friend Thomas who always does what she asks. 1967 Caldecott Award book.

Smith, Samantha, **Journey to the Soviet Union**, Little, Brown, 1985, 122p., Nonfiction, ISBN 0-316-801-755; 0-316-801-763 (pbk).

Ten-year-old Samantha Smith describes her trip to Russia after writing to one of the Russian leaders about her fears of a nuclear war. 1986 Jane Addams Honor Book.

SAMMY
See also Sam, Samantha, Samuel

Byars, Betsy, **House of Wings**, illustrated by Daniel Schwartz, Viking, 1972, 142p., Fiction, ISBN 0-670-38025-3.

Sammy is angry when his parents leave him with his grandfather in an old house in the woods. A wounded crane helps Sammy with his feelings.

Sebestyen, Ouida, **On Fire**, Little, Brown, 1985, 207p., Fiction, ISBN 0-316-77934-2.

Twelve-year-old Sammy lives a very hard life in a frontier mining town in 1911. He has many family problems including a father who drinks and an older brother who is bossy. He also has a good friend. 1982 Jane Addams Award.

Voight, Cynthia, **Dicey's Song**, Atheneum, 1983, 196p., Fiction, LC 82-3882, ISBN 0-689-39044-9.

Sammy Tillerman and his brother and sisters had spent the whole summer looking for their grandmother after their mother abandoned them. Living with grandma in her Chesapeake Bay country home is not easy, and old problems and sorrows do not go away easily. 1983 Newbery Award book.

SAMUEL
See also Sam, Sammy

Quackenbush, Robert, **Mark Twain? What Kind of Name Is That? A Story of Samuel Langhorne Clemens**, Prentice-Hall, 1984, 33p., Nonfiction, ISBN 0-671-66294-5.

Samuel Clemens decided that he wanted to be a writer after working with his older brother and printing a newspaper. This brief biography tells of his travels and how he took the name of Mark Twain.

Raskin, Ellen, **Westing Game, The**, Dutton, 1978, 185p., Fiction, LC 77-18866, ISBN 0-525-42320-6.

Samuel W. Weston was a very rich man. Sixteen people were invited to the reading of his strange will and each had the chance to become a millionaire, depending on how the tricky and dangerous Westing Game was played. 1979 Newbery Award book. 1978 Boston Globe-Horn Book Award. Michigan 1982.

SAN YU

Handforth, Thomas, **Mei Li**, illustrated by Thomas Handforth, Doubleday, 1938, 52p., Picture Book, ISBN 0-385-07401-8.

San Yu and his sister live in Peiping, China. They hope that their three lucky pennies and three lucky marbles will be enough to go to the New Year's Fair in the city. 1939 Caldecott Award book.

SANDY

Williams, Vera B., **Chair for My Mother, A**, illustrated by Vera B. Williams, Greenwillow, 1982, 32p., Picture Book, LC 81-7010, ISBN 0-688-00914-X; 0-688-00915-8 (lib).

A young girl and her mother save coins in a jar to buy a new chair to replace furniture destroyed in a fire. When there is enough money her Uncle Sandy helps them get the chair. 1983 Boston Globe-Horn Book Award. 1983 Caldecott Honor book.

SANTIAGO

Clifford, Eth, **Wild One**, illustrated by Arvis Stewart, Houghton Mifflin, 1974, 206p., Fiction, ISBN 0-395-19491-1.

Santiago was a juvenile delinquent as he was growing up in a small Spanish town. As he matured he decided to be a research doctor and won the Nobel Prize. A fictionalized biography about a real person.

SARA
See also Sara-Kate, Sarah

Byars, Betsy, **Summer of the Swans, The**, illustrated by Ted Coconis, Viking, 1970, 142p., Fiction, ISBN 0-670-68190-3.

At fourteen, Sara has already known many tragedies. Her mother is dead, and her father has become remote, leaving Sara and her younger brother to be raised by an aunt in West Virginia. Sara's brother has been left mentally retarded and speechless following a severe illness. A monotonous summer turns quite eventful. 1970 Newbery Award book.

Gretz, Susanna and Alison Sage, **Teddy Bears Cure a Cold**, illustrated by Susanna Gretz and Alison Sage, Four Winds, 1984, 32p., Picture Book, LC 84-4015, ISBN 0-590-07949-2.

William the bear feels sick and spends several days in bed while Sara and the other bears take care of him. A Reading Rainbow book.

Lapp, Eleanor J., **Orphaned Pup**, Scholastic, 1988, 139p., Fiction, ISBN 0-590-40885-2 (pbk).

Sara finds a puppy and keeps him in an abandoned shed since she doesn't think her mother and stepfather will allow her to keep the dog. As she tries to keep the dog a secret, Sara causes problems for herself and the family.

Levy, Elizabeth, **Lizzie Lies a Lot**, illustrated by John Wallner, Dell, 1976, 102p., Fiction, ISBN 0-440-44714-3.

Sara tries to help her friend to stop telling lies since people never trust a liar.

Schulman, Janet, **Big Hello, The**, illustrated by Lillian Hoban, Greenwillow, 1976, 32p., Easy Reader, LC 75-33672, ISBN 0-688-80036-X; 0-688-84036-1 (lib).

Sara is a doll that moves to California with her family. They take an airplane and are busy getting settled upon arrival at their new house. When Sara is lost, her little girl becomes very upset. A Reading Rainbow book.

Schwartz, Amy, **Begin at the Beginning**, illustrated by Amy Schwartz, Harper & Row, 1983, 26p., Picture Book, LC 82-48257, ISBN 0-06-025227-8; 0-06-025228-6 (lib).

Sara has been selected by her teacher to do the class painting for the art show. At home, Sara has trouble deciding what to paint until her mother helps her decide where to begin. A Reading Rainbow book.

SARA-KATE
See also Kate, Sara, Sarah

Lisle, Janet Taylor, **Afternoon of the Elves**, Orchard, 1989, 122p., Fiction, LC 88-35099, ISBN 0-531-05837-9; 0-531-08437-X (lib).

Sara-Kate lives in a big, gloomy house with her mysterious, silent mother. She has a miniature village in her backyard and she tells her friend that it was built by elves. 1990 Newbery Honor book.

SARAH
See also Sara

Bilson, Geoffrey, **Goodbye Sarah**, illustrated by Ron Berg, Kids Can Press, 1982, 64p., Fiction, ISBN 0-919964-38-9.

Set in Winnipeg, Canada, in 1919. Sarah's father is active in the committee that causes a General Strike, which has violent outcomes.

Bulla, Clyde Robert, **Shoeshine Girl**, illustrated by Leigh Grant, Crowell, 1975, 84p., Fiction, ISBN 0-690-00758-2.

Ten-year-old Sarah is a tough, angry, and obnoxious girl. When her family sends her to live with an aunt for the summer, Sarah learns about both earning money and friendship. Arkansas 1978. Oklahoma 1978. South Carolina 1980.

Cowen, Ida, **Spy for Freedom: The Story of Sarah Aaronsohn**, Lodestar, 1985, 156p., Nonfiction, ISBN 0-525-67150-1.

Sarah Aaronsohn led a spy organization in Palestine during World War I. She shot herself rather than reveal any secrets to the Turkish officials. This biography tells about Sarah and her organization.

Dalgliesh, Alice, **Courage of Sarah Noble, The**, illustrated by Leonard Weisgard, Scribner, 1954, 55p., Fiction, LC 54-5922, ISBN 0-684-18830-9.

Sarah Noble was an actual child who went to cook for her father in 1707 while he built the first house in New Milford, Connecticut. Her mother had told her to keep her courage up and Sarah found she had to be very courageous, particularly when her father left her with Indians while he went to get the rest of the family. 1955 Newbery Honor book.

Haas, Jessie, **Keeping Barney**, Greenwillow, 1982, 160p., Fiction, ISBN 0-688-00859-3.

Although Sarah wants a horse of her own, her parents aren't sure that she can take care of one, so Sarah answers an ad to care for a horse for the winter.

Hermes, Patricia, **You Shouldn't Have to Say Good-Bye**, Harcourt Brace Jovanovich, 1982, 117p., Fiction, ISBN 0-15-2999-442.

Thirteen-year-old Sarah has a difficult time when she learns that her mother has cancer and will die. California 1987.

Lee, Beverly Haskell, **Secret of Van Rink's Cellar**, Lerner, 1979, 174p., Fiction, ISBN 0-8225-0763-3.

After the death of her father during the American Revolution, Sarah and her brother move to New York City with their mother who has taken a job as a lady's maid. The children discover a 'ghost' in the cellar and become involved as spies for General Washington.

Little, Jean, **Mine for Keeps**, illustrated by Lewis Parker, Little, Brown, 1962, 186p., Fiction, ISBN 0-316-52793-9.

Sarah has cerebral palsy. After spending five years away from home at a special center, she returns home thinking she will receive special privileges but learns that she has to change her thinking.

MacLachlan, Patricia, **Sarah, Plain and Tall**, Harper & Row, 1985, 58p., Fiction, LC 83-49481, ISBN 0-06-024101-2; 0-06-024102-0 (lib).

When their father invites a mail-order bride named Sarah to come live with them in their prairie home, Caleb and Anna learn to like her and want Sarah to stay. 1986 Christopher Award. 1986 Golden Kite Award. 1986 Newbery Award book. 1986 Jefferson Cup Award. 1986 Scott O'Dell Award. Arkansas 1988.

O'Dell, Scott, **Sarah Bishop**, Houghton Mifflin, 1980, 184p., Fiction, ISBN 0-395-29185-2.

Fifteen-year-old Sarah runs away and becomes a recluse after her father is killed, and she sees numerous brutalities during the Revolutionary War.

Scott, Elaine, **Ramona: Behind the Scenes of a Television Show**, illustrated by Margaret Miller, Morrow, 1988, 88p., Nonfiction, LC 87-33313, ISBN 0-688-06818-9; 0-688-06819-7 (lib).

Numerous black-and-white photographs show the making of the ten-part television series about Beverly Cleary's famous character, Ramona Quimby. Included are the way a book is adapted to become a script, auditions, filming and editing. Eight-year-old Sarah Polly plays the part of Ramona. A Reading Rainbow book.

Van Allsburg, Chris, **Polar Express**, illustrated by Chris Van Allsburg, Houghton Mifflin, 1985, 30p., Picture Book, LC 85-10907, ISBN 0-395-38949-6.

Sarah finds the last small package under the Christmas tree. The gift contains a special bell that reminds her brother of a magical train ride to the North Pole on Christmas Eve. 1986 Caldecott Award book. Kentucky 1987. Ohio 1991.

Williams, Jay, **Magic Grandfather, The**, illustrated by Gail Owens, Four Winds, 1979, 149p., Fiction, ISBN 0-02-793100-5.

Sarah and her cousin discover that their grandfather is an enchanter and when he is accidentally sent to another world, the two must search through his magic books to find a way to bring their grandfather back.

SASHA

Corcoran, Barbara, **Sasha, My Friend**, illustrated by Richard L. Shell, Atheneum, 1971, 203p., Fiction, LC 69-18968.

Hallie adjusts to an isolated life in Montana with the help of an orphaned wolf pup named Sasha. Kansas 1972.

SCOTT
See also Scotty

McGraw, Eloise Jarvis, **Money Room**, Atheneum, 1981, 182p., Fiction, ISBN 0-689-50208-7.

Thirteen-year-old Scott, his mother, and sister move to the farm they have inherited. In this mystery, they search for the Money Room, which they have heard stories about as a way to provide added income.

Mitchell, Barbara, **Raggin', a Story About Scott Joplin**, Carolrhoda, 1987, 55p., Nonfiction, ISBN 0-87614-310-9.

Biographical information about the famous black musician, Scott Joplin, and the struggles and determination it took for him to become a major composer.

Van Steenwyk, Elizabeth, **Three Dog Winter**, Walker, 1987, 144p., Fiction, ISBN 0-8027-6718-4.

Twelve-year-old Scott races sled dogs for a hobby. Scott becomes unhappy when his life changes due to a move and a new family situation, which put constraints on his hobby.

Wisler, G. Clifton, **Antrian Messenger, The**, Lodestar, 1986, 117p., Fiction, ISBN 0-525-67174-9.

Fourteen-year-old Scott has unusual intuitive powers that lead him into danger. In this science fiction thriller, Scott discovers that he is an alien.

SCOTTY
See also Scott

Joyce, William, **Dinosaur Bob and His Adventures With the Family Lazardo**, illustrated by William Joyce, Harper & Row, 1988, 32p., Picture Book, LC 87-30796, ISBN 0-06-023047-9; 0-06-023048-7 (lib).

While on a family safari to Africa, young Scotty Lazardo finds a dinosaur, which the family names Bob. When Bob returns to America with the family, he creates quite a sensation. A Reading Rainbow book.

SEAN

Battles, Edith, **Witch in Room 6**, HarperCollins, 1987, 144p., Fiction, ISBN 0-06-020413-3.

Sean becomes friends with Cheryl, an eleven-year-old apprentice witch, although her family does not want her to associate with 'regular' kids.

Morpurgo, Michael, **Twist of Gold**, Heinemann, 1987, 226p., Fiction, ISBN 0-7182-3971-7.

Sean O'Brien and his sister leave Ireland in the mid-1800s during the potato famine to search for their father who has immigrated to California.

SEBASTIAN

Howe, James, **What Eric Knew**, Atheneum, 1985, 156p., Fiction, ISBN 0-689-31159-1.

Sebastian Barth is a teen detective and he and his friends solve an exciting and frightening case. There are other books about these characters.

Lyon, David, **Runaway Duck, The**, illustrated by David Lyon, Lothrop, Lee & Shepard, 1985, 28p., Picture Book, LC 84-5677, ISBN 0-688-04002-0; 0-688-04003-9 (lib).

Sebastian's favorite toy is a wooden pull-toy duck named Egbert. When Sebastian forgets that his toy is tied to the car, Egbert begins an adventure that takes him to sea. A Reading Rainbow book.

SELINA

Godden, Rumer, **Mr. McFadden's Halloween**, Viking, 1975, 127p., Fiction, ISBN 0-670-49271-X.

Selina and her pony rescue the dour old farmer, Mr. McFadden, who they have befriended.

SETH

Budbill, David, **Bones on Black Spruce Mountain**, Dial, 1978, 126p., Fiction, ISBN 0-8037-0691-X.

Seth's camping trip to a lonely mountaintop becomes a journey into a painful past that must be confronted. Vermont 1980.

Pryor, Bonnie, **Seth of the Lion People**, Morrow, 1988, 117p., Fiction, ISBN 0-688-07327-1.

Set in prehistoric times, Seth realizes that his skills are not valued by his people and sets out to find another clan.

SEYMOUR

Sharmat, Marjorie Weinman, **Gila Monsters Meet You at the Airport**, illustrated by Byron Barton, Macmillan, 1980, 28p., Picture Book, LC 80-12264, ISBN 0-02-782450-0.

When a young boy from New York and his family move to the West, he imagines it will be very different and knows that he will miss his best friend Seymour. A Reading Rainbow book.

SHABANU

Staples, Suzanne Fisher, **Shabanu, Daughter of the Wind**, Knopf, 1989, 240p., Fiction, ISBN 0-394-84815-2; 0-394-94815-7 (lib).

Set in present-day Pakistan, Shabanu must balance her own wishes against the obligations she has to her family and to centuries of tradition when she is pledged by her father to marry a despised landowner. 1990 Newbery Honor book.

SHANG

Young, Ed, **Lon Po Po: A Red-Riding Hood Story from China**, illustrated by Ed Young, Philomel, 1989, 30p., Picture Book, LC 88-15222, ISBN 0-399-21619-7.

Shang and her two sisters live with their mother in the countryside of northern China. While their mother goes to visit their grandmother, a wolf comes to visit the children and claims to be their grandmother. 1990 Caldecott Award book.

SHARI

Adler, C. S., **Fly Free**, Coward-McCann, 1984, 159p., Fiction, ISBN 0-698-20606-1.

Thirteen-year-old Shari is an abused and unhappy child. She dreams of escaping and seeks comfort by watching the birds fly near her mountain home.

SHE-WHO-IS-ALONE

dePaola, Tomie, **Legend of the Bluebonnet, The**, illustrated by Tomie dePaola, Putnam, 1983, 28p., Picture Book, LC 82-12391, ISBN 0-399-20937-9.

A retelling of the Comanche Indian legend of a little girl named She-Who-Is-Alone and how her sacrifice brought the flower called the bluebonnet to Texas. A Reading Rainbow book.

SHEILA

Blume, Judy, **Otherwise Known as Sheila the Great**, Dutton, 1972, 118p., Fiction, LC 72-78082, ISBN 0-525-36455-2.

Although Sheila wants to go to Disneyland, her father has made arrangements for the family to spend the summer at a professor's house in another town. During the summer, Sheila has her own room away from her sister, makes new friends, has humorous adventures, and learns to swim. South Carolina 1978.

SHERLOCK

Bromberg, Andrew, **Computer Overbyte; Plus Two More Codebreakers**, illustrated by May Kornblum, Greenwillow, 1982, 47p., Fiction, ISBN 0-688-00943-2.

Sherlock and Amanda Jones solve three mysteries by breaking codes and identifying clues.

SHIRLEY

Burningham, John, **Come Away from the Water, Shirley**, illustrated by John Burningham, Crowell, 1977, 22p., Picture Book, LC 77-483, ISBN 0-690-01360-4; 0-690-01361-2 (lib).

While Shirley's parents sit on their folding chairs on the beach offering advice, Shirley and her dog share imaginary adventures with pirates. A Reading Rainbow book.

Cole, Joanna, **Magic School Bus Inside the Earth, The**, illustrated by Bruce Degen, Scholastic, 1977, 40p., Picture Book, LC 87-4563, ISBN 0-590-40759-7.

Shirley and the rest of Ms. Frizzle's class learn firsthand about different kinds of rocks and the formation of the earth when they take a field trip in the magic school bus. A Reading Rainbow book.

Lord, Bette Bao, **In the Year of the Boar and Jackie Robinson**, illustrated by Marc Simont, Harper & Row, 1984, 169p., Fiction, ISBN 0-06-024004-0.

After moving to the United States from China, Shirley wants to become an American but finds she is an outsider until she learns to play baseball. 1985 Jefferson Cup Award.

Martin, Ann, **Yours Truly, Shirley**, Holiday House, 1988, 133p., Fiction, ISBN 0-8234-0719-5.
Shirley has many challenges to learn to cope with as a fourth grader. She is dyslexic and feels that she has to compete with the gifted Vietnamese girl that her parents adopt.

Wolitzer, Hilma, **Introducing Shirley Braverman**, Farrar, Straus & Giroux, 1975, 153p., Fiction, ISBN 0-374-43597-9.
Shirley lives in Brooklyn, New York, and faces the challenges of growing up during World War II. She is particularly concerned about winning a spelling bee, and about her little brother who is afraid of everything.

SID
See also Sidney

Corbett, Scott, **Deadly Hoax**, Dutton, 1981, 86p., Fiction, ISBN 0-525-28585-7.
Sid and his best friend become involved with aliens from outer space who want to destroy an atomic power plant.

SIDNEY
See also Sid

Poitier, Sidney, **This Life**, Knopf, 1980, 374p., Nonfiction, ISBN 0-394-505-492.
Biographical information about the famous black actor, Sidney Poitier. 1981 Coretta Scott King Award book.

SIGRID

Lindquist, Jennie, **Golden Name Day, The**, illustrated by Garth Williams, Harper & Row, 1955, 248p., Fiction, LC 55-8823, ISBN 0-06-023881-X.

While nine-year-old Nancy is staying with her adopted Swedish grandparents, Sigrid and the others try to figure out how Nancy can celebrate a name day since her name is not Swedish. 1956 Newbery Honor book.

SIMON

Aiken, Joan, **Black Hearts in Battersea**, illustrated by Robin Jacques, Doubleday, 1964, 240p., Fiction, LC 64-20376, ISBN 0-8446-6255-0.
Simon is a fifteen-year-old orphan who arrives in nineteenth-century London and immediately becomes entangled with a wicked group scheming against the king.

Aiken, Joan, **Wolves of Willoughby Chase, The**, Doubleday, 1962, 168p., Fiction, LC 63-18034, ISBN 0-385-03594-2.
Simon is a friend to two girl cousins. The three conquer the many obstacles that surround them in Victorian England, including a grim governess and wicked wolves.

Christopher, John, **Fireball**, Dutton, 1981, 148p., Fiction, ISBN 0-525-29738-3.
Simon's American cousin visits him for the summer in England. The two boys become involved in an exciting adventure when they discover themselves in the Roman Britain of 2,000 years ago.

Cooper, Susan, **Over Sea, Under Stone**, Harcourt Brace Jovanovich, 1966, 252p., Fiction, ISBN 0-15-259034-X.
Simon is one of the characters who battles the dark forces of evil while searching for the treasures that will permanently vanquish them.

Drescher, Henrik, **Simon's Book**, illustrated by Henrik Drescher, Lothrop, Lee & Shepard, 1983, 30p., Picture Book, LC 82-24931, ISBN 0-688-02085-2; 0-688-02086-0.
While drawing a story about Simon and a monster, a young boy becomes drowsy and falls asleep. As the boy sleeps, Simon has an adventure as he tries to escape from the monster and is aided by the ink pens. A Reading Rainbow book.

Wrightson, Patricia, **Nargun and the Stars**, Macmillan, 1986, 184p., Fiction, ISBN 0-689-50403-9.

Simon lives on a large sheep ranch in Australia. When he and his cousin are threatened by an ancient, stonelike creature, the youngsters have to think of ways to overpower it.

SIRI

Jones, Adrienne, **Hawks of Chelney, The**, illustrated by Stephen Gammell, Harper & Row, 1978, 245p., Fiction, ISBN 0-06-023057-6.

Siri lives in a small village near the sea and his best friends are a pair of ospreys, or fish hawks. When the villagers decide their poor fishing is caused by the birds and try to force Siri to capture them, Siri flees to the cliffs to live a lonely life.

SOHO

Otsuka, Vuzo, **Soho and the White Horse: A Legend of Mongolia**, illustrated by Suekichi Akaba, Viking, 1981, 46p., Picture Book, LC 80-26789, ISBN 0-670-68149-0.

This Mongolian folktale tells the story of Soho and his horse and how their parting led to the creation of the horsehead fiddle used by shepherds in Mongolia. A Reading Rainbow book.

SONIA

Jukes, Mavis, **No One Is Going to Nashville**, illustrated by Lloyd Bloom, Knopf, 1983, 48p., Fiction, ISBN 0-394-95609-5.

Sonia plans on becoming a veterinarian and wants to keep a stray dog she finds even though her father thinks they already have too many animals.

Singer, Marilyn, **It Can't Hurt Forever**, illustrated by Leigh Grant, Harper & Row, 1978, 186p., Fiction, LC 77-25657, ISBN 0-06-025681-8; 0-06-025682-6 (lib).

Sonia is one of the other patients who eleven-year-old Ellie Simon meets when she goes into the hospital for heart surgery. Minnesota 1983.

SOPHIE

Aiken, Joan, **Black Hearts in Battersea**, illustrated by Robin Jacques, Doubleday, 1964, 240p., Fiction, LC 64-20376, ISBN 0-8446-6255-0.

Sophie is a lady's maid in nineteenth-century London. She assists a teenage orphan who becomes entangled with a wicked group scheming against the king. The two have many madcap adventures including a wild balloon ride and an unexpected sea voyage.

Jones, Diana Wynne, **Howl's Moving Castle**, Greenwillow, 1986, 212p., Fiction, ISBN 0-688-06233-4.

Sophie has been changed into an ugly old woman. As she tries to figure out how to break the spell, she becomes the housekeeper for the Wizard of Howl in his unusual castle.

Mathers, Petra, **Sophie and Lou**, illustrated by Petra Mathers, HarperCollins, 1991, 30p., Picture Book, ISBN 0-06-024071; 0-06-024072-5 (lib).

Sophie is very shy and decides to teach herself to dance after seeing the dance studio across the street. A Reading Rainbow book.

Vinke, Hermann, **Short Life of Sophie Scholl, The**, Harper & Row, 1980, 216p., Nonfiction, LC 82-47714, ISBN 0-06-026302-4; 0-06-026303-2 (lib).

Sophie Scholl was only twelve when Hitler came into power and she joined the Hitler Youth like other good German children. However, Sophie questioned what she saw happening and she, her brother, and a few friends started a small, nonviolent resistance movement called the White Rose. 1985 Jane Addams Award book.

SPRING

Johnson, Emily Rhoads, **Spring and the Shadow Man**, illustrated by Paul Geiger, Dodd, Mead, 1984, 160p., Fiction, ISBN 0-396-08330-7.

Spring Weldon has a vivid imagination. Just before she starts sixth grade, a blind neighbor teaches Spring that her imagination is something to be valued and used.

STACEY
See also Stacy

Martin, Ann, **Kristy's Great Idea**, Scholastic, 1986, 153p., Fiction, ISBN 0-590-41985-4.

Stacey and her friends decide to form a babysitter's club. There are numerous books about this group of friends.

Taylor, Mildred, **Friendship, The**, illustrated by Max Ginsburg, Dial, 1987, 53p., Fiction, LC 86-29309, ISBN 0-8037-0417-8; 0-8037-0418-6 (lib).

When Stacey, his two brothers, and sister are sent to a small rural store, trouble begins as an old black man keeps calling the white storekeeper by his first name. Set in Mississippi in 1933. 1988 Boston Globe-Horn Book Award. 1988 Coretta Scott King Award book.

Taylor, Mildred, **Let the Circle Be Unbroken**, Dial, 1981, 394p., Fiction, LC 81-65854, ISBN 0-8037-4748-9.

The story of the Logan family continues in this sequel. Set in 1935 during the Depression, Stacey and the other three children and their parents watch their poor sharecropper neighbors in Mississippi being victimized by the large landowners. Hard times increase racial tensions and their friend is charged with murder. 1982 Coretta Scott King Award book. 1982 Jane Addams Honor book.

STACY
See also Stacey

Bauer, Marion Dane, **Shelter From the Wind**, Clarion, 1976, 108p., Fiction, ISBN 0-395-28890-8.

Twelve-year-old Stacy runs away from family problems and finds shelter with an old woman who has had a hard life but still appreciates being alive.

Nixon, Joan Lowery, **Other Side of Dark, The**, Delacorte, 1986, 185p., Fiction, ISBN 0-385-29481-6.

At seventeen, Stacy awakens from a four-year coma. She learns that she had been shot by the stranger that killed her mother. Her life becomes terrifying when she realizes that she is the only one who can identify the stranger and that he is following her. 1987 Edgar Allan Poe Award.

STAN
See also Stanley

Cleary, Beverly, **Fifteen**, illustrated by Joe Krush and Beth Krush, Morrow, 1956, 254p., Fiction, LC 56-7509, ISBN 0-688-2185-9.

Sixteen-year-old Stan meets fifteen-year-old Jane and the two develop a friendship that has its ups and downs. Vermont 1958.

STANLEY
See also Stan

Allard, Harry, **Stupids Die, The**, illustrated by James Marshall, Houghton Mifflin, 1981, 31p., Picture Book, LC 80-27103, ISBN 0-395-30347-8.

Stanley Q. Stupid wakes up with the feeling that something is about to happen. When the lights go out, he and his family think they are dead. Arizona 1985.

Lewis, Marjorie, **Wrongway Applebaum**, illustrated by Margot Apple, Coward-McCann, 1984, 63p., Fiction, ISBN 0-698-20610-X.

Stanley Applebaum is known as the fifth-grade klutz because of his lack of athletic abilities. He joins the baseball team, which is coached by his grandmother, and has a surprise during the championship game.

STEFFIE
See also Stephanie

Law, Carol Russell, **Case of the Weird Street Firebug**, illustrated by Bill Morrison, Knopf, 1980, 118p., Fiction, ISBN 0-394-84480-7.

After taking a correspondence course on how to be a detective, Steffie becomes involved in a case involving a firebug who has set several fires.

STEPHAN
See also Estaban, Steve, Steven

Lee, Beverly Haskell, **Secret of Van Rink's Cellar**, Lerner, 1979, 174p., Fiction, ISBN 0-8225-0763-3.

After the death of his father during the American Revolution, Stephan and his sister move to New York City with their mother who has taken a job as a lady's maid. The children discover a 'ghost' haunting the cellar and become involved as spies for General Washington.

STEPHANIE
See also Steffie

Caudill, Rebecca, **Tree of Freedom**, illustrated by Dorothy Bayley Morse, Viking, 1949, 279p., Fiction, ISBN 0-8446-6401-4.

In 1780, Kentucky was full of both hardship and promise. Thirteen-year-old Stephanie took an apple seed with her when she and her family left Carolina to move to Kentucky to homestead. Stephanie would plant a 'tree of freedom' to symbolize the new life that the pioneers intended to build. 1950 Newbery Honor book.

STERLING

North, Sterling, **Rascal**, illustrated by John Schoenherr, Dutton, 1963, 189p., Nonfiction, ISBN 0-525-18839-8.

This autobiographical reminiscence tells about the year that the author was twelve and had a pet raccoon. 1964 Newbery Honor book. Kansas 1966. Oklahoma 1966. Pacific Northwest 1966. Vermont 1965.

STEVE
See also Estaban, Stephan, Steven

Bauer, Marion Dane, **Rain of Fire**, Clarion, 1983, 153p., Fiction, ISBN 0-89919-190-8.

Twelve-year-old Steve is confused by his older brother when he returns from serving in World War II. Steve wants to make a hero of his brother and creates a very difficult situation. 1984 Jane Addams Award book.

Radin, Ruth Yaffe, **Tac's Island**, illustrated by Gail Owens, Macmillan, 1986, 74p., Fiction, ISBN 0-02-775780-3.

While spending a vacation on a Virginia island, Steve becomes friends with a boy who lives on the island and the two have quiet adventures. There is another book about these two friends.

STEVEN
See also Estaban, Stephan, Steve

Leather, Michael, **Picture Life of Steven Spielberg**, Watts, 1988, 64p., Nonfiction, ISBN 0-531-10497-4.

A biography of the famous and popular movie director, Steven Spielberg. Included is his interest in film as a teenager.

STUART

Burke, Susan, **Island Bike Business**, illustrated by Betty Greenhatch and Graeme Base, Oxford, 1982, 78p., Fiction, ISBN 0-19-554297-5.

Stuart and his friends have a dangerous adventure as they try to recover missing bicycles.

White, E. B., **Stuart Little**, illustrated by Garth Williams, Harper & Row, 1945, 131p., Fiction, ISBN 0-06-026396-2.

Stuart Little is a mouse who is born into a human family. He has many humorous and unusual adventures.

SUDAN

De Veaux, Alexis, **Enchanted Hair Tale, An**, illustrated by Cheryl Hanna, Harper & Row, 1987, 42p., Picture Book, LC 85-45824, ISBN 0-06-021623-9; 0-06-021624-7 (lib).

Sudan gets ridiculed for his wild, strange-looking hair. When he runs off for the day, he meets a family friend who helps Sudan accept and enjoy both his hair and himself. 1988 Coretta Scott King Honor book. A Reading Rainbow book.

SUE
See also Susan, Susanna, Susannah, Suzy

Means, Florence Crannell, **Moved-Outers, The**, illustrated by Helen Blair, Houghton Mifflin, 1945, 154p., Fiction, LC 45-2267, ISBN 0-395-06933-5.

Sue Ohara and her family were Japanese-Americans living in California. On December 7, 1941, their life was changed forever. On that day the Japanese attacked Pearl Harbor. Mr. Ohara was taken into custody by the FBI and Sue, her mother, and brother were moved to a Relocation Camp. 1946 Newbery Honor book.

Nostlinger, Christine, **Marrying Off Mother**, Harcourt Brace Jovanovich, 1982, 140p., Fiction, ISBN 0-15-252138-0.

When their parents separate, Sue and her sister are moved to an all-female household with their mother, grandmother, and aunts. Sue attempts to find a husband for her mother with disastrous results.

Stolz, Mary, **Wonderful, Terrible Time, A**, illustrated by Louis S. Glanzman, Harper & Row, 1967, 182p., Fiction, ISBN 0-06-026064-5.

Sue Ellen and her best friend get to leave the city and go to summer camp for two weeks where they have experiences that are both wonderful and terrible.

SUNDAY

Shyer, Marlene Fanta, **Adorable Sunday**, Scribner, 1983, 182p., Fiction, ISBN 0-684-17848-6.

Thirteen-year-old Sunday becomes a model because of her mother's ambitions but the price is too high. Sunday doesn't have time for friends and problems arise in her family life.

SUSAN
See also Sue, Susanna, Susannah, Suzy

Clinton, Susan, **Story of Susan B. Anthony, The**, illustrated by Ralph Canaday, Children's Press, 1986, 31p., Nonfiction, ISBN 0-516-04705-1.

Susan Anthony realized that women had limited rights when she worked in her father's mill as a young girl. Throughout her life she was a leader in the movement against slavery and for women's rights. A brief biography about Susan B. Anthony.

Erwin, Betty, **Go to the Room of the Eyes**, illustrated by Irene Burns, Little, Brown, 1969, 180p., Fiction, LC 71-77446, ISBN 0-316-24946-7.

When they move into an old house in Seattle, Susan and the other five Evans children discover a strange message left by children who lived there thirty years earlier. The message leads the children on a treasure hunt. Vermont 1971.

Gee, Maurice, **Halfmen of O**, Oxford, 1982, 204p., Fiction, ISBN 0-19-558081-8.

Susan Ferris is the only person who can retrieve the Half stones of Good and Evil and restore balance to the world of O. Her cousin rescues her after Susan is captured by evil characters and she continues on her adventures. There are other titles in this series of adventure and fantasy.

Lewis, C. S., **Lion, the Witch, and the Wardrobe, The**, illustrated by Pauline Baynes, Macmillan, 1950, 154p., Fiction, ISBN 0-02-758110-1.

Susan and three other children meet a witch, a mighty lion, and the other characters that live in the land of Narnia. This is the first of the seven titles in the Chronicles of Narnia series.

Ormondroyd, Edward, **Time at the Top**, illustrated by Peggie Bach, Bantam, 1986, 176p., Fiction, ISBN 0-553-15420-6 (pbk).

Susan lives in a six story apartment building. One day she gets off the elevator at the seventh floor and finds herself in 1881 where she has an amazing adventure that changes history.

Ransome, Arthur, **Swallows and Amazons**, illustrated by Arthur Ransome, Cape/Random House, 1981, 351p., Fiction, ISBN 0-224-60631-X.

Susan Walker and her siblings sail to an island and spend the summer camping by themselves. There are other books about the adventures of this family.

Whitney, Phyllis A., **Mystery of the Haunted Pool, The**, illustrated by H. Tom Hall, Westminster, 1960, 223p., Fiction, LC 60-9715, ISBN 0-644-32241-7.

While her father is in the hospital, twelve-year-old Susan goes to stay with her aunt in an antique shop. Susan helps her family by solving an old mystery. Oklahoma 1963.

SUSANNA

See also Sue, Susan, Susannah, Suzy

Jakes, John, **Susanna of the Alamo: A True Story**, illustrated by Paul Bacon, Harcourt Brace Jovanovich, 1986, 32p., Nonfiction, ISBN 0-15-200592-7.

Susanna Dickinson was one of the Americans who fought against the Mexican Santa Anna at the Alamo in San Antonio, Texas, during the siege in 1836.

SUSANNAH

See also Sue, Susan, Susanna, Suzy

Elmore, Patricia, **Susannah and the Blue House Mystery**, illustrated by John C. Wallner, Dutton, 1980, 164p., Fiction, ISBN 0-525-70525-9.

Susannah is an amateur detective. She and her partner help find a missing will and an inheritance in this mystery. There is another book about Susannah and her friends.

SUZY

See also Sue, Susan, Susanna, Susannah

Carlson, Natalie Savage, **Family Under the Bridge, The**, illustrated by Garth Williams, HarperCollins, 1958, 97p., Fiction, LC 58-5292, ISBN 0-06-020991-7.

Armand, the old hobo, disliked children until Suzy, Paul, and Evelyne moved to his bridge with their mother after being evicted from their apartment. Bridges were the only free shelter in Paris, but Armand didn't think it was the proper place for a family to live. Armand learned that when families stay together they make a home no matter where they live. 1959 Newbery Honor book.

SYDELLE

Raskin, Ellen, **Westing Game, The**, Dutton, 1978, 185p., Fiction, LC 77-18866, ISBN 0-525-42320-6.

Sydelle is one of the sixteen people invited to the reading of the very strange will of the very rich Samuel W. Westing. She could become a millionaire, depending on how she plays the tricky and dangerous Westing Game. 1979 Newbery Award book. 1978 Boston Globe-Horn Book Award. Michigan 1982.

SYLVESTER

Steig, William, **Sylvester and the Magic Pebble**, illustrated by William Steig, Simon & Schuster, 1969, 30p., Picture Book, LC 69-14484, ISBN 0-671-66511-1; 0-671-66512-X (lib).

Sylvester Duncan lives with his parents. He collects pebbles and one day he finds a magic pebble that can grant wishes. When Sylvester is frightened by a lion on his way home, he makes a wish that causes great sorrow. 1970 Caldecott Award book.

SYLVIA

See also Sylvie

Aiken, Joan, **Wolves of Willoughby Chase, The**, Doubleday, 1962, 168p., Fiction, LC 63-18034, ISBN 0-385-03594-2.

Sylvia, her cousin, and a friend conquer the many obstacles that surround them in Victorian England, including a grim governess and wicked wolves.

SYLVIE

See also Sylvia

Pendergraft, Patricia, **Miracle at Clement's Pond**, Philomel, 1987, 199p., Fiction, ISBN 0-399-21438-0.

Sylvie and her friends find a baby near the pond. They cause many problems in their small town when they leave the baby on a front porch.

-T-

TANYA

Flournoy, Valerie, **Patchwork Quilt, The**, illustrated by Jerry Pinkney, Dial, 1985, 30p., Picture Book, LC 84-1711, ISBN 0-8037-0097-0; 0-8037-0098-9 (lib).

Tanya helps her grandmother make a patchwork quilt from scraps of fabric that have meaning to each member of their family. When her grandmother becomes ill, Tanya decides to continue working on the quilt by herself. 1986 Christopher Award. 1986 Coretta Scott King Award book. A Reading Rainbow book.

TAO

Young, Ed, **Lon Po Po: A Red-Riding Hood Story from China**, illustrated by Ed Young, Philomel, 1989, 30p., Picture Book, LC 88-15222, ISBN 0-399-21619-7.

Tao lives with her two sisters and mother in the countryside of northern China. When their mother goes to visit their grandmother, a wolf appears to visit the children and claims to be their grandmother. 1990 Caldecott Award book.

TARA

Jacob, Helen Pierce, **Garland for Gandhi**, illustrated by Lillian Sader, Parnassus, 1968, 47p., Fiction, ISBN 0-87466-046-7.

Tara lives in India and her unexpected meeting with Mahatma Gandhi makes a deep and lasting impression on her.

TARAN

Alexander, Lloyd, **Black Cauldron, The**, H. Holt, 1965, 224p., Fiction, LC 65-13868, ISBN 0-03-089687-8.

Taran, Assistant Pig-Keeper and would-be hero, wears his first sword when he joins the warriors of Prydain as they set out to find and destroy the great Black Cauldron. The Black Cauldron is the chief tool of the evil forces and is used to bring the stolen bodies of slain warriors to deathless combat. This is the second book of the Prydain Chronicles. 1966 Newbery Honor book.

Alexander, Lloyd, **High King, The**, H. Holt, 1968, 285p., Fiction, LC 68-11833, ISBN 0-03-089504-9.

This is the last book of the Prydain Chronicles and Taran, the Assistant Pig-Keeper, has his last and greatest quest. Taran and his companions raise an army to seek the most powerful weapon in the kingdom which has fallen into evil hands and threatens the country with annihilation. 1969 Newbery Award book.

TARO

Dunn, Marylois and Ardath Mayhar, **Absolutely Perfect Horse**, Harper & Row, 1983, 186p., Fiction, ISBN 0-06-021774-X.

Taro Chan is adopted by a family when their father returns from the military. His stepsister buys a horse that looks like a loser but turns out to be a winner when it saves the family cattle from a wild dog pack.

Snyder, Dianne, **Boy of the Three-Year Nap, The**, illustrated by Allen Say, Houghton Mifflin, 1988, 32p., Picture Book, LC 87-30674, ISBN 0-395-44090-4.

Taro is a very lazy boy who lives with his widowed mother near a river in Japan. When a wealthy merchant moves nearby, Taro plans a way to marry the merchant's daughter, and Taro's mother makes plans to change her son's lazy habits. 1988 Boston Globe-Horn Book Award. 1989 Caldecott Honor book.

TED
See also Edward, Edwardo, Theo, Theodore

Godden, Rumer, **Dark Horse**, Viking, 1981, 202p., Fiction, ISBN 0-670-25664-1.

Ted Mullins is the stable boy to the race horse, Dark Invader. When the horse is sold and sent to race in India, Ted goes along.

Naylor, Phyllis Reynolds, **Solomon System**, Atheneum, 1983, 210p., Fiction, ISBN 0-689-30991-0.

Ted Solomon and his older brother have a difficult summer at camp knowing that their parents aren't getting along. The boys become closer as they adjust to their family situation.

TEMPERANCE

Gauch, Patricia Lee, **This Time, Tempe Wick?**, illustrated by Margot Tomes, Shoe String, 1974, 43p., Fiction, ISBN 0-936915-04-8.

Temperance Wick lives near Morristown, New Jersey, in 1780. She can wrestle and race her horse. When the 10,000 soldiers camping on her family's farm decide to mutiny, Temperance decides she has to do something. Based on a true story.

TERRI
See also Terry

Mazer, Norma Fox, **Taking Terri Mueller**, Morrow, 1983, 190p., Fiction, ISBN 0-688-01732-0.

Thirteen-year-old Terri Mueller lives with her father and has been told that her mother died when Terri was young. When she finds divorce papers, Terri realizes her mother is still alive and searches for her. 1982 Edgar Allen Poe Award. California 1985.

TERRY
See also Terri

Fleming, Susan, **Pig at 37 Pinecrest Drive**, illustrated by Beth Krush and Joe Krush, Westminster, 1981, 127p., Fiction, ISBN 0-664-32676-5.

Terry is having problems with his mother who has decided to run for mayor and has brought a pig home for a pet.

THAD
See also Thaddeus

Archer, Myrtle, **Young Boys Gone**, Walker, 1978, 218p., Fiction, ISBN 0-8027-6304-9.

Thirteen-year-old Thad is the last Woodruff son after his father and brother are killed during the Civil War. Thad and his mother and sisters escape from their farm and spend three years in safety deep in the wilderness of the Ozarks.

Sharmat, Marjorie Weinman, **Getting Something on Maggie Marmelstein**, illustrated by Ben Shecter, Harper & Row, 1971, 101p., Fiction, ISBN 0-06-025552-8.

Thad Smith dislikes Maggie Marmelstein and he is determined to get something on her, especially since she knows something about him. There are several other books about Maggie.

THADDEUS
See also Thad

Brittain, Bill, **Wish Giver: Three Tales of Coven Tree, The**, illustrated by Andrew Glass, Harper & Row, 1983, 181p., Fiction, LC 82-48264, ISBN 0-06-020686-1; 0-06-020687-X (lib).

Thaddeus Blinn was a funny little man who appeared from out of nowhere and put his tent by the annual Coven Tree Church Social. He said he had the power to give people exactly what they asked for. People find that wishes often have unexpected results when they come true. 1984 Newbery Honor book.

Herzig, Allison Cragin and Jane Lawrence Mali, **Thaddeus**, illustrated by Stephen Gammell, Little, Brown, 1984, 85p., Fiction, ISBN 0-316-35899-1.

Although his birthday falls on Christmas day, Thaddeus has very special and unusual celebrations with the help of his eccentric uncle.

THATCHER

Bates, Betty, **Thatcher Payne-in-the-Neck**, illustrated by Linda Strauss Edwards, Holiday House, 1985, 130p., Fiction, ISBN 0-8234-0584-2.

Thatcher and Kib are friends who plot to get their widowed parents together, and then realize that being brother and sister could ruin their friendship.

THEO
See also Ted, Theodore

Alexander, Lloyd, **Westmark**, Dutton, 1981, 184p., Fiction, LC 80-22242, ISBN 0-525-42335-4.

Theo is an orphan who works as an apprentice to a printer. When Theo agrees to publish a particular pamphlet, he has no idea of the trouble that it will lead to. The printing press is destroyed and Theo becomes a fugitive outside of the law. An intricate and exciting adventure. 1982 Jane Addams Award book.

Bawden, Nina, **Peppermint Pig**, illustrated by Charles Lilly, Lippincott, 1975, 191p., Fiction, ISBN 0-397-31618-6.

Life changes when their father loses his job and the family has to move in with relatives. Theo has problems with a local bully and a mischievous pig.

Raskin, Ellen, **Westing Game, The**, Dutton, 1978, 185p., Fiction, LC 77-18866, ISBN 0-525-42320-6.

Theo is one of the sixteen people invited to the reading of the very strange will of the very rich Samuel W. Westing. Theo could become a millionaire depending on how he plays the tricky and dangerous Westing Game. 1979 Newbery Award book. 1978 Boston Globe-Horn Book Award. Michigan 1982.

THEODORE
See also Ted, Theo

Force, Eden, **Theodore Roosevelt**, Watts, 1987, 94p., Nonfiction, ISBN 0-531-10313-7.

A biography about former President Theodore Roosevelt who overcame a weak body and illness to become a political figure interested in preservation and changes in government.

Judson, Clara Ingram, **Theodore Roosevelt, Fighting Patriot**, Follett, 1953, 218p., Nonfiction.

A biography of Theodore Roosevelt who was a president of the United States. 1954 Newbery Honor book.

THOMAS
See also Tom, Tommy

Adler, David A., **Thomas Jefferson, Father of Our Democracy**, illustrated by Jacqueline Garrick, Holiday House, 1987, 48p., Nonfiction, ISBN 0-8234-0667-9.

This is a biography of Thomas Jefferson, one of the United States's most talented presidents.

Byars, Betsy, **Pinballs, The**, Harper & Row, 1977, 136p., Fiction, LC 76-41518, ISBN 0-06-020917-8; 0-06-020918-6 (lib).

Pinballs don't get to settle where they want to, and neither do foster children. Thomas, Carlie and Harvey are three lonely children who have been disappointed by their own parents. With the help of their foster parents and each other, they decide they aren't really pinballs after all. Arkansas 1980. California 1980. Georgia 1979. Kansas 1980. Minnesota 1986. Missouri 1980.

Fritz, Jean, **Stonewall**, illustrated by Stephen Gammell, Putnam, 1979, 152p., Nonfiction, ISBN 0-399-20698-1.

Thomas Jackson was a famous military leader during the Civil War. He was given the nickname of Stonewall Jackson because of his complex and contradictory personality.

Hamilton, Virginia, **House of Dies Drear, The**, illustrated by Eros Keith, Macmillan, 1968, 246p., Fiction, ISBN 0-02-742500-2.

Thomas and his family rent a large old house that had once been part of the underground railroad. The house holds many secrets and danger, which Thomas unravels in this exciting mystery.

Hartling, Peter, **Crutches**, Lothrop, Lee & Shepard, 1986, 163p., Fiction, ISBN 0-688-07991-1.

Following World War II, Thomas searches for his mother in Vienna with the help of a German war veteran on crutches. Batchelder Award book.

Kennedy, John F., **Profiles in Courage**, illustrated by Emil Weiss, Harper & Row, 1955, 164p., Nonfiction, LC 64-17696.

Thomas Hart Benton showed political courage under pressure. He is one of the eight statesmen featured in this book. 1964 Jane Addams Award book.

Neimark, Anne E., **Deaf Child Listened: Thomas Gallaudet, Pioneer in American Education**, Morrow, 1983, 116p., Nonfiction, ISBN 0-688-01719-3.

Thomas Gallaudet became interested in educating deaf children when he cared for a deaf neighbor. This biography provides information about his life and his work.

Ness, Evaline, **Sam, Bangs and Moonshine**, illustrated by Evaline Ness, H. Holt, 1966, 36p., Picture Book, LC 66-10113, ISBN 03-059805-2; 03-059810-9.

Thomas does anything that his friend Samantha, called Sam, asks him to do. Sam has the bad habit of lying because she has trouble telling the difference between real and moonshine. Her moonshine causes problems for Thomas. 1967 Caldecott Award book.

TIEN PAO

DeJong, Meindert, **House of Sixty Fathers, The**, illustrated by Maurice Sendak, Harper & Row, 1956, 189p., Fiction, LC 56-8148, ISBN 0-06-021481-3.

Young Tien Pao is alone in his family's sampan when it breaks loose from its moorings and is carried by the rushing river. The sampan finally lands in Japanese territory. With only his pig for company, Tien Pao starts the long journey back to his family. Set during the Japanese occupation of China, this story is based on the author's experiences during World War II. 1957 Newbery Honor book.

TIM
See also Timmy, Timothy

Collier, James Lincoln and Christopher Collier, **My Brother Sam Is Dead**, Four Winds, 1974, 216p., Fiction, ISBN 0-02-722980-7.

The American Revolution is graphically portrayed through the experiences of eleven-year-old Tim Meeker and his family who live in southern Connecticut. Tim's sixteen-year-old brother, Sam, joins the rebel army in this exciting book. 1975 Newbery Honor book.

Lively, Penelope, **Revenge of Samuel Stokes, The**, Dutton, 1981, 122p., Fiction, ISBN 0-525-38205-4.

When Tim and his family move to a new house unusual things begin to happen as the ghost of a gardener from the eighteenth century tries to get them to move.

Selden, George, **Genie of Sutton Place, The**, Farrar, Straus & Giroux, 1973, 175p., Fiction, ISBN 0-374-32527-8.

Tim Farr remembers an unusual summer filled with magic and unique characters. It all began with his personal genie.

Walker, David, **Big Ben**, illustrated by Victor Ambrus, Houghton Mifflin, 1969, 134p., Fiction, LC 74-82477, ISBN 0-395-07167-4.

Tim and his sister acquire Big Ben, a gentle, bumbling St. Bernard puppy. The children discover that living with a fast-growing dog has its hazards as well as joys. Arkansas 1972.

Wescott, Nadine, **Lady with the Alligator Purse, The**, Little, Brown, 1988, 24p., Picture Book, ISBN 0-316-931-357.

The character Tiny Tim is featured in this old jump-rope rhyme. Kentucky 1990.

TIMMY
See also Tim, Timothy

Carlson, Natalie Savage, **Ghost in the Lagoon**, illustrated by Andrew Glass, Lothrop, Lee & Shepard, 1984, 40p., Fiction, ISBN 0-688-03794-1.

Timmy decides to catch catfish one night and finds himself frightening the ghost of a pirate who is guarding a buried treasure.

TIMOTHY
See also Tim, Timmy

Blackwood, Gary, **Wild Timothy**, Atheneum, 1987, 153p., Fiction, ISBN 0-689-31352-7.

Although he does not want to go, thirteen-year-old Timothy is taken on a camping trip by his father. When Timothy becomes lost, he discovers that his survival in the wilderness depends on his ability to learn the ways of nature.

Downie, Mary Alice and George Rawlyk, **Proper Acadian**, illustrated by Ron Berg, Kids Can Press, 1980, 64p., Fiction, ISBN 0-919964-29-X.

Set in the mid-1700s, Timothy leaves Boston to visit relatives in Nova Scotia (Acadia). He grows to love the life of the Acadians and goes with them when they are exiled from their homes.

O'Brien, Robert, **Mrs. Frisby and the Rats of NIMH**, illustrated by Zena Bernstein, Atheneum, 1971, 233p., Fiction, ISBN 0-689-20651-8.

Timothy the mouse is so ill that his mother seeks help from the super-rats that have been experimented on in a famous laboratory. 1972 Newbery Award book. Kansas 1974. Massachusetts 1978. Mississippi 1973. Missouri 1973. Pacific Northwest 1974.

TINA
See also Christina

Robinson, Nancy, **Oh Honestly, Angela!**, Scholastic, 1985, 114p., Fiction, ISBN 0-590-41287-6.

Eleven-year-old Tina wants her family to adopt a less fortunate orphan and has problems with her own little sister who causes many surprises. A humorous story of family life.

Thiele, Colin, **Fight Against Albatross Two**, Harper & Row, 1976, 243p., Fiction, ISBN 0-06-026099-8.

Tina lives in a small fishing village in Australia. Conflict arises when an oil crew arrives with a large drilling rig and the fishermen fear for their livelihood. An oil spill creates environmental problems.

TOBY

Boston, Lucy, **Children of Greene Knowe**, illustrated by Peter Boston, Peter Smith, 1955, 157p., Fiction, ISBN 0-8446-6288-7.

Toby is one of the children who had lived in the ancient house at Green Knowe during the seventeenth century. The children meet a boy from the present and have many adventures together. There are five books in this series.

Boston, Lucy, **Sea Egg**, illustrated by Peter Boston, Harcourt Brace Jovanovich, 1967, 94p., Fiction, ISBN 0-15-271050-7.

Toby and Joe buy a wonderful egg-shaped stone while they are on a seaside holiday. When it hatches, the children discover an unusual playmate and the three have amazing adventures.

Howe, Deborah and James Howe, **Bunnicula: A Rabbit Tale of Mystery**, illustrated by Alan Daniel,

Atheneum, 1979, 98p., Fiction, LC 78-11472, ISBN 0-689-30700-4.

The Monroe children, Toby and Pete, find a baby bunny at the movie and take it home. The rabbit only sleeps from sunup to sundown and the family finds two fang marks on vegetables that have been drained of their color. Harold, the dog, and Chester, the cat, become concerned that the rabbit is a vampire. Florida 1984. Hawaii 1983. Iowa 1982. Nebraska 1981. New Mexico 1982. Oklahoma 1982. Pacific Northwest 1982. South Carolina 1981. Vermont 1981.

TOM
See also Thomas, Tommy

Byars, Betsy, **Midnight Fox, The**, illustrated by Ann Grifalconi, Viking, 1968, 157p., Fiction, ISBN 0-670-47473-8.

Tom is an individualist who has a long list of fears and does not enjoy athletics. When his parents send him to spend the summer on a farm, Tom thinks he will be miserable until he begins seeing a black fox over and over.

Christopher, Matt, **Great Quarterback Switch**, illustrated by Eric Jon Nones, Little, Brown, 1984, 97p., Fiction, ISBN 0-316-13903-3.

Using mental telepathy, Tom receives football plays from his brother who is in a wheelchair.

Edmonds, Walter D., **Bert Breen's Barn**, Little, Brown, 1975, 270p., Fiction, LC 75-2157, ISBN 0-316-21166-4.

When Tom Dolan was five, his father deserted the family and Tom and his family lived with the constant threat of poverty. When Tom is fourteen, he takes a job and when he hears that Bert Breen's old barn is for sale, Tom is sure that his life will change if he could just buy the barn and raise cows. 1976 Jane Addams Award book.

Fitzgerald, John D., **Great Brain Does It Again, The**, illustrated by Mercer Mayer, Dial, 1975, 129p., Fiction, LC 74-18600, ISBN 0-8037-5065-X; 0-8037-5066-8 (lib).

Tom Fitzgerald is known as the The Great Brain by his family and friends in Adenville, Utah. He has many creative ways of earning money including operating a homemade carnival ride. Set during the early part of the twentieth century, there are several books about The Great Brain's hilarious escapades. Georgia 1980. Pacific Northwest 1979.

Fitzgerald, John D., **Great Brain Reforms, The**, illustrated by Mercer Mayer, Dial, 1973, 165p., Fiction, ISBN 0-8037-3068-3.

Tom, also known as 'The Great Brain', returns to his home in southern Utah after a year away at school. His summer exploits are outrageous and his brother tries to make him reform. There are other books about this character. Pacific Northwest 1976.

Gurko, Leo, **Tom Paine: Freedom's Apostle**, illustrated by Fritz Kredel, Crowell, 1957, 213p., Nonfiction, LC 57-6567.

The biography of Thomas Paine, one of the most important people of the American Revolution. Tom arrived in America penniless, yet made numerous contributions within a few years of his arrival. 1958 Newbery Honor book.

Hamilton, Virginia, **Justice and Her Brothers**, Greenwillow, 1978, 217p., Fiction, LC 78-54684, ISBN 0-688-80182-X.

Tom and his twin brother are thirteen and able to communicate with each other telepathically. While their parents work during the summer, the boys have to watch out for their younger sister. 1979 Coretta Scott King Honor book.

Pearce, A. Philippa, **Tom's Midnight Garden**, illustrated by Susan Einzig, Lippincott, 1984, 229p., Fiction, ISBN 0-397-30475-7.

Tom discovers a secret Victorian garden that only exists at night. In the garden he meets many unusual characters who had once inhabited the old house. 1958 Carnegie Medal book.

Quackenbush, Robert, **What Has Wild Tom Done Now? A Story of Thomas Edison**, Prentice-Hall, 1981, 102p., Nonfiction, ISBN 0-13-952168-2.

Cartoonlike illustrations tell about Thomas Edison's early years as a newsboy and telegraph operator and then his years as an inventor.

Rockwell, Thomas, **How to Eat Fried Worms**, illustrated by Emily McCully, Watts, 1973, 115p., Fiction, LC 73-4262, ISBN 0-531-02631-0.

Billy is willing to eat anything and agrees to eat fifteen worms to win a bet. Tom and his other friends watch to see if Billy will really eat them. Arizona 1979. California 1975. Hawaii 1976. Indiana 1977. Iowa 1980. Massachusetts 1976. Missouri 1975. Oklahoma 1976. South Carolina 1976.

Twain, Mark, **Adventures of Tom Sawyer, The**, illustrated by Ted Lewin, Messner, 1982, 279p., Fiction, ISBN 0-671-45647-4.

The classic story of Tom Sawyer, his friend Huck, and their adventures in Missouri in the late 1800s.

TOMMY
See also Thomas, Tom

Lofting, Hugh, **Voyages of Doctor Doolittle, The**, illustrated by Hugh Lofting, Fred A. Stokes, 1922, 364p., Fiction, ISBN 0-397-30004-2.

As an old man, Tommy Stubbins writes of his adventures when he was nine years old and went off to seek his fortune with the great Dr. Doolittle who could speak the animals' language. 1923 Newbery Award book.

TONY
See also Anthony, Anton, Antonia, Antonio

Barbour, Karen, **Little Nino's Pizzeria**, illustrated by Karen Barbour, Harcourt Brace Jovanovich, 1987, 30p., Picture Book, LC 86-32006, ISBN 0-15-247650-4.

Tony enjoys helping his father Nino make and serve the best pizza in the world at their small restaurant. When his father decides to open a large, expensive, restaurant, Tony feels left out. A Reading Rainbow book.

Blume, Judy, **Then Again, Maybe I Won't**, Bradbury, 1971, 164p., Fiction, ISBN 0-02-711090-7.

At thirteen, Tony Miglione is having to adjust to a new home and physical changes, while trying to figure out what to do about a friend who shoplifts.

Herzig, Alison Cragin and Jane Lawrence Mali, **Ten-Speed Babysitter, The**, Dutton, 1987, 134p., Fiction, ISBN 0-525-44340-1.

When fourteen-year-old Tony babysits, there is a major storm and sinister happenings.

Key, Alexander, **Escape to Witch Mountain**, illustrated by Leon Wisdom, Jr., Westminster, 1968, 172p., Fiction, ISBN 0-664-32417-7.

Tony and his sister know that they have special and unusual gifts. The two hunt for their home, which is filled with magic, and they are followed by an evil man as they try to get to Witch Mountain.

Sommer-Bodenburg, Angela, **My Friend the Vampire**, illustrated by Amelie Glienke, Dial, 1984, 155p., Fiction, ISBN 0-8037-0046-6.

Tony discovers that having a vampire for a friend can cause unusual problems. There are several other books about these unlikely friends.

TRACY

Hermes, Patricia, **Friends Are Like That**, Harcourt, 1984, 123p., Fiction, ISBN 0-15-229722-7.

Thirteen-year-old Tracy is caught in a dilemma. She wants to be part of the popular crowd but has to give up her best friend who she has known since first grade in order to belong.

TRAVIS

Gipson, Fred, **Old Yeller**, illustrated by Carl Burger, Harper & Row, 1956, 158p., Fiction, LC 56-8780, ISBN 0-06-011546-7.

Fourteen-year-old Travis and his five-year-old brother, Arliss, live with their parents on Birdsong Creek in the Texas hill country during the 1860s. Life isn't easy but they have a snug cabin, their own cattle and hogs, and they grow most of their own food. When a big, ugly yellow dog comes out of nowhere and steals a whole side of pork, Travis hates the dog but Arliss protests hurting it. 1957 Newbery Honor book. Hawaii 1966. Kansas 1959. Oklahoma 1959. Pacific Northwest 1959.

TROY

Smith, Doris Buchanan, **Karate Dancer**, Putnam, 1987, 1987p., Fiction, ISBN 0-399-21464-X.

Fourteen-year-old Troy Matthews is very involved in karate although his parents don't understand his interest.

TY
See also Tyrone

Walter, Mildred Pitts, **Ty's One-Man Band**, illustrated by Margot Tomes, Four Winds, 1980, 40p., Picture Book, LC 80-11224, ISBN 0-02-792300-2.

On a hot summer day, Ty encounters an interesting man with one wooden leg. The man is a one-man band and can make music with a comb, washboard, and wooden spoons. A Reading Rainbow book.

TYRONE
See also Ty

Jordan, June, **New Life: New Room**, illustrated by Ray Cruz, Crowell, 1975, 52p., Fiction, ISBN 0-690-00212-2.

Tyrone and his family have a problem trying to fit a new baby into their already crowded two-bedroom apartment.

-U-

UNA

Hodges, Margaret, **Saint George and the Dragon**, illustrated by Trina Schart Hyman, Little, Brown, 1984, Picture Book, LC 83-19980, ISBN 0-316-36789-3.

George, the Red Cross Knight, is sent by the Queen of Fairies to rid a dreadful dragon from the kingdom of Princess Una. A retelling of a story from the *Faerie Queene* by Edmund Spenser. 1985 Caldecott Award book. Pennsylvania 1985.

-V-

VAL

Vail, Virginia, **Pets Are For Keeps**, Scholastic, 1986, 122p., Fiction, ISBN 0-590-40181-5 (pbk).

Val works at her father's veterinary clinic, Animal Inn. A Saturday accident at a nearby stable results in an injury to a champion horse. There are other books about this clinic in the Animal Inn series.

VELVEL

Singer, Isaac Bashevis, **Fearsome Inn, The**, illustrated by Nonny Hogrogian, Scribner, 1967, 42p., Fiction, LC 67-23693, ISBN 0-689-70769-X.

All roads lead to the inn and when helpless winter travelers stumble in, they become victims of the owners, a witch and her husband. Velvel and his companions break the spell cast over the inn and rescue three girls held captive as servants. 1968 Newbery Honor book.

VERN

Byars, Betsy, **Not-Just-Anybody Family, The**, illustrated by Jacqueline Rogers, Delacorte, 1986, 149p., Fiction, ISBN 0-440-50211-X.

Vern and Maggie Blossom try to straighten out their family's affairs when their grandfather is jailed for disturbing the peace and their brother breaks both of his legs. There are other books about the Blossom family.

VERNA

Stevenson, Drew, **Case of the Horrible Swamp Monster, The**, illustrated by Susan Swan, Dodd, Mead, 1984, 95p., Fiction, ISBN 0-396-08466-4.

Verna and her sixth-grade friends film a monster movie at the swamp and when their film is developed, they make a discovery that involves them in an exciting mystery.

VERON

Kherdian, David, **Road from Home: The Story of an Armenian Girl, The**, Greenwillow, 1979, 238p., Nonfiction, ISBN 0-688-80205-2.

This biography of the author's mother concentrates on her childhood in Turkey in the early part of the twentieth century before the Turkish government deported the Armenian people. 1980 Jane Addams Award book. 1980 Newbery Honor book. 1979 Boston Globe-Horn Book Award.

VERONICA
See also Ronnie

Lowry, Lois, **Rabble Starkey**, Houghton Mifflin, 1987, 192p., Fiction, ISBN 0-395-43607-9.

When her mother suffers mental illness, Veronica's friend Rabble Starkey and her mother move in with them. Both families face major changes in their lives. 1988 Child Study Children's Book Award. 1988 Golden Kite Award.

VICKY
See also Victoria

L'Engle, Madeleine, **Ring of Endless Light, A**, Farrar, Straus & Giroux, 1980, 324p., Fiction, LC 79-27679, ISBN 0-374-36299-8.

This is the fourth book about the Austin family. Vicki Austin begins her summer by attending the funeral of an old family friend, and his son soon turns to Vicky for romance. Vicky has several young men seeking her attention as she watches her grandfather's health deteriorate from leukemia. Vicky also discovers she can communicate with dolphins through nonverbal communication. 1981 Newbery Honor book.

Nordstrom, Ursula, **Secret Language**, illustrated by Mary Chalmers, Harper & Row, 1960, 167p., Fiction, ISBN 0-06-024576-X.

Vicky makes a special friend while she is at boarding school and the two girls share their own private language.

Sleator, William, **Among the Dolls**, illustrated by Trina Schart Hyman, Dutton, 1975, 70p., Fiction, ISBN 0-525-25563-X.

When Vicky receives an antique dollhouse for her birthday, she becomes involved in a horror fantasy where she finds herself reduced in size and a slave to the dolls.

VICTOR

Pinkwater, D. Manus, **Lizard Music**, Bantam, 1988, 136p., Fiction, ISBN 0-553-15605-5.

Eleven-year-old Victor is left alone for two weeks and while watching late-night television he discovers a music group consisting of lizards. Humorous incidents occur as he tries to locate the group.

VICTORIA
See also Vicky

Fox, Paula, **Place Apart, A**, Farrar, Straus & Giroux, 1980, 183p., Fiction, ISBN 0-374-359-857.

After her father's death, Victoria and her mother move to a small village outside of Boston. Victoria meets a wealthy teenage boy and learns a painful lesson about life. 1983 Jane Addams Award book.

VICTORY

Conford, Ellen, **Dreams of Victory**, illustrated by Gail Rockwell, Little, Brown, 1973, 121p., Fiction, ISBN 0-316-15294-3.

Victory Benneker is a sixth grader with an enormous imagination. She daydreams about success, but success eludes Victory in real life until she has the opportunity to share what she is best at.

VINCENT

Brown, Marcia, **Stone Soup: An Old Tale**, illustrated by Marcia Brown, Scribner, 1947, 40p., Picture Book, ISBN 0-684-92296-7; 0-684-16217-2 (pbk).

Vincent and the other peasants hid their food when they saw three hungry soldiers coming down the road. The soldiers then taught the villagers how to make soup from three stones and soon a village feast was prepared. An old folktale. 1948 Caldecott Honor book.

VIOLA

Allard, Harry, **Miss Nelson Is Back**, illustrated by James Marshall, Houghton Mifflin, 1982, 32p., Picture Book, LC 82-9357, ISBN 0-395-32956-6.

The students in Room 207 plan to act up while their teacher, Miss Nelson, is gone having her tonsils removed. The class decides to behave when the mean substitute teacher, Miss Viola Swamp, appears. A Reading Rainbow book. Nebraska 1984.

Allard, Harry, **Miss Nelson Is Missing!**, illustrated by James Marshall, Houghton Mifflin, 1977, 32p., Picture Book, LC 76-55918, ISBN 0-395-25296-2.

The students in Room 207 took advantage of their good-natured teacher, Miss Nelson, until she disappeared. When Viola Swamp comes to class as a substitute, the children learned to appreciate Miss Nelson. Arizona 1981. California 1982. Georgia 1980.

VIOLET

Isenberg, Barbara and Marjorie Jaffe, **Albert the Running Bear's Exercise Book**, illustrated by Diane de Groat, Clarion, 1984, 63p., Picture Book, LC 84-7064, ISBN 0-89919-294-7; 0-89919-318-8.

Violet has been trained as a gymnast and a stunt bear. She knows numerous exercises to teach Albert so he can become a better runner. Pictures show the reader how to do the exercises with Albert. A Reading Rainbow book.

VIRGINIA
See also Genny, Jen, Jennifer, Jenny, Jinny

White, Ruth, **Sweet Creek Holler**, Farrar, Straus & Giroux, 1988, 215p., Fiction, ISBN 0-374-37360-4.

Virginia and her family move to Sweet Creek Holler in the Appalachian Mountains of Virginia in 1948, when she is six. Over a six-year period, Virginia learns a great deal about people and living in a coal-mining community.

-W-

WAINO

Stong, Phil, **Honk, the Moose**, illustrated by Kurt Wiese, Dodd, Mead, 1955, 80p., Fiction, ISBN 0-396-07358-1.

Waino and Ivar live in the rolling hills of the Iron Range in Minnesota where their parents had moved from Finland. During a very cold winter, the boys find a moose in the stable and the moose refuses to leave. 1936 Newbery Honor book.

WALLIS

Conford, Ellen, **Anything for a Friend**, Little, Brown, 1979, 180p., Fiction, ISBN 0-316-15308-7.

Wallis dislikes her name. Her family moves quite often and she finds it hard to always be the new girl. When she discovers a murder has taken place in their new house, Wallis meets someone who says he will take care of it.

WALT
See also Walter

Fisher, Maxine P., **Walt Disney**, Watts, 1988, 72p., Nonfiction, ISBN 0-531-10493-1.

Walt Disney had many struggles as a child and a young man, but he overcame them to become a famous film animator.

WALTER
See also Walt

Buff, Conrad, **Apple and the Arrow, The**, Houghton Mifflin, 1951, 74p., Fiction.

Eleven-year-old Walter Tell awaits the skillful demonstration by his father William who will shoot an apple from the top of Walter's head with a bow and arrow. 1952 Newbery Honor book.

Kendall, Carol, **Gammage Cup, The**, illustrated by Erik Blegvad, Harcourt Brace Jovanovich, 1959, 221p., Fiction, LC 59-8953, ISBN 0-15-230572-6.

In an imaginary world, the Minnipins have lived for generations in an isolated valley. The Min-nipins are a sedate and sober people who dress in greens and browns, mind their own jobs, and never question the authority of the leading family, the Periods. Walter the Early questioned the wisdom of the Periods and he was exiled. The exiles discover ancient enemies who plan to attack the Minnipins. 1960 Newbery Honor book.

Nelson, Theresa, **Devil Storm**, Orchard, 1987, 212p., Fiction, ISBN 0-531-08311-X.

Thirteen-year-old Walter Carroll and his family are caught in a terrible hurricane that hits Texas in 1900.

Sufrin, Mark, **Payton**, Scribner, 1988, 151p., Nonfiction, ISBN 0-684-18940-2.

Biographical information about Walter Payton, the famous football player with the Chicago Bears football team.

WANDA

Estes, Eleanor, **Hundred Dresses, The**, illustrated by Louis Slobodkin, Harcourt Brace Jovanovich, 1944, 80p., Fiction, ISBN 0-15-237374-8.

Wanda Petronski is a quiet girl who always wears the same clean, faded dress to school. The other girls tease her and Wanda doesn't have any friends. When Wanda tells the other girls that she has 100 dresses in her closet they laugh at her. 1945 Newbery Honor book.

Hildick, E. W., **Case of the Bashful Bank Robber, The**, illustrated by Liesl Weil, Macmillan, 1987, 138p., Fiction, ISBN 0-02-743870-8.

Wanda and her friends solve mysteries from their basement headquarters. There are several other books about this group of friends.

WARREN

Byars, Betsy, **Two-Thousand-Pound Goldfish, The**, Harper & Row, 1982, 153p., Fiction, ISBN 0-06-020890-2.

Eight-year-old Warren and his sister are left with their grandmother when their mother flees from the FBI. Warren expects his mother to return at any time and has trouble accepting the reality of his life.

Roos, Stephen, **My Horrible Secret**, Delacorte, 1983, 119p., Fiction, ISBN 0-385-29246-5.

Eleven-year-old Warren can't throw or catch a ball, while his brother is a superathlete. Warren tries to hide his lack of abilities as he prepares to go to Camp Hit-a-Homer. Arkansas 1986.

WATSON

Gilden, Mel, **Return of Captain Conquer, The**, Houghton Mifflin, 1986, 153p., Fiction, ISBN 0-395-40446-0.

Thirteen-year-old Watson Congruent is the hero of this humorous story in which an old television superhero is thought to return to save the world from aliens.

WAYNE

Paulsen, Gary, **Winter Room, The**, Orchard, 1989, 103p., Fiction, LC 89-42541, ISBN 0-531-05839-5; 0-531-08439-6 (lib).

Wayne and his brother Eldon live with their family on a northern Minnesota farm. Eldon describes the scenes around him and recounts his old Norwegian uncle's tales of an almost mythological logging past. 1990 Newbery Honor book.

WENDY

Adler, C. S., **Always and Forever Friends**, Clarion, 1988, 164p., Fiction, ISBN 0-89919-681-0.

Wendy looks for a new friend when her best friend moves. She learns that both friendship and family relationships require nurturing and care.

Barrie, James M., **Peter Pan**, illustrated by Trina Schart Hyman, Scribner, 1980, 183p., Fiction, ISBN 0-684-16611-9.

The classic adventures of Wendy Darling and her two brothers when they are taken to Never-Neverland by Peter Pan.

Snyder, Carol, **Leftover Kid, The**, Putnam, 1986, 158p., Fiction, ISBN 0-448-47773-4.

Wendy has an eighth-grade project to do on her family, and plenty of family to give her assistance since there are four generations trying to live together.

WILBUR

See also Will, Willie, Willy

Brown, Marc and Laurene Krasny Brown, **Bionic Bunny Show, The**, illustrated by Marc Brown and Laurene Krasny Brown, Little, Brown, 1984, 32p., Picture Book, LC 83-22211, ISBN 0-316-11120-1; 0-316-11122-8 (pbk).

Wilbur is an ordinary rabbit in real life, but when he goes to work he becomes the television superhero Bionic Bunny. As Bionic Bunny struggles to outwit the Robber Rats, the reader is taken behind the scenes to a television show to see how an episode is made. A Reading Rainbow book.

Freedman, Russell, **Wright Brothers: How They Invented the Airplane**, Holiday House, 1991, 128p., Nonfiction, LC 90-48440, ISBN 0-8234-0875-2.

The story of Wilbur Wright and his brother as they went from their bicycle shop in Dayton, Ohio, to build and fly the first powered, sustained, and controlled airplane near Kitty Hawk, North Carolina, in 1903. The biography is illustrated with photographs taken by the Wright Brothers. 1992 Newbery Honor book.

White, E. B., **Charlotte's Web**, illustrated by Garth Williams, Harper & Row, 1952, 184p., Fiction, LC 52-9760, ISBN 0-06-026385-7.

Fern saved the runt of the pig litter and named him Wilbur. Wilbur lives in the barn and has a beautiful grey spider named Charlotte for a friend. 1953 Newbery Honor book. Massachusetts 1984. Michigan 1980. Missouri 1980.

WILEY

Fleischman, Sid, **Humbug Mountain**, illustrated by Eric von Schmidt, Little, Brown, 1978, 149p., Fiction, LC 78-9419, ISBN 0-316-28569-2.

Wiley and his sister, Glorietta, live near Humbug Mountain. They have many humorous adventures as they discover a petrified man; their mother's chicken discovers a gold rush; and Wiley discovers notorious villains. 1979 Boston Globe-Horn Book Award.

WILL
See also Wilbur, William, Willie, Willy

Carrick, Carol, **Elephant in the Dark**, illustrated by Donald Carrick, Clarion, 1988, 133p., Fiction, ISBN 0-89919-757-4.

Will is an orphan living in Massachusetts in the mid-eighteenth century. He becomes friends with an elephant that has been left for the winter by a traveling showman. This story is based on an actual incident.

Christopher, John, **White Mountains**, Macmillan, 1967, 184p., Fiction, ISBN 0-02-718360-2.

Set in the future when the Tripods rule the earth, Will and his friends attempt to escape and run away to the White Mountains. One of the Tripod series.

Cooper, Susan, **Dark Is Rising, The**, illustrated by Alan E. Cober, Atheneum, 1973, 216p., Fiction, LC 72-85916, ISBN 0-689-30317-3.

On his eleventh birthday, Will Stanton discovers that he is the last of the Old Ones—immortals dedicated throughout the ages to keeping the world from domination by evil forces. Will begins a quest for six magical signs that will provide aid in the final battle between the Dark and the Light. 1974 Newbery Honor book. 1973 Boston Globe-Horn Book Award.

Cooper, Susan, **Grey King, The**, illustrated by Michael Heslop, Atheneum, 1984, 208p., Fiction, LC 75-8526, ISBN 0-689-50029-7.

This is the fourth of five books in The Dark Is Rising series. In North Wales there is an old tradition that a harp of gold will be found by a boy followed by a white dog with silver eyes—a dog that can see

the wind. Will meets the boy and discovers his own long-appointed quest. 1976 Newbery Award book.

Reeder, Carolyn, **Shades of Gray**, Macmillan, 1989, 152p., Fiction, ISBN 0-027-758-109.

Twelve-year-old Will reluctantly leaves his family home at the end of the Civil War to go live in the Virginia countryside with an uncle. Will considers his uncle to be a traitor since he refused to take part in the war. 1990 Child Study Children's Book Award. 1990 Jane Addams Honor Book. 1990 Jefferson Cup Award. 1990 Scott O'Dell Award.

WILLA

MacLachlan, Patricia, **Unclaimed Treasures**, Harper & Row, 1984, 118p., Fiction, ISBN 0-06-024094-6.

Willa looks back to a special summer when she learned about friendship, family, and herself.

WILLIAM
See also Bill, Billie, Billy, Will, Willie, Willy

Bodecker, N. M., **Carrot Holes and Frisbee Trees**, illustrated by Nina Winters, Atheneum, 1983, p., Fiction, ISBN 0-689-50097-1.

A tall tale about William and the gigantic carrots that grow in his garden.

Buff, Conrad, **Apple and the Arrow, The**, Houghton Mifflin, 1951, 74p., Fiction.

William Tell is a Swiss freedom fighter who is going to prove his skill with a bow and arrow by shooting an apple from the top of his eleven-year-old son's head. 1952 Newbery Honor book.

Chambers, Aidan, **Seal Secret**, Harper & Row, 1981, 122p., Fiction, ISBN 0-06-021259-4.

William and his family vacation in an old cottage on the coast of Wales. William meets a Welsh boy who has captured a seal pup and becomes involved in a dangerous adventure when he decides to rescue the seal.

Cox, David, **Tin Lizzie and Little Nell**, illustrated by David Cox, Bodley Head, 1982, 30p., Picture Book, ISBN 0-370-30922-7.

William Winterbottom owns an old blue car that he calls Tin Lizzie. His neighbor, Billy Benson, has an old grey mare named Little Nell. Each of the Australian farmer's think that his form of transportation is best and so they have a Saturday race. A Reading Rainbow book.

Craven, Carolyn, **What the Mailman Brought**, illustrated by Tomie dePaola, Putnam, 1987, 35p., Picture Book, LC 85-19076, ISBN 0-399-21290-6.

William had missed the first week at his new school due to illness and needed to rest another week. While he is home, a mysterious mailman begins bringing William unusual packages every day. A Reading Rainbow book.

Daugherty, James, **Landing of the Pilgrims**, Random House, 1978, 151p., Fiction, ISBN 0-394-90302-1.

A fictionalized story of the Pilgrims as told through the life of William Bradford.

du Bois, William Pene, **Twenty-One Balloons, The**, illustrated by William Pene du Bois, Viking, 1947, 180p., Fiction, ISBN 0-670-73441-1.

Professor William Waterman Sherman has gotten tired of teaching so he sails across the Pacific Ocean in a large hot-air balloon and experiences the explosion of the island of Krakatoa. 1948 Newbery Award book.

Dubanevich, Arlene, **Pig William**, illustrated by Arlene Dubanevich, Bradbury, 1985, 28p., Picture Book, LC 85-5776, ISBN 0-02-733200-4.

Pig William dawdles in the morning and misses his bus to the school picnic. He makes the best of the situation and a sudden turn of events brings the picnic to him. A Reading Rainbow book.

Fitz-Gerald, Christine Maloney, **William Henry Harrison**, Children's Press, 1987, 100p., Nonfiction, ISBN 0-516-01392-0.

A biography about William Henry Harrison who became president of the United States after showing leadership abilities while he was in the army during the War of 1812.

Garfield, Leon, **Footsteps**, Delacorte, 1980, 196p., Fiction, ISBN 0-440-40102-X.

After his father's death, twelve-year-old William Jones continues to hear footsteps from his father's room. The sounds lead William on an adventure in London to help end his father's torment.

Gretz, Susanna and Alison Sage, **Teddy Bears Cure a Cold**, illustrated by Susanna Gretz and Alison Sage, Four Winds, 1984, 32p., Picture Book, LC 84-4015, ISBN 0-590-07949-2.

William the bear feels sick and spends several days in bed while the other bears take care of him. A Reading Rainbow book.

Konigsburg, Elaine, **Throwing Shadows**, Atheneum, 1979, 151p., Fiction, ISBN 0-689-30714-4.

The story of William as he helps his mother find a new career is one of the five stories in this book.

Magorian, Michelle, **Good Night, Mr. Tom**, Harper & Row, 1982, 318p., Fiction, ISBN 0-06-024079-2.

During World War II, eight-year-old William Beach is evacuated from London and placed in an English village with a widower. Both boy and man learn to trust and develop affection for one another.

Paterson, Katherine, **Great Gilly Hopkins, The**, Crowell, 1978, 148p., Fiction, LC 77-27075, ISBN 0-690-03837-2; 0-06-440201-0 (pbk).

William's mother becomes the foster parent of Galadriel Hopkins, known as Gilly. This is Gilly's third foster home and she has learned in her short life that you have to be tough to survive. Gilly thinks William is freaky and she despises both him and his mother. It takes time for Gilly to learn about love and caring. 1979 Newbery Honor book. 1979 Jane Addams Award book. Georgia 1981. Iowa 1981. Kansas 1981. Massachusetts 1981.

Pinkwater, D. Manus, **Fat Men from Space**, illustrated by D. Manus Pinkwater, Dell, 1980, 57p., Fiction, ISBN 0-440-44542-6 (pbk).

When William goes to the dentist and has a tooth filled, his tooth begins acting as a radio and transmits messages from a UFO.

Rayner, Mary, **Mrs. Pig's Bulk Buy**, illustrated by Mary Rayner, Atheneum, 1981, 30p., Picture Book, LC 80-19875, ISBN 0-689-30831-0.

William and his nine brothers and sisters like to put ketchup on everything they eat. Mrs. Pig has a plan to cure the piglets of this habit, which changes their skin from white to pink. A Reading Rainbow book.

Willard, Nancy, **Visit to William Blake's Inn: Poems for Innocent and Experienced Travelers, A**, illustrated by Alice and Martin Provensen, Harcourt Brace Jovanovich, 1981, 44p., Picture Book, ISBN 0-1529-38-222.

Illustrations and poems about the curious group of guests who go to William Blake's Inn. 1982 Boston Globe-Horn Book Award. 1982 Caldecott Honor book. 1982 Newbery Award book.

Winthrop, Elizabeth, **Castle in the Attic, The**, illustrated by Trina Schart Hyman, Holiday House, 1985, 180p., Fiction, LC 85-5607, ISBN 0-8234-0579-6.

William is afraid that his mother will leave him after his father dies. When William receives a toy castle as a gift, complete with a silver knight, he is taken on an adventure involving magic and a personal quest. California 1989. Vermont 1987.

WILLIE
See also Wilbur, Will, William, Willy

Brenner, Barbara, **Wagon Wheels**, illustrated by Don Bolognese, Harper & Row, 1978, 64p., Easy Reader, LC 76-21391, ISBN 0-06-020668-3; 0-06-020669-1 (lib).

Shortly after the Civil War, Willie, his two brothers, and their parents left Kentucky to travel to Kansas and take advantage of the free land offered through the Homestead Act. After their mother dies, the men build a dugout where they spend the winter and where the three boys wait while their dad searches for new land. Based on a true story. A Reading Rainbow book.

Gault, William Campbell, **Wild Willie, Wide Receiver**, Dutton, 1974, 147p., Fiction, ISBN 0-525-42788-0.

Willie Wagen is a superathlete. He and his coach have problems as their team, the Chicago Miners, fights its way to the Super Bowl.

Hamilton, Virginia, **Willie Bea and the Time the Martians Landed**, Greenwillow, 1983, 208p., Fiction, ISBN 0-688-02390-8.

Twelve-year-old Willie Bea is excited about Halloween but doesn't anticipate what will happen when a radio broadcast announces an invasion by landing aliens.

Hildick, E. W., **Case of the Bashful Bank Robber, The**, illustrated by Leslie Weil, Macmillan, 1987, 138p., Fiction, ISBN 0-02-743870-8.

Willie and his friends solve mysteries from their basement headquarters. There are several other books about this group of friends.

Keats, Ezra Jack, **Peter's Chair**, illustrated by Ezra Jack Keats, Harper & Row, 1967, 32p., Picture Book, LC 67-4816, ISBN 0-06-023112-2.

Peter is upset when his parents paint his old crib and high chair for his new baby sister. Peter decides to run away with his dog, Willie, taking his special chair before it can be painted. A Reading Rainbow book.

WILLY
See also Wilbur, Will, William, Willie

Eige, Lillian, **Kidnapping of Mister Huey**, Harper & Row, 1983, 153p., Fiction, ISBN 0-06-021798-7.

Willy and an elderly friend run away to Wisconsin together because they don't want to go where their families want to send them.

Gardiner, John Reynolds, **Stone Fox**, illustrated by Marcia Sewall, Crowell, 1980, 85p., Fiction, ISBN 0-690-03984-0.

When his grandfather loses his will to live, Willy decides to help make their Idaho potato farm prosperous. Utah 1985.

Showell, Ellen, **Ghost of Tillie Jean Cassaway, The**, illustrated by Stephen Gammell, Four Winds, 1978, 118p., Fiction, ISBN 0-590-07559-4.

Twelve-year-old Willy Barbour and his sister pursue the ghost of a young girl who died in their Appalachian community. Pacific Northwest 1982. South Carolina 1982.

WILMA

Cleaver, Vera and Bill Cleaver, **Queen of Hearts**, Lippincott, 1978, 158p., Fiction, ISBN 0-397-31771-9.

Twelve-year-old Wilma takes care of her grandmother when the elderly woman has a stroke. Wilma learns a lot about what it means to be old and to be young.

WINNIE

Babbitt, Natalie, **Tuck Everlasting**, Farrar, Straus & Giroux, 1975, 139p., Fiction, ISBN 0-374-37848-7.

Winnie Foster has many adventures with the Tuck family including a kidnapping, a murder, and a jail break. The Tuck family is unusual since they had once found a spring with water that gave them everlasting life.

Meltzer, Milton, **Winnie Mandela: The Soul of South Africa**, illustrated by Stephen Marchesi, Viking Kestrel, 1986, 54p., Nonfiction, ISBN 0-670-81249-8.

Winnie Mandela and her husband have been major leaders in South Africa's struggle for equal rights for blacks. This biography tells about Winnie's strengths and gives background information on the political problems of the country.

Milne, A. A., **Winnie-the-Pooh**, illustrated by Hilda Scott, Dutton, 1974, 161p., Fiction, ISBN 0-525-44443-2.

The classic adventures of the stuffed toy bear, Winnie-the-Pooh, and his friends.

WINSTON

Rice, Eve, **Remarkable Return of Winston Potter Crisply, The**, Greenwillow, 1976, 185p., Fiction, ISBN 0-688-84145-7.

Winston has a younger brother and sister who are suspicious of his activities and suspect that Winston is a spy. A humorous family story.

-Y-

YOUNG FU

Lewis, Elizabeth, **Young Fu of the Upper Yangtze**, illustrated by Ed Young, H. Holt, 1932, 266p., Fiction, LC 72-91654, ISBN 0-03-007471-1.

Young Fu is a coppersmith's apprentice in China. His life and experiences with artisans, bandits, scholars, and soldiers are vividly portrayed along with the turmoil of life in China in the 1920s. 1933 Newbery Award book.

YUKI
See also Yukio

Uchida, Yoshiko, **Journey to Topaz**, illustrated by Donald Carrick, Creative Arts, 1984, 149p., Fiction, ISBN 0-916870-85-5.

As a Japanese-American family, the Sakanes face many changes when Pearl Harbor is bombed by the Japanese in 1941. Yuki's father is taken away by the FBI and the rest of the family is sent to a desert concentration camp.

YUKIO
See also Yuki

Garrison, Christian, **Dream Eater, The**, illustrated by Diane Goode, Macmillan, 1978, 28p., Picture Book, LC 85-26771, ISBN 0-689-71058-5 (pbk).

Yukio is having recurring nightmares. As he talks with his father, mother, and grandfather, Yukio finds that they are also having bad dreams and sleeping poorly. None of the villagers are sleeping well because of nightmares and bad dreams until Yukio rescues a hungry baku that eats nightmares. A Reading Rainbow book.

-Z-

ZACH
See also Zachary

MacLachlan, Patricia, **Seven Kisses in a Row**, illustrated by Maria Pia Marrella, Harper & Row, 1983, 56p., Fiction, ISBN 0-06-024084-9.

Zach and his sister are being cared for by relatives while their parents are at a convention. They discover life is different but not bad.

ZACHARY
See also Zach

Lord, Athena, **Today's Special: Z.A.P. and Zoe**, illustrated by Jean Jenkins, Macmillan, 1984, 160p., Fiction, ISBN 0-02-761440-9.

Eleven-year-old Zachary has to take care of his younger sister who gets them both in trouble. Set in a small New York town during 1939. There is another book about these two characters.

ZAN

Knudson, R. R., **Zanbanger**, Harper & Row, 1977, 162p., Fiction, ISBN 0-06-023214-5.

Zan is taken off the girls' high school basketball team. With the support of her classmates she goes through a court battle to try to get back on. There is another book about Zan.

ZEKE

Domke, Todd, **Grounded**, Knopf, 1982, 186p., Fiction, ISBN 0-394-85163-3.

Zeke and his friends produce a play to raise money with humorous results.

Weik, Mary H., **Jazz Man, The**, illustrated by Ann Grifalconi, Atheneum, 1967, 42p., Fiction, LC 66-10417, ISBN 0-689-30021-2.

Zeke lives with his parents on the top floor of an old brownstone in Harlem. The music from a Jazz Man that moved nearby brings Zeke happiness and helps him when he is deserted by his parents. 1967 Newbery Honor book.

ZELDA

Hall, Lynn, **In Trouble Again, Zelda Hammersmith?**, Harcourt Brace Jovanovich, 1987, 138p., Fiction, ISBN 0-15-238780-3.

Zelda is a third grader who gets into a greal deal of mischief, including faking an accident because of her report card and stealing a dog.

ZERUAH

Coblentz, Catherine Cate, **Blue Cat of Castle Town, The**, illustrated by Janice Holland, Countryman, 1949, 122p., Fiction, ISBN 0-914378-05-8.

The folklore of Castleton, Vermont, includes the story of a blue cat and a carpenter who built the most beautiful church pulpit in the state. The girl, Zeruah Guernsey, designed and made a carpet of these two and other citizens who lived in her time: a carpet so beautiful that it hangs at the Metropolitan Museum in New York. 1950 Newbery Honor book.

ZIA

O'Dell, Scott, **Zia**, Houghton Mifflin, 1976, 179p., Fiction, ISBN 0-395-24393-9.

Zia is the young niece of the Indian girl who lives on the Island of the Blue Dolphins. Zia is torn between the worlds of her tribe and that of the padres at the mission where she lives.

ZOE

Conrad, Pam, **Stonewords: A Ghost Story**, HarperCollins, 1990, 130p., Fiction, ISBN 0-060-213-167 (lib); 0-060-213-159.

Zoe discovers the ghost of an eleven-year-old girl living in her house. The ghost takes Zoe back to the day of her death in 1870 to try to change the day's events. 1991 Edgar Allan Poe Award.

Lord, Athena, **Today's Special: Z.A.P. and Zoe**, illustrated by Jean Jenkins, Macmillan, 1984, 160p., Fiction, ISBN 0-02-761440-9.

Four-year-old Zoe is constantly in trouble as her older brother takes care of her during the summer of 1939. There is another book about these two characters.

AUTHOR/TITLE INDEX

TITLE INDEX